Personal Finance in Your 50s

ALL-IN-ONE

for
dummies®

A Wiley Brand

Personal Finance in Your 50s

ALL-IN-ONE

by AARP, Ray Brown, Bob Carlson,
N. Brian Caverly, Esq., Kerry Hannon,
Jack Hungelmann, Aaron Larson,
Sarah Glendon Lyons, John E. Lucas,
Jordan S. Simon, Eric Tyson

Personal Finance in Your 50s All-in-One For Dummies®

Published by: **John Wiley & Sons, Inc.**, 111 River Street, Hoboken, NJ 07030-5774, www.wiley.com

Copyright © 2018 by John Wiley & Sons, Inc., Hoboken, New Jersey

Certain materials excerpted from:

Getting the Job You Want After 50 For Dummies, Copyright © 2015 by AARP

Personal Finance After 50 For Dummies, 2nd Edition, Copyright © 2015 by Eric Tyson and Bob Carlson

Selling Your House For Dummies, Copyright © 2018 by Eric Tyson, Ray Brown, and John Wiley & Sons, Inc.

Published simultaneously in Canada

No part of this publication may be reproduced, stored in a retrieval system or transmitted in any form or by any means, electronic, mechanical, photocopying, recording, scanning or otherwise, except as permitted under Sections 107 or 108 of the 1976 United States Copyright Act, without the prior written permission of the Publisher. Requests to the Publisher for permission should be addressed to the Permissions Department, John Wiley & Sons, Inc., 111 River Street, Hoboken, NJ 07030, (201) 748-6011, fax (201) 748-6008, or online at http://www.wiley.com/go/permissions.

Trademarks: Wiley, For Dummies, the Dummies Man logo, Dummies.com, Making Everything Easier, and related trade dress are trademarks or registered trademarks of John Wiley & Sons, Inc., and may not be used without written permission. All other trademarks are the property of their respective owners. John Wiley & Sons, Inc., is not associated with any product or vendor mentioned in this book.

For general information on our other products and services, please contact our Customer Care Department within the U.S. at 877-762-2974, outside the U.S. at 317-572-3993, or fax 317-572-4002. For technical support, please visit https://hub.wiley.com/community/support/dummies.

Wiley publishes in a variety of print and electronic formats and by print-on-demand. Some material included with standard print versions of this book may not be included in e-books or in print-on-demand. If this book refers to media such as a CD or DVD that is not included in the version you purchased, you may download this material at http://booksupport.wiley.com. For more information about Wiley products, visit www.wiley.com.

Library of Congress Control Number: 2018937027

ISBN: 978-1-119-47151-6 (pbk); ISBN: 978-1-119-47153-0 (ebk); ISBN: 978-1-119-47146-2 (ebk)

Manufactured in the United States of America

10 9 8 7 6 5 4 3 2 1

Contents at a Glance

Table of Contents

Introduction

Welcome to *Personal Finance in Your 50s All-in-One For Dummies*!

So, you've hit your 50s, your job is fulfilling and lucrative, your kids got full-ride scholarships to college, your mortgage is paid off or close to it, you invested early and wisely, your early retirement is on track, and you have an updated, signed will and a plan for your estate that will ensure that exactly what you want to happen to your stuff when you die will in fact happen. Nicely done! Go and be well. You can put this book down now.

What? You're still reading? Hmmm. That must mean you hit a snag or two along the way to personal financial nirvana. Well, don't worry. You're hardly alone. By picking up this book, you've already shown you want to get yourself on a better track, and you've taken your first step toward doing so. This book is all about understanding and improving your financial health from late middle age heading into retirement.

REMEMBER

It's never too late to right the ship! There's a whole lot you can do — even in your 50s — to help yourself have a more comfortable life as you head into your more advanced years, and this book is chock full of juicy advice on that stuff.

About This Book

You hold in your hands a big ol' conglomeration of some of the best For Dummies material on the topic of bettering your economic picture in your later working years. It's divided into six sections, each of which is itself a miniature "book" that focuses on one aspect of personal finance. Check out the Contents at a Glance to see how the book is organized.

You can peruse this book in the way most books have been perused since time immemorial — from cover to cover, starting on Page 1. Or you can use it as a reference guide, looking up specific topics in the Index or Table of Contents.

To make reading and understanding personal finance topics a bit easier, this book uses some conventions to help you along the way:

>> **Italics:** Newly defined terms are set in *italics.*

>> **Acronyms:** Acronyms are spelled out on first use.

>> **Websites:** You'll find references to websites that may provide additional information or make some task easier. Every effort has been made to make sure the links are functional at the time of publishing. If you ever see a website URL split from one line to the next, rest assured there are no extra hyphens, so type the address in your browser just as it appears. If you're reading the e-book, just tap the link to go to that website.

Foolish Assumptions

Here's what this book assumes about you:

>> **You're middle-aged.** You're no spring chicken. You did not just fall off the turnip truck. You've been, as it were, around the block. As such, you probably know very well what a mortgage is, for example, but may not know what a *reverse* mortgage is exactly. You know there are these mysterious programs called Medicare and Social Security headed your way in a few years, but as for details, well . . . you haven't exactly studied up on them — yet.

>> **You know you can do better with your money.** You're busy — work and family duties have had you running around for years. You have a vague sense that you're not as well off as you should be, and you know there must be things you're not doing that you should be doing, and vice versa. You've come to the right place.

That's it! If those two descriptions apply to you, you're ready to read on for hundreds of ideas and expert advice on whipping your finances into shape.

Icons Used in This Book

This book uses the following icons to point out certain insights:

This one indicates short summaries of subject matter you've just read about and also points out important things to keep in mind for later. If you hesitate for a moment when reading the core content, check for one of these to keep progressing smoothly.

This icon flags stuff that may be more technical than you really need to know. The information included with this icon isn't necessary to your understanding of the topic at hand, and you can safely skip it.

This icon is just what you think it is. It highlights something particularly helpful, useful, surprising, or efficient that is well worth paying extra attention to.

This icon flags stuff that could get you in trouble or hurt you financially. Ignore these at your peril!

Beyond the Book

In addition to the material in the print or e-book you're reading right now, this product also comes with some access-anywhere goodies on the web. Check out the free Cheat Sheet and other free articles at www.dummies.com. Just search for "personal finance in your 50s all-in-one."

Where to Go from Here

Ready to go? You're about to dive into lots of valuable advice. As mentioned, feel free to pour a mug of coffee (or, heck, beer), sink into your favorite chair, and plunge into Book 1, Chapter 1. Or if you're really interested in something specific, look it up in the Index or Table of Contents.

Maybe you're in better shape in some areas than others. Maybe your mortgage *is* actually paid off or close to it. However, you hate your job and want to finally strike out on your own and be your own boss, but you've never had the courage to do it. Try Book 1, Chapter 3.

Or perhaps you really *do* have an up-to-date will, but you're terrible at managing a budget. Check out Book 4, Chapter 2 for loads of tips on budget management.

Or you do *indeed* love your job, but you've put away next to nothing for retirement and you're starting to get nervous you'll never be able to. Get thee to Book 1, Chapter 6 to get started on that. (And, no, it's never too late.)

No matter where you begin, you're sure to find a wealth of great ideas in this big old book that can make your life better. Heck, even if you pick up only one or two great ideas and implement them — such as buying an umbrella insurance policy (Book 3, Chapter 4), figuring out what you're worth so you can plan where it should go after you're gone (Book 5, Chapter 2), or turning the equity in your home into a steady income stream that *pays you* every month (Book 6, Chapter 2) — then the book already paid for itself many times over.

Congratulations on recognizing that you *can* and *should* be doing better than you are financially. Really, that's all of us. Because who has time to become an expert on all the dizzying aspects of personal finance? Oh, right . . . the authors of the following pages! So let our hard-earned wisdom guide you. It's time to dive in!

1

Managing Your Career and Retirement

Contents at a Glance

Chapter **1**

Finding a New Job after 50

Welcome, job seekers! Finding a job at any age takes work and dedication. Some older job seekers assume that employers would rather outsource jobs to cheaper workers overseas or hire younger, less experienced workers for lower wages. Although these suspicions are confirmed by the hiring practices of some organizations, current studies show that employers are increasingly willing to consider older candidates and that age alone isn't necessarily the reason some employers are unwilling to consider older candidates.

This chapter aims to help you shift your attitude about job hunting from one of apprehension to one of hope and possibility and to show you a few simple ways to rev up your job-search mojo to today's new workplace reality for job seekers age 50 and older.

Recognizing the Need for and Value of Experienced Workers

The times really are a-changin', and that's good news for your job-hunting prospects. Whether you want to work in an office job, teach yoga, or head up a company, more employers are starting to realize that hiring workers age 50 and older is good for business, and more and more employers are discovering the value of experienced workers. Unfortunately for job seekers 50 and older, the fact that demand for experienced workers is on the rise is a well-kept secret. Realizing that employers need you is an important first step in the process of finding and landing the job you want. It gives you the enthusiasm and confidence to set out on what may be a long and arduous journey. This section reveals the reasons that the demand for older workers is rising — to invigorate you for the journey ahead and remind you of just how valuable you are to employers who need your skills, talents, and experience.

REMEMBER

A job search can be disheartening for anyone, regardless of age. And if that's what you're feeling, never show it to a prospective employer. Always highlight the value you have to offer in every job-search communiqué you send out. If you need a confidence lift, take some time and review all your previous achievements.

Noting a change in the current workforce

Many CEOs are increasingly aware that they need to have older, more experienced workers on board. As the population ages, the workforce is aging right along with it. U.S. employees 65 and older now outnumber teenagers in the workforce for the first time since 1948. In 2002, workers 50 and older comprised 24.6 percent of the workforce. By 2012, they represented 32.3 percent. And by 2022, they're projected to be 35.4 percent of the total workforce.

This emerging trend isn't likely to change anytime soon. More than one in three workers age 45 and older expects to retire at age 66 or older, compared to just over one in five 10 years ago. Moreover, 72 percent of workers ages 45 to 74 envision working in retirement.

Employers are getting worried about their future workforce. In a recent survey by the Society for Human Resource Management (SHRM), one-third of HR professionals predicted that the loss of talent resulting from retirements or departures of workers age 55 and older would be either a problem or a crisis for their organization in the next six to ten years. The Manpower Group 2014 Talent Shortage Survey found that 40 percent of U.S. employers reported difficulty in filling jobs.

Seeing experienced workers as an affordable option

The old concerns that hiring someone your age would probably be too pricey are being debunked. Contrary to common perception, workers age 50 and older don't cost significantly more than younger workers, according to the report "A Business Case for Workers Age 50+: A Look at the Value of Experience 2015," commissioned by AARP and conducted by Aon Hewitt.

Shifting trends in reward and benefit programs mean that adding more age 50-plus talent to a workforce results in only minimal increases in hard dollar total labor costs. These trends include a broad move by large employers to performance-based versus tenure-based compensation, the decline in traditional benefit pension plans, and the fact that healthcare costs are increasing at a slower rate for older workers compared to younger workers.

Meanwhile, in today's global and fast-paced workplace, firms often don't have the time to squander while a younger worker ramps up skills and knowledge. Companies are slowly realizing that to stay competitive, it's smarter to seek out and hire experienced workers. That means you're on the cutting edge of a sweeping change in the demographics of the workplace.

Recent surveys show that companies are realizing that it's strategically smart to pay more attention to recruiting and retaining workers age 50 and older. When organizations need someone to step in and do the job right now and solve an existing problem, they're eager to hire the experienced worker.

That's what the AARP report unveiled. Findings from a 2014 SHRM survey of HR professionals also back up that trend. SHRM's *The Aging Workforce* survey also found that two-thirds of HR executives canvassed reported that their organization employed older workers who retired from other organizations or careers before joining their organization. Gold stars all around.

The *Aging Workforce* survey, part of a three-year national Aging Workforce Initiative by SHRM and the SHRM Foundation and funded by the Alfred P. Sloan Foundation, also found that 61 percent of the 1,900 randomly selected SHRM HR professionals indicated that their organization had attempted to capitalize on and incorporate the experience of older workers in recruitment and retention strategies. (Kudos to them.) The top advantages of older workers were having more work experience (cited by 77 percent of respondents), being more mature/professional (71 percent), and having a stronger work ethic (70 percent).

Capitalizing on lower turnover

Employers find that workers age 50 and older are more loyal and aren't as likely as younger workers to job jump. And that lower staff turnover benefits the bottom line, because the costs of high turnover are tangible. Finding, hiring, and training a new employee is a costly venture, and it becomes even costlier when that well-trained employee decides to jump ship and work for a competitor.

RETAINING OLDER WORKERS PAYS DIVIDENDS, TOO

Depending on your position and industry, the total cost of replacing you can range from thousands of dollars to as much as one-and-a-half times your annual salary. Retaining older workers reduces the one-time costs of turnover, which range from $7,400 to $31,700 or more per employee, according to AARP's most recent survey. This cost includes the time and money that go hand in hand with recruiting and advertising your job, bringing people in for an interview, and training a new hire.

Plus, it's hard to put a price on the institutional knowledge that goes out the door with a departing employee. Now tack on the stress that managers and coworkers must shoulder to make up for the work that falls between the cracks when an employee leaves. And, finally, toss in the toll of lost morale that accompanies the departure of a valued team member. Now the employer has a serious problem. And that's clearly a big incentive for hiring a worker over 50. Older workers often anchor a team.

Harnessing the power of highly engaged workers

Aon Hewitt data show that older workers, in general, *love* their jobs more than younger workers do. Yes, we're more engaged than our younger counterparts. Perhaps we're grateful for the jobs in a way that someone new to the workforce has yet to learn to value and appreciate.

For example, 65 percent of employees age 55 and up in large companies are "engaged," compared to fewer than 60 percent of employees under age 45. Although this gap may seem small, it represents a statistically significant difference in engagement that can have a noticeable impact on business outcomes, according to the AARP report.

In addition to being the most highly engaged age group in the labor force, workers age 55 and older are also the most motivated. A whopping 81 percent of workers age 55 and up are "motivated" — meaning they say that they exert extra effort and contribute more than is normally required in their job — compared to 76 percent of their peers age 25 to 34. Talk about selling points for older workers on the job hunt!

Reaping additional benefits

In addition to all those wonderful attributes already mentioned, older workers typically have the following:

- ➤➤ Ability to make quick decisions and solve problems

- ➤➤ Greater maturity and professionalism

- ➤➤ Superior communication skills, both written and oral

- ➤➤ Ability to serve as mentors

- ➤➤ Critical qualities of reliability and dependability

- ➤➤ More knowledge, wisdom, and overall life experience

Shoulders back. You're valued. Put all this positive juju in your back pocket and never forget how much you have to offer on the job.

Tallying the Benefits of Staying in the Workforce

To get you even more fired up about your job search, here are five money-wise reasons to stay in the workforce as long as you can:

- ➤➤ **The more years you contribute to your retirement plans, the better off you'll be down the road.** You'll be able to delay taking Social Security, which will dramatically boost your eventual payout. If your full retirement age is 66, for example, and you start collecting at age 70, your monthly check will be 32 percent higher than if you begin benefits at 66 and 76 percent more than if you start taking benefits at 62 (when most people do).

  The longer you work, the longer you delay tapping retirement funds, which can continue to grow.

- ➤➤ **Working longer provides income to pay for health insurance until you're eligible for Medicare at 65.** Fewer employers are offering their retired workers medical benefits, and those who do are ramping up the amount retirees must contribute to the cost of coverage. Even better, you may find a job that offers you access to a health plan.

TIP

  Consider the advantage of a health savings account (HSA). If your employer provides one, take advantage of it. It's a good way to save as a tax deduction and use the dollars tax free for qualified medical expenses.

>> **Money aside, you may want to keep working to maintain a sense of well-being.** For people over 50, being engaged, not just involved, is important, according to a report by The Sloan Center on Aging & Work at Boston College. Similarly, when asked about their life and careers, 75 percent of people in their 40s and 50s said they want to make their life more meaningful, while 82 percent said they want to give back more, according to a study commissioned by Life Reimagined, which was created by AARP to help people with midlife transitions. Nearly 30 percent plan to make a career change in the next five years; top reasons include having the opportunity to learn more and giving more back to the community. Work gives you a sense of purpose and of feeling connected and needed. It makes you feel relevant. Pinning a dollar figure to that is difficult, but it's real.

>> **Work sharpens the mind.** Researchers from the RAND Center for the Study of Aging and the University of Michigan published a study showing that cognitive performance levels decline faster in countries that have younger retirement ages. What? Brain cells dying from lack of use? You bet. It's the old "Use it or lose it" axiom. Many aging experts say that to stay healthy, older adults have to learn new things, stay active socially, and exercise.

Bottom line: We're living longer, healthier lives. As a result, we're staying longer in the workforce because we can and often because we need to in order to have a financially secure retirement.

Reorienting Yourself to Today's Job-Search Realities

What's new since your last job hunt? If it's been a while, you'll quickly find that technology has made job searching easier in some ways but more complex than ever in others. Although the Internet has improved access to openings, it has also increased competition for those same openings. Typically, an average of more than 250 résumés are submitted for every job posting, and the first résumé appears within 200 seconds of the posting "going live," according to online job-search expert Susan P. Joyce, publisher of WorkCoachCafe.com.

Although job-search sites make finding jobs easier, online applications and automated screening technologies pose additional obstacles to getting past the gatekeepers. According to a study by job-match site TheLadders (www.the ladders.com), many companies use talent-management software to screen résumés, weeding out up to 50 percent of applications before anyone ever looks at a résumé or cover letter.

REMEMBER

Little wonder then that a recent CareerXroads survey shows that only 15 percent of positions were filled through online job boards. So visiting job boards and applying for jobs is probably not the best use of your time, even though you feel like you have to. Most jobs are either filled internally or through referrals. Yes, the old-fashioned way. In fact, only about half of the roughly 5 million jobs now open in the United States are *ever* advertised publicly. Employers still prefer to hire people they know either directly or indirectly through a referral. In studies of many different employers going back to 2001, employee referrals are the top source of people hired into a company — not job postings. In fact, employee referrals provided more than 55 percent of the hires in one of the studies.

In other words, employers want to hire someone who has already been vetted in some way, which can save a lot of hassle and cost of the hiring process and of replacing people who don't work out, even if they looked great on paper and interviewed like pros. Employers love it when someone who already works for the organization can vouch for the person. And the employee making the referral often has some skin in the game, so to speak. Many employers pop a bonus reward of up to $1,000 or more for referring someone who's hired and does a good job in the first few months on the job.

Does this mean that applying for a job on job boards isn't worthwhile? Not at all! Scanning the boards gives you a sense of who's hiring, what types of openings are out there, and salary ranges. But it does mean that other approaches, such as networking and marketing yourself, may ultimately forge a better route to landing a job.

Deciding What (Else) You Want Out of Work

For many, their paychecks aren't generally what get them juiced about going to work. Most people say they're motivated by the people they work with, the opportunity to keep learning and growing, or the mission or cause of their employer's services or the products it makes. Sometimes they say they love the travel opportunities. So don't get locked into a must-have salary. When searching for jobs and comparing offers, be sure to account for other benefits, including the following:

>> **Flexible workday:** Being able to work from home or having flexible hours or a compressed schedule are biggies. It comes down to being treated as a responsible adult and weaving work more seamlessly into the fabric of your life. And that may be getting easier to achieve. A Bank of America Merrill Lynch survey of 650 human resources executives recently found that half of

employers are willing to offer flexible arrangements, such as working part time or job sharing, to their most skilled and experienced workers.

>> **Healthy work-life balance:** Three in five people interested in a second career midlife say it's very important that the job leaves free time for things they want to do, such as travel, education, or engagement in other activities they enjoy, according to a report by Encore.org, a nonprofit organization that's building a movement to tap the skills and experience of those in midlife and beyond to improve communities. Indeed, many of those interested in encore careers appear eager to mix fewer hours of work per week with more years of work in total. Finding more flexibility may make working a few more years more palatable.

>> **Meaningful work:** More than 25 million Americans 50 to 70 years old are eager to share their skills, passions, and expertise in encore careers that address social needs, typically in education, healthcare, human services, and the environment, according to a 2014 study by Encore.org and Penn Schoen Berland. Of those 25 million, more than 4.5 million are already working for social impact. Another 21 million are ready to join them within the next five years.

>> **Opportunities to interact with others and stay productive:** Human beings are hard-wired to create, produce, and collaborate, and rewarding work provides opportunities to remain active and productive. A Pew Research Center survey found that working for non-financial reasons, such as job enjoyment or the desire to be productive, increases with age.

>> **Competitive benefits:** An AARP/SHRM survey of workers age 50 and up suggested older workers place significance on having competitive benefits and flexible work arrangements. When these workers consider a job offer, health insurance, retirement savings plans, and paid time off benefits play an important role in their decisions. For example, approximately eight in ten workers age 50 and older consider the availability of benefits such as health insurance (82 percent); a pension, 401(k), or other retirement plan (77 percent); and paid time off (80 percent) to be "very" or "somewhat" important considerations in the decision to accept a job.

>> **Learning opportunities:** Boomers tend to be curious, eager, and adventure-some. They're not geared to be couch potatoes passively absorbing entertain-ment. As such, they value learning opportunities both on the job and through employer-sponsored continuing education programs.

Employers are increasingly tuning in to these incentives. So though they worry that they may not be able to meet your salary expectations, they're discover-ing that workers 50 and older are attracted to more than pay. So employers are increasingly offering such non–financial perks as flexible work schedules, tele-commuting options, and training and education opportunities.

Pursuing Your Passion and Finding Purpose

When it comes to finding a successful and meaningful second act, most people simply don't know what they're passionate about, even when they know that they want to move in another direction. This section encourages you to explore other careers and check out some of the fastest-growing job markets to find the right fit. It also provides some tips and cautions to help guide you as you set out to pursue your passion and add purpose to your life.

REMEMBER

Pursuing your passion is fine, but you don't want to end up in the poorhouse doing it. Look for ways to align your passion with what's in demand.

Considering other careers

One way to discover a passion that you can transform into gainful employment is to consider other careers. If you've ever thought to yourself, "I'd like to have her job," you have a head start. Think about those jobs you've always dreamed of having. Maybe you've always wanted to be a writer, graphic artist, wedding planner, interior designer, private investigator, or sports announcer. Perhaps you've always dreamed of owning a bed and breakfast, brewing your own beer, making candy, or producing movies.

No, it's not too late to start thinking about pursuing a totally new career, and many your age have done so successfully. Think of it this way: If you live to 100 and look back 50 years or so, will you still think you were too old back then to pursue that dream job?

TIP

Start now. Pursuing a new career is likely to require a significant commitment of time, money, and effort. The longer time frame you have to plan, the better. Start working at age 50 on a career you might not get around to until age 60. You can start now to research a career you're interested in, take classes, and perhaps even secure an internship in the field to take the new career for a test drive to gauge your true interest in it before going all in.

Test-driving a career in some form is always a good idea. Career changers may enter a period of mourning after starting their new careers. All of a sudden, they realize how much they miss their old careers and aren't really open to replacing what they once had. Internship opportunities are one way to test-drive different work.

FINDING INSPIRATION IN SUCCESS STORIES

Many people find that their passion is something they did when they were younger, often in childhood.

One woman moved from working in a management position at an insurance company to launching her own business making pillows out of old wedding dresses and crafting other customized pillows and quilts. When Marilyn Arnold was 9 years old, her mother, a skilled seamstress, patiently taught her to sew on a vintage Singer treadle sewing machine. As her feet pumped away at the machine in her family's farmhouse near Paris, Missouri, she was smitten. "I was in love with sewing, even when I stuck my finger and it bled," Arnold told me. But she never dreamed that now, at the age of 66, she would be running her own small business, Marilyn Arnold Designs, in Lee's Summit, Missouri.

Bill Skees has been a bibliophile for as long as he can remember. His favorite haunt growing up in Midland, Texas, was a bookstore called Miz B's. "I'd look at her behind the counter and think, 'That's got to be the greatest job in the world.'" In the decades that followed, Skees crossed the country for various jobs in IT, most recently heading development for a gaming company. But the work was stressful, and every chance he got, he slipped off to a bookstore. All the while, he dreamed of opening his own shop. And at 56, he did. He now owns and manages Well Read Books in Hawthorne, New Jersey.

Someday, you'll be able to add your success story to this list.

REMEMBER

Money is the biggest roadblock for most career changers. When you start over in a new field or move to a nonprofit, chances are you need to take a salary cut at least initially. If you have an emergency fund to buy you time, you can do a more thoughtful job search. If you need to, pare back your discretionary living expenses to reflect a more realistic view of what you'll earn. See the later section "Navigating a career change" for details.

Checking out fast-growing job markets

One way to pursue your passion while ensuring your marketability is to consider employment in fast-growing markets. Certain industries, such as energy and healthcare, are experiencing more profound talent shortages than others. According to the ManpowerGroup's 2014 Talent Shortage Survey, here are the top ten jobs that U.S. employers are having trouble filling:

>> Skilled trades (welders, electricians, machinists, and so on, prevalent in construction and manufacturing)

- >> Restaurant and hotel staff

- >> Sales representatives

- >> Teachers

- >> Drivers

- >> Accounting and finance staff

- >> Laborers

- >> IT staff

- >> Engineers

- >> Nurses

Occupations with the most robust job growth by 2022, according to the Bureau of Labor Statistics (BLS), range from personal care and home health aides to interpreters and translators, brick masons and stonemasons, electricians' helpers, and event planners.

Although most of the job growth is expected to be in fields that don't require postsecondary education, jobs that require a college degree or higher are actually growing faster (14.0 percent versus 9.1 percent). And those higher-skilled jobs will pay, on average, more than double ($57,770 per year versus $27,670).

The following sections describe the sectors that are likely to be the hottest over the next few years.

TIP

Look for jobs and opportunities that leverage experience. Check out job websites, including www.aarp.org/work, encore.org, www.Job-Hunt.org, retiredbrains.com, and Workforce50.com to get a flavor for what others are doing and what jobs are out there now.

Healthcare

Look for opportunities in healthcare support, such as nursing assistants, physical and occupational therapists and assistants, skincare specialists, physician assistants, genetic counselors, and social workers. According to projections released by Georgetown University in 2015, the United States faces a shortage of 193,000 nursing professionals by 2020. Additionally, a 2015 report from The Association of American Medical Colleges estimates that, by 2025, the United States will experience a shortfall of anywhere from 46,100 to 90,400 physicians. Here again, recruitment and retention efforts aimed at the 50 and older workforce can help address this shortage.

According to the BLS, occupations related to healthcare, healthcare support, construction, and personal care services, such as physical therapists, skincare specialists, and social workers are expected to add a combined 5.3 million jobs in the United States, an increase representing approximately one-third of all employment gains over the coming decade.

The dietitian, nutritionist, and nursing assistant occupations are each projected to grow 21.1 percent between 2012 and 2022, according to BLS data. Given the comparatively small size of the dietitians and nutritionists profession, projected growth is expected to result in the addition of 14,200 new jobs. The nursing assistants occupation, however, is far larger. The upshot: The same anticipated growth rate in that occupation is expected to add 312,200 new jobs to the economy by 2022.

Leisure and hospitality

The leisure and hospitality sector is growing. People will be spending money to eat out and go on vacation. Chefs, cooks, waiters, bartenders, and restaurant and hotel managers will be in demand.

Software development

The software developer and programmer sector is expected to add 279,500 jobs by 2022, accounting for about four out of ten new jobs in the computer and math occupations group, according to BLS.

Cybersecurity

Although projected growth in jobs for information security analysts, at 27,400 new positions, is tiny compared to jobs for software developers and programmers, the rate of growth for information security analysts is expected to be 37 percent, making this the fastest-growing job in this sector.

Engineering

According to 2013 Current Population Survey data, 22 percent (or 447,000) of engineers in the United States are age 55 and up. As these workers approach retirement age, there may not be enough new workforce entrants to replace their loss in key roles. Focused efforts to retain and recruit older workers can mitigate these gaps.

AARP EMPLOYER PLEDGE: EXPERIENCE VALUED

The AARP Employer Pledge: Experience Valued program (www.aarp.org/work/job-search/employer-pledge-companies/?intcmp=AE-WOR-MAIN) is a national initiative to direct job seekers to employers that value and are hiring experienced workers *and* help employers solve their current and future staffing challenges. Employers who sign the pledge agree that they will do the following:

- Recognize the value of experienced workers
- Believe in equal opportunity for all workers, regardless of age
- Recruit across diverse age groups
- Consider all applicants on an equal basis
- Have immediate hiring needs

More than 460 employers have signed the pledge, including AlliedBarton, American Red Cross, AT&T, Charles Schwab, CVS Caremark, General Mills, Google, Kimberly Clark, Manpower, National Institutes of Health (NIH), New York Life, Scripps Health, S&T Bancorp, Toys "R" Us, United Health Care, Walgreens, and WellStar Health Systems.

Skilled labor

BLS projections show that considerable job growth is expected in skilled labor professions, including brick masons, block masons, stonemasons, and tile and marble setters (and their helpers), and electricians' helpers. As mentioned earlier, employers are currently having the most trouble filling openings in these and other skilled trades.

Translators

For those who speak foreign languages, labor experts also project that there will be a rising need for interpreters and translators in courtrooms and other settings.

Taking the first steps in pursuing your passion

"Pursue your passion" is the kind of advice you receive from a friend or relative who either never pursued her passion or knew from the day she was born what she wanted to do. It sounds like great advice until you pause to think about it and realize that you have no idea what your passion is or how to take that first step from point A to point B. Here are some suggestions to ease you into those first steps, with a tip of the hat to career coach Beverly Jones:

>> **Find a place to start.** You don't need a precise definition before you get going. Start by making a list of what you want in the next phase of your career. Don't look for a perfect path or ideal starting point.

>> **Get things moving by taking small steps.** Get moving in the general direction of where you want to go. One small step may be calling someone who works in a field that appeals to you to discuss possibilities.

>> **Silence your inner enemy.** If you have a negative refrain that goes through your head and sabotages your efforts to make a change, such as, "I'm too old to do that," make note of it. Write that thought down in a notebook and reframe it with a positive thought, such as, "I have these specific skills, and I'm going to use them in a new career." You need to get rid of that old blocking message to move forward with your dreams.

>> **Ask the basic questions.** Does your second act fit your lifestyle? Can you afford it? What does your partner think? Ask yourself how a certain career will work with your social life, your spending habits, and your family situation. It will help you to dig deeper and get a clearer picture of what you truly want in your life and your options to get there.

>> **Keep a journal.** Journaling is a great way to map your new career direction. Make lists: the best times in your life, the things you really like, the experiences you've enjoyed, what you've excelled at, the best moments in your current career. These lists will help you hone in on your passion and visualize yourself harnessing it to pursue something new and exciting.

>> **Get a business card.** Want to be an artist but still working as a lawyer? Get an artist's business card. As soon as you have a card, it makes the career real. You can get your second-act card long before you finish your first act. Printing your new information on a card can be transformative.

>> **Have a mental picture of where you want to go.** Tape a photograph to your office wall of what your new career might look like. Or create a collage. Journal about your goals.

>> **Be practical.** You may need to upgrade your skills and education, but take one class at a time. You can add more classes as your direction and motivation become clear.

>> **Get your life in order.** Get physically and financially fit. Change is stressful. When you're physically fit, you have more energy. Less debt gives you more choices. Debt is a dream killer. With your finances in order, you have more options. You can be more nimble.

WARNING

Don't ruin your hobby. For example, you may love to garden, and you may start thinking about becoming a landscape designer. But you may also quickly realize that you're lonely in the garden all day; you actually prefer working with people. Gardening is a great hobby and escape from work, but it wouldn't be the right career move for you (in this example). Make sure that you think hard about how your passion will look and feel as a *career*.

Putting Proven Success Strategies into Practice

You're not the first person to be looking for a job later in life, and that's good news for you. Others have led the way from unemployment to rewarding work in their 50s and beyond. And although these trailblazers haven't beaten down a path for you to follow (because there are so many paths to follow), they have revealed some strategies and techniques that have survived the test of time. The following sections introduce you to several of the more effective strategies for securing employment, most of which apply to all job seekers, but a couple of which apply specifically to job seekers age 50 and older.

Starting sooner rather than later

The sooner you start looking for a job after losing a job, the more likely you'll find a new job. According to the AARP Public Policy Institute report "The Long Road Back: Struggling to Find Work after Unemployment," by Gary Koenig, Lori Trawinski, and Sara Rix, those who waited three months or longer before beginning their job search were less likely to have become reemployed.

Why wait so long to look for work? The most popular answer was that they needed a break. Other reasons survey respondents cited include that they took time to think about what they wanted to do next (57 percent), had savings or other sources of income (56 percent), and found it hard to get motivated (42 percent). Twenty-five percent of respondents waited to begin their job search because of caregiving responsibilities, about the same number who waited because they didn't know how to get started. Whatever the reason, postponing the search for three months or longer worked against them.

Giving yourself a full-body makeover

Being physically fit, well groomed, and properly dressed is better than Botox. Aim to look and dress with an eye toward a vibrant, youthful appearance:

>> **If you aren't physically fit, make that a priority.** Eat healthy, avoiding sugary and starchy foods and sugary drinks. Exercise at least 30 minutes every other day. Quit or cut back on caffeine, nicotine, and alcohol, if you're so inclined to use those substances.

Maintain a well-groomed appearance. Get a haircut. Try a new 'do to give yourself a fresh look.

>> **Spruce up your wardrobe.** Get the right look for the job that you're seeking. Free personal shoppers are available at many department stores to help. Or you can also ask friends for tips on looking your best. If you wear glasses, consider getting contacts, Lasik surgery, or new glasses with more contemporary frames.

People do judge a book by its cover. Showing up for an interview looking vigorous, well groomed, and sharply dressed demonstrates that you're up for the job and have the requisite stamina, which is often a concern for employers when they consider hiring someone over 50. This advice also applies to any headshots you use for your social media and networking profiles.

Using the most effective means to get a job

When reemployed workers were asked about the most effective steps they took in finding their current jobs, the overwhelming majority attributed their success to networking, according to the AARP's "The Long Road Back: Struggling to Find Work after Unemployment." Here are the most effective steps:

>> Reaching out to a network of contacts

>> Asking relatives and friends about jobs

>> Contacting employers directly

>> Using a headhunter

>> Consulting professional associations

If you're interested in a particular industry, join an association connected with it and seek out volunteer openings. Go to industry and professional meetings and conferences. You never know who will know someone who is hiring. And many college and university career centers are reaching out to alumni to help, too.

Consider volunteering while you're out of work. By putting your volunteering on your résumé, you won't show a blank period of unemployment. To the extent that you can, be out in the world using your skills.

Be aggressive in your job search. Network as much as you can as well as keep an eye out for openings. The people who are aggressive are more likely to be reemployed.

REMEMBER

Networking is not optional. The good news is many older folks have better networks than do younger people. Employers want to hire someone who comes with the blessing of an existing employee or colleague. It makes their job easier. That's a card younger workers, who often have smaller networks, can't play as often as older workers. LinkedIn, for instance, is a great way to pull together your professional network. And you have got to pick up that darn phone. Ask for help and advice. Here are some concrete ways to network:

>> **Pick up the phone and call everybody you ever worked with and every employer you ever worked for.** That's the way to get an interview. If you don't establish a personal connection to the company, submitting an application is probably a waste of time.

Call friends of friends, people in your faith community, athletic club, volunteer organizations, and parents of your children's friends. Heck, call your children's friends, too.

Contact trade and professional associations you belong to. Many have job boards.

>> **Connect with alumni associations and your fraternity or sorority if you belong to one.** College and university placement offices are there to help no matter how long ago you graduated.

Canvas local lawyers, accountants, and bank officers in town and see whether they know of any clients who are hiring. In short, you really have to "kiss a lot of frogs" to find a prince. Leave no stone unturned.

>> **Get social.** Join LinkedIn and Facebook, find and reconnect with people you know, and let everyone know you're looking for a job.

TIP

For a treasure trove of job-search tips and information, head to `www.aarp.org/work`.

The next sections introduce additional strategies and techniques that are effective in landing a job.

Broadening your job search

Broadening your job search simply means being open to other possibilities — considering a different profession in a different industry, making trade-offs in terms of salary and flextime, stitching together a full-time position with part-time gigs, and so on. It doesn't mean applying to every job opening you find. You really want to focus your efforts in one area for maximum impact, but you don't want to pass up a golden opportunity just because it doesn't happen to conform to your notion of the ideal job.

MAKING TRADE-OFFS

Broadening your job search often requires making trade-offs. According to the AARP Public Policy Institute report, "The Long Road Back: Struggling to Find Work after Unemployment," those who manage to find a job often accept lower pay and benefits, and many have to change occupations.

Although some unemployed people have succeeded in finding work with better pay and benefits and more favorable working conditions, others accepted lower wages and fewer benefits, possibly indicating a desire for more flexible work options for work-life balance. Here are some of the ways participants in the study reported broadening their job search:

- Looking for a job in a different field. This was the most common response overall (by 41 percent) for both the currently reemployed and the unemployed (43 percent of each).

- Looking for a job with lower pay or benefits (37 percent of the reemployed and 39 percent of the unemployed). Perhaps job seekers became more realistic as time went on about the possibility of finding the types of jobs and pay they had before becoming unemployed.

Occupational change was a common occurrence among the reemployed; more than half (53 percent) had an occupation different from the one they had before becoming unemployed. Almost two-thirds (63 percent) of the long-term unemployed had a job in a different occupation than the one they had before becoming unemployed. By comparison, 46 percent of the short-term unemployed were in a different occupation.

Among the reemployed working in new occupations, 40 percent were earning "a lot less" and 17 percent were earning "somewhat less" on their current jobs. By comparison, 18 percent and 20 percent, respectively, of the reemployed working in the same occupations said they were earning "a lot less" or "somewhat less." Working in a new occupation often means lower pay because a worker's experience may not be as applicable in the new job.

One way to broaden your search is to think less in terms of job title and more in terms of skills, knowledge, and experience — all these assets may be transferrable to a different profession, a different line of work. If you're focused on a full-time job, you can broaden your search by considering contract work or a temporary assignment, which may lead to a full-time position or even starting your own business.

Considering a patchwork approach to your career

As Henry Ford once said, "Nothing is particularly hard if you divide it into small jobs." You may be able to apply this maxim to piecing together full- or part-time work. For example, you could take on one or two part-time jobs, do some contract work or consulting on the side, and still have plenty of free time and enough money to enjoy that time. Or you may do full-time seasonal work for part of the year and take on a part-time job the rest of the year. And you may want to gradually scale down your workweek over the years as you make a smooth transition into retirement.

Don't be surprised if you find yourself testing a number of different kinds of jobs to find what you really shine at or want to do in the years ahead. You may even strategically build an income stream from a tapestry of work you enjoy and are skilled at doing.

TIP

Consider opening a consulting practice and making yourself available for short-term projects. Alternatively, you might find that creating a patchwork of income streams will give you the flexibility you crave.

Navigating a career change

Fifty-five percent of U.S. workers want to change careers, according to a University of Phoenix survey. To make a switch, you'll probably have to learn new skills, make new professional contacts, sock away cash, and more. Here are the best moves to make your change a successful one:

» Be adaptable and embrace change.

» Do your research. Reach out to people doing the work you want to do, and ask them all you can about their jobs. How did they get started? What do you need to succeed? And what can you expect to earn, both at first and later on? Because you aren't asking for a job, the discussion should be relaxed. Be inquisitive.

>> Moonlight or apprentice yourself to someone already in the field.

>> If you want to work for a nonprofit in a cause meaningful to you — a common goal among career changers — then volunteer; you'll not only see what the day-to-day work entails but also meet people in the organization.

>> Identify the skills you need. Be prepared to spend the time and money to get the skills, credentials, and contacts you need to get relaunched, but don't assume that you'll need a costly degree. See the next section, "Getting the training you need," for details.

>> Get financial aid. Fifty-four percent of employers offer tuition assistance to employees, reports the Society for Human Resource Management. You may have to repay the funds, though, if you don't stay with the company for a certain number of years afterward.

>> Assess your finances. Following your passion is great, but make sure you can afford your dream job. As a general rule, you should try to have at least your first year's worth of expenses covered.

Getting the training you need

Once you reach a certain age, you may be branded with stereotypes that make you vulnerable: resistant to change, technologically challenged, complacent. In a survey by staffing agency Adecco, 39 percent of employers said the greatest challenge with older workers is their difficulty learning new technologies. Of course, this is a misconception — Pew Institute research shows 87 percent of American adults use the Internet — but you may need to demonstrate your tech aptitude to disprove this perception. To increase your market value, obtain the education, training, and certifications required to do the job you're seeking.

WARNING

Before taking classes or training for new skills, research the demand for those skills locally. In the AARP Public Policy Institute study of unemployment, of the 31 percent who participated in training or education programs in the past five years, more said doing so "did not help at all" than those who said it "helped a great deal." This could be pointing to a mismatch between the training they received and current job openings. Before enrolling in expensive courses or classes, do your due diligence:

>> Contact a local community college and ask about skills that local employers are looking for. In certain cases, the American Association of Community Colleges partners with AARP Foundation and local workforce agencies and employers to do this; you can find those community colleges in the Back to Work 50+ section on www.aarp.org/foundation.

Talk to graduates and employers to find out whether the educational and training programs are truly valuable.

>> Consider what you can afford and the return on your investment. Look at free options as well as paid.

Seeking help

During your job search, don't hesitate to ask others for help. People are generally glad to assist if you ask politely for what you need. After all, wouldn't you be eager to help friends or relatives revamp their résumé or assist in any other way you could if they were looking for a job? Sometimes, the most generous people are the least likely to ask for help, never realizing that others may need the opportunity to help someone else. Sometimes, you have to be a taker. Here are common areas where older job seekers often need help:

>> Writing or updating a résumé

>> Getting emotional support (someone to listen)

>> Searching for jobs online

>> Using a computer (navigating LinkedIn, Facebook, Twitter, and other social media and networking sites)

Here are some resources to consider checking out when you need help:

>> Family and friends

>> Workforce centers/one-stop job centers

>> Online job-search sites

>> Career or job coaches

>> Your local library

>> Educational institutions, including placement services

Dealing with Ageism

News from the job front isn't all roses. Ageism is real. If you're over 50 and pounding the pavement these days, you will face certain challenges. Once becoming unemployed, it typically takes an older worker longer to find a job than it does a younger person, according to the Bureau of Labor Statistics (www.bls.gov/web/empsit/cpseea36.pdf). If you've felt the disappointment of a floundering job hunt at a gut level, you have plenty of company. Many are frankly furious, discouraged, and dumbfounded by their inability to land a job that suits their experience and desired salary.

The key to overcoming ageism is to understand employers' concerns and address those concerns, the topics of the next sections.

Knowing what employers are so worried about

Some employers figure that your salary demands are out of their ballpark, and that if they hire you for less, you'll resent it and probably jump ship if you get a better offer. They often perceive, true or not, that you're set in your ways or lack the cutting-edge skills or even the energy to do the job.

Then, too, some hiring managers might surmise that you have age-related health problems, or are likely to, and you'll be taking too much sick leave. And, of course, there's the nagging issue that you're not in it for the long haul, even if that's far from the truth. Finally, there's concern about reverse ageism — the employer may think you won't want to take orders from a younger boss who is probably making more than you.

REMEMBER

Landing a job is difficult for everybody, and everyone seems to have a different take on what it takes to break through. It's not automatically your age that's holding you back. Employers want to hire people they know or can trust. In addition, employers want to reduce their exposure to risk, and you may present a risk regardless of your age. For example, if you made more money than the employer has budgeted for the position, you've been out of work for six months, you've held a higher position (and may be unable to accept a drop in status), or you've had three jobs in the past three years, you may be perceived as a risk. Some of those risks come with age, but they're not caused by age.

Laying their worries to rest

One way to sell a product is to take away every reason a prospective customer has for saying no, and that's the strategy for overcoming ageism. If you do everything else right in terms of revamping your résumé, marketing yourself online, networking, and so forth, you've already given employers plenty of reasons to say yes. Now, you just have to take away their reasons for saying no. Here are some suggestions for doing just that:

>> **Look your best.** Be physically fit, well groomed, and properly dressed.

>> **Keep up with the times.** Do everything you can to keep up with technology and changes in your field or research the skills or certifications required for your new venture. Add the essential expertise and degrees before you apply for a new job. If you've recently updated any software certifications, or you are proficient in social media, let the recruiter or hiring manager know, even if that's a side comment in your discussion.

>> **Build and maintain a strong online presence.** Invisibility is a liability, demonstrating that someone is out-of-date and unable to navigate the online world.

>> **Establish your ability to learn and adapt.** Speak up about your flexibility in terms of management style, your openness to report to a younger boss, your technological aptitude, your energy, and your knack for picking up new skills. For many employers, it's not only about the candidate with the best credentials; it's about who's the best fit overall for the team. You have to make the case that you're the person who is going to both play your position masterfully and help the team.

>> **Downplay the risks.** If you held a higher position or earned more money in the past, or if you've been unemployed for some time or worked several jobs over the course of several years, find ways to downplay yourself as a flight risk. If there's a gap in employment, you may explain, for example, that you were financially solvent and could wait for the job you really wanted, and this is it.

>> **Market your age as a plus.** Think brand management. You're responsible for your own image. Workers 50 and older tend to be self-starters, know how to get the job done, and don't need as much hand-holding as those with less experience. A great benefit to being older is that you have a good deal of knowledge and leadership ability. And whether you realize it or not, you have a network. You have a lot more resources to draw on than do people in their 20s and 30s. So pitch your age as a plus. You need to be able to articulate your value. Strut your stuff.

>> **Practice positivity.** In truth, one of the biggest stumbling blocks to landing a job is negativity. You probably don't need a face lift. What works better is a *faith* lift. You've got to believe in yourself. When you do, it shows from the inside out. People dwell on the bad news. "I've been unemployed for too long. I'm too old." Have faith in yourself. After you've been out of work for a while, you forget your value. You take for granted your accomplishments and contributions.

>> **Stay present.** Don't chatter on in interviews about successes you had ten years ago. Focus on what you've done lately.

TIP

Sometimes it's hard to toot your own horn. Self-promotion is uncomfortable, especially if you've always thought of yourself as a team player. Ask people who know you well, whose opinions you value and trust, to evaluate you in writing: your best skills and talents, your personality, the roles you've been really good at.

Guess what comes back? All the accomplishments, all the positives that you need to be reminded of to prove to yourself that you're a talented individual who has a contribution to make. Then when you're in the interview, networking, or doing informational conversations, you can say, "Well, people have said about me that blah, blah, blah." All of a sudden, you have all the words to use, and it's easier to talk about your attributes because you're using someone else's tribute.

Chapter **2**

Dealing with Changes in Employment

Whether you're unemployed, underemployed, or planning to change careers or start your own business, a solid financial platform gives you the time and options needed to successfully navigate your transition. You'll want to make sure you can afford the basics: food, shelter, healthcare, and so on. If you're out of work, you may need to slash expenses and take advantage of government-sponsored safety-net programs to support yourself and your family through a period of unemployment. If you're planning a career change, you may need to take a job for significantly less money than you had been making to get started in the new field. And if you're planning to start a business or become a contract worker, you can expect to work for several months before you see any income or profit.

Being unemployed is a double whammy; you have no income plus some added expenses. If you need additional training to enter the workforce, for instance, you may have to pay for it, along with transportation to and from the training center or school. Creating, printing, and mailing applications, résumés, and cover letters also cost money, especially if you need to hire someone to help you. And if your employer supplied health insurance, even if you choose to continue that coverage through COBRA, you're faced with paying the entire premium or dropping coverage.

This chapter offers guidance on how to tighten your belt and take advantage of tax breaks and other government programs. This two-pronged attack — spending less while tapping available resources — puts you in a better position to support yourself and your family as you work toward achieving your career goals.

Filing for Unemployment Benefits

When you lose a job, you may be able to apply for unemployment benefits. To qualify, you must meet the following conditions:

>> You're unemployed through no fault of your own, meaning you didn't quit or get fired for *gross misconduct* — committing a dangerous or illegal act, such as stealing from your employer.

>> You received enough wages to establish a claim. Requirements on wages earned vary among states. Contact your local unemployment office or visit your state's unemployment website for details.

>> In most states, you also need to be physically able to work, actively looking for work, and ready and willing to accept work.

REMEMBER

If you qualify, don't let pride get in the way of filing for unemployment insurance benefits. These programs are in place to alleviate some of the financial pain and pressure of being unemployed.

Getting Your Financial House in Order

When money gets tight, your options are limited. You can earn more money, spend less, or do both. You may need to make some painful choices, such as downsizing or even moving to a more affordable city or town. In dire circumstances, you may even consider asking friends or family members for help or taking advantage of government-sponsored assistance programs.

This section aims to help you get motivated to make the changes that are often necessary to firm up your finances. It suggests ways to cut expenses and tap your own financial resources for temporary relief.

Motivating yourself to get started

Spending money is much more fun than cutting expenses, but debt is a dream killer. It drives people to make choices out of desperation that often limit their opportunities to achieve future wealth. If you need additional motivation to get started, consider the following reasons to strive toward financial fitness:

>> **When you're nimble financially, you have more choices.** You can accept a job that may not pay as much as your last one because you *want* the job instead of *need* the job. You can turn down a job that's not right for you, because you can afford to wait for the right opportunity. You can choose to become a contract worker or start your own business knowing that you can survive for months without pay as you establish yourself.

>> **You're more confident and less apt to appear desperate or needy.** As you search for a job, engage in interviews, and negotiate the terms of your employment, you can operate from a position of strength, and your confidence shows.

>> **You can focus on finding your ideal job.** Having to worry less about paying bills, you can focus more time, energy, and effort on finding the job you want or launching your own business.

>> **You can afford to pay for the additional training and services you need to pursue your career goals.** By having savings socked away, you have the resources available to ramp up your skill set.

Focusing on the fundamentals

If you never had to concern yourself with finances in the past, focus first on these fundamentals:

>> **Chart a budget.** Write down your income, what you owe, and what you have socked away. Look at what you're spending every day, every month, and every year. This will help you find ways to pare back your spending. Begin by keeping track of how much you spend each day and on what. (Pay in cash or put everything on a credit or debit card, as long as that doesn't lead to increased spending.) Then, on a monthly basis, study your credit card, bank statements, and log of cash payments to see where your money is going and what can be trimmed back or eliminated. Do you dine out too often? Are you traveling too much? Do you spend a lot on groceries or clothes? Do you have magazine or newspaper subscriptions you don't even read? (See Book 4, Chapter 2 for more about budgeting.)

TIP

Track your finances on a website or smartphone app, such as Mint (www. mint.com) or You Need a Budget (www.youneedabudget.com). These services are designed to help you streamline your bill paying and dissect your monthly spending.

>> **Increase your savings.** If you're unemployed, increasing your savings obviously is not an option, but if you're still working and planning ahead for a career change or business startup, grow your nest egg. A savings cushion of six months to a year of living expenses will stave off dipping into your retirement savings or taking on debt. (Aim for a year's worth of expenses, if you can swing it.)

TIP

>> **Stay liquid.** Emergency funds typically belong in bank accounts or money market funds that don't fluctuate in value and are easily accessible by check, ATM, or teller window. You might also put some of your emergency cash in bank CDs with maturity dates of six months or less so you can eke out a little more interest than from a savings account. You generally find the highest rates at online banks and credit unions. A great place to comparison shop is Bankrate (www.bankrate.com).

>> **Review your credit report and score.** Get a free annual report at www. annualcreditreport.com and check it for errors. Pay a little extra to get your credit score. Your credit score is important for two reasons:

- With a higher score, you can borrow more money at lower interest rates, which gives you more choices. Good credit can provide the funds you need to start a business or pay bills as you transition to contract work.

- Many employers are now checking credit scores prior to hiring. (They must ask your permission to do so.)

>> **If your credit score is lower than 700, work toward improving it.** Pay all bills on time, don't open new accounts, transfer balances, and pay off balances on credit cards. **Note:** It's usually a better idea to keep a paid-off credit card account open, with no balance, than to close it. Part of your credit score is age of credit, which looks at how long you've had each credit account, and the longer the better.

TIP

Consider opening an account with creditkarma.com — it's free and gives you real-time updates to your credit score.

>> **Consolidate debt.** If you have several sources of debt, you may be able to consolidate loans and credit card balances into a single loan with a lower overall interest rate.

>> **Review credit card offers.** Paying 0 percent on balance tansfers is a great way to pay off debt without interest. Just make sure to pay off the debt before the 0 percent promotion ends.

- >> **Reduce or eliminate debt.** Pay down credit card balances and refinance your mortgage at a lower rate, if possible. Consider downsizing your home, depending on where you live and the real estate market. If you have enough equity built up in your current home, you may be able to sell it and pay cash for a more affordable home, eliminating your mortgage.

TIP

If you've experienced a financial setback, such as unemployment, contact your creditors and try to negotiate payment options. Banks are often willing to work out arrangements with people who are responsible enough to call them and make a sincere effort to work out a solution.

- >> **Consult with a fee-only financial planner.** Look for experienced, credentialed advisers. As a rule, an adviser should have the Certified Financial Planner (CFP) designation, awarded by the nonprofit Certified Financial Planner Board of Standards. These national groups of financial planners offer searchable databases with contact information: the Certified Financial Planner Board of Standards (www.cfp.net), Financial Planning Association (www.plannersearch.org), Garrett Planning Network (www.garrett planningnetwork.com), and National Association of Personal Financial Advisors (www.napfa.org).

- >> **Take a personal finance course or read a book.** Many community colleges offer personal finance courses. Check out *Personal Finance After 50 For Dummies,* by Eric Tyson and Bob Carlson (Wiley, 2015).

Tapping your financial resources

If you're over 50, you may have built up quite a nest egg in the form of equity in a home, savings and retirement accounts, and other valuable possessions. Although you don't want to deplete these resources, you may be able to borrow against some of them and cash out portions of others to make it through a rough patch or fund a career change or business startup. Think creatively — and then consult with your financial adviser. Here are a few suggestions to kick your imagination into gear:

- >> **Take out a home equity line of credit.** If you have equity built up in your home, a home equity line of credit enables you to cash out that equity on an as-needed basis.

WARNING

Use a home equity line of credit only as an emergency fund — perhaps to cover mortgage payments to avoid foreclosure while you try selling the property. It's a great safety net to have in an emergency.

>> **Downsize.** Look for a more affordable housing option. Many people who downsize enjoy the resulting increase in financial freedom and wish they had made the move sooner.

>> **Use your assets to earn money.** For example, you may be able to lease one or more rooms in your home (or your entire home, if you move to more affordable accommodations). You can use your car or van to provide delivery services or work as a driver for a service such as Uber (www.uber.com) or Lyft (www.lyft.com).

>> **Sell your assets.** You can always sell your assets, for example on eBay or Craigslist, to turn them into cash. (For guidance on listing and selling items on eBay, check out *eBay For Dummies,* 9th Edition, by Marsha Collier (Wiley, 2016).

Financing Any Additional Education and Training

If you need additional education or training to return to the workforce or to change careers and you can't find it for free, you need to come up with the cash to cover the costs of the training and any books and other materials required for the courses you take. Fortunately, student financing is available even for older students, some of which is available exclusively for older students. This section helps you explore your options.

Paying for your education

Although certain educational offerings are entirely free, many programs, especially those that offer a degree or certification, cost money. If you're currently employed, you may be able to take advantage of employer-reimbursed education and training opportunities, or you may have enough money and time to work on your degree or certification one course at a time. If you're unemployed and strapped for cash, the financial aid department at the school you're interested in can help you explore available options, including scholarships, grants, fellowships, and student loans. This section reveals several options to help pay for your education.

Taking advantage of employer education/training opportunities

Roughly half of employers offer tuition assistance to employees, according to the Society for Human Resource Management. Many employers offer tax-free tuition-assistance programs (up to $5,250, not counted as taxable income), and the contribution doesn't have to be attached to a full-degree program.

IBM'S TRANSITION TO TEACHING PROGRAM

IBM's Transition to Teaching program, launched in 2006, is one of a growing number of corporate-sponsored programs that help current workers make a smooth transition to their next chapter. The program reimburses $15,000 of educational expenses to become certified as a math or science teacher. The program also allows employees to continue working while going to school and to work with their managers to adapt class work to day-to-day job responsibilities. The program even provides networking assistance when the time comes to help employees get a foot in the door for initial job interviews with the school district.

You may have to repay the funds, though, if you don't stay with the company for a certain number of years afterward. And you may need to earn a minimum grade or get your manager's approval for the curriculum to be eligible for this workplace perk.

Admittedly, if you choose a field that doesn't directly relate to your current employment, you may need to convince your boss that your course of study will resonate, even tangentially, with your job. But nothing ventured, nothing gained. In essence, you'll need to explain how continuing education will make you a more productive and creative worker. In other words, what's in it for the company?

Getting a break from Uncle Sam

The federal government has a vested interest in keeping you in the workforce. The longer you continue to work, the more tax revenue you generate. So don't hesitate to seek out government assistance to fund your continuing education. Government assistance typically comes in the form of tax breaks and low-interest loans. Here are a few resources to check out:

>> Visit the Tax Benefits for Education Information Center on the IRS website (www.irs.gov/newsroom/tax-benefits-for-education-information-center). The Lifetime Learning Credit, for example, can give you a tax credit of up to $2,000 to cover up to 20 percent of annual tuition; you don't have to be enrolled in a degree program. (The benefit phases out completely for married couples earning $131,000 and singles earning $65,000.)

>> Consider a low-interest federal Stafford loan. There's no age limit, and you're eligible as a part-time student, too.

Search the web for your state followed by "college financial aid" to find links to sites that contain information about state financial aid programs for higher education.

Certain forms of financial aid are often available only to students working toward their first bachelor's degree, but some schools will waive this requirement for older students returning to college to pursue a career change.

TIP

Go to FinAid.org (`www.finaid.org/otheraid/nontraditional.phtml`) and Edvisors.com (`www.edvisors.com`) for information on scholarships and grants for older students.

Considering Pell grants

For an undergraduate degree, check out federal Pell grants. They're interest-free and don't need to be repaid; the most recent maximum award is $5,730. The amount you'll qualify for depends on factors such as your financial need, tuition costs, and whether you'll be a full- or part-time student. For more on this type of aid, go to the Pell grant area of the U.S. Department of Education's website at `www2.ed.gov/programs/fpg/index.html`.

Paying with tax-free money: 529 plans

To make the most of the money you have available to pay for classes, consider socking away money in a 529 plan. This tax-favored program, run by the states, isn't just for your child's or grandchild's college tuition. People of any age can invest money in a 529 plan and use the cash for their future education costs. A 529's earnings are tax-free when you withdraw the money to pay higher education expenses. Some states even let residents deduct 529 contributions from their state income taxes. And if you wind up not using some or all of the money, you can transfer the funds to another beneficiary, such as your child or grandchild. You can research 529 plans at the College Savings Plans Network (`www.college savings.org`).

Scoring scholarships, grants, and fellowships

Try to score an older-student grant, scholarship, or fellowship. Some groups and foundations offer them, though it may take some investigating to track down this interest-free financing. The American Association of University Women, for example, offers fellowships and grants for women going back to school to advance their careers, change careers, or reenter the workforce. For more on grants, scholarships, and fellowships, check out the sites `www.fastweb.com` and `www.finaid.org`.

Choosing the right loan for you

If you must borrow, be conservative. The Consumer Financial Protection Bureau (`www.consumerfinance.gov`) has excellent college financing advice to help you choose the right loan and pay the least amount of interest. Try to get a Federal Direct Loan. Rates on these loans are fixed and low.

TIP

You may be able to get your monthly student loan payments reduced if you work in public safety, public health, education, social work, or the nonprofit sector. Learn more at the Public Service Loan Forgiveness Program area of the Department of Education site (`www.studentaid.ed.gov/repay-loans/forgiveness-cancellation/public-service`).

Avoiding additional debt

WARNING

Consider your future finances before taking on any significant student debt. Look at it as a short-term investment and weigh the potential return on that investment and the risk. Ask yourself how likely each educational opportunity will produce a return on your investment. Consider your future financial condition if everything goes as planned and if the outcome doesn't live up to your expectations. Is it worth the risk?

If you're already strapped for cash, do your best to avoid taking on more debt. Spending $5,000 for training to become a truck driver, for example, may make sense if you're certain to land a job soon after graduation that pays enough to cover your expenses and the loan in your first year on the job. If you can find a trucking company to cover the cost, even that expense can be avoided.

Applying for student financial aid

The first step to take to pay for additional education and training is to contact the financial aid department at the school or training center you plan to attend to find out whether the program you plan to enroll in is eligible for student financial aid. If it is, you'll probably be required to submit a Free Application for Federal Student Aid (FAFSA). Nearly all educational institutions require that students submit their FAFSA to become eligible for any form of student financial aid, regardless of whether the aid is based on financial need. Students of any age can submit the FAFSA and are eligible for federal student financial assistance. Soon after submitting your FAFSA, schedule an appointment to meet with someone in the financial aid department of the school or training center you plan to attend.

TIP

If you're quitting a job to return to school, request a "professional judgment" review to adjust your income, so your financial aid package is based more on projected income than on your past year's income.

The school's financial aid rep will put together a financial aid package for you that shows the various forms of financial aid and the amounts you qualify for and how much cash you're expected to contribute. For example, a financial aid package may show the amounts you qualify for in the form of scholarships, grants, fellowships, work-study programs, and subsidized student loans. You may be able to secure additional student loans not included as part of your financial aid package if you can't come up with the cash to meet your projected obligation.

REMEMBER

Be sure to submit your FAFSA by your state's or school's deadline — typically early to mid-February for the school year starting in the fall. You'll need information from your tax return to complete the FAFSA, which is kind of tricky; if you don't have all your W-2s and other documents to complete your tax return, you'll have to estimate your income for the year and then file an amended FAFSA later if your estimates are off.

TIP

If you're currently employed, ask your employer's human resources office about the availability of employer tuition assistance. Many large employers provide some form of tuition assistance. Up to $5,250 (in some cases more) in such assistance is excluded from gross income for income tax purposes. They may require you to maintain a minimum GPA to get the assistance and commit to working for the organization for a certain number of years after receiving the assistance (or you have to pay it back). Often the assistance is provided as a reimbursement after the fact, so you'll need to budget for your cash flow needs.

TIP

Visit FinAid (www.finaid.org), click Other Types of Aid, and click Other and Non Traditional for more information. FinAid is a free comprehensive source of student financial aid information, advice, and tools — on or off the web.

Applying for grants and scholarships

Although your financial aid package may contain one or more grants or scholarships, you can find and apply for additional grants and scholarships on your own. Research scholarships at Fastweb (www.fastweb.com), where you can find more than 50 awards that have a minimum age restriction of 30 years or older, more than 230 awards with a minimum age restriction of 25 years or older, and more than 1,800 awards with no age restrictions.

TIP

Ask the financial aid rep at the school you plan to attend about Silver Scholarships. The Serve America Act authorizes the Corporation for National and Community Service (CNCS) to award fixed-amount grants to community-based nonprofit entities to carry out a Silver Scholarship Grant Program, which provides $1,000 higher education scholarships to individuals age 55 or older who complete at least 350 hours of service in a year in an area of national need. The grant may be transferred to a child, grandchild, or foster child.

Leveraging tax breaks to lower costs

The federal government provides tax deductions and credits to offset educational costs. (A *deduction* lowers the income on which taxes are calculated, whereas a *credit* lowers the taxes owed by a certain amount.) Here are a few of the more substantial federal tax deductions and credits available:

>> You can deduct the interest you paid on student loans. This benefit applies to all loans (not just federal student loans) used to pay for higher education expenses. The maximum deduction is $2,500 a year. ***Note:*** The deduction is gradually reduced and eventually eliminated by phaseout when your modified adjusted gross income (MAGI) amount reaches the annual limit for your filing status.

>> The Lifetime Learning Credit allows you to claim up to $2,000 per student per year for any college or career school tuition and fees as well as for books, supplies, and equipment required for the course.

>> You may be able to withdraw from an IRA to pay for qualified higher education expenses for yourself, your spouse, your child, or your grandchild without having to pay an early withdrawal penalty. You will still owe federal and state income tax on the amount withdrawn.

Consult a tax specialist to find out more about federal, state, and local tax breaks to help cover education expenses.

TIP

For more information, read IRS Publication 970, "Tax Benefits for Education" (www.irs.gov/publications/p970) to see which federal income tax benefits may apply to your situation.

Writing Off Your Job-Hunt Expenses

When you're looking for a job, you need all the breaks you can get, and depending on your situation, you may qualify for federal and state income tax deductions to help offset your job-hunting costs. Be obsessive about saving receipts.

WARNING

Job-hunting deductions apply only to searching for a job *in your current field.* If you're switching careers, you can't use them.

Depending on your situation, you may be able to itemize your expenses for a tax deduction, using Form 1040 and Schedule A. You can claim a federal tax deduction only for job-hunt costs exceeding 2 percent of your adjusted gross income. That said, you may want to seek professional tax help for your situation. Here are a few deductions that may apply:

- » **Outplacement and employment agency fees:** These costs are acceptable whether or not you land a new job, assuming, of course, that you're looking for a job in the same line of work. Career-coaching fees may also be deductible.

- » **Résumé preparation and postage:** Paper, ink-jet cartridges, fees paid to a résumé writer, printing costs, and postage are all probable write-offs.

- » **Dues, subscriptions, and association fees:** Membership dues to professional organizations and subscriptions to certain industry publications may be deductible if you use the services provided in your job search. If challenged, you will need to show documentation that a job board at your professional association, for example, was a direct source of leads for you.

- » **Business travel:** You can deduct the IRS standard mileage rate if you use your personal vehicle for business, but be sure to keep travel mileage logs in case you're asked for documentation. Airfare, train tickets, and taxi fare are deductible, provided they're specifically related to your job hunt. You can't, for instance, take a five-day trip to Washington, D.C., to visit the museums, spend a single day interviewing, and then count the entire trip as a write-off.

- » **Business meals:** If you're job searching and meeting with sources or other business contacts, keep track of whether you pick up lunch or coffee, as 50 percent of the total cost of those meals can be deducted.

- » **Moving costs:** If you accept a job that requires you to relocate, you may be able to write off all expenses associated with your move if your new employer doesn't offer to reimburse you. Your new workplace must be at least 50 miles farther from your old home than your old job location was from your old home. If you use your vehicle to move, you can deduct mileage. For more information, see IRS Publication 521 "Moving Expenses" (www.irs.gov/publications/p521).

- » **Internet access:** You should be able to deduct work-related Wi-Fi expenses and fees for online job sites and networking services such as LinkedIn (if you upgrade to a paid, professional account). Again, you must be able to show evidence that these were tools used in your job search.

- » **Home office deduction:** If you're working as a freelancer, contract worker, or consultant while you pound the pavement for a new full-time gig, you can write off some of your home office costs if you have set aside a specific place solely for work. You must file Form 8829 "Expenses for Business Use of Your Home." The IRS now allows a "Simplified Option for Home Office Deduction," which permits you to deduct $5 per square foot of your home office on your tax return, with a maximum write-off of $1,500 (based on a maximum of

300 square feet). It's usually a better option to take the traditional home office deduction, but you should run the numbers. You can read all the home office rules in IRS Publication 587, "Business Use of Your Home" (www.irs.gov/publications/p587).

>> **Skill building:** The cost of job-search seminars and networking events is generally deductible, but again, you must be certain you can prove that they're connected to your job search. Tuition money to acquire or improve job skills may qualify for the Lifetime Learning Credit, which has limitations and income restrictions that are explained in IRS Publication 970, "Tax Benefits for Education" (www.irs.gov/publications/p970).

Accounting for Social Security Benefits Reductions When You Work

If you start receiving Social Security retirement benefits before reaching your full retirement age, your benefits are reduced if you earn more than a certain amount. For example, in 2017, if you're younger than full retirement age, $1 is deducted from your benefits for each $2 you earn above $16,920. If you reach full retirement age during 2017, $1 is deducted from your benefits for each $3 you earn above $44,880 until the month you reach full retirement age. For people younger than full retirement age during 2017, here's the breakdown:

If your monthly Social Security benefit is . . .	And you earn . . .	You'll receive yearly benefits of . . .
$700	$16,920 or less	$8,400
$700	$18,000	$7,860
$700	$20,000	$6,860
$900	$16,920 or less	$10,800
$900	$18,000	$10,260
$900	$20,000	$9,260
$1,100	$16,920 or less	$13,200
$1,100	$18,000	$12,660
$1,100	$20,000	$11,660

If you work for someone else, only your wages count toward Social Security's earnings limits. If you're self-employed, only your net earnings from self-employment count. Other income, such as other government benefits, investment earnings, interest, pensions, annuities, and capital gains, don't count toward your earnings limit. For details, read the pamphlet "How Work Affects Your Benefits" at www.ssa.gov/pubs/EN-05-10069.pdf.

For more about Social Security, read *AARP Social Security For Dummies,* by Jonathan Peterson (Wiley, 2016).

REMEMBER

The amount your benefits are reduced, however, isn't truly lost. Your benefit will be increased at your full retirement age to account over time for benefits withheld due to earlier earnings.

Taking Advantage of Additional Public Benefits

If you're unemployed or experience a significant reduction in income, you may qualify for benefits from federal, state, and local governments that you hadn't previously qualified for, including the following:

>> Unemployment insurance benefits (see the earlier section "Filing for Unemployment Benefits")

>> Subsidized health insurance

>> Food assistance

>> Gas or electricity subsidies

>> Free or low-cost phone service

>> Low-cost auto insurance

When you work, a portion of your taxes goes toward funding these benefits for others. When you're unemployed or underemployed, take advantage of these benefits to get back on your feet (after all, you paid for them), so you can start paying taxes again to help other unfortunate souls.

TIP

To find out which federal benefits you may be eligible to receive, visit www.benefits.gov. To find out about benefit programs in your state, mouse over Benefits in the menu bar near the top, click By State, and click the state you reside in. To find out about local benefit programs, contact a family services organization, community center, or church.

Providing Benefits for Yourself

If you're self-employed, unemployed, or underemployed, you don't have access to employer-sponsored benefits, such as health insurance and pension programs, so you need to provide them for yourself or make do without them. The good news is that if you're not earning enough to fund these benefits yourself, the government may help by subsidizing your health insurance premiums and expanding your tax breaks for any surplus you may be able to squirrel away in a retirement account. This section helps you explore your options.

Planning for retirement

If you're starting a business, working on contract, moving to a nonprofit, or joining a small firm without an employee retirement plan, open your own. Your three key options are solo 401(k), SEP-IRA, and Simple IRA.

>> **Solo 401(k):** This plan is best if you're self-employed with no employees and have income of $100,000 or more. The maximum amount you can contribute is 20 percent of net self-employment income plus $18,000, up to $53,000 in 2015; if you're 50 or older, you can contribute up to $6,000 more. The deadline to open an account to be eligible for a deduction is December 31. You can make contributions until your business's tax-filing deadline.

>> **SEP IRA (Simplified Employee Pension):** A SEP is a good choice if you're running your own business with no employees. The maximum contribution is 25 percent of self-employment income, up to $54,000 for 2017. The SEP has no "catch-up" provision allowing people age 50 or older to invest more than younger people. The deadline to open is April 15 to be eligible for a deduction for the previous tax year or October 15, if you file for an extension.

>> **Simple IRA:** You may opt for a Simple IRA if you have fewer than 100 employees. You can also have a Simple IRA if you don't have employees. If you do have employees, you typically must match up to 3 percent of their compensation. The maximum contribution is $12,500 up to $15,500 if you're 50 or older. The deadline to open an account is October 1 to be eligible for a deduction in the current tax year.

Don't worry about having to max out your contribution; save as much as you can. Opt for an auto-deposit program if your bank and financial firm permit so that you can have a set amount automatically shifted from your business's bank account into a retirement plan every month.

Low-income individuals or couples can qualify for a special Savers Credit of up to $2,000 for an individual or $4,000 for a couple for retirement plan contributions. To be eligible in 2017, single taxpayers couldn't earn more than $31,000 (or $62,000 for married couples).

Getting health insurance

If you're not eligible for an employer-sponsored health insurance plan, shop for insurance on the new healthcare exchanges via Healthcare.gov (www.healthcare.gov). Don't drop your current job insurance (you can continue it for a time under a law known as COBRA) until you have a new policy in place. Note that with COBRA, you're likely to lose your employer's contribution, so be prepared for your health insurance premium to double or worse.

Check your state insurance department website, too, because it may list health insurance choices for residents. Also be sure to ask your doctors which insurance carriers they accept. (See Book 3, Chapter 1 for more about health insurance, and Book 3, Chapter 3 for more on Medicare.)

Crunch the numbers when comparing health insurance plans. You may save money by choosing a high-deductible plan and using a health savings account (HSA) to pay for medical, dental, and medication costs with untaxed money from your HSA. But you may not. To compare plans, take the following steps:

1. **Multiply your monthly health insurance premium by 12 months under one of the plans you're considering.**

2. **Calculate or estimate your total annual out-of-pocket costs under this particular plan.**

   This is the tricky part. If the plan covers everything except a small deductible, simply use the deductible as your total. Likewise, if the deductible is high and you expect your out-of-pocket costs will meet the deductible, use the deductible as your total. But if you're healthy and rarely meet your deductible, you may want to estimate your annual out-of-pocket costs based on previous years' amounts.

3. **Perform Steps 1 and 2 for each plan you're considering.**

4. **Compare the plans.**

For example, suppose that you're comparing a *gold* plan that covers everything except for a $200 deductible and costs $680 per month to a *bronze* plan with a $3,000 deductible that costs $180 per month, and you think you'd probably meet that $3,000 deductible under the bronze plan:

» Annual cost of gold plan = $\left(\$680 \times 12\right) + \$200 = \$8,360$

» Annual cost of bronze plan = $\left(\$180 \times 12\right) + \$3,000 = \$5,160$

In addition, you could have an HSA under the bronze plan and use it to pay your out-of-pocket expenses with non-taxed dollars, saving you additional money, so the bronze plan would be best, all other things being equal (such as whether the doctors you want to see accept that particular plan).

You may be charged a small annual fee of about $40 for a health savings account from a no-load mutual fund company, such as Vanguard or Fidelity. You can contribute up to $3,400 (2017, going up to $3,450 in 2018) to a health savings account for individual coverage (a maximum of $4,350 if you're 55 or older). For families, the limit on contributions is $6,750 (2017, rising to $6900 in 2018) and $7,650 if you're 55 or older. Most banks also have HSAs.

If you're shopping for an individual health policy, you can also compare premiums, deductibles, and out-of-pocket costs at such websites as eHealth (www.ehealthinsurance.com), GoHealth (www.gohealthinsurance.com), Insure.com (www.insure.com), and NetQuote (www.netquote.com). Always check to see whether your preferred doctors are in-network before you select a plan. Or have a local health insurance agent shop around on your behalf. Look for one at the National Association of Health Underwriters website (www.nahu.org).

Chapter **3**

Joining the Ranks of the Self-Employed

f you're like many workers in the United States, your American Dream is to be your own boss and set your own hours. If you've ever freelanced, owned your own business, or worked on contract, you know how silly that notion really is. Instead of being your own "boss," a self-employed worker has dozens of bosses. They're just called something else, such as "customers" and "clients." "Setting your own hours" means choosing to work between 60 and 80 hours whenever you want across all seven days of the week instead of working five 8-hour days.

Still, the dream is alluring. You become the master of your own destiny, sinking or swimming according to your talents, skills, and vision. Although you do face the risk of your enterprise going belly up, you don't have to worry about landing a job; you simply hire yourself. And you're a lot less likely to get fired or laid off.

If you're not scared off yet and you're still interested in flying solo, you've come to the right place. This chapter presents four approaches to becoming your own boss:

» Finding gainful employment as a contract worker

» Starting your own business

>> Working as a social entrepreneur

>> Buying a pre-fab business (a franchise)

Working on Contract

Part-time and contract staffing is on the rise. Recently, the big online job site CareerBuilder released a Harris Interactive survey of more than 3,000 hiring managers and human resource professionals, showing that more than a third of U.S. companies are operating with smaller staffs than before the latest recession. To keep business trucking along, these companies hire contract or temporary workers. It's an easy way for employers to get great, experienced staff and save money at the same time. That can be good news for you.

Being a contractor has its downsides, of course, such as, typically, no health insurance and no paid holidays or sick leave.

Getting sold on the idea

Contract work can be great, especially for people who are retired or are considering a job or career change, for several reasons:

>> **It gives you something to do if you're not currently employed.** Don't discount this. Having a sense of purpose improves your mood and attitude.

>> **It gets you in the door.** It may lead to full-time work with an employer eventually. Don't miss the opportunity.

>> **It brings in some cash.** You can make your experience a plus. Employers are typically willing to pay you generously, providing you have the chops and can solve their problem or meet their need quickly. It lets them bypass the hand-holding and learning-curve stage that a younger, less experienced but lower-paid worker may require. And when you're making money, you feel better about yourself. You feel valued, more confident.

>> **It provides an opportunity to test drive different jobs.** With a short-term "dip in the pool" assignment, you can find out whether this is something you really want to do. Do the job first — moonlight, apprentice, volunteer. If you can get paid for it, go for it. That's the only way you'll know whether the new career is all you dreamed it would be.

- **It builds your professional network.** Nurture relationships with coworkers during your assignments. You never know where contacts may lead you.

- **It secures new and up-to-date references for future employers to contact to find out about what you've been up to lately.**

- **It pads your résumé with current experience.** It's a great way to fill the gaps in your résumé.

- **It sharpens your skills.** You know the mantra: Use it or lose it.

- **It gets you psyched about a work project without the pressure of long-term expectations.** No job is forever, anyway. This one may be shorter than most, and that can be tremendously liberating.

TIP

Consider yourself the CEO of your own small business, even if you have a full-time job. Your primary employer is simply your largest client. Consider doing side jobs if you have a full-time position. That prepares you for self-employed status and starts building a ready list of clients.

TIP

Hone your yarn spinning. Even if the assignment was the pits, and that's always possible, find a clever way to use the experience in a positive way. It can be a great example of your work ethic or your ability to helicopter in and solve a problem, or it can fill a professional need for a company. Make the time spent part of your personal career story. Exercise your poetic license.

Lining up contract gigs

Lining up contract gigs isn't all that different from finding a job, except that you now must find *jobs*, plural. Your former employer may become your first and biggest client, and then you can expand out from there, perhaps working for your former employer's competitors, clients, and vendors (assuming you don't have an agreement not to do so). To expand your clientele, network, search the job boards, and let people know that you're looking for projects or temporary assignments. You may also want to tap temp agencies. Another way to expand is to add services, if you have additional skills that weren't needed in your previous position but that your clientele would be willing to pay for.

TIP

When you're engaged in a project or temporary assignment, collect names and contact information for all the people you work with. One project or temporary assignment often leads to others.

TIP

You can drum up additional work online by using service marketplaces that connect freelancers with clients. Setting up an account is free, but you usually pay the marketplace a percentage of your earnings. Here are a few sites you can use to hawk your services:

>> **Elance** (www.elance.com) is for freelancers in many fields, including writers, editors, graphic designers, translators, marketing specialists, and web developers. Elance keeps 8.75 percent of whatever you earn.

>> **Fiverr** (www.fiverr.com) is another freelancer marketplace like Elance. Fiverr keeps $1 for every $5 gig you sell.

>> **Freelancer** (www.freelancer.com) enables clients to post projects they need done and allows talented freelancers to bid on them. Freelancer generally collects 3 percent of all payments from clients and 10 percent from the freelancer.

>> **Guides.co** (www.guides.co) is a service that "connects people who know with people who want to grow." You create a multimedia guide with text, images, audio, video, and so on, and interested members can purchase your guide. When they do, you receive 95 percent of the proceeds.

>> **Guru** (www.guru.com) helps businesses connect with freelance workers in more than 160 fields of expertise.

>> **HourlyNerd** (www.hourlynerd.com) is an online, on-demand freelance marketplace connecting MBA graduates and students with businesses looking for a flexible, cost-efficient way to address business challenges. Those who work for HourlyNerd can make as much as $300 an hour. Many of the companies are seeking marketing, funding, or strategic planning advice. HourlyNerd charges the client 15 percent and the contractor 5 percent.

>> **Skillshare** (www.skillshare.com) connects teachers in all fields with students interested in those fields, so if you have valuable skills and a knack for teaching those skills to others, check out Skillshare. Compensation is based on the number of students enrolled in your courses. You're also paid a referral whenever someone clicks your unique teacher referral link and becomes a member.

These types of marketplaces generally value older workers, says Jeff Williams, CEO of Bizstarters (www.bizstarters.com), a company that provides coaching and training to older entrepreneurs. "If you can deliver the solution, your age is not important." The keys to success: a solid knowledge about a specific subject, a knack for consulting, and an ease with selling services online.

Running your contracting operation as a business

When you work as a contractor, you're a business, and you need to run your operation as a business. Here are some of the business chores you must attend to:

>> **Become a legitimate business entity.** Check with the Small Business Administration (SBA at www.sba.gov) in your area to find out what you need to do in terms of registering your business with the state and obtaining a business license and permits to operate in your area. You also need to determine whether you want to operate your business as a sole proprietor or as a corporation, such as a Limited Liability Company (LLC), S Corporation, or C corporation. Certain legal protections and tax benefits and responsibilities are associated with each. Consult an attorney and tax specialist to find out more about your options.

>> **Withhold and pay estimated quarterly income taxes.** Independent contractors are required to pay quarterly estimated income taxes to the federal government, the state, and perhaps even the county and city in which they live, or pay a fine. Consult a local tax expert to find out more about your tax obligations, get assistance estimating the amounts you're obligated to pay, and find out when and where to send payments.

>> **Pay attention to the paperwork.** You'll need to keep a detailed record of payments received and expenses, including travel expenses (mileage, restaurant and hotel receipts, and so on). In addition, unless you get all your work through a third party, such as Freelancer.com, you'll need to invoice clients for payments and perhaps provide them with receipts. You may also need to draw up a standard contract (with the assistance of a contract attorney).

>> **Check your insurance.** Add a rider to your homeowner's or renter's policy to cover any business equipment and supplies. You may also need liability insurance, just in case a client decides to file a lawsuit against you. Each state has rules about insurance that can be offered to home-based outfits. Talk to your insurance agent to assess your needs.

Avoiding common pitfalls

Not everyone makes it as a contract worker. Some workers perform better in a standard workplace setting where nearby coworkers provide social interaction and hold one another accountable just by being in close proximity. To boost your success, consider these suggestions:

» **Set and keep a regular work schedule.** A schedule serves two purposes. First, it helps to ensure that you work a set number of hours per week. Second, it prevents work from bleeding into the rest of your life.

» **Set a monthly financial goal.** If you need $30,000 a year to survive and $60,000 to live your desired lifestyle, add 30 percent or more to cover income taxes and expenses. That's $39,000 to $78,000 you need to gross, which represents $3,200 to $6,400 a month.

» **Know what you're worth.** Research the going rate for what you do. Many contract workers have websites where they post their rates. Contact other contract workers in your field and discuss rates. If they're reluctant to share, tell them that you're looking into entering the field and you don't want to undercut others on price; they should be more cooperative after hearing your concern.

» **Don't agree to a fixed price for unlimited work.** Be very specific about how much work you're going to do for X dollars. Otherwise, you either find yourself earning about $1.75 an hour or upsetting clients who feel as though you're changing the terms of the agreement. Setting a fair price is a huge challenge, because many times you enter into a project not knowing the amount of time involved. If you can charge by the hour, that's usually best.

» **Calculate a day rate.** Some clients hire contractors for three- to six-month assignments and require them to work onsite like a standard 9-to-5 job. If you're working in a client's office, consider charging a day rate — for instance, $500 to $600 per day. Some clients will pay overtime by the hour above that amount.

» **Track the time you spend on projects.** By tracking your time and knowing the total paid for a project, you can calculate your hourly wage and adjust your quotes for projects accordingly.

» **Expect and plan for tech crises.** If you're working remotely, make sure you have an in-house or on-call tech support person to assist you if you encounter a technical glitch or have a question.

» **Find or start a professional group for people in your line of work.** A group provides a forum for human interaction that's essential for your mental and emotional well-being. In addition, you may need to talk shop with others to vent frustrations with clients and share advice on how to overcome common challenges.

Launching Your Own Business

According to the State of Entrepreneurship 2015 report released by the Kauffman Foundation, which specializes in studying and promoting entrepreneurship, many Baby Boomers (born between 1946 and 1964) who became entrepreneurs during the information technology revolution in the 1980s and 1990s are today's serial entrepreneurs.

Data shows that these 50- and 60-year-old entrepreneurs have started more and more businesses in the last decade, whereas in the meantime, the rate of business creation among 20- to 30-year-olds has slowed. With life expectancy rising, Boomers continue to be an important economic force for years to come, as the Foundation concludes:

>> Boomers have been, and will continue to be, an entrepreneurial generation.

>> As they work longer and live longer, Boomers also will be entrepreneurs for longer periods of time.

>> The aging of Baby Boomers will create numerous challenges and entrepreneurial opportunities — and Boomers will be the ones who start companies to capitalize on them.

>> The promise of lifetime employment has declined dramatically for people age 35 to 64 over the past 50 years.

>> With older generations living longer, healthier lives, they're likely to continue starting new businesses and mentoring young entrepreneurs.

>> Transaction costs and the barriers to entry have fallen for entrepreneurs of every age.

If you're ready to become a member of one of the greatest generations of entrepreneurs in the United States, read on. This section helps you prepare for what's ahead so you don't get discouraged by unrealistic expectations. It also covers the fundamentals of getting your business up and running. For additional guidance, check out *Starting a Business All-In-One For Dummies* (Wiley, 2015).

Managing your expectations

Opening a business takes a lot of time, energy, drive, and commitment, especially in the initial stages. Expect to work long hours away from friends and family unless, of course, you're launching a family business or partnering with friends. Juggling the whole work-life balance thing when work is your life is tremendously difficult. Work seems to be embedded in every nook and cranny.

As with most endeavors in life, however, substantial investment often leads to substantial rewards — the joy of pursuing your passion; potentially more time with friends and family and more money to enjoy it; enough money to help friends, relatives, and others in need; a chance to make the world a better place; the health benefits of remaining physically and mentally active; and much more. And with years of business and life experience and an expansive professional network, you're far better equipped than a 20- or 30-something to start a business.

Entrepreneurs typically exhibit confidence, tenacity, and hope. No one questions how challenging starting and running a business can be, but for most, the reward is an inner payout that blows right past the struggles and sacrifice.

Here are some quick tips to get you over the first speed bump:

>> **Don't think that you're too old to start your own business.** The median age of founders is 39 — right at the midpoint of a typical professional career — and 69 percent are 35 or older. Nonprofit entrepreneurs tend to be older on average than their traditional counterparts. The average age for nonprofit founders is around 53, according to a study, "Profiles of Nonprofit Startups and Nonprofit Entrepreneurs," by David M. Van Slyke, professor of public administration at Syracuse University and Jesse D. Lecy, assistant professor of public policy at Georgia State University.

>> **Get comfortable with salesmanship or team up with someone who already is.** Sales is a key ingredient for success. Your confidence is only part of the battle; the other part is marketing yourself as you move along from those heady first few months or even years.

>> **Brace yourself for greenhorn blues.** Moving into a new arena requires psychological preparation. You're the boss now and probably making a few mistakes. A supportive partner or best friend may be all the shoring up you need, but don't ignore the possible emotional setbacks you may experience as you work through the transition phase.

>> **Make mistakes with grace.** Face it: The older you are and further along on your professional success ladder, the harder it is to accept criticism and responsibility for screwing up. Your ego just isn't as nimble and forgiving as it once was. Accept that trying new things means learning from your mistakes along the way. You'll be in a healthier, stronger place to move ahead. Doing things poorly is just another step toward doing them well.

Coming up with a business idea

When you're looking to start a business, opportunities are endless, but you need to pick one idea and make sure it's the right fit for you and your future customers or clientele. This section explores various approaches to discovering a business idea that's right for you. As you peruse your options, use the following criteria as test strips to determine whether the business idea has legs:

>> The idea is going to be something you enjoy working on (because you're going to be doing it a lot).

>> The idea serves a need that's not being met or solves a problem that's not being addressed satisfactorily.

>> People want or will want the product or service you're selling. You can often gauge the marketability of a product by looking at its benefits. If it's going to solve a huge problem or save the buyer a huge amount of money, they'll want it. In other cases, you may need to perform market research; for example, without giving away your brilliant idea, talk to as many potential customers as possible to gauge future demand.

>> You can offer the product or service for a price that customers or clients are willing to pay and that produces a sufficient profit to make it worth your efforts. Do your homework to estimate costs for manufacturing the product or making the service available, marketing it, delivering it, covering overhead, and so on. After you deduct the costs, is the profit that remains worth your efforts and the risk you're taking? Do some additional market research to find out how much prospective customers would be willing to pay for such a product or service.

>> The idea is within your risk tolerance. If it's not, you're going to be a nervous wreck until the business turns a significant profit, which may take months or even years.

Now that you have a few benchmarks for judging ideas, you're ready to start brainstorming ideas to judge. Get your pen and paper handy and read on.

Looking to your current occupation for ideas

One of the easiest, quickest, and least risky business ideas is to keep doing what you were doing as an employee but do it as a contractor. (See the earlier section "Working on Contract" for details.) But that's not the only option for transitioning from employee to business owner in your own field. You can start a business that serves the needs of your industry in other ways, perhaps by inventing a product or service that solves a common problem your former employer had but never managed to solve. Or perhaps you thought of a way to use the service or product your former employer sells to make money in a different way.

As an expert in some aspect of the industry or field you're already in, you have the knowledge to innovate in that industry or field, so that's the first place to look for new business ideas.

Turning a hobby into a profit

Turning a hobby into a business may really pay off, but doing so can take a while. That's the finding of a recent study that looks at entrepreneurs who start a business based on a personal pursuit. In the study, published in the *Journal of Business Venturing,* these entrepreneurs lagged behind other founders in the first few years of developing their enterprises. But they caught up after 45 months in terms of pace. In the end, the hobby-to-business founders were more likely than others to produce revenue, achieve a profit, and have a deep commitment to their business.

So look to your hobbies and pastimes for business ideas. Are you musically inclined? Do you like to garden, bake, do crafts, write, take photography, or play games? Whatever it is you do, you may be able to turn it into a money-making venture. Just try not to ruin your avocation by making it your vocation, to borrow a play on words from Robert Frost.

Cashing in on your natural gifts

Some things can't be taught. They just come naturally to you. We're all born with a distinctive set of talents that are as singular as fingerprints. These aren't skills that we learn along the way or passions discovered over the years. These are inborn gifts. It's the way your voice sounds, for instance, or your athletic prowess, or your inner mechanical capability.

If you aren't certain what you have a knack for, ask friends, relatives, and colleagues. They may point out things you simply take for granted. Think about what you've been good at since you were a kid. If you're uncertain, though, several organizations, including the Rockport Institute (www.rockportinstitute.com), provide career-testing programs that can help you assess your natural talents. And AARP's LifeReimagined.org offers interactive programs that help you identify your interests, values, goals, and purpose.

Here are a few jobs where you can follow your talent to make money. These jobs may offer flexible hours and can be on a full- or part-time basis:

>> **Voice-over actor/artist:** If you've been blessed with a deep, resonating timbre, or perhaps a smoky, husky purr, it may be time to put it to work. The need for voice talent is rising, thanks to the increase in online multimedia websites and audiobooks. The variety of possible gigs ranges from commercials to podcasts, web videos, audiobooks, documentaries, business and training videos, telephone messages, and applications. Last year, the freelance website Elance (www.elance.com) touted voice acting as one of the fastest-growing fields, with a threefold increase in job postings on the site.

>> **Organizer:** If you're great at and enjoy organizing offices, kitchens, bathrooms, garages, sheds, and other spaces, consider creating a business that offers your organizational skills to others. Your skills can come in particularly handy for retirees who are seeking to downsize. You may even offer additional services, such as selling property on eBay and through various other means.

>> **Medical equipment maintenance and repair:** Were you the kid who always took things apart in the garage for the sheer fun of putting them back together? From wheelchairs to gurneys, if you've got the fix-it gene, this is a fast-growing job that plays right into your innate mechanical ability. Employment of medical equipment repairers is projected to grow 31 percent from 2010 to 2020, according to the Bureau of Labor Statistics (BLS), much faster than the average for all occupations. You can start your own business or work for someone else.

>> **Calligraphy artist:** Harness your power of penmanship. In the digital world, where the electronic signature is becoming status quo, those who can create flowing cursive writing with smooth coordination and fine motor skills are few and far between. You can use your dexterity to create fonts and scripts for company logos, wedding invitations, place cards, and menus, among other word-based undertakings. You probably won't get rich, but there's work for someone who practices the antique art of calligraphy.

>> **Seamstress and tailor:** Sewing like a pro requires a mixture of sharp hand-eye coordination and artistic flair. The job boils down to dexterity and details. And, truth is, for many people, simply threading a needle is maddening. Old-fashioned sewing has become a fading art, even though finding someone who can perform the job with panache has been in steady demand. Nearly half of all seamstresses and tailors are self-employed, according to the BLS.

>> **Senior fitness trainer:** The nitty-gritty: If you're a natural athlete, working out is in your blood. That's why teaching active adult exercise classes might just be your dream job. More fitness clubs and gyms across the country are offering classes catering to the silver-hair set, according to fitness industry experts. Overall, employment of fitness trainers and instructors is expected to grow by 24 percent from 2010 to 2020, faster than the average for all occupations.

Getting help

Although starting a business carries a ring of independence, you have a better chance of succeeding if you reach out for help. Here are some resources you can tap for help in starting a business:

>> AARP's Life Reimagined (www.lifereimagined.org) has a number of ideas to help plan your next career move to become a business owner.

>> The Association of Small Business Development Centers (www.america ssbdc.org), a joint effort of the Small Business Administration (SBA), universities, colleges, and local governments, provides no-cost consulting and low-cost training at about 1,000 locations.

>> The Kauffman Foundation's FastTrac Boomer Entrepreneur program (www. fasttrac.org/entrepreneurs.aspx), in collaboration with AARP, is piloting specialized ten-week courses in both English and Spanish in select cities. Up to 20 applicants will be accepted in each course.

>> Lawrence N. Field Center for Entrepreneurship at the Zicklin School of Business at Baruch College offers a free, online, open-source entrepreneurship curriculum intended for people over 50. It includes help with developing business plans, obtaining loans, gaining access to business start-up incubators, and meeting mentors to serve as sounding boards. For more information, visit www.blogs.baruch.cuny.edu/fieldcenter/.

>> SCORE (www.score.org) is a nonprofit that provides education to entrepreneurs. At SCORE, working and retired executives and business owners donate their time and expertise free of charge in person or online.

>> Senior Entrepreneurship Works (www.seniorentrepreneurshipworks.org) is a nonprofit organization designed to engage, empower, and connect would-be entrepreneurs over the age of 55.

>> The Small Business Administration (www.sba.gov) has loads of information about starting and managing a business. You'll find pages that cover nearly every aspect of starting and managing a business, from thinking about starting a business to paying taxes and hiring employees.

TIP

The SBA website has a section specifically for entrepreneurs 50 and older at www.sba.gov/content/50–entrepreneurs. Also check out AARP's small business site, www.aarp.org/startabusiness.

>> Startup Nation (www.startupnation.com) is packed with practical information from quality sources relevant to starting, managing, and growing a business. In addition, it encourages and enables small-business owners and people seeking to become small-business owners to connect with and learn from one another.

TIP

Find a mentor. Connect with someone who started a business similar to yours and ask the person to be your mentor. Try finding someone in your existing network who fits the bill. If you can't find someone you're already connected with, track down candidates online. Look for an entrepreneur mentor who has the following qualities:

>> Knowledge and confidence in the skills you lack

>> Business acumen and a successful track record in starting and running a business — someone who's walked the walk and succeeded

>> Ability to be practical, honest, and supportive all at the same time

If you're planning to launch a major business venture that requires financing possibly through investors, consider assembling an advisory board — a diverse group of three to eight individuals who have a proven track record in various areas of starting and running a business. *Diverse* means some men, some women; some older and some younger; conservative players and risk takers; creative and practical. They can guide you and may lead you to investors and customers.

To find prospective board members, tap your network of people who have experience with your type of business (and maybe some who don't) and invite about three to five of them to join your board. Then, conduct either virtual or in-person meetings with them on a periodic basis to discuss two to three issues of key importance. Board members are typically compensated by a certain percentage of equity in the company (0.25 to 2.0 percent is common). But you may find friends and other associates willing to offer their expertise pro bono.

Writing a solid business plan

Writing a business plan before launching your business is essential for two reasons: process and product. The process of writing the plan forces you to consider key factors to achieving success and helps you define your vision. The product (the finished plan) provides a road map of how to get from point A to point B. Although you may need to take some detours along the way to get around roadblocks, having a plan in place keeps you on track. The product is also necessary if you need to apply for a loan or other financing.

There's no strict model to follow, but in general, a simple plan should be about 20 pages and contain the following sections:

>> An **executive summary** that explains what your business will do, who the customers will be, why you're qualified to run it, how you'll sell your goods and services, and your financial outlook.

>> A **detailed description** of the business, its location, who your management team is, and what your staffing requirements are. Also include information about your industry and your competition.

>> A **market analysis** that targets your customers more specifically (demographically), including age, gender, and where they live. The analysis also describes your sales and promotional strategy to reach them.

>> A **realistic forecast** of start-up outlays — cost of raw materials, equipment, employee salaries, marketing materials, insurance, utilities, and fees for attorneys and accountants — along with projections for gross and net annual profit.

TIP

Search the web for "business plans." You may even want to narrow your search for business plans in a specific industry or for a specific type of business, service, or product. You'll find plenty of examples. Another great resource is *Business Plans Kit For Dummies*, by Steven D. Peterson and Peter E. Jaret (Wiley, 2016).

Financing your enterprise

For most businesses, securing capital is the biggest obstacle. Research the start-up costs for your business and develop a plan with your financial adviser to ensure that you'll have the funds you need. Here are some sources of financing to explore:

>> **Personal savings:** Most start-ups are financed with an entrepreneur's own money.

>> **Loans from banks and credit unions:** For many who want to start a business, the local bank is frequently a first stop for financing, but don't hold your breath; many banks won't approve loans for start-up businesses. In the off chance that you find a bank that will, you'll need a clean credit record, an excellent credit score (720 or higher), a solid business plan, and probably a good chunk of your own change invested in the business.

TIP

For more about securing a small-business loan, check out BusinessUSA (www.business.usa.gov), the federal government's site for entrepreneurs seeking small-business loans. An SBA-guaranteed bank loan can lower your down payment and monthly payments. To find a bank offering one of these loans, check the Local Resources section of the SBA's website as well as the site's loans and grants search tool.

>> **Home equity credit lines or loans:** If you've built up some equity in your home, a home equity line of credit is a fairly easy route to gain access to cash, and interest is generally manageable. Lenders typically let you borrow 75 to 80 percent of your home's value, minus the amount of money you still owe on the mortgage. With a line of credit, you borrow money on an as-needed basis up to the amount of the approved loan.

With a home equity line of credit, you're putting your house up as collateral. If you can't make the monthly payments or pay the loan in full when it becomes due (typically 10 to 15 years down the line), you risk losing your home.

>> **Friends and relatives:** Members of your inner circle may be willing to lend you cash interest-free or at a low rate. Put everything in writing to avoid misunderstandings that may arise over the loan's terms, including repayment dates.

>> **Equity investors:** Equity investors may back you in exchange for equity or partial ownership. The SBA's Small Business Investment Company program (www.sba.gov/category/lender-navigation/sba-loan-programs/sbic-program-0) can offer leads. These investors typically fall into two groups:

- *Angel investors* are high-net-worth individuals who generally invest $25,000 to $100,000 and may consider investing in a good idea. Visit AngelList (www.angel.co) to get in touch with an angel investor.

- *Venture capitalists* are also high-net-worth individuals, but they're more likely to invest more, require much more than just a good idea, and perform much more due diligence. In many cases, they band together to form a venture capital firm to pool their investments.

  Both types are typically swamped by requests, extremely careful with their money, and prefer growth-oriented sectors, such as technology and bioscience.

>> **Crowdfunding websites:** A relative newcomer in start-up financing is *crowdfunding,* virtual fundraising campaigns intended to typically raise relatively small amounts of money from donors who are not repaid. For details, visit crowdfunding sites, including Kickstarter (www.kickstarter.com), Gofundme (www.gofundme.com), and Indiegogo (www.indiegogo.com).

>> **Crowdlending websites:** *Crowdlending* is a variation on the crowdfunding theme, but in this case, people expect to get their money back. Crowdlending sites include Fundingcircle.com (www.fundingcircle.com), Onevest (www.onevest.com), Accion (www.accion.org), and Kiva Zip (zip.kiva.org). Many crowdlending sites specialize in making no- or low-interest microloans (up to $25,000) to impoverished individuals who want to start businesses. The SBA also issues microloans up to $50,000. In general, interest rates range from 8 to 13 percent.

>> **Economic development programs:** You'll need to do some legwork for this type of financing, but it could be well worth your time. Getting your firm certified as a woman-owned business, for example, can help you qualify for money that's only available to companies with that designation. Certification can also help you land government and big-business clients. For example,

Michelin North America, based in Greenville, South Carolina, has provided $1 million in low-interest financing — loans range from $10,000 to $100,000 — to certain businesses, including women-owned firms, in parts of South Carolina.

>> **State and local economic development agencies:** Some states and municipalities provide funding for economic development that's available for starting specific businesses in certain locations. Check the SBA's online directory and contact the office in your area to see whether any money is available and find out restrictions on its use.

>> **Grant programs:** The SBA operates a network of nearly 100 Women's Business Centers around the country. They provide state, local, and private grant information to women eager to start for-profit or nonprofit businesses. Grants.gov (www.grants.gov) lists information on more than 1,000 federal grant programs. BusinessUSA (www.business.usa.gov) is another great resource to find out about federal government financing for businesses.

WARNING

Here are a couple of financing sources to steer clear of:

>> **Credit cards:** Avoid using personal plastic at all costs. Most cards carry high double-digit interest rates, which is an outlandish price to pay for starting a business.

>> **Retirement savings:** Don't put your future financial security at risk. Not only will you owe income taxes by taking money out, but you'll also lose the tax-deferred compounding and, if you're younger than 59½, you'll owe Internal Revenue Service withdrawal penalties. Please don't do that. No business is worth it. Furthermore, if the business fails, and your nest egg goes with it, the loss comes at a point in your life when it will be tough to rebuild that retirement fund.

A recent twist is *rollovers as business start-ups* (ROBS), which raise the risks a bit higher, according to some experts. With this approach, business owners use their retirement funds, such as 401(k) assets, to finance or expand a business without incurring taxes or penalties. The account is rolled over into a new retirement fund. And that new retirement fund, in effect, becomes a shareholder in the start-up. It's legitimate, according to the Internal Revenue Service, but it's complicated. And if not set up perfectly, it could result in penalties and a big tax bill.

Here are seven tips for people who are keen to launch businesses and who need to attract money to their start-up (with input from Jeanne Sullivan, a noted venture capitalist):

>> **Hone your story.** You need one or two lines that sum up your product or service. The key is to be able to get that company story out of your mouth in a clear, succinct, short pitch. You'll also want to include a clear example of how a customer would use your product or service.

>> **Know your market.** To get a solid grip on the potential size of your customer base, ask yourself: How big is it? Is it crowded? What niche are you trying to serve?

>> **Be able to reel off your business's current finances and financial needs.** It's basic math — adding, subtracting, and percentages. Investors want to see that you're accounting for all the costs and not just dreaming of the profits.

TIP

Brush up on the lingo. You need to be able to answer questions such as these: What are the capital needs of the business over time? What are the gross margins? What's your break-even time frame?

>> **Prepare for show and tell.** If you're selling a product, make sure you have a prototype and get it in the hands of early pilot customers. Then you'll have something real to discuss with an investor.

>> **Have a strategy for hiring your team.** Outline the key people you need over the next 18 months and recruit them — knowing that they may work for you now for equity or part time until you get some funding.

>> **Surround yourself with an advisory board — a brain trust.** Your advisers can be formidable references for you with investors. (See the earlier section "Getting help" for more about assembling an advisory board.)

>> **Prepare to work harder than you ever have**. Most small-business owners work more than 60 hours a week, according to a new survey by small business loan provider Kabbage. Prepare for the inevitable setbacks.

If all this sounds overwhelming, don't let that get you down. In all likelihood, you'll wish you'd only done it sooner.

REMEMBER

Becoming a Social Entrepreneur

A *social entrepreneur* is a person who creates a business venture with the goal of making the world a better place. With more and more people over 50 seeking meaningful employment and facing a job market that makes it tough for workers over 50 to get hired, social entrepreneurship is becoming an attractive option for the 50–plus crowd.

This section explains the ins and outs of getting started and making it as a social entrepreneur. But first, before you head down the path of making a living by doing good deeds, answer these five questions:

>> **What social problem or need are you truly passionate about?** The first step is finding an unmet need or a problem that's yet to be solved. Selecting your area of focus must come from your heart, from what you genuinely care about, so think carefully about your mission.

>> **What's your plan for cracking the problem or meeting the need you've identified?** An innovative idea or creative approach to meeting the need or solving the problem is essential. Consult with several people who share your passion. The idea is to put something on paper that's adequate to show possible advisers, financers, and colleagues what you have in mind.

>> **Do you have the skills and conviction required?** Gut check time. To run a successful operation, you need to be a CEO, CFO, marketing and sales specialist, and more. How good are you at rallying the troops, motivating others to join your cause and contribute their time, talents, and energy? Do you have the eagerness and energy to work long hours, perhaps with little or no pay for weeks or months on end?

>> **Are you comfortable engaging with the public and asking for help?** As the founder of a nonprofit, you're typically the face of the organization. That means you need to be prepared for public exposure. In addition, you must be comfortable asking everyone in your network for support — friends, relatives, community members, and so on.

>> **Can you obtain the funds?** Do you already have (or know how you can secure) the monetary and in-kind donations needed to support the organization for the foreseeable future?

REMEMBER

Although its primary goal is to do good rather than make a boatload of money, a social entrepreneurship is still a business. Follow the guidance in the earlier section "Launching Your Own Business" to establish a firm foundation for your venture to give yourself the best chance of achieving your goal.

Making a nonprofit start-up to-do list

To start off on the right foot, take the following steps:

1. Research the field you're entering and develop a detailed plan for getting from point A to point B.

2. **Obtain first-, second-, and third-hand knowledge of how nonprofits operate.**

   - **First-hand:** Work with other nonprofits if you haven't done so already. Volunteer so you know what you're getting into and the challenges involved.

   - **Second-hand:** Talk with people who've started nonprofits to glean their perspectives and experience.

   - **Third-hand:** Read up on nonprofits and take workshops on how to get started.

3. **Complete the IRS paperwork to establish a nonprofit entity.**

   IRS publication 557 (`www.irs.gov/pub/irs-pdf/p557.pdf`) contains information on all the organizational categories and instructions on qualifying for and applying for 501(c) status.

4. **Secure the funding to launch your nonprofit and sustain it for the foreseeable future.**

   See the earlier section "Financing your enterprise" for details, but ignore the parts about using your own money and borrowing against your personal assets. Don't put any of your personal assets at risk.

Here's some additional advice:

>> **Don't underestimate the burnout factor.** Starting this kind of venture typically demands long hours with low or no pay (for some time), and the final responsibility for your project's success falls to you and you alone. And don't hold your breath for all the backslapping for a job well done. It may be years before your organization's work is acknowledged, if it ever is.

>> **Be aware of your time commitment.** As founder, you may play a huge and active role in the early days, but eventually you'll need to have a plan in place to step off the stage. Making room for a new generation of leaders to take the reins is never easy, but it's critical to sustaining an organization over time.

>> **Be careful not to lose your own identity in that of the nonprofit.** With all the time, energy, and passion that go into starting and nourishing a nonprofit, drawing the line between yourself and the organization can be harder than you think. This kind of work is personal and takes passion.

LESSONS FROM THE PINK FUND

Molly MacDonald is founder and CEO of The Pink Fund, a nonprofit that provides financial aid to breast cancer patients. As a breast cancer survivor, she offers the following
ten tips to others who are eager to launch nonprofits around causes that are dear to
them:

- **Start out by volunteering your time.** You may have to work for nothing for the
  first year.

- **Go slow.** Some people will applaud your mission but will hang back before offering
  funding until they see that you're successful.

- **Invite a well-known speaker to an event.** Bringing in someone with a following
  could gin up interest in your nonprofit when you're just starting out and under the
  radar.

- **Create a vision board to inspire you.** That's a collage on a big white poster board
  with images and magazine cutouts that home in on your dreams and goals for your
  nonprofit.

- **Use your connections to get the word out through the media**. MacDonald got
  one of her former employers, the *Detroit Free Press,* to run a story on her effort, and
  more than a dozen other newspapers picked it up.

- **Seek out nonfinancial donations or barter for services**. The Pink Fund's office
  space, legal work, brochure, and website are all donated. Even its logo was
  designed by one of MacDonald's friends in exchange for a table.

- **Make sure your financials are in good shape**. Run a lean organization, keep
  impeccable records, file your taxes on time, and have a treasurer who advises you
  on how to spend money and stay within your budget.

- **Develop an intern program**. It saves some costs and gives interns work experience for ten weeks or so.

- **Use social media relentlessly.** Follow people on Facebook, Google+, LinkedIn, and
  Twitter to network and tap into their collective knowledge.

- **Network, network, network.** Attend community events and volunteer to speak at
  local Rotary Clubs and similar organizations. You never know who you'll meet or
  where your networking will lead.

You can read Molly MacDonald's story along with expanded tips at www.kerryhannon.
com/?p=4214.

Getting help: Organizations that support social entrepreneurs

When you're starting a nonprofit, you're not alone. Many people have traveled the path, and almost everyone wants you to succeed. After all, you're striving to make the world a better place. One of the first steps is to get schooled in how to become a social entrepreneur and how to start a nonprofit. Here are several resources to check out:

» The Bridgespan group (www.bridgespan.org) offers information and guidance along with support and networking opportunities to help you get started.

» The Chronicle of Philanthropy (www.philanthropy.com) provides information and advice for leaders of philanthropic enterprises. You can also use this site to recruit people who want to work for a nonprofit.

» CommonGood Careers (www.commongoodcareers.org) recruits for nonprofit careers at management level.

» Encore.org (www.encore.org) is a go-to site for anyone interested in a career with social meaning and purpose; it includes a list of nonprofit job opportunities.

» GuideStar (www.guidestar.org) is a leading source on nonprofit organizations.

» Idealist (www.idealist.org) provides leads to more than 10,000 job opportunities nationwide in the nonprofit sector. This is a great place to go to recruit volunteers and interns.

» Independent Sector (www.independentsector.org) has research and resources of more than 600 charities, foundations, corporations, and individuals.

» The National Council of Nonprofits (www.councilofnonprofits.org) is a network of state and regional nonprofit associations serving more than 20,000 organizations.

Exploring Franchising Opportunities

Many who are eyeing a second career fancy the idea of running their own business. Yet the risk and work involved in starting a business from scratch can be daunting. One way to ease into entrepreneurship is to purchase a franchise. Many franchises provide a full range of services, including site selection, training, product supply, marketing plans, and even assistance in obtaining financing.

But franchising can be a tricky and expensive road. An initial investment ranges from tens of thousands of dollars up to $500,000. And it's not unusual to hear franchisees gripe about ongoing royalty and advertising fees. For example, to own a Subway franchise store costs an estimated $116,000 to $263,000 in the United States. On top of that, however, franchisees pay fees of 12.5 percent of gross sales (minus sales tax) every week to corporate headquarters: Eight percent is for franchise royalties, and 4.5 percent goes to advertising. That's a lot of bread.

This section sheds light on franchising opportunities and offers advice on how to get started and what to watch out for.

Don't rush in

WARNING

One of the biggest mistakes franchisees make is to hurry into business without doing enough research and soul-searching to determine whether franchising is right for them or whether a certain franchise is really a good match. Don't let the fear of missing out on a golden opportunity drive you to make a rash decision.

Take your time to evaluate your options and research franchises you may be interested in buying, including talking to other franchise owners, particularly owners of the same franchises you're interested in. Find out what they like and dislike about the franchise. For more about reality-testing a franchise opportunity, see the later section "Do your due diligence."

Do a self-assessment

Buying a franchise is a huge time and money commitment. You're putting tens or even hundreds of thousands of your own dollars on the line and will be working 60 or more hours every week to make your franchise a success. Before making that commitment, answer the following questions:

>> **Is this concept, product, or service something I'm passionate about?** The answer had better be yes, because passion provides the drive to help you overcome the inevitable setbacks and frustrations.

>> **Am I prepared to work hard?** Although the franchisor provides you with a ready-made business, its success is entirely up to you. You need to show up and work hard to satisfy your customers and attend to all the details of running a business. The franchisor won't do that for you.

>> **Am I customer-focused?** To succeed, you need to be honest, fair, personable, service-oriented, and customer-focused. If you're not, you're more likely to drive away customers than attract them.

>> **Am I optimistic and confident?** Optimism and confidence are contagious and convey to customers and clients your belief in the products and services you're selling.

>> **Do I have the skills to run a business?** Franchisors are looking for people with transferable business skills, such as sales, marketing, management, communication, customer service, and an ability to balance the books.

>> **Am I a quick learner?** The learning curve is steep. You need to be able to read and follow instructions and "catch on" to the way the franchise wants the business run.

>> **Am I willing to follow orders?** As explained next, franchisors make the rules, and franchisees follow them. If you're not comfortable with that, you may be better off starting your own business.

For more on navigating the world of franchising opportunities, check out *Franchise Management For Dummies*, by Michael Seid and Joyce Mazero (Wiley, 2017).

Accept that you don't call the shots

Franchising is a cookie-cutter approach to expanding a business. It's important to realize that, regardless of the sales pitch, you're not really your own boss. You must follow the formula. There's little wiggle room for innovation. Franchises depend on the by-the-book execution of a business plan. For the most part, you have to be willing to do what you're told. And if you don't, you could lose your right to own the franchise.

Franchise guidelines may cover site selection, marketing materials, signage, employee uniforms, bookkeeping procedures, sales area, which vendors you use, and more. If you're independent and like to call the shots, franchising may not be your thing.

Do your due diligence

When researching franchise opportunities and narrowing the field, perform your due diligence to select a franchise that's likely to succeed and meet your goals. To perform your due diligence, take the following steps:

1. **Gauge demand for the franchisor's products or services.**

Is there a need in your community that's not being met or a problem that's not being addressed that the franchise is uniquely positioned to meet or solve?

2. **Assess potential competitors.**

   Are other businesses addressing the same need or problem successfully within your community or online? What makes the franchise you're considering that much better that potential customers would choose it over what's already available? If the franchise has competitors and isn't significantly better than them, cross it off your list.

3. **Evaluate brand recognition.**

   Does the franchise have a strong brand presence and a good reputation in your community for delivering quality products and services? Do people talk about a desire to have that particular brand available locally?

4. **Search the web for complaints about the franchise.**

   Visit the franchise's website and find it on Facebook, LinkedIn, and Twitter, and read what others (customers and franchisees) post about it. Search the web for the company's name followed by "complaints" or "rip-off" to find out what customers and perhaps former employees and franchisees have to say about the franchise. Check also with the Better Business Bureau or local consumer protection agency for any complaints that have been filed.

5. **Find out how long the franchise has been in the franchising biz.**

   A long track record proves that the franchise is doing something right.

6. **Find out how supportive the franchise is.**

   Support often comes in the form of training and advertising. In addition, some franchises may offer financing to get up and running. If you get the feeling that the franchisor is more interested in its own wealth at the expense of franchisee success, cross it off your list.

7. **Obtain and read the franchisor's disclosure agreement.**

   It provides contact information for previous purchasers in your region, audited financial statements, a breakdown of start-up and ongoing costs, and an outline of your responsibilities and the franchisor's obligations. Pay close attention to the pages in the document showing franchisee turnover. Names and phone numbers of former and current franchisees in your area should be listed.

TIP

Check whether the franchise you're exploring has the SBA's stamp of approval (www.sba.gov/content/franchise-registry-approved-brands). SBA-approved franchises are ones whose disclosure agreements have been reviewed and accepted by the SBA.

8. **Contact current and former franchise owners.**

   Ask them what they like and dislike about the franchise and what they think could be done better. Contacting former franchisees may take some legwork, but the key is to find out why they're no longer in business.

TIP

Interview franchisees in person. Chances are that they'll be more forthcoming in a face-to-face meeting. Be aware that some may have signed confidentiality agreements that prevent them from talking to you.

Consult an accountant or attorney with experience in franchising to help you gauge the entire franchise package, including costs, projected profits, tax implications, and your ability to sell the franchise later, if desired.

Be sure you have enough money

How much can you afford to lose? Do you have a financial cushion or another source of income to cover your living expenses for a year or more? If not, pump the brakes. Create a budget and figure out how much you will need to live on while your start-up gains traction.

Although some franchises break even quickly, most take 12 months or longer before a newcomer can draw a salary. The initial fee for a franchise is clearly stated in the disclosure documents, but newcomers often underestimate operating costs.

Consider getting a loan

Many franchisees take out a loan to cover initial investment and start-up costs. You may want to try a bank where you've been a longtime customer or one that's familiar with the franchise field.

TIP

Applying for a preapproved franchise loan is often easier and quicker. To find the green-lighted list, go to the Franchise Registry (www.franchiseregistry.com) or to FRANdata.com (www.frandata.com). You can search by name if you have a certain franchise in mind or by industry. Plan on a down payment of 20 to 30 percent of the loan amount.

Check out additional resources

For more information and guidance on buying and running a franchise, check out these resources:

>> American Franchisee Association (AFA) at www.franchisee.org is a national trade association of franchisees and dealers with more than 7,000 members.

>> American Association of Franchisees & Dealers (AAFD) at www.aafd.org has developed fair franchising standards for franchisors and franchisees to adopt.

>> Blue MauMau (bluemaumau.org) presents accounts of the ins and outs of franchising.

>> The Federal Trade Commission's (FTC's) Franchises, Business Opportunities, and Investments page at www.ftc.gov/tips-advice/business-center/selected-industries/franchises,-business-opportunities,-and-investments features links to several relevant areas on the site.

TIP

>> The Federal Trade Commission's (FTC's) "Buying a Franchise: A Consumer Guide" (www.ftc.gov/tips-advice/business-center/guidance/buying-franchise-consumer-guide) which is available on the web or as a downloadable PDF. It's a 16-page booklet that's well worth the time required to read it.

>> International Franchise Association (IFA) at www.franchise.org is a great place to go to find out more about franchising and specific franchise opportunities.

>> Small Business Administration's (SBA) Franchise Businesses page at www.sba.gov/content/franchise-businesses provides a good overview of franchising.

>> Unhappy Franchisee (www.unhappyfranchisee.com) features stories of franchises gone wrong. What a way to end a section on franchising, eh?

Chapter **4**

Tracking Small Business Revenues and Costs

Running your own business means hard work and long hours.

One of the ways that you keep score of how you're doing is to track your business revenue and expenses; the difference between the two is the profit or loss for your company. You should utilize a system for accounting for your business inflows and outflows to stay on top of what's going on in your business — and to ease the pain of completing the never-ending stream of tax forms required by state and federal government tax authorities quarterly and annually.

This chapter explains the basics of developing a business accounting process for your small business. It also discusses how to fulfill the myriad filing requirements of the tax authorities by keeping proper records.

Establishing an Accounting System for Your Business

If you're thinking about starting a business or are already in the thick of running one, make sure you keep a proper accounting of your income and expenses. If you don't, you'll have a lot more stress and headaches at tax time.

Besides helping you over the annual tax-filing hurdle and fulfilling quarterly requirements, accurate records allow you to track your company's financial health and performance during the year. How are your profits running compared with last year? Can you afford to hire new employees? Analyzing your monthly or quarterly business financial statements (profit and loss statement, balance sheet, and so on) can help you answer these important questions.

WARNING

Here's another reason to keep good records: The IRS may audit you, and if that happens, you'll be asked to substantiate particular items on your return. Small business owners who file IRS Form 1040 Schedule C, "Profit or Loss From Business," with their tax returns are audited at a much higher rate than other taxpayers. Although that dubious honor may seem like an unfair burden to business owners, the IRS targets small businesses because more than a few small business owners break the tax rules, and many areas exist where small business owners can mess up.

REMEMBER

If your small business *is* audited, well-prepared and organized financial records will help. Auditors are so used to "shoebox" accounting that being organized in and of itself helps establish you in the auditor's eyes as a responsible business person.

The following sections cover the key tax-organizing things that small business owners need to keep in mind and get right.

Separating business from personal finances

One of the IRS's biggest concerns is that, as a small business owner, you'll try to minimize your company's profits (and therefore taxes) by hiding business income and inflating business expenses. Uncle Sam thus looks suspiciously at business owners who use personal checking and personal credit card accounts for company transactions. You may be tempted to use your personal accounts this way because opening separate accounts is a hassle — not because you're dishonest.

TIP

Take the time to open separate accounts (such as bank accounts and credit card accounts) for your business and your personal use. Doing so not only makes the tax authorities happy but also makes your accounting easier. And don't make the mistake of thinking that paying for an expense through your business account proves to the IRS that it was a legitimate business expense. If the IRS finds that the expense was truly for personal purposes, it will likely dig deeper into your company's financial records to see what other shenanigans are going on.

Documenting expenses and income in the event of an audit

It doesn't matter whether you use file folders, software, or a good old-fashioned shoebox to collate receipts and other important financial information. What does matter is that you keep complete and accurate records of both expenses and income.

WARNING

>> **Expenses:** You'll probably lose or misplace some of those little pieces of paper that you need to document your expenses. Thus, one advantage of charging expenses on a credit card or paying by check is that these transactions leave a trail, which makes it easier to total your expenses come tax time and prove your expenses if you're audited.

Just be careful when you use a credit card because you may buy more things than you can really afford. Then you're stuck with a lot of debt to pay off. Only charge on a credit card what you can pay off in full by the time your statement payment due date rolls around.

On the other hand (as many small business owners know), finding lenders when you need money is difficult. Signing up for a low-interest-rate credit card can be an easy and quick way for you to borrow money without groveling to bankers for a loan.

>> **Income:** Likewise, leave a trail with your revenue. Depositing all your checks in one account helps you when tax time comes or if you're ever audited. Be sure to use a dedicated account for your business; don't be tempted to deposit business income into a personal account.

The later section "Keeping Good Tax Records for Your Small Business" provides full details on the process of stashing the right items.

Keeping current on income and payroll taxes

When you're self-employed, you're responsible for the accurate and timely filing of all your income taxes. Without an employer and a payroll department to handle the paperwork for withholding taxes on a regular schedule, you need to make estimated tax payments on a quarterly basis, or pay a fine.

If you have employees, you need to withhold taxes from each paycheck they receive, and you must make timely payments to the IRS and the appropriate state authorities. In addition to federal and state income taxes, you must withhold and send in Social Security and any other state or locally mandated payroll taxes, and you need to issue W-2s annually for each employee and 1099-MISCs for each independent contractor paid $600 or more. Got a headache yet?

For paying taxes on your own self-employment income, you can obtain Form 1040-ES, "Estimated Tax for Individuals." This form comes complete with an estimated tax worksheet and four payment coupons to send in with your quarterly tax payments. It's amazing how user-friendly government people can be when they want your money! The form itself has some quirks and challenges, but you'll be happy to know that Book 1, Chapter 5 explains how to deal with them.

To discover all the amazing rules and regulations of withholding and submitting taxes from employees' paychecks, ask the IRS for Form 941, "Employer's Quarterly Federal Tax Return." Once a year, you also need to complete Form 940, "Employer's Annual Federal Unemployment (FUTA) Tax Return," for unemployment insurance payments to the Feds.

TIP

If your business has a part-time or seasonal employee and the additional burden of filing Form 941 quarterly, the IRS has made the paperwork a tad easier. You may be able to file Form 944, "Employer's Annual Federal Tax Return," if your tax withholding on behalf of employees doesn't exceed $1,000 for the year (which translates to about $4,000 in wages). If you qualify, you need to file only once each year. To see whether you qualify, call the IRS at 800-829-0115 or visit its website at www.irs.gov. If you do qualify, the IRS will send you something in writing.

Also check to see whether your state has its own annual or quarterly unemployment insurance reporting requirements. Look for your state's Department of Labor or use the links on the U.S. Department of Labor website at www.dol.gov/whd/contacts/state_of.htm. And, unless you're lucky enough to live in one of those rare states with no state income taxes, don't forget to get your state's estimated income tax package.

Falling behind in paying taxes ruins some small businesses. When you hire employees, for example, you're particularly vulnerable to tax land mines. If you aren't going to keep current on taxes for yourself and your employees, hire a payroll company or tax adviser who can help you jump through the necessary tax hoops. Payroll companies and tax advisers are there for a reason, so use them selectively. They take care of all the tax filings for you, and if they mess up, they pay the penalties. Check with a tax adviser you trust for the names of reputable payroll companies in your area. Generally, using a payroll service for form preparation and tax deposits is money well spent. The cost is much less than the potential penalties (and time) if you prepare them yourself.

Reducing your taxes by legally shifting income and expenses

Many small business owners elect to keep their business accounting on what's called a *cash basis.* This choice doesn't imply that all business customers literally pay in cash for goods and services or that the company owners pay for all expenses with cash. Cash-basis accounting simply means that, for tax purposes, you recognize and report income in the year you received it and expenses in the year you paid them.

By operating on a cash basis, you can exert more control over the amount of profit (revenue minus expenses) that your business reports for tax purposes from year to year. If your income fluctuates from year to year, you can lower your tax burden by doing some legal shifting of income and expenses.

Suppose that you recently started a business. And assume that you have little, but growing, revenue and somewhat high start-up expenses. Looking ahead to the next tax year, you can already tell that you'll be making more money and will likely be in a much higher tax bracket. Thus, you can likely reduce your tax bill by paying more of your expenses in the next year. Of course, you don't want to upset any of your company's suppliers. But you can pay some of your bills after the start of the next tax year (January 1) rather than in late December of the preceding year (presuming that your business's tax year is on a regular January 1st through December 31st calendar-year basis). *Note:* Credit card expenses are recognized as of the date you charge them, not when you pay the bill.

Likewise, you can exert some control over when your customers pay you. If you expect to make less money next year, don't invoice customers in December of this year. Wait until January so you receive more of your income next year.

WARNING

Be careful with this revenue-shifting game. You don't want to run short of cash and miss a payroll! Similarly, if a customer mails you a check in December, IRS laws don't allow you to hold the check until January and count the revenue then. For tax purposes, you're supposed to recognize the payment as revenue when you receive it.

Note: One final point about who can and who can't do this revenue and expense two-step. Sole proprietorships, partnerships (including limited liability companies, also known as LLCs), S corporations, and personal-service corporations generally can shift revenue and expenses. On the other hand, C corporations and partnerships that have C corporations as partners may not use the cash-accounting method if they have annual receipts of more than $5 million per year.

Keeping Good Tax Records for Your Small Business

Tax records pose a problem for many people because the IRS doesn't require any particular form of record keeping. In fact, the IRS recommends, in general terms, that you keep records only to file a "complete and accurate" return. This section explores what records you should keep, where you should maintain them, and for how long.

Ensuring a complete and accurate tax return

In case you don't feel like flipping through countless pages of government instructions on what constitutes a "complete and accurate" return, here are some common tax situations at a glance and the types of records normally required:

>> **Business expenses:** The IRS is especially watchful in this area, so be sure to keep detailed proof of any expenses that you claim. This proof can consist of many items, such as receipts of income, expense account statements, and so on. Keep in mind that the IRS doesn't always accept canceled checks as the only method of substantiation, so make sure you hang on to the bill or receipt for every expense you incur.

>> **Car expenses:** If, for the business use of your car, you choose to deduct the actual expenses rather than the standard mileage rate (which is 53.5 cents per mile for tax year 2017), you need to show the cost of the car and when you started using it for business. You also must record your business miles, your

total miles, and your expenses, such as insurance, gas, and maintenance. You need a combination of a log and written receipts, of course! Stationery and office supply stores carry inexpensive logbooks that you can buy for your vehicle usage and expense tracking. You can also find smartphone apps to serve the same purpose.

>> **Home expenses:** If you own your home, you need to keep records of your mortgage and real estate tax payments, the purchase price and purchase expenses, and the cost of all the improvements and additions you make over time (save your receipts). Although you may not be selling your house this year, when you do, you'll be thankful you have all your receipts in a neat little file. If you rent a portion of your house or run a business from it, you also need your utility bills, general repair bills, and housecleaning and lawn-mowing costs to calculate your net rental income or your home office expense.

Setting up a record-keeping system

TIP

The tax year is a long time for keeping track of records that you need (and where you put them) when the filing season arrives. So here are some easy things you can do to make your tax-preparation burden a little lighter:

>> **Use an accordion file.** You can buy one with slots already labeled by month, by category, or by letters of the alphabet, or you can make your own filing system with the extra labels. All this can be yours for less than $15.

>> **Set up a manila file folder system.** Decide on the organizational method that best fits your needs, and get into the habit of saving all bills, receipts, and records that you think you may use someday for tax purposes or for things that affect your overall financial planning. This basic advice is good for any taxpayer, whether you file a simple tax return or a complicated one with far more supplemental schedules. Note that this plan, which should set you back about $5, is only minimal, but it's much better than the shoebox approach to record keeping. (A scanning program for documents may also be of interest here.)

>> **Track tax information on your computer.** A number of financial software packages enable you to keep track of your spending for tax purposes. Just don't expect to reap the benefits without a fair amount of upfront and continuing work. You need to figure out how to use the software, and you must enter a great deal of data for the software to be useful to you. Don't forget, though, that you still need your receipts to back up your claims; in an audit, the IRS may not accept your computer records without verifying them against your receipts.

If you're interested in software, consider a business-oriented program, such as QuickBooks, for your small-business accounting. For really simple businesses, consider Quicken. You can merge data into QuickBooks at a later date if you desire. Whichever software you choose, keep in mind that the package tabulates only what you enter or download into it. So if you use the software to write your monthly checks but neglect to enter data for things you pay for with cash, for example, you won't have the whole picture.

Deciding when to stash and when to trash

REMEMBER

One of the most frequently asked questions is how long a taxpayer needs to keep tax records. The answer is easy — a minimum of three years. That's because the statute of limitations for tax audits and assessments is three years. If the IRS doesn't adjust or audit your 2017 tax return by April 15, 2021 (the three years start running on April 15, 2018), it missed its chance. (If you filed after April 15 because you obtained an extension, you must wait until three years after the extension due date rather than the April 15 tax date. The same is true when you file late — the three-year period doesn't start until you actually file your return.)

TIP

Save all records for the assets that you continue to own. These records can include stocks and bonds, automobiles, your home (along with its improvements), and expensive personal property, such as jewelry, video cameras, or computers. Keep these records in a safe-deposit box in case you suffer a (deductible casualty) loss, such as a fire. You don't want these records going up in smoke!

Some taxpayers take the practical step of videotaping their home and its contents, but if you do, make sure that you keep that record outside your home. You can save money on safe-deposit box fees by leaving your video with relatives who may enjoy watching it because they don't see you often enough. (Of course, your relatives may also suffer a fire or an earthquake.)

WARNING

In situations where the IRS suspects that income wasn't reported, IRS agents can go back as far as six years. And if possible tax fraud is involved, forget all time restraints!

Watching out for state differences

Although the IRS requires that you keep your records for only three years, your state may have a longer statute of limitations with regard to state income tax audits. If you're curious what your state's rules are, check with your state's income tax collecting authority. Also, some of your tax-related records may be important to keep for other reasons. For example, suppose that you throw out your receipts after three years. Then the fellow who built your garage four years ago sues you, asserting that you didn't fully pay the bill. You may be out of luck in court if you don't have the canceled check showing that you paid.

The moral: Hang on to records that may be important (such as home improvement receipts) for longer than three years — especially if a dispute is possible. Check with a legal advisor whenever you have a concern because statutes of limitations vary from state to state.

Replacing lost business records

If your business records have been lost or destroyed, you can often obtain duplicate bills from major vendors. You shouldn't have a great deal of trouble getting copies of the original telephone, utility, rent, credit card, oil company, and other bills. Reconstructing a typical month of automobile use can help you make a reasonable determination of the business use of your car. If that month's use approximates an average month's business use of an auto, the IRS usually accepts such reconstructed records as adequate substantiation.

If you deposited all your business income in a checking or savings account, you can reconstruct that income from duplicate bank statements. Although banks usually don't charge for copies of bank statements, they do charge for copies of canceled checks if you can't obtain them online. These charges can be quite expensive, so do some legwork before ordering copies of all your checks. For example, obtain a copy of your lease and a statement from your landlord saying that all rent was paid on time before you request duplicate copies of rent checks.

By ordering copies of past returns with Form 4506, "Request for Copy of Transcript of Tax Form," you can have a point of reference for determining whether you accounted for typical business expenses. Past returns reveal not only gross profit percentages or margins of profit but also the amounts of recurring expenses.

Chapter **5**

Estimated Taxes and Self-Employment Taxes

I f you're self-employed or running a small business, you have plenty to keep you busy each day, week, month, and year. Adding employees to the mix increases the complexity of what you're doing.

For tax purposes, when you're running your own show, you need to submit estimated income taxes each quarter during the year. When you hire employees, you need to submit the taxes that you're required to withhold from their paychecks. This chapter tackles both of these issues.

Likewise, when it comes time to file your annual income tax return, you need to file forms to calculate your self-employment taxes (for Social Security and Medicare, for example). And you may want to contribute to a health savings account (HSA) for yourself or your employees — or simply to allow your employees to tap into this valuable benefit. Both of these topics are addressed here as well.

Form 1040-ES: Estimated Tax for Individuals

The U.S. tax system actually has a simple rule that most people don't think about: It's a pay-as-you-owe system, not a pay-at-the-end-of-the-year one. That's why *withholdings* (having your taxes deducted from your paycheck and sent directly to the government) are great — what you don't see, you don't miss, and your tax payments are periodically withheld and submitted for you throughout the tax year.

If you're self-employed or have taxable income, such as retirement benefits, that isn't subject to withholding, you need to make quarterly estimated tax payments on Form 1040-ES (which you can find easily at www.irs.gov).

WARNING

When you don't pay your taxes on your income as you earn it, you may get hit with penalties and interest when you do pay them, on or before April 15 of the following year. Some small business owners are constantly taking current year's cash flow to pay last year's taxes and never quite catch up. In some cases it can help to make payments *more* often than quarterly. Some business owners take a fixed percentage out of cash receipts and transfer that money to a separate account to make sure they have the money needed for their estimated tax payments.

You can avoid paying a penalty on tax underpayments if you follow these guidelines: You must pay in at least 90 percent of your current year's tax, either in withholdings or in estimated tax payments, as you earn your income, or you can use the safe harbor method (see the next section).

Comparing the safe harbor method to the 90 percent rule

If your income isn't constant or regular, you may choose to follow the so-called *safe harbor rule* and pay 100 percent of last year's tax on an equal and regular basis during this current tax year. This method is simpler than it sounds. If, for example, you have a $3,000 tax liability showing on your most recent year's Form 1040, you may make four quarterly payments of $750 during this current tax year. Provided that you do that, you won't owe any penalty for a current year tax underpayment, even if your current year's tax liability is substantially more — such as $15,000.

Because the safe harbor rule is so easy, you can simply choose to use that when calculating your estimated taxes. Note, though, you do still have to pay the balance of tax due by the return filing date (April 15) to avoid late payment penalties and interest.

In comparison to the safe harbor rule, the 90 percent rule is tricky to calculate. In paying 90 percent of your current year's tax, you need to adjust your payment amounts every quarter during the year that your income rises or falls. Using this method leads to increased paperwork. Still, because it's one of your tax payment options, we explain how to calculate your estimated taxes using the 90 percent rule in the following section.

WARNING

If your current (prior) year's income is (was) more than $150,000, you have to make estimated tax payments equal to 110 percent of your previous year's tax to escape an underestimating penalty if your current year's total federal income tax bill turns out to be substantially more than your previous year's bill. As long as you do this, even if you end up paying a sizable tax bill on April 15, you won't have to pay any penalty or interest on the remaining balance due, despite the fact that your estimated tax payments were less than 90 percent of your tax. (*Note:* This rule doesn't apply to farmers or fishermen.)

Completing and filing your Form 1040-ES

You need to accompany your estimated tax payments with Form 1040-ES (payment voucher), "Estimated Tax for Individuals." This small form requires only your name, address, Social Security number, and the amount that you're paying. For your current year estimated federal income tax payments, make sure that you use the current tax year's 1040-ES.

When mailing in payment with your form 1040-ES, write your checks made payable to the "United States Treasury," making sure your name, Social Security number, and the words "20XX Form 1040-ES" (whatever the current tax year is) are clearly written on the face of the check, and then mail to the relevant address listed in the Form 1040-ES booklet.

TIP

For each tax year, quarterly estimated tax payments are due on April 15, June 15, and September 15 of the current calendar year and January 15 of the next calendar year. (If the 15th falls on a weekend, the actual due date is the next business day, which could be the 16th or 17th of a month.) If you file your completed current year's tax return and pay any taxes due by January 31, you can choose not to pay your fourth quarter estimate (which is due January 15) without incurring any penalty.

If you're not sure how much you need to pay in estimates, Form 1040-ES also contains instructions and a worksheet to help you calculate your current year's estimated tax payments. If you're using the safe harbor method to calculate your estimated tax requirements (see the preceding section) and you have nothing withheld from any source, you can skip the worksheet, take the number from line 61 of your last year's Form 1040, divide it by 4, and drop that number into each of the vouchers. You're done! Now you just need to remember to pay your quarterly bills.

If, on the other hand, some, but not all, of your income has taxes withheld on it or you want to pay only 90 percent of your current year's tax liability upfront (maybe because your income this tax year is going to be considerably less than it was in the previous tax year), you have to complete the worksheet that comes in the Form 1040-ES packet to calculate your estimated payment amounts.

The Estimated Tax Worksheet contained in the Form 1040-ES packet is a preview of your upcoming year's tax return, or what you think that tax return will show. On it you include your adjusted gross income (AGI), your deductions, whether you itemize or take the standard deduction, any credits you're entitled to, and any additional taxes you may be subject to. The worksheet can help you calculate the minimum amount you must pay during the current tax year to avoid paying penalties and interest when it comes time to file your annual tax return.

REMEMBER

You're only estimating when you're making these quarterly tax payments. If your circumstances change and your income rises or falls, you can adjust any payments you haven't yet made. After you make a payment, though, you're stuck with it, and you need to wait until you file your income tax return for the year before you can claim a refund.

WARNING

Don't include your first estimated tax payment for a new tax year with your previous year's Form 1040 or Form 1040A. Instead, mail it separately to the address shown in the instructions for Form 1040-ES. The IRS routes different types of payments to different post office boxes to help eliminate confusion on its end, and a payment sent to the wrong address may be more likely to be credited against the wrong year.

TIP

If you need an extension of time to file your most recent tax year's Form 1040 and you ordinarily make estimated tax payments, you can skip making a separate first quarter estimated tax payment for the next (upcoming) tax year. Instead, add the amount of your first quarter estimate to what you think you still owe on your tax return, and then pay that resulting balance due with your extension. Place the total of your projected most recent tax year's liability and your first quarter estimate on line 4 of Form 4868, "Application for Automatic Extension of Time to File U.S. Individual Income Tax Return," and pay the balance shown on line 6. If your most recent tax year's projections are correct, apply the overpayment (which should equal what you would have paid with your first quarter Form 1040-ES) to your next year's tax return. If your projections are off, though, and your most recent year's tax liability is higher than you thought it would be, you've protected yourself from owing penalties and interest on the underpayment of your tax. Although you may owe a small penalty for underpaying your next year's estimates, it will be minor compared to the penalty and interest you'd owe on your most recent year's tax return.

Keeping Current on Your Employees' (and Your Own) Tax Withholding

When you're self-employed, you're responsible for the accurate and timely filing of all your income taxes. Without an employer and a payroll department to handle the paperwork for withholding taxes on a regular schedule, you need to make estimated tax payments on a quarterly basis, as mentioned.

When you have employees, you also need to withhold taxes on their incomes from each paycheck they receive. And you must make timely payments to the IRS and the appropriate state authorities.

This section covers what you need to do for yourself and your employees.

TIP

Falling behind in paying taxes can cause all kinds of trouble. When you hire employees, for example, you're particularly vulnerable to tax land mines. If you aren't going to keep current on taxes for yourself and your employees, hire a payroll company or tax adviser who can help you jump through the necessary tax hoops.

Form W-4 for employee withholding

If an employee owes a bundle to the IRS when it comes time to complete their annual federal income tax return, chances are they aren't withholding enough tax from their salary. Unless that employee doesn't mind paying a lot on April 15, he needs to adjust his withholding to avoid interest and penalties if he can't pay what's owed when it's due.

TIP

Relying on the worksheet on Form W-4 to accurately calculate the correct number of exemptions an employee should be claiming would be easy, but it's not that simple. Instead, employees should check out the IRS website (www.irs.gov), which has a nifty W-4 calculator that they can use at any time during the year to make sure they're having enough tax withheld from their paychecks. The calculator is easy to use and gives a reasonably accurate picture of how much they'll owe (or have refunded) next April 15.

Tax withholding and filings for employees

In addition to federal and state income taxes, you must withhold and send in Social Security and any state or locally mandated payroll taxes. You must also annually issue W-2s for each employee and 1099-MISCs for each independent contractor paid $600 or more.

To discover all the rules and regulations of withholding and submitting taxes from employees' paychecks, ask the IRS for Form 941, "Employer's Quarterly Federal Tax Return." Once a year, you also need to complete Form 940, "Employer's Annual Federal Unemployment (FUTA) Tax Return," for unemployment insurance payments to the Feds. Also check to see whether your state has its own annual or quarterly unemployment insurance reporting requirements. And, unless you're lucky enough to live in a state with no income taxes, don't forget to get your state's estimated income tax package.

TIP

If your business has a part-time or seasonal employee and the additional burden of filing Form 941 quarterly, the IRS has made the paperwork a bit easier. You may be able to file Form 944, "Employer's Annual Federal Tax Return," if your tax withholding on behalf of employees doesn't exceed $1,000 for the year (which translates to about $4,000 in wages). If you qualify, you need to file only once each year. If you think you may qualify, call the IRS at 800-829-0115 or visit www. irs.gov. If you do qualify, the IRS will send you something in writing.

Schedule SE: Self-Employment Tax

If you earn part or all of your income from being self-employed, use Schedule SE to figure another tax that you owe — the Social Security tax and Medicare tax.

>> The first $118,500 of your self-employment earnings is taxed at 12.4 percent (this is the Social Security tax part) for tax year 2016.

>> The Medicare tax doesn't have any limit; it's 2.9 percent of your total self-employment earnings. For amounts of $118,500 or less, the combined rate is 15.3 percent (adding the two taxes together), and for amounts above $113,700, the rate is 2.9 percent (see the exception in the following paragraph).

If your self-employment earnings are under $400, you aren't subject to self-employment tax.

Note: Effective with tax year 2013, to help pay for federally mandated health insurance, higher income earners began paying a greater Medicare tax rate. The additional Medicare tax amount is 0.9 percent on earned individual income of more than $200,000 (married couples filing jointly pay the additional tax on amounts above $250,000).

Your self-employment earnings may be your earnings reported on the following:

>> Schedule C (line 31)

>> Schedule C-EZ (line 3)

>> Schedule K-1, Form 1065 (box 14, code A) or Form 1065-B (box 9, code J1); use Form 1065-B if you're a partner in a firm

>> Schedule F (line 36) or Schedule K-1, box 14, code A (Form 1065) if you're a farmer

>> Form 1040 (line 21); your self-employment income that you reported as miscellaneous income

Choosing a version of Schedule SE: Short or long?

Wouldn't it be nice if Schedule SE simply said, "If you're self-employed, use this form to compute how much Social Security and Medicare tax you have to pay"? Paying this tax ensures that you'll be entitled to Social Security and Medicare when you're old and gray.

You have three choices when filling out this form:

>> **Section A — Short Schedule SE:** This section is the shortest and easiest one to complete — six lines. But if you were also employed on a salaried basis and had Social Security tax withheld from your wages, you'll pay more self-employment tax than required if you use the short schedule. Moonlighters beware.

>> **Section B — Long Schedule SE:** Use this part of the form if you received wages and are self-employed on the side. Suppose that you have wages of $40,000 and have $90,000 in earnings from your own small business. If you use the Short Schedule SE, you'll end up paying Social Security tax on $130,000 when the maximum amount of combined earnings that you're required to pay on is only $113,700. You pay Medicare tax, however, on the entire $130,000.

This section isn't all that formidable. Make use of it so you don't end up paying more Social Security tax than you have to.

REMEMBER

>> **Part II — Optional methods to figure net earnings:** If your self-employment earnings are less than $5,200 (for 2017), you can elect to pay Social Security tax on at least $5,200, so you'll build up Social Security (and Medicare) credit for when you reach retirement age. You may do this for up to five years.

TIP

You may be able to use Section A of Schedule SE (the short schedule) if your only income subject to Social Security and Medicare tax is self-employment income. If you're self-employed and also are employed by someone else, you have to use the long form (Section B); otherwise, you may end up paying more Social Security than you're required to because Social Security tax has already been withheld from your salary. To prevent this disaster, enter the total of the amounts from boxes 3 and 7 of your W-2 on line 8a of page 2 of Schedule SE. (And if you file Form 4137, "Social Security and Medicare Tax on Unreported Tip Income," enter the amount from line 9 of that form on line 8b of Schedule SE.)

Half of your self-employment tax is deductible. Complete Schedule SE and note the following: The amount on line 5 of Schedule SE is the amount of tax that you have to pay (on the long form, it's line 12); you carry it over to Form 1040 (line 56) and add it to your income tax that's due. Enter half of what you have to pay — the amount on line 6 of Schedule SE (that's line 13 of the long form) — on Form 1040 (line 27).

Completing the Short Schedule SE

Here's the lowdown on completing Section A — Short Schedule SE:

» **Line 1:** If you're not a farmer, you can skip this line. If farming is your game, enter the amount from line 34 of Schedule F or box 14, Code A, Form 1065, Schedule K-1 for farm partnerships.

» **Line 2:** Enter the total of the amounts from line 31, Schedule C (line 3, Schedule C-EZ) and box 9, Code J1, Form 1065-B, Schedule K-1 (for partnerships). This is how each partner pays his Social Security and Medicare tax. You may also have to pay Social Security and Medicare tax on the miscellaneous income reported on line 21 of Form 1040. This includes income such as from directors' fees, finders' fees, and commissions.

Note: The following aren't subject to self-employment tax: jury duty, notary public fees, forgiveness of a debt even if you owe tax on it, rental income, executor's fees (only if you're an ordinary person, and not an attorney, an accountant, or a banker, who may ordinarily act in this capacity), prizes and awards, lottery winnings, and gambling winnings — unless gambling is your occupation.

» **Line 3:** A breeze. Add lines 1 and 2.

» **Line 4:** Multiply line 3 by 92.35 percent (0.9235). Why? If you were employed, your employer would get to deduct its share of the Social Security tax that it would have to pay, and so do you.

>> **Line 5:** If line 4 is $118,500 or less (for tax year 2016), multiply line 4 by 15.3 percent (0.153) and enter that amount on line 56 of Form 1040. For example, if line 4 is $10,000, multiply it by 15.3 percent, and you get $1,530.

If line 4 is more than $118,500, multiply that amount by 2.9 percent (0.029) and add that amount to $14,099. (This is the maximum Social Security tax that you're required to pay.) For example, if line 4 is $120,000, multiply that amount by 0.029 (2.9 percent is your Medicare tax), which comes to $3,480. Now add your Medicare tax ($3,480) to your Social Security tax ($14,099) for a grand total of $17,579. Enter $17,579 on line 56 of Form 1040. (**Note:** You get to use cents on Schedule SE if you so desire, but the IRS wants you to use the whole dollar method on Form 1040.)

>> **Line 6:** Multiply line 5 by 50 percent (0.5). You can deduct this amount on line 27 of your 1040.

Form 8889: Health Savings Accounts (HSAs)

Health savings accounts (HSAs) allow people to put money away on a tax-advantaged basis to pay for healthcare-related expenses. This section explains how they work and the tax form — Form 8889 — that you must file with the IRS to claim an HSA deduction for contributions.

Understanding how HSAs work and who can use them

Money contributed to an HSA is tax-deductible, and investment earnings compound without tax and aren't taxed upon withdrawal as long as you use the funds to pay for eligible healthcare costs. So, unlike a retirement account, HSAs are actually triple tax-free!

The list of eligible expenses is generally quite broad — surprisingly so in fact. You can use HSA money to pay for out-of-pocket medical costs not covered by insurance, prescription drugs, dental care (including braces), vision care, vitamins, psychologist fees, and smoking cessation programs, among other expenses. IRS Publication 502 details permissible expenses.

Now, some folks think that it's not worth contributing to an HSA if the money won't be left in the account for long because of current medical expenses. However, simply passing money through the account before paying medical expenses gains you the highly valuable upfront tax break. For example, suppose that you have $1,000 in medical expenses currently (for an office visit and diagnostic test). By contributing the $1,000 to your HSA, if you're in a moderate tax bracket, you could easily save yourself about $300 in income taxes.

Most insurance premiums aren't eligible for being paid with HSA money, but some are. According to the IRS, you may "treat premiums for long-term care coverage, healthcare coverage while you receive unemployment benefits, or healthcare continuation coverage required under any federal law as qualified medical expenses for HSAs." Also, if you have a balance in your account at age 65, you can use that money to reimburse for Medicare costs.

Employers with fewer than 50 employees can offer HSAs. Self-employed folks can use them as well. Anyone (as long as you aren't covered by Medicare) who has a compatible policy may have an HSA.

Most HSAs require that some amount of money ($1,000, for example) be invested in a safe option like a money fund or savings account that is accessed with a debit card or checks that enable you to pay for medical expenses. Many HSAs offer a menu of investments — typically mutual funds. So, when comparing HSAs, you should compare the quality of those offerings.

Also be sure to examine fees, which can really add up on some HSAs. In addition to the fees of the offered funds, beware of load fees and maintenance fees of about $5 per month (which may be waived for regular automatic investments or once you meet a certain minimum).

TIP

So far, mostly banks and brokerages linked with banks offer HSAs. Investment companies have held off on offering HSAs themselves until they're convinced that the market for them is large enough to make it worth their while. HSAs have also found themselves in the political crosshairs in Congressional debates and possible regulatory changes, but an erosion of HSA tax benefits seems unlikely.

Completing Form 8889

Form 8889, "Health Savings Accounts," is one of those IRS forms that looks much worse than it actually is, at least from the standpoint of the actual experience of most folks who get stuck filling it out. That said, for a minority of folks, Form 8889 can be cumbersome and time-consuming.

If you're contributing to an HSA, you generally need to concern yourself with only Part I of the form. Here are the primary issues you need to address in this part of the form:

>> **Line 1:** This is where you indicate whether your health insurance covers just you or your family.

>> **Line 2:** Enter the amount of your HSA contributions (and those made on your behalf).

>> **Line 3:** This is where you enter your maximum allowable HSA contribution. Note that the maximum is more for those age 55 and older at the end of the most recent tax year (see line 7).

>> **Line 4:** If you have one of the older Archer MSAs, you need to enter the amount, if any, that you and your employer contributed to said account during the tax year, because that will reduce your allowable HSA contribution.

If you took any distributions from an HSA during the tax year, you address that in Part II of this form. You must track and report your distributions so that the IRS gets the taxes owed on them.

Finally, in Part III, if you failed to maintain a high-deductible health plan for the entire tax year, you may owe additional tax, which is determined and calculated here.

Chapter 6

Developing a Retirement Plan

Many folks dream about retiring. No more racing to catch the commuter train or beat the worst of rush-hour traffic, saying goodbye to endless meetings about topics for which you have little or no interest. Instead you'll have plenty of free time to do the things you can rarely find the time and energy to do while you're working. It sure sounds appealing, doesn't it?

Although many folks dream about it, few are preparing for retirement. A survey conducted by the Employee Benefit Research Institute regarding Americans' planning for retirement found that

» Only about 64 percent of working adults surveyed are actually saving for retirement.

» Of those who are saving, 69 percent have a nest egg of less than $50,000.

» About half of survey participants simply guess at the amount of their retirement needs.

Your future plans are important enough to deserve more than a guess, but, yes, you're busy. So this chapter promises to provide plenty of retirement-planning insights and tips without spending gobs of your time. First, this chapter discusses some general retirement topics you need to understand.

Deciding When to Retire

Retiring sounds so appealing when you've had a frustrating stretch at a job you're not particularly enjoying. But some folks really enjoy working and aren't eager to have wide-open daily schedules day after day, week after week. Deciding when to retire and what to do in retirement is an intensely personal decision. You need to consider many financial and personal considerations and questions, and we thoroughly address them in this chapter.

WHAT FOCUS GROUPS SAY ABOUT PLANNING FOR RETIREMENT

The Society of Actuaries conducted some interesting focus groups with folks early in their retirement years. They honed in on people who had investment portfolios of at least $100,000 and who needed that money along with their Social Security and pension benefits to meet their retirement expenses.

Most of these people didn't consult advisers and plan all that much for their retirement. Instead, they were more concerned with quitting work by a particular age. A number of focus group participants commented that their retirement decision came down to a "feeling" that they could swing it. Consider these comments from three different retirees:

- "I thought you were supposed to retire when you are about 65 and thought I would try it."

- "I never sat down and thought 'I am 59, and in 30 years I'll be 89. Have I allocated enough for 30 years?' I never did that. Theoretically, I should have."

- "We take it day by day. I can't worry about what is going to happen tomorrow."

The focus groups also found that retirees were spending more than they expected on entertainment and travel, prescription drugs, and gas. It also wasn't unusual for retirees to overlook inflation. And finally, although retirees were concerned about the potential for high medical and long-term care expenses, they did little planning around those expected expenses.

Even when you're healthy, the job market may not be. Your employer could suffer financial hardship and reduce its workforce. Or maybe you'll be lucky enough to retire early (even though it's unplanned) because your employer offers you a buy-out package that's too good to turn down. Or worse, you may lose your job with little notice and few benefits.

Ideally, when caught in one of these situations, you would obtain another job and continue it until your planned retirement age. Unfortunately, events may not unfold that way. The economy, the job market, and your age could work against you. Finding another job, at a compensation level you're willing to work for, may not be possible.

Even when you leave a full-time career voluntarily, you may plan to work part time for a few years. Or you may assume that if the first years of retirement are more expensive than planned, you could return to work at least part time. Yet a part-time job you assumed would be easy to find may not be available at all or may be available at a much lower level of pay than you expected.

Knowing How Much You Really Need for Retirement

Most people have a long-term financial goal of retiring someday. For some, doing so means leaving paid work behind entirely. To others, simply cutting back on work or doing something completely different on a part-time basis is most appealing.

If you don't plan to work well into your golden years, you need a reasonable chunk of money to maintain a particular lifestyle in the absence of your normal employment income. The following sections help you get started on determining how much money you need and come to grips with those numbers.

Figuring out what portion of income you need

If you're like most people, you need less money to live on in retirement than during your working years. That's because in retirement most people don't need to save any of their income, and many of their work-related expenses (commuting, work clothes, and such) go away or greatly decrease. With less income, most retirees find they pay less in taxes, too.

On the flip side, some categories of expenses may go up in retirement. With more free time on your hands, you may spend more on entertainment, meals out, and travel. The costs for prescription drugs and other medical expenses also can begin to add up.

So what portion of your income do you really need as you make your retirement plan? The answer isn't simple. Everyone's situation is unique, so examine your current expenditures and consider how they may change in the years ahead. (Check out the chapters in Book 4 for more information on budgeting and managing your expenses.)

To help figure out how much money you need, keep the following statistics in mind. Studies have shown that retirees typically spend 65 to 80 percent of their pre-retirement income during their retirement years. Folks at the lower end of this range typically

>> Save a large portion of their annual earnings during their working years

>> Don't have a mortgage or any other debt in retirement

>> Are higher-income earners who don't anticipate leading a lifestyle in retirement that's reflective of their current high-income lifestyle

Those who spend at the higher end of the range tend to have the following characteristics:

>> Save little or none of their annual earnings before retirement

>> Still have a significant mortgage or growing rent to pay in retirement

>> Need nearly all current income to meet their current lifestyle

>> Have expensive hobbies that they have more time to pursue

Carefully look at all your expenses and anticipate how they may change.

Grasping what the numbers mean

When determining how much money you need for your retirement plans, you want to think in terms of your goals and how much you should save per month to reach your desired goal given your current situation.

Some folks hear a number — a big, bad number like $3.8 million — and it gets stuck in their head. That number is the size of the nest egg they believe they need to achieve a particular standard of living throughout their retirement.

TIP

Instead of obsessing about a large number, it's better to examine your own standard of living that can be provided by the assets you've accumulated or will likely accumulate by a preferred retirement age. You can then begin to put the numbers into perspective for your own individual case (see the later section "Crunching the Numbers").

Eyeing the Components of Your Retirement Plan

To meet your retirement goals, you need a firm grasp of what resources are available to help you. In addition to government benefits such as Social Security, company-provided pensions and personal investments round out most people's retirement income sources. This section takes a closer look at these elements.

Social Security retirement benefits

Social Security is intended to provide a subsistence level of income in retirement for basic living necessities, such as food, shelter, and clothing. However, Social Security wasn't designed to be a retiree's sole source of income. When planning for retirement, you'll likely need to supplement your expected Social Security benefits with personal savings, investments, and company pension benefits. If you're a high-income earner, you particularly need to supplement your income — unless, of course, you're willing to live well beneath your pre-retirement income. (See Book 4, Chapter 4 for more discussion on Social Security.)

TIP

If you're still working, you can estimate your Social Security retirement benefits by looking at your most recent Social Security benefits statement, which the federal government sends annually to adults age 25 and older. Statements usually are mailed three months before your birthday. If you can't locate your most recent statement, you can get one fairly quickly either by requesting it online at www.ssa.gov (click on the Your Social Security Earnings Statement tab on the home page) or by calling 800-772-1213 and requesting form SSA-7004 ("Request for Social Security Statement"). You also can set up a "my Social Security" account on the Social Security website that lets you obtain updated benefits estimates, verify your earnings, and take other actions.

REMEMBER

Like many people, you may be concerned about your Social Security. You may be afraid that it won't be there when you retire. Although you may have to wait until you're slightly older to collect benefits or endure more of your benefits being taxed, rest assured — Congress has been reluctant over the years to make major negative changes to Social Security, because doing so would risk upsetting a large and highly active voting bloc of retirees and near retirees.

With your Social Security benefits statement in hand, you can see how much in Social Security benefits you've already earned and review how the Social Security Administration (SSA) determines these numbers. With this information, you can better plan for your retirement and make important retirement planning decisions.

Looking at your estimated benefits statement

Your Social Security benefits statement can give you important information about your estimated retirement benefits. On Page 2 of this annual statement, you see information like the following (unless you don't have enough *work credits*, which are awarded for every year you earn money):

> *You have earned enough credits to qualify for benefits. At your current earnings rate, if you continue working until:*

- *Your full retirement age (67 years), your payment would be about $1,543 a month*

- *Age 70, your payment would be about $1,924 a month*

- *If you stop working and start receiving benefits at age 62, your payment would be about $1,064 a month*

These statements are pretty self-explanatory.

Assumptions: Discovering how your benefits are estimated

Along with your benefits estimates, the SSA also discloses the assumptions used to come up with your numbers and some important caveats. You should understand the assumptions behind the estimates we talk about in the preceding section. Why? These are projections, and depending on your earnings in the years ahead, your expected benefits may change. Here's what the SSA says:

> *Generally, the older you are and the closer you are to retirement, the more accurate the retirement estimates will be because they are based on a longer work history with fewer uncertainties such as earnings fluctuations and future law changes.*

REMEMBER

If you stop and consider this assumption, it does make sense and is true of about any forecast or estimate. The further into the future you try to project something, the more likely it is that the estimates may be off base.

To understand what could throw off future estimates, keep the following in mind as you dig a little deeper into the SSA's assumptions:

If you have enough work credits, we estimated your benefit amounts using your average earnings over your working lifetime. For 2017 and later (up to retirement age), we assumed you'll continue to work and make about the same as you did in 2015 or 2016. We can't provide your actual benefit amount until you apply for benefits. And that amount may differ from the estimates stated above because:

(1) Your earnings may increase or decrease in the future.

(2) After you start receiving benefits, they will be adjusted for cost-of-living increases.

(3) Your estimated benefits are based on current law. The law governing benefit amounts may change.

In other words, the SSA assumes that your future earnings will annually be about the same as your earnings in the most recent couple of years. Therefore, as their own cautions highlight, if you expect your future work earnings to change from your most recent years' employment earnings, your expected Social Security retirement benefits also will change.

Don't get hung up over expected cost-of-living increases. Later in this chapter, these increases are incorporated into the analysis. The third point about future benefit law changes is considered in Book 4, Chapter 4.

TIP

If you want to delve into different scenarios for your Social Security benefits, you can try the SSA's online Retirement Estimator at www.socialsecurity.gov/estimator.

Pensions

When putting together your retirement plan, you also want to consider any pensions you have available to you. You may have previously worked for an employer offering pension benefits, or you may currently work for a company with such a plan. Also known as a *defined benefit plan,* a company pension plan is one that your employer actually contributes to and invests money in to fund your future pension payments.

In a typical plan, the employer may put away about 8 to 10 percent of your salary (this money is actually in addition to your salary, because the money isn't taken from your income as it would be if you were contributing to a retirement plan such as a 401(k) plan). The money is then invested mostly in a mix of stocks and bonds (as it is in a balanced mutual fund).

Two terrific attributes of pension plans are as follows:

>> **The savings happen automatically.** Unlike a retirement savings plan like a 401(k), you don't have to think about your pension plan. You don't have to cut back on your spending or complete any forms. Your employer is putting away money on your behalf month in and month out.

>> **You don't experience any investment hassles or challenges.** The pension fund manager does all the heavy lifting with regard to investing the money. So there's no need for you to research or monitor financial markets or investments.

If your current or previous employers have a pension plan and you may have accumulated benefits, request a copy of each plan's benefit description and a recent statement of your earned benefits.

Based on your years of service, your benefits statement will show you how much of a benefit you've earned. Your current employer's statement or the person or department that works with benefits may also be able to show you how your pension benefits will increase based on working until a certain future age.

Investments

The many types of investments you may have are an important component of your retirement plan. These investments may come in various forms, such as bank accounts, brokerage accounts, mutual fund accounts, and so on. Your investments may or may not be in retirement accounts. Even if they aren't, they still can be earmarked to help with your retirement.

Take an inventory of your savings and investments by gathering recent copies of your statements from the following types of accounts or investment options:

>> Bank accounts — checking (especially if it holds excess savings), savings, CDs, and so on

>> IRA accounts

>> Taxable accounts at brokers and mutual funds

>> Employer retirement accounts, including

- Profit-sharing plans

- Employee stock ownership plans (ESOPs)

- 401(k)s, 403(b)s, and so forth

>> Investment real estate

IN GOOD HANDS: KNOWING YOUR PENSION IS PROTECTED

Many people don't realize how safe their pension benefits actually are. Even if the company goes under, pension assets are held separately and are backed up by the Pension Benefit Guaranty Corporation (PBGC). The PBGC is a federal agency created by the Employee Retirement Income Security Act of 1974 (also known as ERISA) to protect pension benefits in private-sector pension plans, also known as *defined benefit plans.* PBGC guarantees basic pension benefits earned, subject to limits, including

- Pension benefits at normal retirement age
- Most early retirement benefits
- Disability benefits
- Annuity benefits for survivors of plan participants

PBGC doesn't guarantee health and welfare benefits, vacation pay, or severance pay. The maximum benefit amount that PBGC guarantees is quite substantial.

You simply need to take an inventory of your current assets and use that information in the later "Crunching the Numbers" section to determine where you stand regarding retirement planning.

Your home's equity

If you've owned a home over the years and it has a decent amount of *equity* in it (the difference between its market value and the mortgage debt owed on it), you can tap into that equity to provide for your retirement. To do so, you have two primary options:

> » **Sell your home.** After you sell your home, you can either buy a less costly one or rent one.

> » **Take out a reverse mortgage.** With a *reverse mortgage,* you draw income against your home, which is accumulated as a debt balance to be paid once the home is sold.

If you're pretty certain you want to tap your home's equity to help with retirement, consider how much equity you would use. And check out the chapters in Book 6, which deal with these two options in detail.

When Setting Up Your Couples Plan

When beginning your retirement planning, make sure that, if you're married, you sit down with your spouse and coordinate each person's plan together. Doing so may seem obvious, but it's an important step. Discussions about retirement plans need to begin long before retirement. Even when one spouse is doing most of the financial planning for retirement, both spouses need to have a meeting of the minds over the nonfinancial aspects of their senior years. And the spouse who is not doing as much of the financial planning still needs to know the overall financial situation.

Following are some questions couples should begin discussing at least five years before retirement:

>> Should each of you retire? If so, when would each prefer to begin retirement?

>> Would retirement be complete, or is part-time work a possibility for either spouse?

>> Where will you live during retirement?

>> How will each of you spend nonworking time during retirement? What things will you do together and which will you do separately?

>> Have you estimated how much money you will need to support your retirement plans? If so, how much will you need and how close are you to having it?

>> What is the plan for spending your retirement funds, and what is the plan for investing the funds?

>> What assets and accounts do you own, where are they, and how are they invested?

>> What legacy do you hope to leave? Is there a plan for fulfilling that goal?

>> What is your estate plan, and where are the documents?

>> What role will children, grandchildren, and parents play in the rest of your lives? Will you move to live near either adult children or aging parents? Do you plan to help or support either of them if needed? If this is a second marriage for either spouse, what are the plans for any children of the prior marriage?

>> What is the attitude of each of you to aging, and how do you expect to react to it?

Crunching the Numbers

For purposes of retirement planning, what matters most is where you stand today as far as reaching your goal. So you need to crunch some numbers to get a handle on your situation. One of the best ways to do so is to use available retirement calculators, either online or with a hard-copy workbook. These resources can walk you through the calculations needed to figure out how much you should be saving to reach your retirement goal. The information you collect and the questions you answer earlier in this chapter allow you to hit the ground running with the number crunching.

TIP

Among the mass market website tools and booklets, try the one from T. Rowe Price at www3.troweprice.com/ric/ricweb/public/ric.do. The T. Rowe Price Web-based Retirement Income Calculator is a user-friendly tool, and the website says it takes about ten minutes to complete. If you're organized and have your documents handy, you may cruise through it that quickly, but otherwise you'll more than likely need 20 to 30 minutes.

The following sections walk you through steps for using the T. Rowe Price retirement planning tools to get a better assessment of your financial numbers as you prepare for retirement. T. Rowe Price is the example, but please note that you can select another company's tool if you prefer.

Understanding assumptions and how they work

Whether you use a retirement calculator online or via a work booklet, make sure you're aware of the different assumptions used. This section details those assumptions. It specifically looks at the T. Rowe Price assumptions and online calculator. To make the best use of this site, review the following important key assumptions. If you choose not to use this online tool, you can use the discussion of the assumptions that follow for other retirement planning tools, including the T. Rowe Price work booklet.

>> **Asset allocation:** The calculator asks you to enter your current *allocation* (mix of major investment classes) and then to select an allocation for after you're retired. For the retirement allocation, you can choose a fixed 40 percent stock, 40 percent bond, or 20 percent money fund, or you can have the mix gradually shift away from stocks each year that you're in retirement. Either choice is fine, but we have a slight preference for the latter of the two options.

REMEMBER

The calculator doesn't include real estate as a possible asset. If you own real estate as an investment, you should treat those assets as a stock-like investment, because they have similar long-term risk and return characteristics. You should calculate your equity in investment real estate.

>> **Age of retirement:** For this assumption, you plug in your preferred age of retirement, within reason of course. (For example, plugging in age 53 is pointless if you've selected that age knowing that the only way to accomplish that date is by winning the lottery.) Depending on how the analysis works out, you can always go back and plug in a different age. Sometimes folks are pleasantly surprised that their combined accumulated resources provide them with a decent enough standard of living that they can actually consider retiring sooner than they thought.

>> **Social Security:** The T. Rowe Price calculator asks whether you want to include expected Social Security benefits. You definitely should include your Social Security benefits in the calculations. Don't buy into the nonsense that the program will vaporize and leave you with little to nothing from it. For the vast majority of people, Social Security benefits are an important component of their retirement income, so do include them.

Based on your current income, the T. Rowe Price retirement program will automatically plug in your estimated Social Security benefits. As long as your income hasn't changed or won't change dramatically, using their estimated number should be fine. Alternatively, you can input your own number using a recent Social Security benefits statement if you have one handy. Or use the Retirement Estimator at the Social Security website (`www.socialsecurity.gov/estimator`).

After you enter your personal information and decide on the preceding assumptions, you're ready to finish the calculations on the T. Rowe Price website. Price's completed analysis shows how much you can live on per month and then compares that with what you're stated goal or amount was. The calculations include doing 1,000 market simulations, and it works 80 percent of the time. (See the nearby sidebar "Monte Carlo retirement simulations" for a more detailed explanation of this type of modeling, if you're interested.)

REMEMBER

The T. Rowe Price analysis allows you to make adjustments, such as your desired age of retirement, rate of savings, and how much you expect to spend per month, to what age you'd like your savings to last. So, for example, if the analysis showed that you have much more than enough to retire by age 65, try plugging in, say, age 62 and, voilà, the calculator quickly shows you how the numbers change.

Making the numbers work

After you crunch the numbers, you may discover you need to save at a rate that isn't doable. Don't despair. You have the following options to lessen the depressingly high savings you apparently need:

» **Boost your investment returns.** Reduce your taxes while investing: While you're still working, be sure to take advantage of retirement savings accounts, especially when you can gain free matching money from your employer or you're eligible for the special tax credit from the government. When investing money outside of retirement accounts, take care to minimize taxes. For more on investing strategies, see Book 4, Chapter 3.

» **Work (a little) more.** Extend the number of years you're willing to work, or consider working part time for a few years past the age you were expecting to stop working.

» **Reduce your spending.** The more you spend today, the more years you'll have to work to meet your savings goal. See Book 4, Chapter 2 to find out how to manage your spending in retirement.

» **Use your home's equity.** If you didn't factor in using some of your home's equity into your retirement nest egg, consider doing so. Some people are willing to trade down into a less costly property in retirement. You also can take a reverse mortgage to tap some of your property's equity. (Book 6, Chapter 2 has more on this.)

Dealing with excess money

Believe it or not, some folks accumulate more than they need to achieve their desired lifestyle. Often, this is a surprise to the client, so some folks have a hard time believing the good news.

If you find yourself with extra money, the good news is at least you don't have to worry about making sure you can continue your current standard of living during retirement. In this situation, consider taking either of the following actions:

» **Enhance your retirement.** Don't be afraid to enjoy yourself. While you're still healthy, travel, eat out, take some classes, and do whatever else floats your boat (within reason, of course). Remember that come the end of your life, you can't take your money with you.

MONTE CARLO RETIREMENT SIMULATIONS

When you start doing number crunching for retirement planning, you begin to realize that the outcome is dependent on many variables. In addition, other factors, such as how investment returns change over time, can have a significant impact, especially over the short term, on your retirement plans.

Over the past century, the rate of inflation has averaged about 3 percent per year. Growth-oriented investments, such as stocks, have returned about 9 percent per year historically. Bonds and other fixed-income investments have returned about 5 percent per year.

Those are long-term averages, which are all well and good, but suppose that a worker decided to retire around the year 2000, and, like most retirees early in their retirement, he still had a healthy chunk of his investments in stocks. Because the stock market experienced severe downturns both early and late in the 2000s, his standard of living and ability and comfort with taking withdrawals from his retirement funds may be impacted.

A *Monte Carlo simulation* runs many different scenarios and calculates the likelihood (percentage of the time) that you will accomplish your retirement goal. The T. Rowe Price retirement calculator we walk you through in this chapter does Monte Carlo simulations and tests about 1,000 market scenarios to see how your retirement plans will work out in many different market conditions.

>> **Earmark a portion of your assets for your beneficiaries.** You may want to leave something for your family members as well as other beneficiaries, such as your place of worship and charities. If so, you need to determine the approximate dollar amount for each of the beneficiaries. Estate planning is so important that the chapters in Book 5 are devoted to it.

REMEMBER

Of course, life can throw you unexpected curve balls that could cause you to incur higher-than-expected expenses. But if you're always preparing for rainy day after rainy day, you may lead a miserly, unenjoyable retirement.

Making Plans for Nonfinancial Matters

Getting caught up in the climb up the career ladder, burning the midnight oil, and accumulating wealth and possessions is easy in a capitalist society. In your pursuit, losing sight of some areas — the ones not about money — is also easy.

These areas are just as important — if not more important — than your finances, which is why you should be working just as hard at planning them.

Personal connections

A lot of research shows that those individuals who have strong and healthy connections in their later years tend to be happier, enjoy better health, live longer, and live longer independently. As you're preparing for retirement, make sure you spend time making and maintaining healthy personal relationships. Doing so is an investment that pays dividends by improving the length and quality of your life.

TIP

If you have children of your own (and perhaps they give you grandchildren), you've got a built-in network of younger folks to keep you actively involved. If you don't have any children or grandchildren, or if you want more personal connections, you can forge friendships with people younger than you through your activities, hobbies, fellowship, and so forth.

Personal health

Your health is much, *much* more important than your financial net worth. Just ask folks who have major medical problems — especially those they could have avoided — if they wish they had taken better care of their health. Although anyone can experience bad luck or bad genes when it comes to health, you can do a lot to stay healthy and enjoy enhanced longevity and the best possible quality of life.

Activities, hobbies, interests

For folks who have had full-time jobs, retiring and having no job to occupy their days sounds alluring. However, some retirees feel a lack of purpose and miss the satisfaction that comes from meeting the challenges of work. A fringe benefit of most people's work is the human interaction that comes along with it.

REMEMBER

When planning for your future, consider the following as good substitutes for work, because they provide challenges and foster friendships and connections with others:

>> **Activities and hobbies:** Exercising is a good choice to include in long-term plans; it provides vast health benefits and opportunities to meet new friends and hang out with old ones. If you're not into exercising, perhaps you can look at different hobbies you like, such as collecting something. You can meet interesting people and make new friends by going to auctions, garage sales, and such. People like to collect all sorts of things; just be careful you don't spend too much money.

>> **Part-time work:** Working part time, especially when you have more flexibility in setting your hours, can be an excellent part of a retirement plan. It can provide enjoyments and a challenge — not to mention some extra dough.

>> **Volunteering:** Giving something back to society pays many dividends. You can find a zillion volunteer opportunities. Your place of worship, organizations that support a cause you believe in (for example, fighting cancer or heart disease), and schools are super places to start looking. Stumped for ideas? Try a service like VolunteerMatch (`www.volunteermatch.org`).

IN THIS CHAPTER

» **Reviewing the features of retirement accounts**

» **Surveying the different types of accounts you can choose from**

» **Taking care of your 401(k) balances**

» **Naming beneficiaries for your retirement accounts**

» **Becoming familiar with RMDs**

Chapter **7**

Grasping Retirement Accounts and Their Rules

One of the virtues and drawbacks of living in the United States is that you have plenty of choices — sometimes too many. And that's certainly the case with the numerous types of retirement accounts and variety of investments; far more options exist here than in just about any other country in the world.

With so many choices, you may be confused about which option is best for you. Selecting the best is important because you can end up saving yourself more tax dollars and making more after-tax money in the long run. And whether you're entering retirement or are still a decade (or more) away, you need to understand the nuances and rules of each type of account so you not only make good decisions but also comply with the myriad tax rules.

This chapter discusses the common types of retirement accounts to which you may contribute. It also discusses early withdrawal penalties, beneficiary decisions, transfer and rollover rules, and borrowing from or against retirement accounts.

Eyeing the Characteristics of Retirement Accounts

Before you can use retirement accounts to your benefit, you first need to know the 4-1-1 on these accounts, including the advantages to using them and the potential drawbacks. The following sections lay out these pros and cons. Keep this important information in mind as you consider the different types of retirement accounts available.

Focusing on the tax benefits

The main attraction of any retirement account is the tax savings it provides. You generally receive upfront tax breaks on your contributions up to a certain limit. For example, suppose that you're able to contribute $1,000 per month ($12,000 per year) into a tax-deductible retirement savings plan. Assuming that, between federal and state taxes, you're paying about 35 percent in taxes on your last dollars of income, you should see your federal and state tax bills decrease by about $4,200 ($12,000 × 0.35). This immediate savings is usually enough of an incentive to encourage folks to build wealth by funding retirement accounts.

Because the money contributed to the retirement account isn't taxed at the federal or the state level in the year in which a contribution is made, your take-home pay shrinks by much less than the $1,000-per-month contribution. Unfortunately, directing money into retirement accounts doesn't allow you to avoid current Social Security and Medicare taxes on wages you earn during the year.

REMEMBER

These upfront tax breaks are just part of the value derived from using retirement accounts. You also can reap these other tax-related benefits when you invest in a retirement plan:

>> **Your investment returns accumulate without taxation.** After you contribute money into a retirement account, any accumulated investment returns aren't taxed in the year earned. So, in addition to reducing your taxes when you make your contribution, you save from this tax-deferred compounding of your investment over time. In other words, all the taxes you would have owed over the years compound in your account and make your money grow faster. You pay tax on this retirement account money only when you make withdrawals.

>> **When you invest, Uncle Sam ends up with less of your money.** If you don't invest money in a retirement account, you start with less *dinero* in your pocket because Uncle Sam and your state's government immediately siphon off some taxes. The longer the money is invested, the more you profit by investing inside a retirement account.

REMEMBER

Some people are concerned that if their tax rate in retirement is high, then funding retirement accounts could lead to higher taxes. Although this scenario is possible, it's unlikely. Because of the tax-deferred compounding, you should come out ahead by funding your retirement accounts. In fact, your retirement tax rate could increase and you'd still come out ahead.

Income tax rates need to rise significantly from current levels to eliminate the tax-deferral benefits. Even though income tax rates for some individuals may rise in the future, the benefits of tax-deferred contributions and investment income should outweigh the increased tax burden you may face when these funds are withdrawn. For example, say that your tax rate at the time of contribution is 35 percent. Table 7-1 shows how high your tax rate would need to increase to wipe out all your tax-deferral benefits over the years.

TABLE 7-1

Retirement Tax Rates That Would Negate Tax-Deferral Benefits

Number of Years Contribution Compounds	Tax Rate That Eliminates Benefits
10	50 percent
15	56 percent
20	61 percent
25	66 percent
30	70 percent
35	74 percent
40	77 percent

As you can see from the table, the longer your money is invested, the higher your tax rate would have to rise to wipe out the tax-deferred compounding benefits. After the money is in the account for 30 years, your tax rate would have to double (from 35 percent to 70 percent) to eliminate the tax-deferred compounding benefits.

TIP

If your employer matches your contributions or contributes additional money to your account, such as with a company-sponsored 401(k) plan, you'll be even better off. Free employer money further enhances the upfront tax benefits by giving you more money working for you that is not subject to tax in the year the contributions are made. Even if you unexpectedly need to withdraw your contribution, you should still come out ahead — the penalties for early withdrawal are only 10 percent and whatever penalty, if any, your state charges. You'll also owe regular federal and state income tax on withdrawals.

Being aware of restrictions and penalties

Some people contribute little or no money to retirement accounts because of worries about having access to their funds. Although investing your money in a retirement account may limit your access to the money in the short term, overall the investment is a smart move for your retirement in the long run.

If you do have to withdraw your money from a retirement account prior to reaching 59½, you may incur a tax penalty. The penalty is 10 percent in federal taxes plus whatever penalty your state assesses. This penalty tax is in addition to the regular income tax that's due in the year you make the early withdrawal.

Some exceptions (called IRS Rule 72(t) exceptions) do allow you to withdraw retirement account money before age 59½ without penalty, though you'll still owe income taxes. (All the exceptions are explained in detail in the free IRS Publication 590-B, "Distributions from Individual Retirement Arrangements".) The most commonly used exceptions are these:

>> **Five years of withdrawals:** You may withdraw retirement account money early as long as you make withdrawals for at least five consecutive years or until age 59½, whichever is later. The withdrawals must be substantially equal each year and be based on your life expectancy according to Internal Revenue Service (IRS) assumptions and reasonable interest rates. IRS rulings provide details for computing the annual distributions.

>> **Health problems:** If you suffer a disability or incur significant medical expenses, you may be allowed to withdraw money early from your retirement account without penalty. See IRS publication 590 for more information.

>> **Borrowing:** Your employer's retirement plan may allow you to borrow from your plan without incurring a penalty. This is generally not a great idea, especially if you seek the money for current spending, such as buying furniture, taking a vacation, and so on. It can make sense, for example, if you need some down payment money to buy a home. But be sure that you understand the repayment rules and terms, because if you're unable to repay the loan, the unpaid money is treated as a retirement account withdrawal and subject to current federal and state income taxes as well as penalties unless you withdrew the money after age 59½.

You can read more about these and other exceptions at www.irs.gov/retirement-plans/plan-participant-employee/retirement-topics-tax-on-early-distributions.

REMEMBER

The best solution for short-term money needs is to ensure that you maintain an emergency reserve of money (three to six months' worth of living expenses) outside your retirement account. If you don't have an emergency reserve account, you may be able to borrow money from other sources, such as a family member or through a line of credit or lower-interest credit card.

Identifying the Different Types of Retirement Accounts

Different employers and employment situations present unique retirement account options. This section explains the common retirement accounts you'll confront and how they work.

Employer-sponsored retirement accounts

When you work for a company or organization, you may have access to an employer-sponsored retirement savings plan. In this case, the company provides access to an investment firm through which you can contribute money via payroll deductions. Plans have rules specifying, for example, how long after becoming an employee you must wait to begin participating in the plan, company matching contributions, and the overall limits of how much you may contribute to your account.

The good news with this type of plan is that your employer has done the legwork and maintenance for the plan. The potential bad news is that you're at their mercy if they don't have a good plan.

For-profit companies may offer 401(k) plans. Nonprofit organizations can offer 403(b) plans. Government employees may have their own plans such as a 457 plan for state and local government workers and the Thrift Savings Plan for federal government employees. These plans are similar in that contributions into them from your employment earnings aren't taxed at either the federal or state level.

REMEMBER

For tax year 2017, the annual contribution limits for these retirement accounts are the lesser of 20 percent of an employee's salary to a maximum of $18,000. If you're 50 or older, your contribution limit is $24,000.

Self-employed retirement savings plans

Another type of retirement plan is the self-employed retirement savings plan. One of the biggest benefits of earning self-employment income is the ability to establish a tax-sheltered retirement savings plan. These plans not only allow you to contribute more than you likely would be saving on a tax-deferred basis for an employer, but they also can be tailored to meet your specific needs.

As with other retirement savings plans, your contributions to self-employed savings plans are excluded from your reported income and are thus exempt from current federal and state income taxes. The earnings that accumulate on your savings over time also are exempt from current income taxes. You pay taxes on your contributions and earnings when you withdraw them, presumably in retirement, which is when you're likely in a lower tax bracket.

A couple of different versions of self-employed retirement plans are available. The following list explains which plan may be right for you:

>> **Keogh plan:** This type of retirement plan is of potential interest to business owners who have employees that are covered by a plan, because you may be able to contribute more to your account relative to contributions for your employees' accounts. Speak with a tax adviser or an investment management company for more information.

You must establish a Keogh plan by the end of the tax year (usually December 31), but you have until the filing of your federal tax return to make your actual contribution to the plan.

The drawback to a Keogh plan is that it requires slightly more paperwork than a SEP-IRA plan to set up and administer. However, the no-load mutual fund "prototype" plans simplify the administrative burden by providing fill-in-the-blank forms.

>> **A Simplified Employee Pension Plan, Individual Retirement Account (SEP-IRA):** This type of plan cuts through much of a Keogh plan's red tape and is somewhat easier to set up and administer.

REMEMBER

As with a Keogh plan, when you as the employer establish a SEP, you must offer this as a benefit to employees if you have them.

With both of these plans, you may contribute up to the lesser of 25 percent of your self-employment income to a maximum of $54,000 for tax year 2017 ($55,000 for 2018). To determine the exact maximum amount that you may contribute from self-employed income, you need to have your completed Schedule C tax form so you know your business's net income for the year. To find out more about setting up these types of accounts, see the nearby sidebar "Establishing and transferring retirement accounts."

Individual Retirement Accounts (IRAs)

What if you work for an employer that doesn't offer a retirement savings plan? You can certainly lobby your employer to offer a plan, especially if it's a nonprofit, because little cost is involved. Absent that, you can consider contributing to an Individual Retirement Account, or IRA. You may contribute up to $5,500 in 2017 as long as you have at least this much employment (or alimony) income. Those folks who are age 50 and older may contribute up to $6,500 in 2017. The limits are adjusted for inflation annually (or not).

WARNING

Whether you can deduct your IRA contribution from your annual taxes depends on whether you participate in another plan through your employer. Check with your employer about this.

TIP

If you can't take the tax deduction for a regular IRA, consider the newer Roth IRAs, which allow for tax-free withdrawal of investment earnings in your later years. For tax year 2017, you may contribute up to maximum limits, which are the same as on a regular IRA, as long as your modified adjusted gross income doesn't exceed $118,000 if you're a single taxpayer or $186,000 for married couples filing jointly.

ESTABLISHING AND TRANSFERRING RETIREMENT ACCOUNTS

Retirement accounts that you establish, such as a SEP-IRA or Keogh (if you're self-employed) and Individual Retirement Accounts (IRAs), can be set up through mutual fund companies, brokerage firms, and other financial firms. You choose what investments you want in these accounts. You also can transfer these accounts to different firms. Simply call the company that you want to move your account into and ask it to send you its account application and transfer forms. You may be able to do this online at the firm's website.

For retirement accounts that your employer maintains, such as a 401(k) plan, you're limited to the investment options that the plan offers. When you leave this employer, you can elect to roll over your account balance into an IRA. Simply contact the investment company that you'd like to use for the IRA, and ask it to send you its account application forms (or complete them on the firm's website). Then instruct your previous employer on the name and contact information for your chosen investment company where you want your money sent. Don't take possession of your money from the 401(k); otherwise, you'll get hit with a 20 percent federal income tax withholding. For more help with investing, check out Eric Tyson's *Investing For Dummies* (Wiley).

Rolling Over Retirement Balances

One of the most important decisions you'll make with your retirement accounts is what to do with your money in your accounts when you retire. Make the right choice and do the transaction properly, and your after-tax retirement income will be greatly increased. Make a mistake, and you'll pay far more taxes than you need to.

The most common rollover is from a 401(k) plan to an IRA. There are other types of rollovers, however. Money can be moved from one 401(k) to another, from one IRA to another, and from a defined benefit pension plan to an IRA, to give three common examples. But the 401(k)-to-IRA rollover is the most common and probably the most important. This section, as an example, focuses on the important (and common) decision of how to handle a 401(k) account balance when leaving an employer.

Deciding what road to take

You should begin planning what to do with your 401(k) account balance well before you leave the sponsoring employer to ensure that you have sufficient time to research and get comfortable with what you're going to do with your money. Too many people make their plans for travel and other activities for the first six months of retirement, but then they give no thought to what to do with their 401(k) balances until presented with their options as they're leaving the job.

Most 401(k) plans offer several options for handling an account balance when you leave your employer. Here are those options and the issues to consider for each one:

REMEMBER

>> **Leave the balance in the plan until distributions begin.** This option can be a good idea when you like the plan because of its investment options, low costs, or other features. The plan also may allow you to take loans from the account, which could make the plan a source of emergency cash.

However, depending on your circumstances, you may not want to leave your money in the plan for several reasons. For example, you will have more investment options by rolling the balance into an IRA. In addition, the employer could increase fees and change plan offerings between the time you quit and the day you begin receiving distributions. As a former employee, you'll be out of the information loop and may learn about important changes long after current employees. Due to rules and restrictions, most 401(k) plans also are less flexible about post-retirement distributions than IRAs.

>> **Look into annuity options.** The plan may offer an annuity option, making fixed, guaranteed payments to you for life or for a period of years, which can be attractive. Look at all your options, though; you may find higher payments available through commercial annuities purchased through an IRA. (For more on annuities, check out Book 4, Chapter 3.)

TIP

When your employer offers an attractive annuity but you don't want the entire account turned into an annuity, you can purchase the annuity with part of the account. The annuity portion can be distributed directly to you, and then taxes are paid only as annuity payments are received. The rest of the account can be rolled over to an IRA.

>> **Take the account balance in a lump-sum payment.** The entire lump sum would be included in gross income, but the tax law provides a special ten-year income averaging treatment that reduces the tax — but only for those born before 1936, so few people taking lump sums now qualify. You may choose this option when you need or anticipate needing the cash to pay expenses within a few years. Otherwise, you probably should take advantage of tax deferral by leaving the balance in the 401(k) plan or rolling it over to an IRA.

>> **Roll over the balance to an IRA.** A *rollover* basically is taking the money from the 401(k) account and moving it to an IRA. The rollover transfers the account to the broker or mutual fund company of your choice for the best combination of fees, investment choices, and other services.

Choosing a custodian and rolling over your balance to an IRA

After deciding that you want to roll over your 401(k) balance to an IRA, determine who will be the IRA custodian. The *custodian* is a broker, mutual fund firm, bank, insurance company, or other financial services company that offers IRAs. When considering which custodian to choose, consider the following:

>> **Research the fees, services, and investment options.** Look for an IRA custodian that has the features and services you desire. You should have an idea of how the account will be invested initially and which types of investments are most important to you.

>> **Decide how you will transact most of your business.** Do you prefer talking on the telephone? Doing transactions in person? Mailing information? Or using the web? Most large custodians offer all these options, but smaller ones may not.

After you select your custodian, you basically have two ways to rollover a retirement account balance:

>> **Option 1:** The trustee for your employer's plan can issue a check to you or make a direct deposit into your bank account. You have 60 days to deposit the check (or an equivalent amount) into an IRA or other qualified retirement plan. If you fail to make the transfer within 60 days, you'll owe income taxes; and if you're under age 59½, you may owe a 10 percent early distribution penalty. In 2014, the IRS revised the rules so that a taxpayer is allowed to do only one of these rollovers per tax year.

WARNING

This type of rollover has a trick. When the check is made out to you, the trustee must withhold 20 percent of the account balance for income taxes. The taxes will be refunded to you after you file your tax return and show that you rolled over the account balance within 60 days. But you must deposit in the IRA the entire 401(k) account balance, not only the amount distributed to you. As a result, you must come up with an amount equal to the 20 percent that was withheld and roll that into the IRA along with the amount that was distributed.

>> **Option 2:** The other form of rollover is the *trustee-to-trustee transfer.* The 20 percent withholding isn't required when the distribution check is made payable to a specific IRA custodian instead of to you.

Here's how this easy transaction works:

1. You open an IRA with the custodian of your choice.

2. You complete a rollover form giving the details of the account you want the balance rolled over from.

3. The IRA custodian contacts the trustee of your 401(k) plan and ensures that the 401(k) trustee transfers your account balance to the custodian.

This method is the easier and safer way to roll over your IRA, because it avoids the possibility of missing the 60-day deadline of the other method and can be done an unlimited number of times. All you have to do is be sure the 401(k) balance is transferred to your IRA. Sometimes a mistake is made, and the transfer is made to a taxable account instead of an IRA. If this isn't corrected promptly, you will owe income tax on the entire amount.

Why would anyone choose Option 1 when you can avoid the hassle of rounding up the extra cash by choosing Option 2? Some employees choose inferior Option 1 because they don't know better and their employers don't warn them before issuing the check. You've now been informed and won't make that mistake!

REMEMBER

No matter which of the preceding options you choose, to be tax-free, a rollover must qualify as a *lump sum,* which means that the entire account must be distributed within the same calendar year. Sometimes a rollover doesn't qualify as a lump sum because some late dividends or other distributions aren't distributed until after December 31. In addition, the employee must be either *separated from service* of the employer (in other words, no longer working for the employer) or over age 59½.

WARNING

If your 401(k) account contains employer stock, don't transfer the entire account to an IRA. Doing so causes you to lose a valuable tax benefit. When the employer stock is distributed to a taxable account, taxes are generally deferred on it until the stock is sold from that account. In this situation, you maximize tax benefits by splitting off the employer stock from the retirement account. Have the employer stock distributed to a taxable (nonretirement) account and the rest of the account rolled over to an IRA.

Choosing Beneficiaries for Your Retirement Accounts

When you create a retirement account, you need to make sure you select the beneficiaries who receive the proceeds. Your will doesn't determine who inherits your IRA and other qualified retirement plans. The account is inherited by whoever is named beneficiary on the beneficiary designation form on file with the plan custodian or trustee.

When choosing your beneficiary, take the time to select the person (or persons) you want to receive your money. Often people don't give much thought to this important designation. Most folks simply write down an obvious beneficiary when they open the account and don't give much thought to it again. In the meantime, they may have been married or divorced, or had children or grandchildren. The account probably has grown into a significant asset over time, yet the beneficiary choice hasn't been reconsidered through all these changes.

You need to give some thought to your beneficiary choice as part of your overall estate plan, and you must review that choice every couple of years. Here are some guidelines to follow:

>> **Take care of your spouse first.** Retirement accounts are a significant part of most estates. Married people whose priorities are taking care of their spouses name their spouses as the primary or sole beneficiaries of their accounts. Of course, you also should name contingent beneficiaries (those who get the

account if the primary beneficiary has passed away) in case your spouse doesn't survive you or passes away while assets are still in the IRA. For most people, the contingent beneficiaries are their children in equal shares. But you can name other contingent beneficiaries, such as other relatives or friends.

>> **Be careful about naming a trust.** A *trust* is an arrangement in which a trustee manages property for the benefit of someone else. You may want to name a trust as beneficiary to ensure that, for example, your sibling who knows something about investing manages the IRA until your teenagers are older. A trustee also can control how much is distributed. A trust also allows you to control who receives the amount left after the initial beneficiary passes away. However, you have the potential of losing the tax deferral for the IRA if the beneficiary isn't a natural person. Certain types of trusts carry a limited exception to this rule about natural persons. In this case, however, the trust must be carefully written by an experienced estate planner to avoid losing the tax deferral.

>> **Consider splitting your IRA.** When you have children but no surviving spouse (or your spouse will have significant non-IRA assets), your children likely will be named equal beneficiaries of your IRA. When children inherit IRA funds, annual distributions are required based on the life expectancy of the oldest beneficiary. The children also must agree on investments and distributions that exceed the minimum required distributions.

TIP

Your children have the right to split the IRA into separate IRAs for each of them. You may want to split the IRA now instead of waiting for the kids to work things out. This split gives you more control over the amount of assets each child inherits. It also allows you to name different contingent beneficiaries for each IRA. If you want a trust to control the inheritance of only one beneficiary, splitting the IRA makes this easier. Otherwise, the other beneficiaries have to coordinate their management of the IRA with the trustee.

>> **Make charitable gifts with the IRA.** All your beneficiaries could receive more after-tax wealth when charitable gifts are made with the IRA and other heirs inherit other assets.

WARNING

Don't name your estate as a beneficiary. A natural person must be beneficiary for the IRA to retain its tax deferral. Name your estate as beneficiary, and the IRA must be distributed on an accelerated schedule. Also, don't *fail* to name a beneficiary; otherwise, your estate will be considered the beneficiary.

Taking Required Minimum Distributions, or RMDs

The main purpose of investing in an IRA or other qualified retirement plan is to help you financially during your retirement years. As a result (and because he wants to collect taxes), Uncle Sam requires that you start taking distributions at a certain age. You must begin annual *required minimum distributions* (RMDs) from IRAs and other qualified retirement plans by April 1 of the year after you turn age 70½.

The following sections help you calculate your RMD with an IRA and with other types of retirement accounts.

REMEMBER

The RMD is a floor, not a ceiling. You're free to withdraw as much in excess of the RMD as you want. An excess distribution doesn't result in any credit the following year. The adjustment is automatic because the next year's RMD is computed using the account balance as of the end of the current year.

Calculating your RMD for an IRA

To calculate your RMD, you can do the following:

1. **Start with your IRA balance as of December 31 of the year before you turn 70½.**

2. **Divide this amount by your life expectancy.**

   The result of dividing your IRA balance by your life expectancy is your RMD for the year. The good news is you don't have to do the math regarding your life expectancy. Instead you must consult the life expectancy tables in IRS Publication 590-B (available for free at www.irs.gov). Most people use the "Uniform Lifetime Table."

   You use a different life expectancy table, the "Joint Life and Last Survivor Expectancy Table," if you're a married IRA owner whose spouse is the primary beneficiary of the IRA and is more than ten years younger.

3. **Repeat the calculation each year.**

WARNING

   For the first RMD, use the IRA balance as of December 31 of the year before you turned 70½, not the year before the April 1 deadline. The first RMD, though delayed until April 1 of the year after turning 70½, really is the RMD for the previous year. If you wait until April 1 to take the distribution, you'll have to take two distributions in that year: the previous year's distribution, and the current year's distribution that's due by December 31. Taking two distributions in one year could push you into a higher tax bracket. Overall taxes may be lower if the first distribution is taken by December 31 of the year you turn age 70½.

So, for example, if Rick turned 70½ in January 2017 and Corrine turned 70½ in December 2017, each must take his or her first RMD by April 1, 2018. Subsequent RMDs must be taken by December 31 of each year. If you fail to take an RMD, the penalty is 50 percent of the distribution that should have been taken. Ouch!

When you own more than one IRA, add all the balances together as one to compute the RMD. You can withdraw that amount from the IRAs in any combination you want. Take it all from one account, equally from the different accounts, or in any other way you want. Just be sure that by December 31 your distributions equal (or exceed) the RMD.

REMEMBER

If a traditional IRA is converted into a Roth IRA, a new RMD is required for the year of the conversion, using the traditional IRA balance as of December 31 of the preceding year. A new RMD also is required for the year of the IRA owner's death, no matter when during the year that occurred. Roth IRAs are discussed in the section "Individual Retirement Accounts (IRAs)," earlier in this chapter.

Computing the RMD for other retirement plans

All qualified retirement plans — profit-sharing, 401(k), and pension plans — must make RMDs. The basic calculation is the same as for IRAs, but employer plans have some important differences.

For employer-sponsored plans (but not for IRAs, SEP-IRAs, and SIMPLE IRAs), the required beginning date is delayed when you're still working for the employer and don't own more than 5 percent of the employer's stock. The first RMD is delayed until April 1 of the year after the year in which you retire. Also, for money contributed to a 403(b) plan before 1987, RMDs may be delayed until age 75.

REMEMBER

The calculations for employer plans can be a bit different from IRA calculations. For instance, when you have multiple employer plans, such as a profit-sharing plan and a 401(k) plan, you compute the RMDs separately for each plan instead of totaling them. Check IRS Publication 590 for details (see www.irs.gov).

WARNING

An employer-sponsored plan can impose stricter rules than the IRS imposes. For example, some employer plans require retired employees to withdraw or roll over their account balances within five years. They may have other stringent restrictions as well. These rules are in the documents describing the employer plan. You're supposed to receive these periodically and can request them at any time from your employer or plan trustee.

2

Getting Your Affairs in Order

Contents at a Glance

IN THIS CHAPTER

» **Understanding the estate planning process**

» **Creating your estate plan**

» **Getting help when you need it**

» **Avoiding common estate planning pitfalls**

» **Making your wishes known**

Chapter **1**

Ensuring That Your Last Wishes Are Honored

You've worked hard all your life, you've accumulated some assets, and you're ready to plan your estate. But you're probably not excited about planning your estate. You have already figured out that you have a lot of work to do. You must also think about unpleasant things, including your death, the possibility of your incapacity, and how your family will cope without you.

What's the primary purpose of an estate plan? Taking care of your loved ones after you're gone. Why plan your estate now? Because the sooner you start, the more certain you can be that your plan will take care of your family's needs in the way that you want.

As you proceed with this process, you'll probably find out your estate planning needs aren't as complicated as you thought. You may discover that all you need is a will, perhaps backed up by a simple living trust. You may discover that your needs are more complicated and enlist the help of an estate planning professional. Yet even then, your understanding of the estate planning process and tools will help you communicate your needs and choose your best options.

Having an estate plan also provides a great deal of comfort. You'll be able to plan for your family's financial needs. And after your death or incapacity, your loved ones won't have to fret about what you would have wanted them to do. They'll know your actual wishes.

What Can Happen When You Don't Plan Your Estate

Simply put, if you don't plan your estate, the government has an estate plan in store for you. Your state's laws of *intestate succession* will apply, and the state will decide who inherits your assets, usually your spouse and children. But that's not all:

>> In the event of your incapacity, a court may appoint people to make decisions for you regarding your personal and medical care and the management of your money. A stranger may end up deciding where you live, what medical treatment you receive, and perhaps even whether you really need $20 for a haircut.

>> If you have minor children, a court will have to decide who will care for them but will not have the benefit of your input.

>> The business you spent a lifetime building may end up failing or in the hands of a court-appointed receiver.

Planning your estate isn't a one-time task. Changes in your life circumstances can dramatically alter both your wishes for your estate and whether your original estate plan even remains viable.

Sometimes it seems like your life doesn't change much, so you may be wondering what sort of changes could occur. Consider the following:

>> Your estate will probably grow substantially over the course of your life, although it may also shrink.

>> You may marry, divorce, separate, have or adopt a child, or experience a death in your family.

>> Your children will grow up and establish their own households.

>> You may move between states, buy and sell property, or start your own business.

>> Your designated trustee or personal representative may no longer be available, or your relationship with that person may change.

>> Laws may change. In fact, they will. You can expect a new estate tax bill to be working its way through Congress within the next year or two, and it won't be the last.

In all probability, you'll update your estate plan several times during your life, and on occasion you may even start over from scratch.

WARNING

If you don't update your estate, over time it may become largely ineffective. When that happens, you're not much better off than you were before you created the outdated estate plan.

Reaping the Benefits of Planning Your Estate

The biggest advantage of planning your estate is that your wishes will be respected, both while you're alive and after your death.

Your estate plan helps you in several ways:

>> Incapacity planning helps ensure that you receive the type of medical care and treatment you want, that your assets are managed according to your own wishes, and that your end-of-life decisions are respected.

>> Your will and trust ensure that your assets are distributed to the heirs you choose, under terms and conditions you define.

>> Your business succession plan helps ensure that your business doesn't fail following your incapacity or death and that control of your business passes to a suitable successor.

When you don't plan your estate, your incapacity plan will be defined by a court, and your estate will be carved up according to state law. The result may be far different from what you desire.

Planning for your care while you're alive

In addition to planning for the distribution of your assets after you die, a complete estate plan looks at what will happen to your estate if an accident or illness leaves you unable to properly care for yourself.

Your incapacity plan includes your durable power of attorney, healthcare proxy, and living will:

>> Your durable power of attorney appoints an attorney-in-fact who can make financial decisions for you if you become incapacitated.

>> Your healthcare proxy appoints a healthcare advocate who can help you make medical decisions if you're unable to make or communicate those decisions yourself.

>> Your living will describes what care you want to receive, and don't want to receive, during the final days of your life.

If you don't appoint people to help with your medical and financial needs, your family may have to go to court to have somebody appointed to make decisions for you. Your loved ones will face unnecessary burdens and confusion:

>> Your family will have to go to court to have somebody appointed to manage your personal and financial needs, at a time when they're already under stress due to your incapacity.

>> The court won't know who you'd prefer to assist with your medical and financial decisions and may appoint somebody who you would find unacceptable.

>> Your helpers won't know your wishes or the limits you'd impose on their choices if you were able to communicate them. They'll have to try to guess what you would have wanted.

WARNING

The impact of these choices may be profound. Whatever your plans, with a court-appointed guardian supervising your medical care, you're more likely to undergo more intrusive medical care and to spend your last days in a hospital or nursing home.

Ensuring that your assets go where you want

When you plan your estate, you pick your heirs and decide how much you want to leave to them. Although state laws do restrict your ability to disinherit certain heirs, especially your spouse, for the most part you can leave your money to family, friends, schools and charities, or anybody else you choose.

In defining your bequests, you may choose to simply distribute your assets to your heirs upon your death. But you may also choose to be very creative in how you distribute your assets.

>> You can defer your bequests to a later date (for example, "When my son turns 25").

>> You can mete out your gifts in installments (for example, "$20,000 to my daughter upon her 18th birthday, $20,000 on her 23rd birthday, and $60,000 upon her 30th birthday").

>> You can impose conditions on your bequests, requiring your heirs to satisfy those conditions before they receive the inheritance (for example, "$50,000 to my son upon his graduation from college").

If you don't plan your estate, the state will make all those choices for you. Your estate will go to your heirs according to your state's laws of intestate succession, described later in this chapter in the section "Realizing What Happens If You Don't Have an Estate Plan." If you have minor children, the probate court may appoint a conservator to look after their assets until they turn 18. But any adult heir will immediately receive their legally defined inheritance. Your wish to support your alma mater or to give to charity? Forget it.

REMEMBER

The only way to be sure that your assets are distributed the way you want is to plan your estate. (See Chapters 2 and 3 in Book 2 for more about planning your bequests and providing for dependents.)

Looking Out for Common Pitfalls

Everybody makes mistakes, but some mistakes get made a lot. Actions that may seem like they'll simplify your estate may in fact make it more complicated, burden your ability to use and enjoy your own assets, or increase the tax burden to your estate and heirs.

At the same time, once you understand the common pitfalls, most are pretty easy to avoid. You can avoid some mistakes simply by planning your estate now rather than putting it off until your health starts to fail.

Benefits and dangers of jointly titling real estate, property, and bank accounts

A common shortcut to estate planning involves adding your desired heir to the title of your real estate, financial account, or other titled asset. You can choose between a number of different types of joint ownership. In all likelihood, when you add somebody as an owner, you'll create a *joint tenancy with right of survivorship*, meaning that this person automatically inherits your share if you die first.

Some huge risks can arise from joint ownership of a home. Take a common example, where you add your child to the deed as a joint tenant:

>> Your son gets divorced, and his wife asks the divorce court to award him half of "his share" of your house.

>> Your son may decide that the home is "more than you can handle" and ask a court to force the sale of the property.

>> Your son decides to move in. It's his home, too, isn't it?

>> Your son suffers financial problems or doesn't pay his taxes, and his creditors or the IRS try to collect against "his share."

Also, adding a joint owner can increase that person's capital gains tax exposure when the property is eventually sold.

Other issues may also arise, such as

>> What happens if you can no longer afford to support your home, or are no longer physically able to care for it, but your child won't agree to a sale?

>> What happens if you want to refinance your mortgage to improve the property, get a better interest rate, or withdraw equity from your home, but your child refuses to cooperate?

>> What if you want to sell your house and move into a smaller home or condo, but your child wants to keep "the family home"?

>> What happens if you have to move into a long-term care facility?

When you give up your full ownership interest, you run the risk that your children will suddenly decide that they know what is best for you and prevent you from making perfectly reasonable decisions relating to your own home.

Similar issues arise with joint ownership of bank accounts. Because the law presumes that both you and your joint account holder have equal rights to the money, your co-account holder may empty the account. His creditors may try to garnish the account to satisfy his debts. If it truly is a joint account, with both of you contributing toward the balance, the IRS will still try to include the entire account balance in your taxable estate, and your child will have to prove to the IRS that he contributed part of the money and that his contribution should not be taxed.

Possible alternatives to joint ownership include the use of a living trust, or transfer-on-death titles and accounts. (Book 5, Chapter 4 discusses trusts.)

"MY CHILDREN WOULDN'T DO THAT TO ME"

You probably have thought at one time or another that your offspring would never do any of these awful scenarios to you. While other people may have children who will abuse joint ownership or empty a joint bank account, your children would never do such a thing. You know what? You're probably right. The worst abuses happen in exceptional cases, and most children try to respect their parents' wishes. But not all the problems arise from malice.

Your child may encounter financial troubles. It's easy to "borrow" a car payment or a house payment from your joint bank account. Maybe your child even repays the loan the first time or two. But then she finds herself having borrowed two or three payments. Then four. And before she even appreciates what she's doing, she's "borrowed" far more of your money than she can realistically pay back. Do you sue your child? Call the police? The odds are that you won't. You'll suffer a strain in your relationship and have a less comfortable retirement than you had previously expected.

On the flip-side, your child may be far more concerned with your financial stability than you are. Every time you make a purchase, your child may be demanding to know what you spent "all that money on" and "did you really need it?" There was a case where a child emptied out her mother's joint bank account, not because her mother was spending inappropriately but because the daughter was afraid she *might*. She didn't approve of her mother's new boyfriend and was concerned that her mother might make excessive gifts.

Benefits and dangers of life estates

You own your home, and you want your children to inherit your home. So how about a life estate? In a *life estate,* you retain the right to use and control your home for the rest of your life, and you provide for your ownership of your home to pass to specific people upon your death. You're called the *life tenant,* and the people who eventually receive your home are your *remaindermen.* You can create a life estate for other property as well, which is called a *retained life estate.*

In a typical arrangement, once you create a life estate, you retain the exclusive right to the use and possession of your home. You pay the day-to-day expenses of your home, including routine maintenance, homeowner's insurance, and property taxes. You pay the interest on the mortgage, but your remaindermen pay the portion of the mortgage payment that goes to the principal balance.

As a life tenant, you face the same type of dependence upon the goodwill and cooperation of your remaindermen as you do with joint ownership (see preceding section). You need your remaindermen's consent to refinance or sell your home, and difficulties can arise if you become unable to pay the home's ongoing expenses.

A life estate may also appeal to you if you have children from a prior marriage who you want to eventually inherit your home but you want your current spouse to be able to live in your home following your death. You can provide in your estate plan for your spouse to receive a life estate in your home, with your children as the remaindermen. But consider the consequences:

>> Say that you're considerably older than your spouse. You die at age 82, and your spouse is 63. At this time, your children are nearing retirement age. If your spouse lives for another 20 years, your children will be elderly by the time they inherit your home. By then, they may have little need for an inheritance.

>> Your spouse may neglect the property, causing your children to have to pay insurance, taxes, and repairs and possibly having to take your spouse to court.

>> You may create acrimony between your spouse and your children, who see your spouse as standing in the way of "their inheritance."

>> Your spouse may remarry. Do you want to subsidize your spouse's new family?

TIP

An alternative? Keep your house in a trust for five to ten years, or whatever other time period you desire, and let your spouse have full use and enjoyment of it during that period. Then have your trust convey your house to your children.

Danger of subjecting an asset to Medicaid spend-down rules

Medicare is a federal health insurance program that provides payment for certain hospital and medical expenses for people age 65 and older. But as you age, you face a huge potential expense that Medicare doesn't ordinarily cover: long-term care.

If you're wealthy enough, lucky enough, or hold sufficient long-term care insurance, you may not need to worry about the cost of your long-term care. But most people, even those with some insurance, can face significant financial hardship from the high cost of residential care.

This is where Medicaid comes in. Medicaid is an additional federal program that covers medical costs, including the cost of long-term care, if you're financially unable to pay for that care yourself.

But before you can qualify for Medicaid, *spend-down rules* apply. If you have too much income or too many assets, you won't qualify for Medicaid until your income or assets are spent down to a qualifying level. The goal here is to make you pay for your own care before the government takes over, while still protecting you and your family from becoming impoverished by the costs of long-term care. Note that spend-down rules don't require that your assets be spent on your medical care, but you do face restrictions on how you can spend your excess money without affecting your qualification for Medicaid.

What if you give your assets away instead of spending them? Can you qualify for Medicaid? That's where *look back rules* kick in. When you apply for Medicaid benefits to pay for long-term care, the government examines your financial transactions over the past five years to determine whether you've transferred assets out of your estate. If you have, the government will impose a penalty period before you can qualify for Medicaid benefits. Any gifts, including payment of tuition for an adult child, charitable donations, and even Christmas presents, can trigger a penalty period for long-term care benefits.

You benefit from a modest Medicaid exemption for income and savings. But you may benefit from a large exemption in the form of your home. If you're in a nursing home but are expected to return to your own home, your home is exempt from the spend-down rules. Note that if you stay in a nursing home for six months or longer, Medicaid assumes that you won't return home. Also, if you're married, as long as your spouse remains in your home, it's exempt from spend-down rules.

So how do you accidentally lose your exemptions? Usually in one of two ways:

» You don't understand the exemptions and believe that the government will take your house no matter what. You transfer title to an heir, probably your children. Your home is no longer yours, and the government will apply spend-down rules to its fair market value.

» You aren't even thinking about Medicaid. You decide that the easiest way to leave your home to your heirs is to add them to the title, giving them outright ownership. The transfer of an interest in your home for less than fair market value during the look-back period can trigger spend-down rules or penalties.

Traditionally, people often used life estates to try to avoid Medicaid spend-down rules. The value of a life estate isn't counted toward your assets when you apply for Medicaid benefits. But states are eager to recover Medicaid expenses and are increasingly imposing liens against the property a Medicaid recipient has placed into a life estate.

One more thing to consider: Even when an exemption applies during your lifetime, the state may seek to recoup its costs by imposing a lien against your property after your death.

Your best approach is to engage in estate planning long before you end up in long-term care. If you plan for your long-term care needs and implement an asset protection strategy before the Medicaid look-back period begins, you can minimize the effect of spend-down rules and recoupment policies on your estate.

TIP

If you believe you or your spouse will require Medicaid benefits later in life, you can consult a lawyer who specializes in Medicaid planning. Your lawyer can help you create a strategy to minimize the effects of Medicaid's spend-down and look-back rules as well as help you avoid or minimize liens Medicaid may attempt to assert against your estate after you die.

Potential for increased tax exposure

Most people won't pay federal estate tax. The current estate tax exemption in 2017 is $5.49 million. Only one in around 500 estates is subject to estate tax. But . . .

WARNING

The estate tax is substantial. After the exemption, the current estate tax rate is 40 percent. If your estate is large enough to pay estate taxes and you do no advance planning, the government may turn out to be a huge beneficiary.

Realizing What Happens If You Don't Have an Estate Plan

Are there drawbacks to not planning your estate? Yes, and some of them are *big*.

If you have a large estate, you will maximize your estate tax liability (see the preceding section). But in addition to the possibility that you'll increase the government's cut, you have two huge reasons to have an estate plan:

>> If you don't plan your estate, the government will decide who inherits your assets.

>> If you don't designate a custodian for your minor children, the state will pick somebody for you.

You may enjoy many smaller benefits as well, including picking the person who will administer your estate and providing instructions for your funeral and memorial service. If you don't draft a will, others will make those choices for you.

Following the laws of intestate succession

If you don't make an estate plan for yourself, the state has already made one for you. State *laws of intestate succession* define who inherits the property of people who die without a will. Typically, your surviving spouse will receive half of your estate, with the remainder divided between your children. If you have no surviving spouse or children, your estate is distributed by formula to other surviving members of your family.

In some cases, the state's plan for your assets may be very similar to your own. In others, it will be wildly different. But the only way to be certain that your estate is distributed the way you want is to create an estate plan.

Even if you plan your estate, intestate succession laws may apply to some of your assets in the following situations:

>> You forget to include an asset in your estate plan.

>> You direct an asset to an heir through your living trust but forget to transfer ownership of the asset into your trust.

>> After all your bequests are made, you'll almost certainly have something left over in your estate, even if just a small amount of cash or your clothing and personal effects.

TIP

You should include a *residuary clause* in your will, describing how any assets left in your estate are to be distributed after all specific bequests have been made. That way, all your assets will be distributed consistent with your own wishes, and not through choices the state makes for you.

Determining the custodian of your minor children

Although uncommon, tragedy can strike your family and kill both you and your spouse. Families tend to travel together, so a terrible car accident or plane crash could leave your children as orphans.

If you draft a will, you may designate custodians for your minor children. You can pick people you trust to care for your children and raise them in a manner you approve. If you want, you can designate one person to care for your children and another person to manage their money.

Although courts aren't bound by your designation, judges usually defer to a parent's wishes. But if you don't make a choice, the judge will pick somebody for you. That person or persons could be

» Your in-laws, who were abusive to your spouse throughout her childhood

» Your sister, whose husband was adamantly opposed to caring for your children until he learned about their Social Security survivor's benefits

» Your cousin, who has never been able to manage money but will now be responsible for overseeing your children's inheritance

Granted, often the court will make a good decision and pick somebody who will provide excellent care for your children. But why take the chance?

TIP

Even if you're divorced from the other parent, you can designate a guardian. That way, you don't have to update your will if something happens to their other parent. If you have custody of your children and have serious concerns about the other parent's ability to properly care for them if something happens to you, you can include with your will an explanation of why you'd prefer somebody else to take custody of your children. Although courts will almost always give custody to a surviving parent, because that's typically what the law requires, you will at least make the court aware of your concerns.

Issues you may face in providing for your children and dependents are discussed in Book 2, Chapter 3.

Creating Your Will or Trust

If you're reading this book, you may be considering drafting your own estate plan. If you don't expect to owe estate taxes, don't want to disinherit your spouse or child, and have the time to work through the process, you should be able to do it yourself. But if you lack the time or inclination, have a very large estate, are disinheriting an heir, are the owner of a business, or have a complicated plan for the distribution of your estate, you'll almost certainly benefit from professional estate planning services.

Whatever you decide, your understanding of the estate planning process will help you. It's essential to planning your own estate, but it will also help you understand your own needs and communicate your wishes to an estate planning professional.

Deciding who should create it

As you embark upon the estate planning process, you need to ask yourself: Are you able to plan your entire estate yourself? You may discover that

>> You're capable but don't have sufficient time or interest to go through the process of planning your estate.

>> You can plan the bulk of your estate but require some specialized estate planning services that should be performed by a lawyer.

>> Whether due to the size and complexity of your estate, or your own discomfort with the process, you should hire a professional to plan your estate.

There's absolutely nothing wrong with getting help with your estate plan. Most *lawyers* don't plan their own estates. It's not a matter of ability, because most are capable of figuring out what they would need to do. It's a matter of getting things done quickly and getting the benefit of an expert's advice and knowledge.

Although you may cringe at the thought of paying money to a lawyer, remember that your time is valuable. How many hours of your time do you want to spend learning the intricacies of estate tax law or business succession when an experienced estate planning lawyer will be able to do a better job in a fraction of the time, by dint of experience? And if you make a mistake, the increased capital gains tax, income tax, and estate tax exposure will probably dwarf the cost of professional estate planning services.

WARNING

The state of Louisiana has chosen to make it very difficult to draft your own will. The steps you must take to execute a valid will are the most complicated in the nation. But that's not all. The state's *forced heirship laws* mandate minimum bequests to certain heirs and restrict your right to reduce their bequests or disinherit them. You can create what by all appearances is a valid, properly executed will yet still have the state restructure your bequests to your heirs. Pretty much everybody in Louisiana, including most lawyers, should have a professional draft his will.

Understanding the process

Planning your estate can be a big job, but it's something you can handle. Approach the process step by step:

1. **Gather your facts.**

   Take stock of your personal situation, including where you live, who lives with you, your extended family, and other potential heirs, including friends and charities.

Take a thorough look at your assets, determining what you own, how you own it, and what it's worth. Also review your debts, including what you owe and who you owe it to.

2. **Determine your estate planning needs.**

Ask yourself the following questions:

- You need a will, but do you also need a living trust?

- Do you want to use other trusts, to delay or structure inheritances, or to protect your heirs?

- Will your estate owe estate taxes? How complex does your estate planning strategy need to be? Do you also need a gifting strategy, to transfer wealth to your heirs during your lifetime?

- Do you own your own business? What sort of business succession plan do you need?

- What other special circumstances do you need to address? For example, do you have children from a prior relationship? Do you want to disinherit an heir?

- Who will serve as your helpers? Your *personal representative* manages your estate in probate court, pays your bills and taxes, and oversees your funeral and burial arrangements. Your *trustee* manages, controls, and distributes assets held in your trust. Your minor children need a *custodian* to take care of them if something happens to you and perhaps a second person to take care of their money.

- If you're creating a trust, what property do you want to put into your trust?

- How will you leave your assets to your heirs? Will they receive their inheritances immediately, or will they be held in trust until some point in time in the future? Will any of your gifts be conditional, with your heirs only receiving their inheritance when a condition (such as college graduation) is met?

- How will your estate pay its bills and expenses? Do you have enough money available to pay your debts and taxes, pay for the administration of your estate and trust, and cover funeral expenses? Should you carry some life insurance to cover those costs?

This process is described in Book 2, Chapter 2.

3. **Prepare your will and living trust, making sure that you address all your major assets, including those with sentimental value.**

For some assets, you'll want to designate contingent beneficiaries, in case an heir dies before you do or declines an inheritance.

You will also include a residuary clause, directing how any assets left in your estate will be distributed after all your specific gifts have been made.

For guidance on drafting your will, see Book 2, Chapter 4. Trusts are covered in Book 5, Chapter 4.

4. **Execute your estate planning documents to give them legal effect, obtaining proper witness signatures and notarization.**

   You can execute all of your documents after you have completed them or, if you prefer, as you complete each document. Guidance for executing your will is provided in Book 2, Chapter 4. Instruction for executing your trust is found in Book 5, Chapter 4.

5. **Lather, rinse, repeat.**

   You'll review your estate plan on a regular basis, perhaps annually (and not less than once every few years), to make sure that it still suits your needs.

   You'll also review your estate plan when you experience major changes in your life, including moving to another state, marriage, divorce, separation, childbirth or adoption, significant change in your financial situation, or the death of an heir.

   For information on reviewing and updating your will, see Book 2, Chapter 4. Guidance for updating a revocable trust is provided in Book 5, Chapter 4.

Throughout this process, ask yourself whether it's realistic for you to plan your estate yourself. You can manage a will and living trust, but tax planning, business succession planning, more complicated trusts, or complicated plans for the distribution of your assets can change that. So can state laws, particularly if you want to leave your spouse less than the law requires, or if you live in Louisiana.

Thinking about your kids, money, life insurance, and more

You need a plan for your incapacity. That plan may include a living trust, granting the trustee authority over the trust's assets if something happens to you. But you should also prepare a durable power of attorney and healthcare proxy and should consider a living will.

If you own a business, you probably need a business succession plan. This plan has two major components. First, how do you convey your business to your heirs while minimizing capital gains taxes and estate taxes, and second, who will take control of your business and manage it if you die or become incapacitated? Without a good succession plan, you risk your business collapsing (see Book 2, Chapter 2).

Do you have retirement accounts? As with your life insurance policies, they'll typically pass to a named beneficiary instead of going through your estate. Have you considered what rollover rights your beneficiary may enjoy? Inheritance of tax-deferred retirement savings can be more valuable to an heir who can roll those savings into his own retirement accounts instead of having to immediately pay taxes.

Do you have life insurance? Take a look at who owns the policy and who you've named as beneficiaries. Ownership will affect whether your insurance proceeds are included in your taxable estate. Your beneficiaries will receive the proceeds out-side of probate, meaning that your beneficiary designation controls who receives the money even if your will says something else. When you review and update your will, you should also review and update your life insurance beneficiaries.

How will your estate pay its bills? Do you have enough cash assets or investments that can be liquidated to pay the costs of your estate? Do you need to have life insurance to help cover those costs? If so, will the insurance proceeds be subject to estate taxes, and can those taxes be avoided?

Will your estate have to pay estate taxes? Are you unsure? If your estate will owe estate taxes, you will almost always benefit from professional estate planning services. Estate taxes are so high that in the long run those services will typically pay for themselves several times over. See Book 5, Chapter 5 for more about mini-mizing estate taxes.

TIP

Keep your estate planning documents safe, perhaps in a bank safety deposit box or with your attorney. Be sure that your personal representative can find your will.

Chapter **2**

Planning Your Bequests

G iving away your assets is easy, right? You just make a list of the people in your life who are closest to you, divide your assets between them, and you're done. Well, maybe not. You have to consider many other factors to be sure that your estate plan is carried out as you intend and that your beneficiaries receive the full benefit of your gifts.

This chapter helps you identify the people, institutions, charities, and other beneficiaries to whom you wish to leave bequests. It also helps you recognize special circumstances that may affect your estate plan, such as the effect of blended marriages and business succession planning. You also discover how to select a trustee or personal representative, when you should get help from an estate planning professional, and how to find and choose a lawyer, accountant, or institutional trustee.

Calculating Your Assets

You need to figure out what assets you have and how you want to leave them to your heirs. You inventory your various assets, including your savings, investments, retirement accounts, real estate, personal property, cars, boats, jewelry, collections, and anything else you own. You consider your debts, including asset-related debts, such as mortgages and car loans. You also consider how your property is held and whether jointly held property will pass to the joint title holder without going through probate (see Book 5, Chapter 3 for a lot more on probate).

For the most part, your estate plan is written on paper and isn't etched in stone. You may change your will or revocable trusts at any time you choose. Similarly, you may change the beneficiaries on your life insurance policies, annuities, and retirement accounts. If you use irrevocable trusts in your estate plan, once you transfer assets into those trusts, you can't change your mind about your gifts.

Determining Your Intended Heirs and Beneficiaries

After you create a list of assets and heirs, you can decide how to divide those assets. Consider your family, including your parents, spouse, children, grandchildren, siblings, and perhaps also aunts and uncles, cousins, nieces and nephews, or more distant relatives. Think about whether you want to make gifts to friends or other nonrelatives. You may also decide to leave bequests to charities, schools, churches, or other organizations.

Even with this list in hand, you're not quite done. You need to think about how your heirs may change over time, through birth, death, adoption, divorce, remarriage, or anything else that may happen in the future. You don't have to write your estate plan to cover every contingency, but your forethought can help you create an estate plan that needs less frequent amendment. You will also have a better picture of what types of changes in your life will necessitate the revision of your estate plan.

REMEMBER

Your estate will have bills and expenses of its own and has to repay your outstanding debts. Your trust will also incur expenses. Make sure that you provide sufficient money for those expenses, or your gifts to your heirs may have to be reduced in amount or sold so that your estate can pay those expenses.

REMEMBER

You should include a clause in your will or trust distributing the *residuary* — anything that is left over after all specific gifts and bequests have been made. This clause will ensure that any gifts or bequests that are declined by an heir, or that lapse due to the death of an heir, are properly distributed. It will also prevent the need to have a court distribute what may be a small amount of money or an asset with limited value, with court costs and legal fees potentially exceeding that value.

Individuals

After you figure out who your heirs are, you need to figure what you want to leave to them. Ask yourself these questions:

>> How much do you want to leave to each heir?

>> Do you want your heirs to inherit equally?

>> Do you want your heirs to inherit immediately upon your death, or do you want to defer part or all of their inheritance to a later date?

>> Do you want to make any bequests conditional, such as requiring a child to marry or graduate from college before they inherit?

>> Do you want to disinherit any heirs so that they receive nothing under your will or trust?

>> What do you want to happen to your bequest if your heir dies before you or declines to accept it?

If you intend to leave specific assets to your heirs, you need to remember that the value of your assets may change over time. In some cases, the asset may be sold, lost, or destroyed before your will or trust is administered. You may include language in your trust that equalizes the value of specific gifts, such that a child receiving a less valuable gift will also receive a sum of cash. You can also give heirs a percentage of your estate instead of specific dollar values to help preserve your intentions in the event that your estate grows or shrinks in size.

If you want to keep an asset in the family, you should designate an alternate beneficiary just in case your primary beneficiary dies. For example, if you leave your daughter your grandmother's engagement ring, do you want it to go to your son-in-law if she dies before you? Or would you prefer that it go to another child or to one of your grandchildren?

You may leave your household furnishings or other personal property to your heir without making an exhaustive list of everything you own. For example, you can leave your clothes to a specific heir or charity. Another option is to describe a mechanism by which your heirs will inherit personal property — for example, you could leave your children your furniture, but provide that they take turns selecting a piece of furniture until all of it has been distributed between them. If you provide for them to take turns selecting items, you should also either indicate who picks first or describe a technique, such as drawing a high card from a deck of cards, to determine who will be randomly selected to pick first.

To make sure that some heirs benefit from your request, you must engage in some extra estate planning. For example, your minor children will require somebody to manage their assets. One of your children may be bad with money, so you may want to create a *spendthrift trust* to prevent them from squandering an inheritance or having it taken by creditors. If you have a child or grandchild with special needs, you may need to create a *special needs trust* to allow him to benefit from your gift instead of the state taking it as reimbursement for the cost of public assistance.

You're not limited to describing your heirs by name. You may also describe your heirs by class, such as "to my children" or "to my grandchildren." Such language may help ensure that children or grandchildren born after you complete your estate plan share in an inheritance. Or, if you prefer, you can expressly exclude after-born children. You may also state whether you want adopted children or stepchildren to be treated as your children or provide for them separately.

WARNING

State law restricts your ability to disinherit your spouse and may also restrict your ability to disinherit your minor children. You should expect that under state law, your spouse will have the legal right to an *elective share* of your estate, possibly including assets held by your living trust. If you leave your spouse less than that amount, your spouse can choose to take the elective share instead of your bequest. The consequence can significantly alter the distribution of your estate to your other heirs. Disinheriting heirs through a trust is easier than disinheriting them through your will.

WARNING

Louisiana has an unusual set of laws described as *forced heirship laws,* which attempt to force you to leave certain minimum bequests to your spouse and children. Louisiana also limits the circumstances under which you can avoid the application of those laws. These laws can make it difficult to plan even a simple estate in Louisiana, unless your wishes happen to accidentally correlate with what state law requires. Most people will benefit from discussing these laws with a lawyer.

Institutions or charities

You may want to leave part or all of your estate to an organization that advances the public good or supports a cause you believe in. Subject to state law restrictions on disinheriting your heirs, discussed in the previous section, you are free to do so. Many charities and educational institutions offer model documents you can use to leave bequests to them.

Charitable giving may also help you avoid estate taxes. A bequest to a tax-exempt organization may provide your estate with a tax deduction.

You may also consider using a *charitable remainder trust* to reduce the size of your taxable estate or to help you avoid capital gains taxes. Typically, the trust is set up to provide an income for yourself while eventually making a gift to charity. The trust may also be reversed, providing an income to a charity from an asset that will pass to your heirs upon your death.

Other bequests

It's your money, so for the most part, you can leave it to whomever you want. You can set up scholarships or memorial funds, support a public garden, or engage in other creative gifting.

You can also create a trust to benefit your pet. Yes, really. Pet trusts are not universally recognized as valid, although a growing number of states have passed laws making them enforceable. In states where they're not formally recognized, try to choose a trustee who will carry out your wishes even though they're not legally binding.

Thinking about Your Family Circumstances

Generally speaking, the complexity of your estate plan increases with the size of your family. It's pretty easy to plan your estate when you're single. Getting married doesn't add much complication. But then you have kids, divorce, remarry, have a blended family. . . . Each new development may complicate your plans and wishes.

WARNING

If you're in a domestic partnership, the odds are your state provides no inheritance rights to your partner if you die. Consistent with your wishes, you must create an estate plan that conveys assets to your partner and grants your partner authority over your estate and person in the event of incapacity.

REMEMBER

Whenever your family circumstances change, whether by birth, death, adoption, marriage, separation, divorce, remarriage, or anything else you can think of, you need to review your estate plan to make sure that it remains consistent with your wishes and goals.

Estate Planning for Second Families

If neither you nor your spouse has children, estate planning for your second marriage is pretty simple. You simply execute new estate planning documents designating your spouse as your beneficiary. In some cases, you may want a more complicated estate plan, leaving some of your premarital assets to other friends, relatives, or charities instead of your spouse.

But if you or your spouse have children from prior relationships, things become a lot more complicated. And the complications compound if you later have children together. Here are some questions to think about:

>> Do you wish to treat all your children equally? Including your stepchildren? Including minor children, who must be supported during their childhood and who may need assistance with college costs?

>> Does your spouse want to treat your children equally with their own children?

>> Is your spouse younger than you? If you leave your estate to your spouse "for life," how will your spouse's age affect things when your children receive their inheritances?

>> If your spouse survives you, will your spouse's estate plan include all your children, or will your children from your prior relationship be effectively disinherited?

You may feel 100 percent certain that your spouse "will take care of" your children and be comfortable leaving your entire estate to your spouse. Most of the time, your instincts will be correct, and your spouse will respect your wishes. But if your spouse chooses not to leave money to your children from the prior marriage or dies intestate, your children are effectively disinherited.

Start thinking about estate planning before you marry. You may find that you need a prenuptial agreement to keep some of your premarital assets from becoming part of your marital estate or subject to your spouse's elective share of your estate. The *elective share* is the amount your spouse may choose to inherit under state law, and your spouse may exercise that right if your will provides for a lesser inheritance.

Giving your new spouse a life estate

A common tool used in estate planning for second marriages is the *life estate.* If you own your marital home as separate property, you can make your spouse a life tenant. Your children receive title to the home upon your spouse's death. But a life estate may prove to be an imperfect tool:

>> **If your spouse is younger than you, your children may be elderly by the time they inherit your home.** As your home is usually the most valuable asset in your estate, this delay can mean that they inherit little or nothing during the years when an inheritance would be most useful to them.

>> **A life estate can put your spouse in conflict with your children.** Your children may believe that your spouse is neglecting the property. At times this is true, with your spouse failing to pay taxes or the principal portion of the mortgage, or failing to fix a leaky roof or other structural problem, putting your children's inheritance at risk.

>> **A life estate may not be consistent with your own wishes.** For example, you may prefer that your home go to your children after your spouse remarries.

PRENUPTIAL AGREEMENTS

As you enter your second marriage, you may want a prenuptial agreement, but be afraid of how your prospective spouse will react to the idea. Another common concern involves the full disclosure of your assets to your spouse. You may not want to make that type of disclosure. Yet a prenuptial agreement may provide significant estate planning advantages. You can help mitigate worries by keeping the agreement simple or, particularly if your primary interest is in your estate plan, by including provisions that will provide generously for your spouse in the event of divorce.

Your prenuptial agreement will clarify what property, which of your assets, and which of your spouse's assets continue to be separate property after you marry, including your interest in a family business. Your prenuptial agreement can waive the rights that you and your spouse have to take an elective share of each other's estates. It will also provide for how property will be divided if you divorce and may limit spousal support.

Even without a prenuptial agreement, if you're careful with your assets, you should be able to keep many of your premarital assets out of your marital estate. This separation is more difficult in community property estates, or if you use marital assets to make loan payments or to maintain or improve the premarital asset. Also, simply keeping your assets separate will not be sufficient to protect those assets from being included in your spouse's "elective share" of your estate. Still, if you leave your spouse a greater inheritance than state law requires, it's very unlikely that your spouse will instead choose to receive the elective share.

If you decide to use a prenuptial agreement, make sure that you introduce the idea well in advance of your marriage ceremony — at least several weeks in advance and preferably several months. You and your spouse should both have independent legal representation to help you understand the agreement. If you have significantly more money than your prospective spouse, you can pay their lawyer fee, but they should pick their own lawyer.

TIP

Even without a prenuptial agreement, you can help mitigate these issues.

>> **If you can afford to do so, you can purchase life insurance for the benefit of your children.** Although their inheritance of your house is delayed, they immediately get the proceeds of your insurance when you die.

>> **You can hold the house in trust and provide for your spouse to reside in the house for a fixed number of years, perhaps five or ten years.** After that period of time expires, the house is conveyed to your children.

Using trusts to hold your assets

Your living trust can be beneficial in directing your separate property to your children. You can also place some of your assets in an irrevocable trust for the benefit of your children before you remarry, but you need to be aware of gift tax consequences. (Estate taxes are discussed in Book 5, Chapter 5.)

A common estate planning tool for second marriages is the *bypass trust,* in which you leave a substantial bequest to your children. This gift takes advantage of your gift tax exemption, by keeping the gift out of your spouse's taxable estate. It also permits you to provide income for the support of your spouse, while directing the principal of the trust to your children.

Another common estate planning tool for second marriages is the *Qualified Terminable Interest Property* (QTIP) trust, which is often used in conjunction with a bypass trust. You can use the bypass trust up to the amount of your estate tax exemption and then use a QTIP trust for other assets, which will be treated as part of your spouse's estate, but which you may still direct to your children upon your spouse's death.

More tools to consider

Some states permit *contract wills,* which can't be changed after the death of the first spouse. However, this type of will can be unduly limiting, particularly if the surviving spouse remarries or has more children, and may complicate probate. Before considering a contract will, be sure you fully understand how the joint estate plan would affect you as the surviving spouse.

A more complicated estate planning tool that may be useful in second marriages is the *Family Limited Partnership* (FLP). You control the assets in your FLP while your children are limited partners who have an ownership share but no control over the assets. The FLP is often costly to create and comparatively burdensome to maintain.

REMEMBER

Don't forget to update the beneficiary designation for your insurance policies and retirement accounts. If you don't, you may find that you leave a windfall to your ex-spouse instead of your current spouse and children.

Estate Planning for Your Business

If you own your own business or a share of a family business, your estate plan should include a business succession plan. A will isn't enough, and your living trust is probably inadequate. Business succession is a complicated process and is usually best implemented over a course of years. If you're a business owner:

>> If you're active in your business, your succession plan should provide for the continued operation of the business in case of your incapacity or death.

>> Your succession plan should describe who will own your interest after your death and who will take over your management role.

>> You may also carry life insurance to help fund the continued operation of the business, to hire additional staff to perform the tasks you previously performed, or to provide a cushion for liability the business may incur as a result of interruptions in its services.

>> Your succession plan should be flexible enough that it can be adapted to the changing needs of your business as well as changes in your wishes and those of your heirs.

WARNING

You need to be aware of possible estate tax consequences of business ownership. Your estate plan should anticipate the possibility that your business could fail upon your death but that when calculating your estate taxes the IRS may try to value your business as if it continues to operate. As part of your estate plan, you should document the factors that may limit the value of your business to a buyer or that may make it difficult to sell. That documentation will make it easier for your family to argue that, upon your death, the business had little or no value.

REMEMBER

Many small businesses falter or fail when their founder leaves the business or dies. Sometimes this failure is unavoidable, particularly if the business is entirely dependent upon the owner. The nature of the business may make its value largely dependent upon the continued involvement of the owner, as with a law practice or dentist's office, or the owner may operate the business in a manner that leaves it with little value to a buyer, such as by choosing to maximize short-term income and not investing profits back into the business. A good succession plan can help ensure that your business continues to function after your death.

Sometimes you will want to transfer business ownership or management to another family member, perhaps a child. Other times, you will want to sell the business to somebody outside of your family. Remember that it can take a long time to find a buyer for your business, and the buyer may expect training and support. If you intend for your business to be sold after your death, you should still implement a plan for its operation and management pending sale and for support of the new owner.

Inheritance of your sole proprietorship

When you're the sole owner of your business and you want to leave it to your heirs, you need to consider many factors:

- ➤➤ **Who will manage your business?** If one of your children is already managing your business, it's easy enough to have your child continue in that role. But if not, are any of your heirs both willing and able to take over the business? If it's necessary to hire a manager, who will make the hiring decision and how will the position be funded? How quickly can the new manager take over to minimize or eliminate any interruption in operations?

- ➤➤ **Will your death cause an interruption in the cash flow of your business?** If so, you may want to purchase insurance to help your business maintain its liquidity.

- ➤➤ **Who will inherit ownership?** Will you give the business to one of your children, balanced against bequests of other assets or life insurance proceeds to your other children? If you give equal ownership interests to your children, will you also give them equal say in the operation of the business? If so, by what mechanism will disputes between them be resolved?

DISCUSSING YOUR SUCCESSION PLAN

You may have a very clear idea of who will take over your business when you die and how your heirs will share ownership or management responsibility. But you need to talk to your heirs about your plans and make sure that you're on the same page. A poor choice of manager, or conflicts between co-managers, creates a substantial possibility that your business will fail.

You may discover that the child who manages your business is losing interest in the business and intends to sell the business upon your death. If your child manager has grown your business, your child may resent the idea that ownership will be shared equally with her other siblings upon your death. Some children will threaten to quit if they feel that their hard work will end up creating a windfall for siblings who have their own lives and careers apart from the business.

You may be inclined to leave your children equal ownership and management roles in your business. Conflicts often arise between co-owners. For example, your children have different visions of how the business should operate, or one wants to invest profits in the business while the other wants to withdraw the maximum salary and dividends. Your conversation with your heirs will help you anticipate and plan for this type of conflict.

The FLP may be a useful tool in leaving your business to your heirs, while also possibly reducing its value for the calculation of estate tax. In a FLP, you retain control of your business as the managing partner, while transferring ownership of shares to your children. Your children are limited partners and thus do not have any say in your management decisions. You can use the annual gift tax exemption, presently $14,000 (in 2017), to gradually transfer ownership to your children while reducing your taxable estate.

Even if you choose not to implement a FLP, perhaps due to its cost or complexity, you may nonetheless use an annual gifting strategy to transfer shares of your business to your children. Annual gifts have an additional benefit, in that as your business grows in value so do the shares you have already transferred. If you wait until you die, today's $14,000 gift may represent a six-figure increase in your taxable estate. Although your children will face increased capital gains tax if they sell the gifted shares, as opposed to getting a step up in basis when inheriting them at your death, the potential tax savings remain substantial. For more on estate taxes, see Book 5, Chapter 5.

You can also sell shares to your children during your lifetime, financing the sale with a low-interest promissory note. Similar to a gift, your children receive the shares at a much lower value than they're likely to be worth at the time of your death. You may still implement a gifting strategy, using your annual gift tax exclusion to forgive part of the debt owed on the note.

Inheritance of your share of a business

Every small business with more than one owner should have a buy-sell agreement addressing the right to purchase shares from a partner who wants to leave the business, or from a partner who becomes incapacitated or dies. You probably don't want a stranger buying or inheriting your partner's interest, or exercising the proxy rights of an incapacitated partner and then trying to assert a say in how your business is operated. Without a buy-sell agreement, you may get exactly that or may give that "gift" to your partners.

If you own a share of a business, whether it's a family business or a business you run with partners or investors, you face many of the same issues as with a sole proprietorship (see previous section). If you manage the business or have a significant management role, you and your partners need to plan for a successor manager.

A key difference is that your partners have an interest in how your shares are distributed. Some businesses have buy-sell agreements, detailing how shares are to be valued and when your shares may be purchased by the other partners. Depending upon what you and your partners decide:

>> The business may buy life insurance to help fund the purchase of a deceased partner's shares.

>> The buy-sell agreement may provide for your partners to pay for your shares in installments.

>> Your partners can purchase your shares for cash, obtaining financing, if necessary.

The buy-sell agreement may be triggered upon a partner's death or incapacity, giving your partners the opportunity to purchase your shares from your estate rather than having them inherited by somebody they would prefer not be involved in the business. You, of course, get the same benefit should misfortune fall upon one of your partners.

Appointing the People Who Will Carry Out Your Estate Plans

You may be used to taking charge of every detail of your life. But no matter how independent you are, you can't administer your own estate. You have to get help from somebody else. So what do you do?

You seek out helpers who are trustworthy, responsible, and financially stable and who are young and healthy enough that they're likely to remain both willing and able to manage your affairs after your death or incapacity. Your choice will usually be a person, but at times you may choose an institutional trustee or lawyer to administer your trust or will. The following sections help you make the right choices and choose helpers who will protect your estate and respect your wishes.

Choosing your personal representative or trustee

Your *personal representative*, also called an *executor*, is the person who manages your estate during the probate process. Your trustee manages the assets held by your trust. During the administration of your trust or estate, your trustee and personal representatives will be the primary target of anybody who is unhappy with your estate plan or the way it is being administered.

Whenever you choose somebody to assist with your estate plan, you should talk to her before adding her to your will or trust. This discussion isn't a sales pitch where you're trying to convince somebody to become your trustee. It's more like a job interview, where you try to be absolutely certain that your candidate is trustworthy, reliable, and willing to perform a difficult job. Find out the answers to the following questions:

>> Does the person want the job?

>> Does the person truly understand how difficult it may be?

>> Does the person have the necessary knowledge and skills to fulfill her role?

>> Does the person have the time to perform her role?

>> Does the person live near you? If not, how much travel will be involved if she accepts the job?

>> Is the person comfortable interpreting your will or trust?

>> Is the person financially stable? Will she have any temptation to "borrow" money she's supposed to safeguard?

>> Does the person expect to be compensated? If so and you wish her to agree to a particular rate or amount of compensation, is the compensation you're offering acceptable?

>> Does the person understand your goals and wishes?

>> Will she stand up for your wishes, even if friends and relatives are pressing her to make a different decision?

REMEMBER

Estate administration involves number crunching. Accountings must be prepared for a probate court and possibly for trust beneficiaries. There may be a lot of bills to pay and savings, retirement, and investment accounts to close out. Tax returns must be filed on behalf of your trust and estate. Your trustee may also be responsible for managing or leasing property and making investment decisions. Either your trustee or personal representative may have to liquidate estate assets — for example, to pay taxes owed by your estate.

Although it's reasonable for your trustee or personal representative to hire professionals to assist with these tasks, you need to choose somebody who is comfortable working with numbers. Her math skills increase the quality of oversight of your assets and reduce the chance that your estate will unnecessarily incur expenses for professional services.

REMEMBER

If your personal representative or trustee will take control of your business, be sure that she's competent to manage your business affairs. Remember the recommendations for business succession planning, discussed earlier in this chapter in the section "Estate Planning for Your Business." Don't let your business falter or fail due to a lack of preparation for your death or incapacity.

SHOULD YOU CHOOSE COPERSONAL REPRESENTATIVES OR COTRUSTEES?

Sometimes you may have more than one person in mind to help with the administration of your estate. For example, one person may be very good with numbers but not have much time to devote to estate administration, while another may have ample time but be terrified of preparing accountings or tax returns. Perhaps you have two children and fear that one will resent the other if you designate one but not the other. A possible resolution is to appoint them as joint administrators of your estate.

There's no limit on how many people can jointly administer your estate, although at a certain point, a saying comes to mind: "Too many cooks spoil the broth." Don't unnecessarily complicate the administration of your will or trust by appointing a panel of administrators. Also, as hard as it is to find a trustee or personal representative who is both qualified and willing, the more people you add, the more likely it is that you will end up including somebody who is not an appropriate choice.

The biggest concern in appointing more than one person as trustee or personal representative is that conflict will occur. Even if you're sure that your choices will get along, include a mechanism for dispute resolution. Your dispute resolution mechanism may involve assigning tie-breaking authority to one person, providing for mediation or arbitration, or even tossing a coin or drawing the high card from a deck of cards.

TIP

One factor you may have in mind when choosing a trustee or personal representative is whether she'll work for free. That expectation may be reasonable if your trustee or personal representative is a primary beneficiary of your estate or if your estate is simple. But working for free is otherwise a lot to ask of somebody. For a larger or more complicated estate, either task can become a part-time job and in some cases a full-time job. Compensation makes it much less likely that your trustee or personal representative will resent the job or will resign when she realizes just how much work is involved.

Choosing a successor

It takes two, baby. Or more. Your first choice as personal representative or trustee may not be able to fulfill that role for many reasons:

>> Your first choice may become ill or die.

>> Completing the tasks involved may take more time and effort than your first choice is willing or able to give.

>> Despite your prior discussions, your first choice may simply change her mind and decline the appointment.

>> Your first choice may not be sufficiently competent or capable and may have to be replaced by a court.

By designating a successor (or more than one successor), your trust or estate will continue to be managed by somebody you choose.

REMEMBER

If the person you chose as trustee or personal representative becomes unwilling or unable to serve, unless you have designated a successor, the probate court will choose somebody to take over the job. The person appointed may be a complete stranger who has no familiarity with your goals and wishes and will charge fees that may significantly exceed what a friend or relative would agree to accept.

Discussing your estate plan with your helpers

After you have chosen your trustee, personal representative, and successors, you need to make sure they understand your wishes. You should sit down with them and have a conversation about your estate plan and goals.

Go over your will or trust and explain what each provision means. Encourage your helper to ask questions.

Finding Professionals to Assist You

The more complicated your estate plan, the more likely it is that you will require assistance when preparing and implementing your plan. Common situations in which professional assistance is recommended include

>> You're planning for business succession.

>> You're using estate tax avoidance strategies.

>> You're doing estate planning for second marriages.

>> You're leaving assets to a disabled heir who receives public assistance.

>> You're disinheriting an heir.

If you're doing anything unconventional with your assets within the state of Louisiana, you can easily run afoul of that state's *forced heirship laws.* You should consult a lawyer to make sure that your estate plan is properly formulated and that it will be upheld by a court.

Getting help from a lawyer

Your first task in getting help from a lawyer is finding a responsible estate planning lawyer. Your ideal lawyer will be experienced not only with planning estates but also with planning estates that are similar to yours. Similarity goes beyond size and extends to similarity of assets. If you have a small business, you need a lawyer familiar with business succession issues. If you're on your second marriage, need to create a special needs trust for a disabled child, or want to disinherit an heir, seek a lawyer who is experienced with those issues. You may want a lawyer who has probate experience and whose estate planning documents have stood up in probate court.

Easier said than done? Certainly. You won't find that type of detail from a Yellow Pages ad, and if you call a law office and ask, you're almost certain to hear that the lawyer you have contacted has qualifications that far exceed your needs (whether or not that is true). So what do you do? Try to get referrals from people you know who have hired estate planning lawyers. If you have an accountant you trust, request a referral. You can also interview members of the American College of Trust and Estate Counsel (ACTEC), using its online directory (available at www.actec.org).

Hiring an accountant

Just as when you hire a lawyer, referrals are very useful when you need to hire an accountant. Your friends, family, business associates, and your lawyer may have suggestions. You can also consult your state's CPA Association. You can find a directory of CPA Associations on The American Institute of Certified Public Accountants website at www.aicpa.org/states/stmap.htm.

When you have selected some possible CPAs, you should interview them. Questions to ask include

» How long have you been in practice?

» What are your qualifications and credentials?

» What is your experience with situations like mine?

» Do you specialize in servicing people with situations like mine?

>> Will you personally handle my needs, or will the work be performed by somebody else within your office?

>> How much do you charge, and does that price include all costs and fees?

>> What services will I receive for that payment?

When you choose an accountant, consider the condition of the accountant's offices. Are they neat and organized? That's what you should expect. You can also rely on your instincts. Do you trust the accountant and feel comfortable with the idea of working with the accountant? If not, it's a big world. You have a lot of other accountants to choose from.

Using professional trust services (institutional trustees)

Your first thought upon hearing the words *institutional trustee* is probably, "that sounds expensive." The most common institutional trustees are banks, brokerages, lawyers, and trust companies. They typically charge annual fees between 1 and 3 percent of the value of the trust.

An institutional trustee is thus likely to charge more than a friend or relative who serves as trustee, and you can't expect that an institutional trustee will waive its fees. Unless your trust is valued at $400,000 or more, using an institutional trustee is probably not financially prudent. In fact, many institutional trustees will decline to service smaller estates.

Using an institutional trustee provides the benefit that your trustee is likely to be in operation for the entire life of the trust. At the same time, responsibility for your trust may be handed off from employee to employee, due to staffing changes or employee turnover. You should inquire about continuity issues when you interview potential trustees.

You should consider having the trust periodically reviewed by a third party, to make sure that assets are being properly invested and maintained. This review adds an additional cost to your trust but helps protect your heirs from mistakes or misconduct. Your institutional trustee should carry insurance to protect you from losses resulting from any such problems.

An institutional trustee is likely to be objective when managing your estate. Except as clearly authorized by the trust, pleas from your children for the extra disbursement of funds will probably fall on deaf ears. An individual may be swayed by a family relationship or feelings of friendship. Similarly, while your children may decide that it makes no difference whether they spend the money that they're supposed to hold in trust for your grandchildren, your institutional trustee will do exactly what you instructed and make sure that your grandchildren receive your gift. Your institutional trustee will also not go through a period of grieving after your death or shy away from recovering trust assets from your friends or relatives.

Institutional trustees are readily able to consult other professionals. While your individual trustee may struggle to find a lawyer or accountant who can give her advice on a minor problem, your institutional trustee can easily obtain advise from lawyers, accountants, investment professionals, and other experts. Also, even with staff turnover, the institutional trustee's experience with trusts avoids the learning curve of an individual trustee who has little or no prior experience managing a trust.

WARNING

Issues of self-dealing may arise with institutional trustees. The trustee may be inclined to invest the trust's assets through the institution. You may want to mandate that part or all of the trust's assets be invested through other institutions so that the trustee will make the most suitable investments instead of favoring his employer's investment vehicles. For smaller trusts, some institutions will restrict investment options. Be aware of your institutional trustee's practices before you choose it.

LOSS OF THE PERSONAL TOUCH

Historically, your institutional trustee may have been your small town bank manager who had worked in the same bank for many years and had a long-term personal relationship with you. The banking industry has evolved. Today, it's exceptional to have that type of personal relationship with your banker.

Although a lack of relationship can help the trustee remain objective, the loss of a personal relationship may also affect your estate. Although each of a succession of professional managers may do a perfectly competent job, one may miss a pattern that may be obvious to a trustee who has managed your trust from its inception.

A story that may not be true, but is illustrative of the problem, involves a wealthy woman who created a pet trust for the benefit of her dog. The trust provided for the woman's housekeeper to remain in her home and to draw a considerable salary to care for the home and dog for the duration of the dog's life. She hired an institutional trustee to manage the trust.

A succession of employees of the trust company made dutiful inspections of the house at least once each year and confirmed that the dog was still alive. More than a decade later, when the dog would have been more than 20 years old, a newly assigned employee recognized that something was amiss. An investigation revealed that the dog had died. The housekeeper had purchased look-alike dogs and was on her third dog when her trickery was detected.

Chapter **3**

Providing for Your Children and Dependents

Providing for children is often the first concern of somebody creating an estate plan. Young children will need somebody to care for them and to manage their assets. An estate plan can also help adult children by providing for college or for supporting children with disabilities.

Choosing a Guardian

As the parent of minor children, you are undoubtedly concerned about who will take care of your children in the event of your death. In most cases, a surviving parent can provide care, but these issues can be particularly pressing for single parents.

If a surviving parent can't provide care for your children, a court will appoint somebody to care for them. Although your choice of *custodian*, or personal guardian, for your minor children is subject to court approval, in most cases, a court will defer to your wishes. To best protect your children, you should select a primary custodian and an alternate custodian, somebody who will care for your children if the primary custodian becomes unable or unwilling to serve.

In some cases, you and your spouse may disagree on who should be the children's custodian. You should strive to reach agreement, even if your choice is less than perfect, because otherwise a court will make the decision for you.

Making the decision

Most of the time, parents want to keep their children together and will choose a custodian who is willing to care for all their children. In some situations, such as where your children have a large difference in age, you may want to designate more than one custodian based on the individual needs of your children. For example, you may provide for a teenager to remain with a nearby family through the end of high school, while a grandparent cares for your younger children.

Questions to consider in choosing a custodian include

>> **How old is the custodian?** Your designated custodian should be a legal adult under the laws of your state. In most cases, that's the age of 18, but in a few states, the age of majority is 21.

>> **How qualified is your custodian?** Does your choice have good parenting skills and an appropriate personality and temperament? Can he provide a stable household environment?

>> **Does your custodian have any physical limitations?** Caring for children, and particularly for young children, can be physically taxing.

>> **Does your custodian have other priorities?** Will your choice have the time to care for your children, even if doing so affects his work life, social life, or lifestyle?

>> **Does your custodian have other children?** If so, how old are they, and how well would your children blend into the household?

>> **Does your custodian share your moral and religious beliefs?** Will he continue to raise your child in your faith or in a manner consistent with your morals?

>> **Can your custodian afford to take care of your children?** If your estate is not sufficient to provide for the financial needs of your children, will your choice be able to make up the difference?

WHAT IF YOU CAN'T AGREE ON A GUARDIAN?

You and your spouse have given a lot of thought to the question of who should care for your children if you die, but you just can't agree. Don't give up yet. The consequences of not choosing a guardian are potentially far more serious than the consequences of picking somebody you believe is second best.

Start by interviewing your candidates. You may find that one of the preferred choices is unwilling to take on the responsibility of your children or that a candidate looks less appealing once you've thoroughly examined his qualifications.

If, after your interviews, you're both convinced that your preferred guardian is the best choice, take a look at the big picture. Are you arguing over the lesser of two evils? Or are you choosing between two qualified, appropriate candidates? If your disagreement is over two suitable, willing guardians, consider a compromise, or even choosing by coin toss. Pick one candidate as guardian and the other as successor.

TIP

You should discuss these issues with possible custodians and interview them prior to making your choice. This is a major decision, and it should be an informed decision. You may also choose to draft a letter to the custodian, to be kept with your will, which will remind them of your wishes for your children's care. Although the letter will not likely have any legal effect, it will remind the custodian of your wishes and may help ensure that they're followed.

Choosing a guardian other than the noncustodial parent

WARNING

In the case of divorce, if the noncustodial parent still has custody rights, the law will presume that custody should go to that parent upon your death. You may be concerned that the noncustodial parent is not a suitable custodian. Although you may not be able to prevent that from happening, you can take steps to help protect your child:

» Designate a preferred custodian in your will. The other parent may die first or may opt not to take custody.

» Discuss your concerns with your designated custodian.

» Document the factual basis for your concerns and keep the documentation with your will.

> » Consult a family lawyer in your state to formulate a plan to help keep the child out of the other parent's custody.

> » If necessary, provide for your estate to retain the services of a family lawyer who handles custody and guardianship proceedings.

If the noncustodial parent has abandoned the child or has a history of mental illness, abusive conduct toward the child, or substance abuse, you may be able to initiate guardianship proceedings shortly before or after your death, in which a court can consider appointing your preferred custodian as the child's guardian. Please remember that custody and guardianship laws are different in each state, and this will not always be possible.

Managing Your Child's Assets

If you're married, you may choose to leave your estate to your spouse and trust that your spouse will take care of your children's needs. If you're separated or divorced, or simply wish to do so, you can make bequests to your minor children. However, from both practical and legal standpoints, children have very limited authority to manage their own assets.

When a child has assets beyond a few thousand dollars, an adult must help manage those assets. If you don't designate a custodian for your child's estate and the other parent is not available to care for your child, the funds will fall under court supervision and may be managed by a stranger, who will charge fees for services provided. Even if the court appoints a relative who does not charge fees, legal and accounting expenses may be incurred when they prepare annual reports for the court.

You will probably choose the same person to be your child's custodian and to manage their assets. Most of the time, that person will be a surviving parent. Yet some people are wonderful with children but terrible with money. If the person you select as caregiver for your children has poor financial skills, you can choose a different person to be custodian of their estate. Similarly, if you're divorced and prefer that your ex-spouse not control your children's inheritance, you may designate a different person or financial institution to serve as custodian.

REMEMBER

The same considerations apply when choosing a custodian to care for your child or your child's estate (see preceding section), but the emphasis shifts to the financial. Your choice should be a legal adult who is responsible with money, trustworthy, and has the time to handle your child's assets. You will want to designate the primary custodian and also identify an alternate.

Conflict may arise between the person who oversees your child's assets and the child's custodian. You can minimize conflicts by

>> Trying to select people who will work in a cooperative, collaborative manner.

>> Discussing in advance your wishes for how your children will be supported and how you want the children's assets to be used for their support.

TIP

Depending on your wishes and the size of your estate, you may create a trust to hold some or all of your children's assets. The trust can include detailed provisions about when money should and should not be paid out and can even provide a mechanism for resolving conflicts between the caregiver and the trustee. For more on trusts, see Book 5, Chapter 4.

Providing for Your Child's Needs

You've taken care of your child's physical care and financial well-being through adulthood. But what about providing for your child's higher education? What if your child has special needs, and an inheritance may jeopardize needed government benefits? What if you want to be sure that your child doesn't fritter away the inheritance you worked so hard to provide?

The principal tool for managing your child's inheritance is the *trust fund*, through which you designate a responsible person to hold and manage your children's inheritance. A trust also gives you greater control over when your children will receive an inheritance, even after adulthood. Although a few states let you postpone a child's inheritance by a few years if you express that intent in your will, a trust is a much more powerful tool for controlling when and how your child will receive an inheritance. (For more on trusts, see Book 5, Chapter 4.)

Your child's education

You may already have a savings account for your children's future education. However, more formal savings tools, such as qualified tuition plans, Coverdell Accounts, and accounts under the Uniform Transfers to Minors Act, may provide tax advantages as you save toward your child's college. Even diligent savings will not be sufficient to cover college expenses, and you may also want to provide for college through an inheritance, insurance, or trust.

You can use any form of trust to help fund your child's college education, but using a trust for college savings does have some drawbacks. The trust will have to file an annual tax return and is taxed on its income, and the balance of the fund may affect your child's eligibility for financial aid.

529 plan

A qualified tuition plan, commonly called a *529 plan*, comes in two forms:

>> **Savings plan:** You deposit funds to later be used for college expenses. Management fees for this type of account are fairly low, but investment choices are limited, though they are improving. Contributions to 529 plans are considered gifts for purposes of taxes. The annual exclusion for 2017 was $14,000 per person — that means $14,000 for you and another $14,000 for your spouse, so you could gift a grandchild $28,000 per year tax-free. If you go over that limit, you have to report it on your taxes using Form 709.

>> **Prepaid college tuition plan:** You can pay toward tuition at in-state colleges, with the savings guaranteed to increase in value at the same rate as college tuition. These plans are usually limited to state residents. You can apply the savings to private and out-of-state colleges, but even a fully funded plan may not fully cover those costs.

Anybody can contribute to a 529 plan, so they provide an easy way for members of your extended family to help contribute to your child's future education costs. Most states offer full or partial tax deductions for contributions to the plan. The assets are exempt from federal income taxes and are often also exempt from state and local taxes, and earnings accumulate on a tax-deferred basis. If your child dies or decides not to go to college, you can transfer the plan to another member of your family. For financial aid purposes, the plan is valued at an amount equal to the refund value of the plan.

Coverdell Account

A *Coverdell Account* (previously known as an education IRA) is funded with post-tax dollars and is maintained for the benefit of one beneficiary. You can contribute to a Coverdell Account for any child below the age of 18. As long as the money is used for education-related expenses, no tax is incurred on either the principal or interest earned when you make a withdrawal. Unlike other savings options, you can use the fund for K–12 education costs as well as for college costs. You have much greater flexibility with the investment of the funds than with a 529 savings plan. As the funds are considered to be an asset of the parents, there is no financial aid consequence to Coverdell Account savings.

Despite their advantages, Coverdell Accounts also have serious disadvantages. Total annual contributions are limited to $2,000 per year, and high-income parents may be subject to even lower limits. Also, your child must use the money from the account by the age of 30, or the account balance will be disbursed to your child subject to a 10 percent penalty and will be subject to taxes on its earnings. It may be possible at that time to change the beneficiary or roll over the account to another beneficiary, so another child or qualifying relative can benefit from the money without incurring those penalties, but the rollover process is very complex. You can find information on transfers and rollovers on the IRS website (presently at www.irs.gov/publications/p970). Due to the low limits on contribution, the account's management costs can consume or exceed its earnings.

UTMA trust

You can also use trusts and similar vehicles to save toward your children's college expenses during your lifetime. One popular option is an account created under the Uniform Transfers to Minors Act (UTMA). Unlike other trusts, the terms of an UTMA trust are defined by statute. Gifts made into an UTMA account are irrevocable. The money you place into the minor's UTMA account will fall under his control when he reaches the age of majority, which in most states is the age of 18. Most states permit you to set a turnover age of 21.

WARNING

If you're concerned that your child is more likely to buy a car than budget for college, then the UTMA trust is unlikely to be your tool of choice.

Section 2503(c) trust

An option very similar to an UTMA is the Section 2503(c) trust, which is also created for the benefit of a person under the age of 21. You can make annual contributions to the trust up to the amount of the annual gift tax exclusion, presently $14,000. You can apply the principal and interest earned to college expenses. You can provide the child with the option to continue the trust past the age of 21, if he chooses not to withdraw his money at that time.

Crummey trust

A popular form of trust that also takes advantage of the annual gift tax exclusion is called a *Crummey trust.* That name is not a judgment on its merits — it was named after its creator.

A Crummey trust can continue past the age of majority, but there is still a catch. The beneficiary is allowed to withdraw the gift only during a window of 30 to 60 days after each contribution. While most children understand that such a choice will probably result in that gift being the last you make, the money can still present a temptation.

WARNING

Few choose this type of trust for college savings, because administrative costs of Crummey trusts tend to be high, and their entire balance will be treated as an asset when your child seeks financial aid.

Life insurance policy

One approach is to purchase a life insurance policy to pay college expenses. The best approach is to create a life insurance trust, to be funded by the policy upon your death. Because your estate is not the beneficiary of the life insurance benefit, the money is not subject to estate taxes. The trust can provide for the payment of tuition and living expenses during college and for having any balance to to be distributed to your child after graduation.

Your child's special needs

If your child has a physical or mental disability that may require a lifetime of care, you may be torn between how to provide for your child and concern about how an inheritance would affect your child's government benefits. Parents sometimes feel that their choices are limited to the following:

>> Disinheriting the child.

>> Directing a bequest to another child, with the understanding that the sibling will use the bequest to benefit their disabled child.

>> Ignoring possible financial consequences, and making a bequest to the disabled child.

TIP

These approaches are all far from perfect, and each can frustrate your goal of providing for your child. Fortunately, you have another option — the special needs trust. This type of trust can hold your child's inheritance without putting government benefits at risk or causing them to be discontinued.

WARNING

Creating a special needs trust is complex, as is the interplay of Medicaid, SSI, and other government benefits. For special needs planning and the creation of a special needs trust, you should get help from a qualified lawyer.

Your child's financial stability

Although your child is not likely to object to inheriting a large sum of money as a young adult, you may be frightened by the idea. No matter how mature and responsible your child may be, he may not be wise with his inheritance.

A few states provide you with a limited ability to delay inheritance, but if you state that wish in your will, most will allow your child to take control of an inheritance at the age of 18. None will delay inheritance past the age of 25.

If you do not want your child to inherit as a young adult or want to provide for inheritance of only a portion of your bequest at that time, your best solution is to create a trust. A trust will not only give you that flexibility but will also allow you to provide for special disbursements in the event of special events, achievements, or emergencies.

TIP

If your child has a history of substance abuse, irresponsible gambling, or wild spending, you can utilize a form of asset protection trust called a *spendthrift trust* to help ensure that your child can't squander his inheritance. The trust disburses money on a schedule or under circumstances you define. Your child can't borrow against the balance of the trust fund, nor can creditors attach it as security for loans. A valid spendthrift trust will even survive your child's bankruptcy.

An *asset protection trust* can also help protect your child's inheritance in the event of divorce. Though most states will compel the trust to pay child support or spousal support from the trust, the funds within the trust will not be considered part of the marital estate and thus will not be subject to division in divorce.

Chapter **4**

Writing and Signing a Will

Your will is an essential part of your estate plan. No matter what else you do to plan your estate, your will serves purposes that no other estate planning document can fill. Through your will, you can

» Designate who will care for your minor children and their money

» Detail your preferences for your funeral and the disposition of your body

» Plan how your estate will pay your bills

» Provide a backup plan in case something is accidentally left out of your estate plan or a bequest fails

Most people are able to compose a simple will, which is all some people need. This chapter outlines what goes into a will and how to properly execute your will.

More complex estate plans utilize both a will and trusts. If your estate is large, you need to engage in tax planning, or you want to do things that may be legally tricky (such as disinheriting an heir), you'll probably benefit from having a lawyer draft your will.

Deciding Whether a Will Serves Your Needs

In one sense, asking yourself whether a will serves your needs is an easy question. Everybody has needs that can be served by a will, so everybody should have a will.

And your estate plan may be able to be managed with *just* a will. If you don't have estate tax concerns, aren't concerned about probate or having your will made part of a public court record, and simply want your estate to be distributed to your heirs when you die, a simple will may be all you need.

TIP

Until you're near retirement age, a living trust probably won't help you, but it will cost you time and money to create and update, and it will be more cumbersome for you to work with assets that you transfer into the trust. Sure, even younger people can suffer a sudden illness or die unexpectedly, but if you're in pretty good health, you can cover your bases pretty well with a will, durable power of attorney, and healthcare proxy.

Trusts are most useful in your estate plan when

>> Your estate may be subject to estate taxes. In 2018, your estate must be worth more than $5.6 million to pay federal estate taxes.

>> You want to avoid probate court.

REMEMBER

Most states have significantly improved the probate process, and smaller estates often qualify for simplified probate. It may be cheaper to probate your estate instead of creating and funding a trust.

Simplicity often leads you to a will

The fewer assets you have, and the less complicated your plans for the distribution of your estate, the more likely it is that a will is all you need.

Similarly, if you're married and want to leave most or all of your estate to your spouse, you probably don't need a complicated estate plan. Your spouse should automatically inherit your share of jointly owned property, and you may not have much left to go through probate.

Do you own real estate in more than one state? The probate court in the state where you die doesn't have authority over real estate located in another state or country. To probate out-of-state real property, the administrator of your estate will have to start a separate probate action in the state where the property is located. You can easily avoid this complication with a *living trust*. (See Book 5, Chapter 3 for more on this process.)

Do you own your own business? If so, even during your prime working years, you should start thinking about business succession. If your business may falter or fail without you, you also need to create a plan for your incapacity. During the time it takes for a probate court to appoint somebody to take over your business, it may suffer significant losses or become broken beyond repair.

REMEMBER

You can create and fund trusts with your will. You can get the estate tax benefits of a bypass trust or restrict when and how your heirs receive their inheritances, by including pour-over provisions in your will to fund an existing trust or providing for the creation and funding of an entirely new testamentary trust.

WARNING

If you live in Louisiana, whatever your circumstances, your estate may be too complicated to plan by yourself. Your state has *forced heirship* laws that require you to leave bequests to certain heirs and has strict requirements for the execution of a valid will. If you reside in Louisiana, you should probably hire a lawyer to draft your will.

For people in other states, the larger and more complex your estate, the more likely it is that you'll benefit from having a professionally drafted will. If you require tax-planning services, want to disinherit an heir, or have children from a prior relationship, a lawyer can help you figure out exactly what you need to do to plan your estate and help you avoid traps that can seriously disrupt your plan for your assets.

For more information on estate planning traps, see the chapters in Book 5.

Assets not covered by a will

As you review your assets, consider whether they're jointly owned or already have a designated beneficiary. If you're married, many of your assets are probably jointly owned with your spouse. Your insurance policies and retirement accounts name a beneficiary.

When joint ownership or a beneficiary designation define who will receive property upon your death, it doesn't matter what you put in your will. Whatever your will says, the assets pass according to the title or beneficiary designation and never become part of your probate estate. These transfers are thus said to occur *outside of probate*.

The following sections address the different types of assets not covered by a will.

Insurance, annuities, and retirement accounts with designated beneficiaries

When you designate a beneficiary for an insurance policy, annuity, or retirement account, the asset is transferred to your beneficiary upon proof of your death. These assets are generally still included in your estate for the calculation of estate tax, but the probate court isn't involved in the transfer of the asset to your beneficiary.

Your heir may receive significant benefits from receiving a retirement account outside of probate. (See Book 1, Chapter 7 for more on retirement accounts.)

Insurance can be a very important part of your estate plan, and it may be possible for you to keep insurance proceeds out of your taxable estate. See the chapters in Book 3 for more on insurance.

Property with a right of survivorship

If you're married, you and your spouse probably jointly own your home. If your deed says that ownership is *by the entireties* or refers to a right of survivorship, your co-owners should receive your interest in the property without going through probate.

Joint bank accounts

The money in your joint bank accounts is available for either account holder to withdraw, at any time. Unless you set up the account to require the consent of all account holders, your joint account holder doesn't need your permission to withdraw funds. When you die, your interest in the account passes to your joint account holders.

WARNING

You need to be careful with joint bank accounts for several reasons:

>> The IRS will try to count the entire balance of your joint account in your taxable estate and will require the joint account holders to prove that they contributed money to the account balance.

>> Your joint account holder can empty your account. There are many sad stories where an elderly person added a younger sibling or child to the account to "help" pay her bills and manage her assets, only to have the "helper" pocket the money.

If you intend to maintain total control over the account until your death, you may be better served by adding a transfer-on-death provision to your account rather than joint ownership (see the next section).

Transfer-on-death accounts and titles

As an alternative to joint ownership, you can give somebody an interest in property or financial accounts that doesn't take effect until you die. Although the asset is included in your estate for gift tax purposes, the *transfer-on-death provision* transfers ownership to your beneficiary upon your death without the necessity of probate. You keep total ownership and control of the asset during your lifetime.

You need to be careful using this technique. If your family circumstances change, your transfer-on-death provision may become outdated, as in the following cases:

>> If you set up a deed to transfer ownership to your three children upon your death and a child dies before you, the property will go to your surviving children unless you included your grandchildren as contingent beneficiaries.

>> If you later have or adopt another child, unless you update the provision, that child won't inherit.

>> If you set up an asset to transfer on death to your spouse, you must remember to update that provision after divorce, or your ex-spouse will receive the asset.

Exploring the Types of Wills

Wills come in many different types. For the most part, the difference is one of complexity. The basic elements of a simple will are also present in a highly complex will, but additional provisions have been added.

The statutory will

Most states offer a *statutory will*, a very simple will that, if properly executed, will be accepted by a probate court. Statutory wills are often made available as fill-in-the-blanks forms, so they're pretty easy to complete. You may be able to get a form by asking your state representative's office to provide one, and in many states, they're available for download from the state legislature or state courts' websites.

At the same time, statutory wills are very simple. They can help you implement a basic estate plan but aren't meant to help with tax planning or more complicated estates. Although unquestionably "better than nothing," a statutory will is most useful if you have a very small estate and desire a very simple estate plan.

The handwritten (holographic) will

A *holographic will* (or in Louisiana, an *olographic* will) is written entirely in your own handwriting and is signed by you but isn't witnessed. Most states disfavor holographic wills and recognize them only under narrow circumstances, such as when they're prepared by a soldier who is engaged in combat.

A cousin of the holographic will is the *oral will*, sometimes called a *nuncupative will*, where there is no written document at all. A court will entertain an oral will in a few circumstances — typically only where the person making the will faces imminent death, where disinterested witnesses produce a written record of the will shortly after the person's death, and where only small amounts of money are involved.

Sometimes you can go through the trouble of writing or articulating a will, but you can't produce a written will that is properly witnessed. Make sure that your wishes will be respected by following your state's formalities for the execution of your will.

A will of your own

Your will is more powerful than you may realize. In addition to parceling out your estate to your heirs, you can create and fund trusts, implement parts of your estate tax avoidance strategy, designate caregivers for your minor children, and outline your preferences for your funeral and memorial service.

As a general rule, when you create a will, it's sensible to

>> **Follow state law formalities for the execution of your will.** Otherwise your will may be rejected by a probate court.

>> **Whenever possible, keep your estate plan simple.** Don't complicate your will unless you're truly convinced that the added complexity is necessary to your estate plan.

Other wills

Usually a will may appoint an administrator, designate people to care for your minor children, and allocate your estate between your heirs. But you can do a lot more with your will:

>> **Testamentary and pour-over wills:** You can create a trust with your will or direct your estate to put assets into a trust.

>> **Joint wills:** You can create a joint estate plan with your spouse and may also be able to make your joint estate plan legally binding even after your death.

>> **Self-proving wills:** You can add an affidavit to your will to simplify the process of submitting it to probate.

Testamentary and pour-over wills

When you create a living trust, you traditionally transfer assets into your trust during your lifetime. That transfer of assets simplifies probate and helps with disability planning.

But what if you never get around to transferring your assets into your trust or want to keep ownership in your own name during your lifetime? You can use your will to create or fund a trust. How is this done?

>> **A pour-over will funds an existing trust.** A pour-over clause may add additional funds or assets to your living trust. But you can also execute a trust that you have no intention of funding during your lifetime and direct assets into the trust from your estate.

>> **A testamentary trust will includes language that creates a trust that becomes operative upon your death.** You can even make the creation of the trust conditional — for example, directing inheritances for your minor children into a trust but allowing them to directly receive their inheritances if they reach adulthood before you die.

Testamentary trusts can be useful as part of a tax-avoidance strategy. For example, if you're married, you can create a testamentary bypass trust to maximize estate tax exemptions for your combined marital estate.

Joint wills

In simple terms, a *joint will* is executed by both you and your spouse. When the first spouse dies, the surviving spouse inherits the entire estate. When the surviving spouse dies, the estate is distributed according to the terms of the will.

A joint will is a simple way to provide for your spouse and heirs, but it's not much more complicated for you and your spouse to both execute your own separate wills.

If your joint will doesn't prevent the surviving spouse from changing the will after you die, your spouse may change your common estate plan. If you're trying to provide for friends or relatives that your spouse doesn't care for, or for children from a prior marriage, that may be a risk you don't want to take.

TIP

If you want to be sure that, if you die first, your spouse can't change your joint estate plan, many states permit you to enter into a contract will. You and your spouse enter into a joint estate plan.

>> As long as you remain alive, you and your spouse may change the plan or even scrap it.

>> Upon your death or the death of your spouse, the estate plan becomes binding and irrevocable.

For a smaller estate, a contract will may be a sufficient means of ensuring that your heirs receive their inheritances, even if your spouse might prefer to disinherit them after your death. But a contract will does have disadvantages:

>> Your spouse may not be able to sell or dispose of assets that are identified in the joint estate plan. For example, will your spouse be able to sell the marital home and move into a condo or apartment? What if your spouse can barely afford the house payments, let alone the cost of maintenance?

>> Your other heirs' inheritances may be tied up for the life of your spouse, which could be 20 or 30 years. Do you want your children to receive their inheritances when they're getting established in their lives or when they're approaching retirement age?

TIP

If you're considering a binding, joint estate plan, you should consider using a trust. The bypass trust is a powerful estate planning tool that lets you direct assets to your heirs while providing lifetime support for your spouse. You can also use trusts to allow your younger spouse to remain in the marital home for a period of years following your death, with the home then being inherited by your children from a prior marriage.

Self-proving wills

It's unlikely that somebody is going to challenge the validity of your will. Most of the time, everybody agrees that the will submitted to the probate court is genuine. But if a disagreement does occur, tracking down witnesses to your will can be difficult. Your witnesses may have moved, and some may even be dead.

A *self-proving will* includes an affidavit, executed and signed by your witnesses in front of a notary public. When the affidavit is properly executed, your will may be submitted to probate without any statements from your witnesses.

Elements of a Will

To be effective, your will must describe who you are, what assets you have, who you want to receive your assets, and how your assets are to be divided. Beyond the basic elements, your will appoints a personal representative to administer your estate and can also appoint caregivers for your minor children. It can create or fund trusts to hold and manage your assets after your death. Your will can also describe your funeral and burial preferences.

Who are you?

The popular conception is that a will commences with the declaration, "I, John Smith, being of sound mind and body. . . ." However, it's not necessary to describe your health. And if you're not mentally competent, it doesn't make any difference to say you are.

REMEMBER

All you really need to do is identify yourself sufficiently so that people will know that it's your will.

What are your assets?

Part of the estate planning process is figuring out what you own. Your possessions will typically include

>> Personal assets:

- Cash, savings, and checking accounts
- Investments
- Home furnishings
- Jewelry
- Art and antiques
- Collectibles
- Your wardrobe

>> Real estate, including your primary residence and any vacation property

>> Insurance policies and annuities

>> Retirement plans

If you're a business owner or are a partner in a small business, your estate also includes your interest in the business.

Not all your assets will go through probate. Insurance policies and retirement plans probably have a designated beneficiary. Your home may automatically go to your spouse as the joint title holder. But you should still consider those assets when planning your estate, because they can affect how you distribute your other assets. For example, if one of your children is the beneficiary of a life insurance policy, you can leave a larger bequest to your other child to balance out the inheritances.

You should also take inventory of your debts, including mortgages and bank loans, credit cards, student loans, and car loans.

REMEMBER

Your estate will pay off your debts before your heirs receive their inheritances. If some of your property has to be sold to pay your debts, a specific bequest of that property will fail, or your estate may not have enough money left over to fill all your bequests.

Who are your beneficiaries?

After you know what you own, you need to figure out who you want to give it to. Put together a list of your possible heirs. Be overinclusive. You don't have to leave something to every person on your list.

Here are a few ideas to get you started:

>> Your family, including

- Spouse

- Children and stepchildren

- Grandchildren and great-grandchildren

- Parents

- Sisters and brothers

- Aunts, uncles, and cousins

- Nieces and nephews

>> Your friends

>> Educational institutions

>> Charities

You need to also consider the circumstances of your heirs. Young children may benefit from having their inheritances left to them in a trust, providing for their support and payment of educational expenses over a period of years. An heir who doesn't manage money well may benefit from a spendthrift trust. An heir who receives public assistance due to a disability may benefit from a special needs trust. You can find more discussion on these special circumstances in Book 2, Chapters 2 and 3.

What are your bequests?

You know what you own. You know who your heirs are. You now need to figure out who gets what (and who gets left out).

REMEMBER

The law limits your ability to disinherit your spouse and sometimes your minor children.

WARNING

When you're drafting a will in Louisiana, you operate subject to your state's *forced heirship laws.* These laws compel you to leave minimum bequests to certain heirs, principally your spouse and children, and define very narrow grounds under which you may disinherit an heir or provide a lesser bequest than the law specifies. These laws make it very difficult for people to plan their estates without the assistance of a lawyer.

Avoiding failed bequests

Your bequests may fail in one of two ways:

>> Your heir may die before you or may decline an inheritance.

>> You may leave a bequest of property that is no longer part of your estate when you die.

The first problem is pretty easy to address. If you have a specific item of property that you want to remain in the family, designate an alternate beneficiary. For example, if you leave your grandmother's engagement ring to your eldest daughter, name her younger sister as the alternate beneficiary.

Naming an alternate beneficiary is also important because your bequest to an heir who dies before you may pass to that heir's descendants instead of staying in your estate. If you don't designate an alternate beneficiary for Grandma's engagement ring, it may end up going to your son-in-law.

If you leave a bequest of a specific asset that is no longer in the estate, your bequest failed. This problem can arise with anything that is sold, lost, spent, or destroyed, including cars, collections, investments, and cash. For example:

>> Your will bequeaths "My house at 1212 Cherry Tree Lane" to your son. You subsequently sell the house, move, and don't update your will to leave your new home to your son. His gift fails. Your first house is no longer in your

estate, and your new home doesn't automatically get substituted for the old. Although a more generic description, such as simply saying "my home," may prevent the failure of your bequest if you own a different home at the time of your death, it won't help if you no longer own a home.

>> You have an investment account worth $500,000. You leave $100,000 to your brother, with the balance to be split between your children. Before you die, you suffer an illness that runs up large medical bills. After your medical bills and the other debts of your estate are paid, only $80,000 remains in the account. Part of your brother's gift fails, because he receives only $80,000 of the $100,000 you intended him to receive. But although you intended them to each inherit $200,000, your children receive *nothing* from the account.

Sometimes a gift will fail by accident or oversight. Say that you have two children, Jack and Peter. Your will leaves bequests to "My children, Jack and Peter." You later have a third child, Sue, but forget to update your will. Even though she's one of your children, you've excluded her from that bequest. Note that this omission may not leave her empty-handed.

With a bit of extra thought, you can help make sure that your bequests succeed.

>> You can use generic descriptions, such as "my personal residence" or "my car" so that changes in your assets are less likely to cause a gift to fail.

>> You can gift in percentages ("20 percent of my stock account to my brother, and the rest divided equally among my children") rather than in specific dollar figures.

>> You can give class gifts, "to my children" or "to my grandchildren," rather than naming specific individuals.

Creating a moral obligation or a binding inheritance

Sometimes you have reasons you don't want to leave property directly to the intended recipient. Here's a common example: Perhaps you have a child who is disabled and receives public assistance. Instead of creating a special needs trust, you may choose to leave that child's share of your estate to another sibling, trusting that your children will take care of each other.

Most of the time, things work out the way you want. Probably 95 percent of the time, the heir who holds an inheritance for the benefit of somebody else will do exactly what you wanted. Sometimes, though, perhaps out of personal financial hardship or out of greed, the person holding the money will spend it, and the person she was supposed to look after has no legal remedy.

Even when things work out, this arrangement can burden a family relationship. The child trusted with the money may come under constant demands for more money, perhaps amounts well in excess of what you left, from her sibling.

If you want to create a moral obligation on your heirs, you can take some comfort in the odds. But be sure that you also consider the burdens and risks you may create.

Reference to a tangible personal property memorandum

Some states allow you to make reference in your will to an external document that lists items of personal property and who inherits them. This memorandum allows you to leave your household furnishings and personal possessions to specific people, change the list to add new items, remove things you no longer possess, or change who gets what, without changing your will.

The formal requirements for the memorandum can be very different, depending on the laws of your state. Some states are content with a list you sign and date, while others require formal witnessing and execution. Not all states permit this type of memorandum.

If your state permits and you create a memorandum, make sure that you keep it in a secure place known to your personal representative. If it gets lost or misplaced, it can't be followed.

What happens with the residue (if any) of the estate?

After all your bequests are made, odds are that something will be left over. Items of personal property that weren't specifically described in your will, some of the money that was set aside to pay the expenses of your estate — your clothes, a bequest that failed — whatever it is, the leftover items are the *residue* of your estate.

A *residuary clause* describes how those leftovers are to be distributed to your heirs. For example, "The residue of my estate is to be divided equally between my children."

If you don't include a residuary clause, anything left in your estate will be distributed according to your state's laws of intestate succession. Truly, including a residuary clause is so easy that you have no excuse not to have one.

Writing and Signing a Will

Payment of debts by the estate

Your estate is obligated by law to pay your debts. Your personal representative provides notice to your creditors, consistent with the laws of your estate, those creditors submit claims for payment, and your estate pays those debts found to be valid.

Help your personal representative by leaving, along with your will, a list of your debts. That list will make notifying your creditors of your death and their obligation to submit claims to your estate so much easier for your personal representative.

Most wills include a clause directing your personal representative to pay your bills. Some are more demanding, suggesting that your personal representative should affirmatively seek out and pay your creditors.

A clause relating to your debts can't reduce your estate's obligations to pay its debts under state law. It can only enlarge the responsibilities of your personal administrator. Some consider this clause to be optional and suggest leaving it out of your will.

Describing your funeral and burial wishes

If you have specific wishes for your funeral and burial, you can describe them in your will. Topics you may want to address include

>> Whether you want to be cremated or buried or have other wishes for the disposition of your body

>> Where you want to be buried

>> What type of funeral and memorial service you desire and any specific people you want to have invited to your service

>> Any poems, scripture, songs, quotations, or readings you'd like shared at your service

Your estate plan should anticipate the payment of funeral expenses. Funeral costs, along with your other bills, are paid before any distributions are made to your heirs.

Designating a personal representative

Your personal representative, also called an *executor*, manages your estate in the probate court. This role is important and sometimes difficult, so you need to choose somebody who has the necessary interest and qualifications to administer your estate. You want somebody who is mature, financially responsible, and trustworthy.

You can describe in your will how your personal representative is to be compensated. Unless your personal representative is your primary heir, you should probably provide for payment.

You should also designate an alternate personal representative, in case your first choice is unable or unwilling to serve. If you don't choose a personal representative or don't have an available alternate when your first choice is unavailable, the probate court will appoint somebody to administer your estate.

Designating a guardian for any minor children

If you're providing for your minor children, you should designate a person you want to care for your children if you die. You can separate physical care from finances, designating one person to take physical care of your children and another person to handle their money.

You'll also want to designate successor caregivers, just in case your first choice is unable to fulfill their duties.

Your signature

After you finish drafting your will, you must sign and date it. Some states require that you sign your will in front of your witnesses. Others allow you to sign it at an earlier time, as long as you inform your witnesses that it's your signature and acknowledge that the document is your last will and testament.

Executing a Valid Will

The specific requirements for executing a will are different in each state. Every state requires your will to be witnessed by two legally competent individuals. Many states limit the inheritance that may be received by a witness to your will, so use witnesses who aren't also your heirs.

Choosing the right witnesses

If someone challenges your will, your witnesses may be crucial to establishing the authenticity of your will and signature. What does that mean? It means that you want your witnesses to be

>> Credible

>> Available

>> Disinterested

Note: Disinterested doesn't mean *uninterested.* It means that they don't stand to profit from their actions. If one of your heirs contests your will and it was witnessed by another heir, a court may be skeptical of your witness's testimony. Also, as a check on self-interested testimony, most states limit the amount you can leave to an heir who serves as a witness. In short, pick witnesses who are not heirs.

TIP

You may also want to pick witnesses who are younger than you are and who have relatively stable addresses. Although some states allow you to use minors as witnesses as long as they're competent to testify in court, most states don't. You're best served by choosing witnesses who are legal adults.

Signing and executing your will

Although the specific requirements for execution are different from state to state, you should probably take a conservative approach to executing your will. If you want to go a bit overboard:

>> Consider using three witnesses instead of two and make sure that they're all legal adults.

>> Don't use your heirs as witnesses.

>> Have a signing ceremony where all your witnesses see you sign your will and sign on as witnesses in front of you and each other and your notary.

>> At your signing ceremony, complete a self-proving affidavit before a notary.

REMEMBER

If you go the extra mile, even if you significantly exceed what your state demands of you, you reduce the chances that a challenge will be made to the validity of your will.

3

Dealing with Insurance

Contents at a Glance

Chapter **1**

Seven Guiding Principles of Insurance

This chapter (and book) is meant to help you take responsibility for your life. It's for people who don't want to be victims — people who want the tools and information to be empowered when they make decisions. If that sounds like you, you're in the right place.

This chapter focuses on seven guiding principles of insurance, covered in detail. Follow these seven principles when making decisions about your insurance program, and your decisions will be good ones.

Keep It Simple

Managing *risk* (the chance of a loss happening) and buying insurance is tough enough without making it any more complicated than it has to be. For every risk, generally more than one strategy exists that effectively minimizes that risk. Using the keep-it-simple principle, you take the simple path. *Simple* means easier and more likely to be implemented — simple is not less effective.

Here's an example of this principle: Following a major fire or burglary, one of the requirements in a homeowners policy is to create an inventory of what was lost or destroyed, including, if possible, any receipts and canceled checks. Does that sound like a nightmare to you? It is! Even harder than *documenting* what you had is *remembering* what you had! Imagine coming home from a hard day at the office and finding either charred remains of what was once your dream home or finding your front door broken and your home torn apart by a burglar. The emotional trauma is bad enough. But in addition, you have to remember what's missing, because you get paid only for what you can remember.

REMEMBER

A policy is the legal contract between you and an insurance company in which the company agrees to pay covered claims when you have them in exchange for a monthly (or some other periodic) payment from you. Any given policy contains many coverages.

Conventional insurance wisdom has always held that the solution to this dilemma is to fill out a household inventory booklet prior to any loss, listing descriptions and values for every piece of personal property you own in every room of the house. Talk about a fun way to spend an evening — or, more realistically, your two-week vacation.

A written inventory isn't such a bad idea, but it violates the keep-it-simple principle because it's complex, and it takes far too much time. As a result, it's rarely accomplished.

TIP

A far simpler strategy for handling this documentation is a video or photographic inventory. This approach is easy, fast (you can video the whole house in an hour or two), and even fun — especially when you add a verbal description: "This vase here that looks like a garage sale reject is really an antique from the Ming Dynasty worth $2.5 million."

The video strategy is a good one because everything you own can be on one hard drive or DVD (or both, or two of both, one of which should be stored off your premises). Your video is easily stored, and, best of all, you can add to it when you acquire new things. If you don't own a smartphone or video camera, you can rent or borrow one. An extra benefit of having filmed documentation at claim time is a reduced need for receipts: Most adjusters will waive that requirement if they can see the item in your home prior to the loss, in some kind of photographic format.

REMEMBER

All in all, the video strategy is superior in every way to the written inventory strategy. Of course, if the house burns down, so will all your records, so be sure to store the hard drive or DVD safely off premises (for example, in a safe-deposit box at your bank).

Don't Risk More than You Can Afford to Lose

Risks can be good if they make economic sense. Carrying large *deductibles* (the amount of a loss that you pay out of your own pocket before insurance kicks in) to lower insurance costs is a smart gamble if you save enough on your *premiums* (the price you pay for the insurance policy covering a defined time period — for example, six months or a year). Not buying collision insurance on older cars that you could afford to replace is another smart gamble. But be sure to insure any risk that is a part of your life if the risk could cause you major financial loss — if it's more than you can afford to lose.

For example, the financial hardship of your paycheck stopping as a result of a long-term illness or injury is substantial. About one-third of all workers, at some point in their career, have a long-term disability. Yet many people who totally depend on their paycheck don't have disability insurance. Big mistake — it's a clear violation of the principle to risk only what you can afford to lose. Disability insurance is the most under-purchased major insurance coverage in this country. (*Coverage* is a promise to pay a certain type of claim if it occurs; other examples include automobile liability coverage, theft coverage, and so on.) If the loss of your income would cause major financial problems in your household, and your employer doesn't provide disability insurance for you, make sure you carry a good disability policy.

Don't Risk a Lot for a Little

Spending a little now (for coverage) makes more sense than spending a lot of your own money later when something happens that you're not covered for.

Most people who buy insurance can't afford to buy unlimited quantities; you probably don't have millions of dollars of liability coverage, for example. So you tend to buy a limit that feels comfortable and doesn't blow your budget. But too many people are considerably underinsured, and, tragically, they're seldom aware that better insurance would cost them very little.

REMEMBER

Liability is your financial obligation to another person (or persons) for injuries or property damage you cause. Liability coverage is a promise in an insurance policy to defend you in court and pay what you owe another person (or persons) for injuries or property damage you cause, up to the liability limits you chose.

Using car insurance as an example, the most commonly purchased liability insurance limit in the United States today is $100,000 per person for injuries you cause to others. Is that enough to pay for a seriously injured person's medical bills and lost wages as well as compensation for that person's pain and suffering? Just the medical bills alone could easily use up the entire coverage limit, leaving you to personally pay all other costs, plus some of your own defense costs. Your personal, uninsured financial loss could easily reach several hundred thousand dollars. Table 1-1 shows some typical annual costs for additional liability coverage for two cars in a metropolitan area.

TABLE 1-1 ## Typical Annual Liability Costs for Two Cars

Liability Limit	Additional Annual Costs beyond the Cost for $100,000	The Amount of Additional Coverage beyond $100,000
$300,000	$50	$200,000
$500,000	$80	$400,000
$1.5 million	$150	$1.4 million
$2.5 million	$225	$2.4 million

Following the rule to not risk a lot for a little means that you shouldn't buy only $100,000 of coverage when each additional $100,000 of coverage costs so little. In fact, you can usually pay for the extra cost simply by boosting your policy deductibles to the next level. Increasing your deductible by $250 to $500 often saves you enough on your insurance bill to pay for most or all of the added cost of additional liability coverage.

Consider the Odds

This rule says that when the odds of a claim happening are virtually zero, and the insurance costs are inappropriately high, you shouldn't buy the insurance. Considering the odds also means buying insurance when the possibility exists that a serious claim could occur.

Homeowners policies exclude earthquake losses. But they do offer an option to buy the coverage for an additional charge. Here are two examples of how the principle of considering the odds applies: It's estimated that only about 20 percent of

California homeowners had earthquake coverage to protect themselves against the devastating California earthquake of 1989, despite the high odds of an earthquake occurring. The 80 percent who were uninsured were in clear violation of both this rule (to consider the odds) and the rule not to risk more than you can afford to lose. As a result, many homeowners suffered ruinous, uninsured earthquake losses that easily could have been avoided with the purchase of insurance.

But if you live in an area that has no prior history of earthquakes and is located nowhere near any known fault lines, the probability of an earthquake may be near zero. In this instance, considering the odds means maybe not buying earthquake insurance if it costs more than a few dollars a year.

Like earthquake damage, flood and surface-water losses are excluded under the traditional homeowners policy. Considering the odds means that if your home is located high on the pinnacle of a hill overlooking a valley and your basement is unfinished, you probably don't need to spend your money on flood insurance. On the other hand, if your home is located in a low-lying flood plain or near a river, you probably should consider buying flood insurance, because the odds of a large loss are good.

TIP

Flood insurance is available from the federal government — check out www.fema.gov/national-flood-insurance-program for details.

Risk a Little for a Lot

This principle encourages you to avoid insurance when the risk is small in relation to the amount of the premium. Say, for example, that you own a 2002 Honda worth $1,000. You were just hit with a DUI, and you're facing premiums of two to three times what you had been paying — not just this year, but for each of the next three to five years. Your collision insurance premium with a $500 deductible has just increased from $100 to $300 a year. If you keep this coverage, the maximum risk to the insurance company is the value of the car ($1,000) minus your deductible ($500) minus the salvage value of the car ($50), which totals $450. This rule advises you not to buy what turns out to be $450 of insurance for a $300 annual premium. Under these circumstances, the smart move is to drop the collision coverage.

Avoid Las Vegas Insurance

WARNING

Avoid any insurance that transfers only part of the risk to the insurance company, leaving you unprotected for the rest. Accidental-death insurance purchased from an airport vending machine is a good example. It often pays only if you die in a plane crash in the next few days! What you really may need is more life insurance, protecting you all the time and from any cause.

With "Las Vegas insurance," you are, in effect, betting that if the claim occurs, it will be the result of a limited cause of loss you bet on. Not smart. Table 1-2 shows some examples of Las Vegas insurance and a better alternative that gets rid of the gamble.

Yes, the last item in Table 1-2 is tongue in cheek — no insurance company has come out with rush-hour insurance yet — but it makes the point. The bottom line? If you buy any insurance that transfers only part of the risk — as these examples of Las Vegas coverage do — you leave yourself vulnerable. Spend a little more money, and get much better insurance.

TABLE 1-2   ## Types of Insurance and the Associated Risks

Type of Insurance	The Pitfalls	Better Solution
Accidental death	Pays only if you die accidentally	Life insurance
Travel accident	Pays medical bills only if incurred on a trip	Major medical health insurance
Cancer or dread disease coverage	Pays only medical bills caused by a specific calamity	Major medical health insurance
Rush-hour liability insurance	Doubles your lawsuit protection if the accident occurs between 7 a.m. and 8:30 a.m. or between 4:30 p.m. and 6 p.m.	Adequately high auto liability limits

Buy Insurance Only as a Last Resort

This principle advises you to buy insurance only when it's the best and most cost-effective solution. You have many options in treating any given risk; insurance is only one. Treat your risks with noninsurance strategies first.

Here's one example of how this principle works: Say you've inherited Grandma's heirloom sterling silver. It's precious to you, so, naturally, you want the best coverage possible. Your agent has you get an appraisal that costs you $100. You buy a special rider to your homeowners policy covering the silver's appraised value of $10,000 at a premium of $90 a year. One year later, burglars break into your home and steal your precious heirloom. In the meantime, the silver has increased in value to $15,000. You collect the $10,000 insurance proceeds from the policy, but you've suffered three disappointments:

» The $5,000 difference between the value of the stolen silver and the amount that insurance covered.

» Grandma's pattern has been discontinued, and it's difficult to find an identical match.

» Even if you find the same pattern, it doesn't have the sentimental value that Grandma's *exact* set had.

Insurance is not the best solution for managing this risk — not only because cash is a poor substitute for treasures but also because of the hassle and cost of the appraisal as well as the insurance premium that's due every year.

A better, noninsurance method for handling Grandma's silver risk (and at the same time following the keep-it-simple strategy mentioned earlier in this chapter) is to store the silver in an off-premises safe-deposit box, thus preventing the loss almost entirely. Or, if that isn't practical because you want to use the silver for special occasions, hide it well, reducing by about 90 percent the chance of a loss through theft. You can further reduce the risk by adding a central burglar alarm.

REMEMBER

When it comes to irreplaceable treasures, preventing the loss altogether is a far better strategy than insurance, without the costs or the pitfalls of insurance coverage.

IN THIS CHAPTER

» **Looking at the dangers of buying insurance based on price alone**

» **Identifying the two components of a great insurance program**

» **Finding a top insurance adviser at no extra cost**

Chapter **2**

Buying Insurance

A great insurance program has two key components:

» Your program is in balance in all major risk areas.

» Each policy that you buy is well designed with high limits for major loss coverages and with all the right endorsements that customize your policy to cover the risks in your life that would not otherwise be covered.

You'll have a better chance of accomplishing both goals if you take time to locate a highly skilled insurance agent who's an expert on every type of personal insurance that you need.

Yes, the cost of insurance is important. You want your costs to be competitive and manageable. But the true cost of your insurance program is not only what you pay upfront in premiums but more importantly what you have to pay out-of-pocket at claim time. Most people who shop for insurance put all the emphasis on the front-end costs — the premiums — and then may end up having to pay thousands or hundreds of thousands of dollars in uncovered claims later.

REMEMBER

When it comes to insurance costs, it's far better to pay a little too much in premiums than to pay for an uncovered major claim later.

Understanding What Makes a Balanced Insurance Program

You face several major risks regularly throughout your lifetime that, if they occur, can cause your financial ruin: major medical bills, major damage to or destruction of your residence, major lawsuits and the cost of defending them, long-term disability, premature death, and — especially for those over age 40 — the risk of extended long-term care.

Your insurance program is in balance if each of these major risk areas is equally well covered and you're not spending too much on one area and too little on another.

Many people have major-loss coverage that's out of balance. They may have a good medical plan with high limits but no coverage for long-term disabilities. They may have $1 million of life insurance on the breadwinner but none on the homemaker. Their home may be fully insured, but they have only $100,000 of coverage for lawsuits and no umbrella liability policy.

REMEMBER

A highly skilled agent can help you identify imbalances in your insurance program and suggest the corrective action needed, which is why taking the time to find the right agent is so important. Most people who buy insurance don't take the time to find the right agent for them. They let whoever answered the phone and gave them the quote be their agent, without any knowledge of that person's skill level. And, in the end, they get a less-skilled agent than they could have had for the same price.

For more information on finding the right insurance agent, see "Choosing Your Professional Adviser," later in this chapter.

Customizing Each Policy to Meet Your Unique Needs

The ideal insurance policy is a single page that simply says, "If you have a loss — no matter what the cause and no matter how high the cost — we will cover it in full." No exclusions. No 20-page policies. Wouldn't that be wonderful?

Because that policy isn't going to be available anytime soon, you want to get as close as possible to that ideal using a combination of several policies.

REMEMBER One of the key guiding principles from Book 3, Chapter 1 is: "Don't risk more than you can afford to lose." That means having all major risk areas in your life well covered. To accomplish that objective, you should work with a highly skilled professional agent.

Choosing Your Professional Adviser

Automobile, home, boat, umbrella, and other personal policies, as they're sold off the shelf, rarely, if ever, cover all your major property and liability risks. But they will cover most, if not all, of those major risks if they're customized to your needs with proper coverage limits and appropriate coverage endorsements. Customizing a policy requires a great deal of coverage expertise and care. And that's why, for most people, locating and hiring the best possible adviser has to be the very highest priority when it comes to buying insurance.

BARGAIN-BASEMENT BRAIN SURGERY

Suppose that you've been told you need brain surgery. If you shop for it the way many people shop for insurance, here's what you do: You start by calling around town, getting quotes over the phone. You probably aren't exactly sure what kind of brain surgery you need, so you decide to get a price for the type that you think you *probably* need. You get quotes from all over — from surgeons, clinics, hospitals, and even medical-school interns. You're not concerned about skill — just price. After all, it's only brain surgery.

You find a clinic that will do the surgery you think you need for the lowest price. You sign up for the brain surgery. The intern who answered the phone when you called does the surgery, even though one of the top brain surgeons in the area works for the clinic and would do the surgery for the same price as the intern. The intern, lacking the expertise to diagnose the exact type of surgery you need, performs the surgery you asked for in the quote. The top brain surgeon would have known enough to recognize that what you requested was the wrong procedure for you and would put you at risk for serious brain damage. She would have recommended a different, more expensive, but much more helpful surgery instead.

Insurance isn't brain surgery, but it isn't a commodity, either. The moral of the story is that if you shop for insurance like this, you'll probably end up with the wrong diagnosis, with possible serious side effects, and with a less-skilled adviser than you need and could have had for the same price.

Understanding how agents get paid

In almost all states, agents selling personal insurance get paid the same commission as every other agent representing that particular insurance company — usually about 10 percent to 15 percent — regardless of the agent's experience, the agent's skill level, or the quality of the insurance plan that the agent designs. This payment structure is both good news and bad news for you.

The good news: Getting an expert for the price of a novice

Although the flat commission compensation system is anti-consumer (rewarding quantity of sales rather than quality), you can really benefit from the system in one way: You can buy the very best talent for not a penny more than you would pay for the worst possible agent! Can you see how ridiculous it is to select your agent based on the warm body who gives you the quote? The vast majority of the time, the person you talk with the first time you call a company will not be one of that insurance company's most skilled agents.

REMEMBER

Almost all insurance buyers see an insurance premium as buying them one thing — an insurance policy. In reality, the premium pays for much more than that. The policy, the coverage, and the insurance company make up about 85 percent of the premium. Professional advice, policy service, and help from a professional agent when there is a problem make up the other 15 percent. Spend that 15 percent wisely! Get the best agent that you can find.

TIP

The more complex your lifestyle and the more of a lawsuit target you are, the more important it is to take the time to find an agent with the most expertise that you can.

The bad news: Finding a needle in a haystack

The "everybody gets paid the same" rule for agent compensation has one big drawback: The marketplace pushes agents with greater skills away from smaller, personal insurance policies and their small commissions into business insurance, where the premiums and commissions more appropriately compensate the best agents' greater expertise. The current compensation arrangement makes finding agents with great personal insurance skills a difficult task.

Knowing what you want in an adviser

Okay, so you're sold on the idea of finding the best adviser that you can for the commission dollars that you're spending. Where do you look for candidates? And when you find two or more candidates, how can you select the one that's best for you?

Build a checklist of what you want in your agent. Ask yourself the following questions:

>> **Do I want my life, health, disability, long-term-care, and other coverages with the same agent?** You'll have the best-designed program if you can find one agent with the expertise to oversee your whole program — expertise in every kind of personal policy. At the very least, it's wise not to have more than two agents that you work with.

>> **Is a regular, yearly review important to me?** If so, add this to your shopping list. Do regular reviews. A well-designed insurance plan starts to rust with coverage gaps if it's not polished up every year or two.

>> **Do I have a home business?** If so, you must find someone with small-business insurance expertise. Add that to your list.

>> **Are top claim skills important to me?** Do you want the best possible claims coaching, to maximize your claim when you file it? Do you want an agent skilled enough to fight, successfully, for your rights if your claim is unjustly denied or underpaid?

Then use the answers to these questions to screen potential candidates.

Searching for candidates

You're looking for an agent to probe your needs, identify coverage gaps, solve problems, help you resolve claim disputes, do annual reviews, and, in short, provide greater expertise. Here are some possible sources for candidates. Try to get at least two to three prospects.

Word of mouth

Word of mouth is always one of the best sources when seeking a professional of any kind. But be careful not to fall into the price trap. Because so many people buy their insurance solely on price, when you ask for a referral for a good agent, you might get: "Call Bob. He's a good guy. He saved me $200 a year. And he always remembers my birthday." So you call Bob, get his quote, save your $200 or more, and end up with a good price for the wrong coverage (and an annual birthday card). And you've done nothing about your uninsured coverage gaps.

TIP

To avoid the price trap, be specific when asking for a referral. You don't necessarily want the best salesman or the one you'd most like to go to a ball game with. You want the person who will give you the best professional advice.

Professional societies

An insurance agent can earn a number of advanced insurance designations by completing a series of courses and passing the exams. Here are just a few:

» Chartered Property Casualty Underwriter (CPCU)

» Certified Insurance Counselor (CIC)

» Certified Life Underwriter (CLU)

» Accredited Advisor in Insurance (AAI)

Many other designations exist as well. Anyone earning any insurance designation has to spend 100 hours to 1,000 hours (for the CPCU) in the classroom and studying on her own as well as pass national exams. These people have gained additional expertise in certain areas and have a commitment to professionalism and ethical behavior. Don't choose an agent based *solely* on professional designations, but weigh these designations (or the lack thereof) heavily in your decision.

MANAGING RISK WITH A PERSONAL RISK MANAGER

When it comes right down to it, buying a bunch of insurance policies, even from very knowledgeable agents who customize all the coverages to your particular needs, still leaves you wanting. For example, you may need help sorting through your group health insurance options at work to pick the plan that offers your family the best all-around coverage for the least cost. If you're married and both you and your spouse have group options from your respective employers, you may need help determining which plan is best to insure your children. What about your group options for additional life insurance? Should you apply for that if you have diabetes or other health issues? How much do you need? If you're 65 and still working, should you apply for full Medicare now or stay on your employer's group plan? The list of questions is endless. . . .

Personal risk managers are insurance agents who are highly skilled in every type of personal insurance policy. They help consumers identify and manage the risks in their lives — not just those covered by policies the agents handle — in exchange for a value-added, annual, risk-management fee in addition to any commission earned by the agents.

There is no society of personal risk managers — at least not yet. You find one by first finding an agent highly skilled in every type of personal policy and then offering them the job. Offer to pay them an annual fee in exchange for helping you manage all the risks in your life — not just those covered by those policies that the agent handles for you.

Insurance companies

If you already know you want to be insured with a particular company, go directly to that company for agent referrals. You can also go to the insurance company for agent leads if you've shopped ahead for a certain type of insurance and found one or two insurers that are the lowest priced.

All you know at this point is that they're the lowest priced for the coverage you shopped for but not necessarily the coverage you need.

What you need to find out from the insurer is who the company's best, most knowledgeable agents are. The insurance company knows who these agents are, but the company is unlikely, for legal and other reasons, to give you their names. So here's an idea: Call the local company office and ask them to fax or email you a list of all their agents in your state who have a CPCU or CIC designation. They may not have a list at their fingertips, but they can get it for you. Whichever method you use, it should yield a small supply of quality prospects.

Making the choice

At this point, you've narrowed down your choice to one or two candidates for your "job opening" for an agent/adviser. You're probably thinking, "How do I, with limited knowledge, make this choice? I don't even know what to ask."

Start by requesting a face-to-face meeting for the purpose of doing an insurance review for every policy that you have, including your group coverage at work. You'll be able to tell by your gut feel whether this is the person for you.

If you've narrowed your field to two candidates, have both of them do the insurance review for you. The agent with the greater expertise and greater care for your well-being will stand out.

The job of protecting you from financial ruin caused by property or liability claims is an important one. Approach it as seriously as you'd approach choosing a doctor, lawyer, or accountant.

Don't get quotes at this stage yet. If you're comfortable and she has the expertise you're looking for, ask her to design a program for you with all the right coverages. Then have her quote what she recommends and meet with her a second time to review the quotes and get her help making choices. Once all those changes are implemented, you should have satisfied both the components of a great insurance program. How about that!

When you've completed the reviews, ask about the agent's background, his educational and practical experience, and the kind of ongoing help you can expect — both in terms of regular fine-tuning of your program and in terms of the kind of assistance you'll get in a serious claim or dispute. Don't consider any candidate who doesn't offer you the big three:

>> The expertise to help you design a great protection plan with the least possible gaps

>> Ongoing reviews and regular contact about new developments so your plan stays current

>> Outstanding assistance at claim time, both coaching you and being a strong advocate for your rights in a dispute

Choosing an Insurance Company

A good agent can advise you on both the financial strength and the quality of claim service of any insurance company that you're considering. If, however, you're buying direct without advice or you just want more information on a particular company, go to www.ambest.com.

A. M. Best analyzes and rates insurance companies based on their overall quality and financial strength. It gives insurers grades, much like school — A++, A+, A, A−, B+, B, and so on. (For more details on each of the grades, go to www.ambest.com/ratings/index.html.) The higher the rating, generally, the safer you are from the risk of the insurance company closing its doors and not being able to pay your claim.

TIP

Don't buy insurance from any insurance company with an A. M. Best policyholder rating of less than A unless you have no other choice.

The larger your exposures and the greater your coverage limits, the stronger the insurance company rating you should seek. For example, if your income and/or assets make you a target for lawsuits, you'll probably buy an umbrella policy (see Book 3 Chapter 4 for more information on an umbrella policy). The A. M. Best rating for that umbrella policy should, ideally, be an A+ or A++. Picking an insurance company can be a gamble. Fortunately, organizations like A. M. Best help improve your odds.

Chapter **3**

Getting the Most Out of Medicare

Medicare, a government-run medical expense insurance program, is the program used by most Americans age 65 and older. Fewer and fewer retirees receive coverage through employers or union plans, leaving most seniors without an affordable alternative to Medicare. Medicare (www.medicare.gov) covers most medical services and supplies received in hospitals, doctors' offices, and in other healthcare settings. The coverage is split among several parts of Medicare, and you may choose which of those parts to use. You also have choices within some of those parts. Medicare doesn't cover all the medical care a senior needs. Some seniors who have Medicare buy supplemental insurance to fill some of the gaps in Medicare coverage.

All the options Medicare offers can make the program confusing, but this chapter sorts out the choices and shows you how to make the best decisions. To muddy the waters even further, Medicare has exhaustive regulations explaining what it covers and how much it will pay. This chapter reviews the essentials to give you a good idea of what's covered and what you'll have to pay from your personal assets (or obtain other insurance to cover).

This chapter explores Medicare's four parts:

>> **Part A:** This part provides hospital coverage.

>> **Part B:** Also called *Original Medicare,* this part covers outpatient medical services such as visits to doctors.

>> **Part C:** Also called *Medicare Advantage,* this part is offered by private insurers as an alternative to Original Medicare and usually provides broader coverage.

>> **Part D:** This part provides prescription drug coverage.

You'll also read about Medicare supplemental insurance policies, which cover some or all the care and supplies not covered by Medicare. Private insurers offer the supplemental policies.

The goal of this chapter is to help you sort through the choices to make decisions that provide the coverage you need while keeping out-of-pocket outlays low. Simply selecting the option with the lowest premium often isn't the best choice.

REMEMBER

Even if you've been in Medicare for a while and are happy with your choices, don't skip this chapter. Costs and options in plans change frequently, and Medicare has an open enrollment period each year that allows beneficiaries to change plans. You should take a fresh look at the options annually. You may find that you can do better this year.

Starting Medicare: A Broad Overview of Enrollment Deadlines

You don't want to miss the first date to sign up for Medicare. Except for in a few circumstances, you may have to pay a cost if you miss the deadline. Some people are confused about the sign-up deadlines, because the deadlines vary depending on the Medicare part. Good news: This section is here to help sort everything out.

REMEMBER

A section of this chapter is devoted to each of these Medicare parts. So, because this is an overview of the enrollment deadlines, you can find more information regarding each part in the respective sections in this chapter. The following lists the Medicare part with its respective deadlines and penalties:

>> **Part A:** This part has no premium for those meeting eligibility requirements, and you're automatically enrolled if you qualify. So you don't have any deadlines to meet. Those who don't qualify may enroll and pay a premium. The initial enrollment period for those who want to pay is three months before your 65th birthday, the month of your birthday, and the three months following your 65th birthday. There's also a general enrollment period each year from January 1 to March 31. Finally, there are special enrollment periods for those who delayed signing up because they had employer coverage during the initial enrollment period.

>> **Part B:** You have a seven-month window for initial enrollment in this part of Medicare. The window is three months before your 65th birthday, the month of your birthday, and the three months following your 65th birthday. You're exempt from the initial sign-up deadline and penalties for delay if you have retiree health coverage from an employer. But beware: Many employer retiree plans require eligible members to sign up for Part B and cover only items Part B doesn't. These plans don't qualify for the exception. Also, not all employer plans qualify for the exemption. For example, a plan with fewer than 20 employees doesn't qualify. If you are nearing age 65 and have employer coverage, ask your employer or insurer if the plan qualifies for delayed Medicare enrollment without penalty.

If you miss the initial enrollment deadline, you can sign up during the six-week enrollment period that begins November 15 each year, but you'll pay a higher premium. The amount of the penalty depends on how long you waited to enroll. (You must sign up for Part B to enroll in a Part C plan.)

>> **Part D:** The eligibility date and initial enrollment periods for this part are the same as for Part B. And if you buy a Part D policy after the initial eligibility periods, a penalty increases your premium. The penalty is 1 percent of the national base premium amount for each full month you delayed enrolling. The penalty can increase each year as the base premium changes. You avoid the penalty if you delayed enrolling in Part D because you had creditable coverage.

>> **Medigap plans:** You're guaranteed an opportunity to buy a Medigap policy during the six months that begin on the first day of the month in which you're both 65 or older and enrolled in Part B. (Some states have other open enrollment periods.) Under Medicare law, you won't incur a premium penalty for enrollment after this period, but you won't be guaranteed an opportunity to buy a policy.

Understanding Part A

Part A covers hospitalization and similar services and is the simplest part of Medicare. In general terms, it covers the following:

>> Inpatient care in hospitals (including critical access hospitals and inpatient rehabilitation facilities)

>> Inpatient stays in skilled nursing facilities (but not custodial or long-term care)

>> Hospice care services

>> Home healthcare services

>> Inpatient care in a *religious nonmedical healthcare institution* (a facility providing nonmedical, nonreligious healthcare items and services to people who need hospital or skilled nursing facility care that wouldn't be in agreement with their religious beliefs)

REMEMBER

Part A is free, which means that unlike other parts of Medicare, most beneficiaries don't pay premiums. Of course, it's not *really* free; you paid for the coverage with taxes while working.

The following sections provide everything you need to know about Part A, including who's eligible and what coverage you can expect to have.

Seeing who's eligible and signing up for Part A

For most people, eligibility for Part A depends on being eligible for Social Security. To receive Part A premium-free, you must be eligible for Social Security. That means you must have paid taxes into the system for at least 40 quarters (10 years) while either an employee or self-employed. (See Book 4, Chapter 4 for more on Social Security.)

Most people who are eligible for Part A are automatically enrolled. Here's the lowdown on automatic enrollment for the different groups:

>> Anyone receiving Social Security benefits or Railroad Retirement benefits is automatically enrolled on the first day of the month he turns age 65. Your Medicare card should arrive in the mail three months before your 65th birthday.

>> If you're under 65 and received disability benefits from Social Security (or in some cases Railroad Retirement disability benefits) for 24 months, you're automatically enrolled after those 24 months. You should receive your Medicare card during your 25th month of disability.

>> If you have ALS (Lou Gehrig's disease), you're automatically enrolled in Part A the month disability benefits begin.

REMEMBER

If you don't qualify for Part A but want to be covered under it, you may be able to enroll and pay premiums. To do so, you must still meet one of the following criteria:

>> You must be 65 or older, entitled to enroll or be enrolling in Part B, and be a citizen or resident of the United States.

>> You're under 65 and disabled and your premium-free Part A coverage ended because you returned to work.

If you choose to pay for Part A, you also must enroll in Part B and pay its premiums. The premiums change each year. The premiums for Part A in 2017 are $413 monthly for those with less than 30 quarters of Medicare covered employment and $227 monthly for those with 30 to 39 quarters of Medicare covered employment. The premiums for Part B are $134 per month in 2017 for most members but increase as your income rises. Your state may help pay the premiums if you meet its income and asset limits.

TIP

Most people who get Social Security benefits pay less than $134 because the Part B premium increased more than the cost-of-living increase for 2017 Social Security benefits. If you pay your Part B premium through your monthly Social Security benefit, you'll pay less ($109 on average). Social Security will tell you the exact amount you'll pay for Part B in 2017.

WARNING

If you don't sign up for Part A when you're first eligible, your premium will increase by 10 percent for a period of time. If you delayed signing up for two years, for example, you'll pay the higher premium for four years.

If you aren't eligible for free Part A and want to buy it, you can enroll only during the following periods:

>> **Initial enrollment period:** This is the period you're first eligible for Medicare, which is three months before you turn 65 to three months after the month you turn 65.

>> **General enrollment period:** This period extends from January 1 to March 31 each year.

>> **Special enrollment period:** This special period is available to you if you delayed enrolling because you or your spouse was employed and had a group health plan from work. It's also available if you are disabled but delayed enrolling because you or your spouse was working and had a group health plan. In either case, you can enroll in Part A anytime while working and under the group health plan or during the eight-month period that begins when either the employment or the group coverage ends.

>> **Special enrollment for international volunteers:** Generally, if you delayed signing up for Part A because you had health insurance while volunteering in a foreign country for a tax-exempt organization for at least a year, you can enroll in Part A during the six-month period that begins the first month any of the following happened:

- You stop volunteering outside the United States.

- You're still outside the United States but no longer have medical coverage outside the United States.

- When the sponsoring organization is no longer tax-exempt.

WARNING

Folks who aren't receiving Social Security benefits but are eligible for them and for premium-free Part A need to sign up for Part A by contacting the Social Security Administration (SSA) three months before turning 65. For example, you still may be working or decided to wait until a later age to receive Social Security.

Defining Part A coverage

Part A of Medicare generally covers hospital stays and similar inpatient care and services. But the coverage isn't unlimited. The types of covered care and the dollar amounts are restricted.

Coverage limits for Part A are based on the *benefit period.* Under Medicare, a benefit period begins the day you enter a hospital or skilled nursing facility. It ends when you haven't received inpatient care in such facilities for 60 days in a row. If you need inpatient care after that, a new benefit period begins.

Medicare's coverage and payment limits for the three main types of inpatient care are described in the following sections. Keep in mind that the dollar amounts included are for 2017; they're adjusted each year. Also, Congress can alter and change what Medicare covers and other details.

REMEMBER

In addition to the following three types of inpatient care, Part A also pays for hospice care and the cost of blood after the first three pints in a calendar year.

Hospital stays

Coverage in this category is for a semiprivate room, meals, general nursing, drugs as part of your inpatient treatment, and other hospital services and supplies. Places where these inpatient services are covered include acute care hospitals, critical access hospitals, inpatient rehabilitation facilities, long-term care hospitals, and inpatient care as part of a qualifying clinical research study. Inpatient mental healthcare is also covered.

Items and services that Part A doesn't cover include private-duty nursing, a television or telephone in your room, or personal care items like razors or slipper socks. A private room isn't covered unless it's medically necessary.

WARNING

Note that services delivered by doctors while you're in the hospital aren't covered by Part A. They may be covered by Part B or other insurance. Otherwise, you must pay for them with your personal resources.

Part A doesn't pay the full cost of all these services. For hospital stays during days 1 through 60 of the benefit period, you pay a deductible of $1,316. For days 61 through 90, you pay $329 per day. After 90 days, you pay $658 coinsurance for each *lifetime reserve day.* Lifetime reserve days are days when you need inpatient hospital or skilled nursing facility care beyond 90 days in a benefit period. You get 60 lifetime reserve days during your lifetime. After exhausting your lifetime reserve day limit, you pay all costs. Coverage for inpatient mental healthcare in a psychiatric hospital is limited to 190 days in a lifetime. These amounts are for 2017 and are adjusted each year.

REMEMBER

Medicare pays all covered costs except for a daily coinsurance amount of $658 for each lifetime reserve day. So you pay $658 per day for each day after 90 days in a benefit period, until your lifetime reserve days are used. You pay all hospitalization costs after using all the lifetime reserve days.

Skilled nursing facilities

This coverage includes a semiprivate room, meals, skilled nursing and rehabilitative services, and other services and supplies for up to 100 days in a benefit period. But the coverage kicks in only after a minimum three-day inpatient hospital stay for a related illness or injury. So only care needed for rehabilitation or recovery from an illness or surgery qualifies. Your doctor must certify that you need daily skilled care, like intravenous injections or physical therapy. Medicare doesn't cover long-term care or custodial nursing-home care.

REMEMBER

The first 20 days of the skilled nursing facility stay are fully covered, and then you pay $164.50 per day for days 21 through 100 of the benefit period. You pay all costs after day 100 in the benefit period.

Home healthcare

As with skilled nursing care, home healthcare is covered only after a hospital stay. Home care is limited to the first 100 home health visits following a hospital stay, and you must be homebound to be covered. The care must be medically necessary part-time or intermittent skilled nursing care or physical therapy, speech-language pathology, or a continuing need for occupational therapy. Care must also be ordered by a doctor and provided by a Medicare-certified home health agency. Home health services also may include medical social services, part-time or intermittent home health aide services, durable medical equipment, and medical supplies for use at home.

REMEMBER

Medicare-approved home healthcare services are fully covered, and you pay 20 percent of the Medicare-approved amount for durable medical equipment.

Exploring Parts B and C

Seniors use Part B or C of Medicare the most, whichever one they choose. Parts B and C are considered together, because they're alternatives; the other parts of Medicare stand alone.

REMEMBER

Here's the process for signing up for Parts B and C:

1. You first must join Part B and pay the Part B premium.

2. You then choose to be covered by either Original Medicare under Part B or a Medicare Advantage plan under Part C.

If you join an Advantage plan, the sponsor may pay all or part of your Part B premium.

Part B is a fee-for-service plan run by the government (though it contracts with insurance companies that administer the details). Part C is offered by private insurers and includes the coverage of both Parts A and B and often additional coverage.

About 70 percent of enrollees chose Part B in 2014, and Part C has been growing rapidly since being introduced in 1997. Its growth rate increased in recent years; only 16 percent of beneficiaries were enrolled in Advantage plans in 2006. The enrollment percentage varies greatly among the states. The following sections review Part B first and then Part C. Each discussion reviews the main features of each plan and the factors to consider when making a choice.

Scoping out Part B

Part B, which is also referred to as Original Medicare, helps cover medical care received outside a hospital or similar facility. It covers medically necessary services like doctors' services, outpatient care, and other medical services. *Medically necessary services* are services or supplies needed for the diagnosis or treatment of a medical condition and that meet accepted standards of medical practice. Part B also covers some *preventive services,* which are to prevent illness or detect it at an early stage. Recently, it began to cover yearly wellness visits.

Part B is a fee-for-service plan. Under a *fee-for-service plan,* you pick the doctor or other medical provider. However, the doctor must choose to participate in Medicare and must be accepting new Medicare patients. You don't need a referral for a specialist or approval from Medicare before incurring an expense. If Medicare covers the care, the program pays its share of the cost. You pay any deductibles, copayments, or other amounts for the covered care. (These costs are discussed in the later section "Paying for Part B.")

WARNING

The list of care covered by Part B is extensive, but still many medical services aren't covered. Services *not* covered include the following: most care needed when traveling outside the United States, acupuncture, most chiropractic services, cosmetic surgery, custodial care, most dental care, eye exams and eyeglasses, foot care, hearing aids, long-term care, many laboratory tests, orthopedic shoes, most prescription drugs (though these may be covered under Part D or a Medicare Supplement policy), many procedures in ambulatory surgical facilities, and syringes or insulin. You must pay for noncovered care with your own funds or by purchasing other coverage, such as a Medicare Supplement policy.

TIP

A summary of covered and noncovered services under Part B is in the book *Medicare & You,* which is available free online at www.medicare.gov or by calling 800-MEDICARE (800-633-4227). You can also obtain this book through your local Medicare office or area Office on Aging. The Medicare website also has many details about coverage.

Signing up for Part B

If you want to be covered by Part B, you generally don't have to take action. If you're receiving Social Security benefits or Railroad Retirement benefits, you're automatically enrolled in Part B on the first day of the month you turn age 65.

You'll receive a Medicare card in the mail about three months before your 65th birthday. Instructions accompanying the card tell you what to do if you don't want Part B, including returning the card. If you keep the card, you'll be enrolled in Part B. Your premiums will be deducted from Social Security benefits.

You may be eligible for Part B even though you aren't receiving Social Security or Railroad Retirement benefits. In that case, you need to sign up for Part B during the initial enrollment period that begins three months before your 65th birthday and ends three months after your 65th birthday.

If you missed the initial enrollment period, you have other opportunities to sign up:

>> **General enrollment period:** Between January 1 and March 31 each year, any eligible person can enroll in Part B.

   You'll incur a penalty for missing the initial enrollment period and signing up during this period. Your premium will increase 10 percent for each 12-month period you didn't sign up for Part B after you could have. The penalty usually lasts as long as you're enrolled in Part B. You may avoid the penalty if you qualify for the special enrollment period.

>> **Special enrollment period:** You may delay signing up for Part B without penalty if you or your spouse were working at the time of your initial eligibility and were covered by a qualified medical plan through work. You may sign up for Part B anytime while you're covered under those circumstances or during the eight-month period, which begins the earlier of two times, when the employment ends or when the qualified group medical coverage ends.

>> **Special enrollment for international volunteers:** Generally if you delayed signing up for Part A because you had health insurance while volunteering in a foreign country, you can enroll in Part A during the six-month period that begins the first month any of the following happens:

- You stop volunteering outside the United States.

- You no longer have medical coverage outside the United States.

- When the sponsoring organization is no longer tax-exempt (whichever comes first).

Medicare reimbursements to doctors have been an issue for years. As a result, a number of doctors won't accept new Medicare patients; some won't accept any Medicare patients at all. Before deciding to join Original Medicare under Part B, check with any doctors you want to verify that they participate in Medicare and will accept you as a Medicare patient.

Paying for Part B

Part B shares most covered costs with the beneficiary — it pays about half the total medical costs of its beneficiaries and requires a 20 percent copayment on most covered care. Part B has three expenses: monthly premiums, a deductible, and copayments. The following sections outline them. The specific amounts generally change annually.

PREMIUMS

Part B has a monthly premium that's deducted from your monthly Social Security benefits. If you're a Part B member not receiving Social Security benefits, you're billed for the premium. The basic premium, which is determined each year, is set so that it covers 25 percent of the actual cost of Part B. In 2017, the basic premium was $134.00.

Medicare became a means-tested program beginning in 2007. Instead of everyone paying the same premium, those with higher incomes pay higher premiums. (The higher premiums are also called a *surtax*.) The premiums are based on a person's *modified adjusted gross income*, or MAGI. Modified adjusted gross income is the adjusted gross income on your tax return increased by any tax-exempt interest, EE savings bond interest used for education expenses, and excluded foreign earned income you earned.

REMEMBER

The higher premiums begin for single taxpayers with a MAGI of $85,000 and for married taxpayers filing jointly with a MAGI of $170,000. The premiums increase on a sliding scale as the MAGI rises; beneficiaries in the highest income bracket are estimated to pay 80 percent of the per capita cost of Medicare for the year.

A 2015 law increased the means-testing of the program. Single beneficiaries with MAGI above $133,500 and married beneficiaries with MAGI above $267,000 will pay higher premiums beginning in 2019.

You'll notice a two-year lag between when your income is earned and when it affects your Medicare premiums. For example, the 2016 income tax returns will be used to determine 2018 Medicare premiums. The Internal Revenue Service (IRS) receives your tax return and transmits the information to the SSA. Then, the SSA processes the information and sends you a letter sometime after mid-November listing your monthly Medicare premium for the following year. You can choose to have the higher premium withheld from your Social Security benefits as with the regular premiums, or you can pay the amount separately. Table 3-1 lists the premiums and surtaxes for different income levels in 2015.

TABLE 3-1

Part B Premiums and Surtaxes Due, According to MAGI

You Pay	If Your MAGI Is:	
	Single	Married Couples
$134.00	$85,000 or less	$170,000 or less
$187.50	$85,001–$107,000	$170,001–$214,000
$267.90	$107,001–$160,000	$214,001–$320,000
$348.30	$160,001–$214,000	$320,001–$428,000
$410.00	Above $214,000	Above $428,000

You can avoid higher Medicare premiums in two different ways. The following list spells out your two options:

REMEMBER

>> **Plan your finances to minimize MAGI.** Most basic tax planning strategies that reduce adjusted gross income (AGI) will also reduce MAGI. The exceptions are for the items that are added back to AGI:

- Tax-exempt interest

- EE savings bond interest used for education purposes

- Foreign-earned income

You can limit withdrawals from retirement plans and annuities to only the amounts needed for spending and required by law or contract. Avoid selling assets to recognize capital gains in taxable accounts, or sell assets with losses to offset the gains. Losses from business activities also will reduce MAGI.

Itemized deductions on Schedule A of the tax return, such as mortgage interest and charitable contributions, don't reduce MAGI.

>> **Appeal the decision.** Because the income used to determine the premiums is two years old, you can appeal the premium if your financial situation has changed. Changes that result in lower premiums include

- Divorce

- A spouse's death

- Job loss

- Reduced working hours

- Retirement

- Bankruptcy

Details about the factors that will be considered regarding the appeal and how to file it are included with the letter announcing your premium.

DEDUCTIBLE

Medicare Part B doesn't begin paying benefits until you pay the annual deductible, which was $183 in 2017. In other words, you pay the first $183 of covered care, and then Part B's coverage kicks in after that. The deductible may be adjusted annually as Medicare's costs change.

COINSURANCE

Many services covered by Part B carry a coinsurance or copayment. The *coinsurance* usually is a percentage of the *Medicare-approved amount* for the service. A *copayment* is a fixed amount you pay per treatment or service. The Medicare-approved amount is the price Medicare sets for the service. For most covered services, you pay 20 percent of the Medicare-approved amount as coinsurance.

TIP

Ask your doctor or other provider whether she accepts the Medicare assignment. If she does, that means she agrees to charge you no more than the Medicare co-insurance or copayment after Medicare pays its share. Providers that don't accept the assignment can charge you a higher amount than the coinsurance percentage of the Medicare-approved amount. The additional charge, however, is limited to an additional 15 percent of the Medicare-approved amount.

Probing Part C: Medicare Advantage

Part C is better known as *Medicare Advantage.* Medicare beneficiaries choose between Part B and Part C. The main difference between the two is this: With Part C, rather than the government offering a plan, many private insurers, both for-profit and nonprofit, offer different plans. You choose which plan to join. The number of plans offered depends on where you live. Areas with a large number of Medicare beneficiaries offer dozens of plans. Some sparsely populated rural areas offer few or no Medicare Advantage plans.

The plans offered under Part C, including their costs, are approved by Medicare before they're offered. Plans must meet certain guidelines for coverage and other features before receiving approval. The plans receive a fixed amount per Medicare member from Medicare every month.

Most Advantage plans charge a monthly or annual premium. It could be the same or less than the monthly premium for Part B. Clarify whether the premium is in addition to the Part B premium or in lieu of it. (Even though you aren't in Part B Original Medicare when you join a Part C plan, you still must enroll in Part B and pay the Part B premium. Either you pay the premium, or the plan pays it on your behalf.)

WARNING

A number of members of Congress don't like Medicare Advantage plans and regularly propose rules that would make them less attractive. The Affordable Care Act of 2010 contained provisions that would reduce their reimbursements from Medicare but also contained provisions allowing bonus payments for those plans that have better healthcare outcomes. The changes were fully phased in in 2017. It's possible that these changes will reduce the attractiveness of Advantage plans. That happened to Medicare+Choice programs, a predecessor to Advantage plans.

The following sections give you the rundown of the Part C details, including the coverage you can expect, how to change plans, and the best ways to research the different plans.

Becoming familiar with the Part C plans

All Medicare Advantage plans must provide at least the same coverage as Original Medicare, both Parts A and B. However, one appeal of Medicare Advantage plans is that they usually cover more than Original Medicare and at a lower out-of-pocket cost to most members. They often have additional coverage, such as prescription drugs, dental, vision, hearing, and health and wellness programs. The Advantage plans set their own deductibles, copayments, and coinsurance. Often, you pay a fixed amount or percentage for a doctor's visit or other treatment.

Most Medicare Advantage plans are a version of managed care in the following two forms:

>> **Health maintenance organizations (HMOs):** If you belong to an HMO and want to use a doctor or other provider who doesn't belong to the network, you pay the full cost. HMOs often must approve certain types of care and treatment by specialists before they're covered.

>> **Preferred provider organizations (PPOs):** If you're covered by a PPO and want to see an out-of-network professional, you pay a higher cost than you would for seeing an in-network provider.

TIP

You have a few other choices with the different Advantage plans available. The following are also options, although they're less common:

>> **Private fee-for-service (PFFS) plans:** This type was the fastest-growing Part C plan until 2009. Now they have less than 2 percent of Medicare beneficiaries. They used to be allowed to cover treatment by any Medicare-approved medical provider. But a rules change in 2011 forced them to create their own networks of doctors and other care providers. So before signing up for a PFFS plan, Be sure that any doctors, hospitals, and other medical providers you prefer are in the PFFS network.

» **Medical savings accounts (MSAs):** These plans combine a high-deductible insurance policy and a bank or savings account. Medicare pays the plan a fixed amount annually for each member, and the plan deposits a portion of this money into your MSA. You pay for all your care until you reach the deductible for the year, using your choice of money from the MSA and personal funds. The amount deposited in your MSA is likely to be less than the deductible for the year. If you don't use the entire MSA during the year, the balance is carried forward to the next year. After your medical spending for covered services reaches the deductible, the plan pays for any care that would be covered under Part B. You pay for any medical care you receive that isn't covered by Medicare. Keep in mind that you may need to pay copayments for some care.

» **Special needs plans (SNPs):** These plans are for people who live in institutions such as nursing homes, who are eligible for both Medicare and Medicaid, or who have certain chronic conditions such as diabetes or congestive heart failure. Members generally have a primary doctor who coordinates all their care. Treatment generally must be by doctors and hospitals in the plan's network.

Before choosing an Advantage plan, make sure you investigate the following two important issues:

» **Verify limits on service providers.** Verify that primary doctors and specialists you like are in the network and, if not, what your cost would be to use them. Most HMOs and PPOs limit specialist treatment and referrals. Be sure you understand the rules and are comfortable with them. Also, ask which hospitals in the area participate. This information is especially important in areas where some hospitals have better reputations than others.

» **Estimate your out-of-pocket costs under different levels of care.** The array of copayments and deductibles in some plans is confusing. Estimate how much you're likely to pay in a typical year. Add up the copayments for your typical annual doctor visits, medications, and any other medical services you normally receive. Assume that your health will change and you need more care. Estimate your out-of-pocket costs for different types of care and treatment. Compare the out-of-pocket costs of an Advantage plan with Original Medicare.

Joining or changing Advantage plans

You are free to join or change membership in Advantage plans or switch from traditional Medicare to an Advantage plan, but you can take the actions only at certain times. You can make your moves during the following times:

» **Initial enrollment period:** When you're first eligible for Medicare, you can join either Original Medicare or an Advantage plan during the usual Medicare sign-up period of three months before the month you turn 65 through three months after turning 65.

>> **Annual open enrollment season:** Medicare has an annual six-week enrollment period, which usually is from October 15 through December 7. During this period, you can switch from Part B to Part C, from Part C to Part B, or from one Part C plan to another. If you missed your initial enrollment period, you can join a plan during this period. The coverage under your new plan begins January 1 of the following year.

>> **General enrollment period:** An enrollment period for Part C takes place between January 1 and March 31 each year. You can join, switch, or drop a plan during this period, but the change won't be effective until July 1. During this period, there are a few actions you can't take. During this period, you aren't allowed to join, switch, or drop a Medicare MSA plan. Also, you can't join or switch to a plan with prescription drug coverage unless you already have prescription drug coverage under Part D.

REMEMBER

Generally, a choice under Medicare is fixed for the calendar year. You can't change until the next enrollment period — and that change isn't effective until January 1 of the following year. At other times, you can change only under the following exceptions:

>> When you move out of a plan's service area

>> When you're covered under both Medicare and Medicaid

>> When you live in an institution, such as a nursing home

>> When you qualify under Medicare's program for help to those with limited income and resources

Researching Part C plans

Medicare reviews and approves all Part C plans and has most of the information about them. Medicare offers the following two ways for you to find out about and compare the plans offered in your area:

>> **You can visit the Medicare website.** This site (which can be found at www. medicare.gov) has a feature called "Medicare Plan Finder." This feature does the following:

• Provides a summary of each plan and lets you dig deeper into the details of individual plans

- Estimates annual out-of-pocket costs if you enter information about your health and medications

- Allows you to compare up to three plans on one screen and to sort the plans for certain features that are priorities for you

The Medicare website also has contact information for each plan so you can get any information you don't find on the website.

>> **You can call 800-MEDICARE (800-633-4227).** If you're not computer-savvy, don't worry. The operators at this toll-free number have the information from the website available to them, so they can discuss all the options with you.

WARNING

Don't buy Part C or Part D by phone. The law contains some protections to consumers considering the purchase of Part C Medicare Advantage plans and Part D prescription drug plans. Sellers and sponsors of these plans aren't allowed to initiate sales contact by telephone or by visiting your home. Anyone who contacts you in these ways representing an insurer or selling these policies is violating the law unless you contacted them first. Make sure you don't buy a policy from them.

You may be able to enroll in the Medicare Advantage plan of your choice directly from the Medicare website. Otherwise, you contact the plan through the mail, telephone, or its website. Most plans allow you to enroll through any of these media.

WARNING

As you're researching the different plans, don't automatically choose the policy with the lowest premium. Check the other costs and estimate your total out-of pocket costs for the year. Also, look at the details of the plans, not just the summaries. Examine the coverage for hospital stays and skilled nursing facility care. Check out limits on items such as chemotherapy, blood transfusions used in transplants or other major surgery, and elective treatments such as hip replacement. Under some plans, if you need these types of care, you could pay more than you would under Original Medicare.

Qualifying for Prescription Drug Coverage with Part D

You can get prescription drug coverage under Medicare in two ways. We discussed one way earlier in this chapter: Join a Medicare Advantage plan under Part C that covers prescription drugs. The other way, for those who chose Original Medicare coverage under Part B, is to buy a prescription drug coverage policy under Part D of Medicare. This section discusses Part D.

Examining Part D plans

Medicare prescription drug plans have similarities to Medicare Advantage plans under Part C. Consider the following details about Part D plans:

>> They're offered by private insurers or other companies.

>> The plans are reviewed and approved by Medicare before they can be offered to the public.

>> Coverage, premiums, and other features of each plan differ.

>> In areas with many Medicare-eligible people, dozens of plans are available. In rural areas, few plans are available.

Unlike Part C plans, however, some national Part D plans are available to every Medicare beneficiary in the country. Medicare requires the plans to provide a minimum level of coverage, and it can ask for other changes and terms in the plans. Providers are free to add coverage beyond the minimum.

The following sections outline how Part D works, explain how to get the coverage you want at the lowest cost, discuss how to deal with Part D's coverage gap, and show you how to compare plans.

Reviewing premiums and other costs

The following list outlines the different costs associated with Part D plans. As with other medical expense plans, make sure you estimate your total out-of-pocket costs when comparing prescription drug plans. With Part D plans, this means comparing several possible types or tiers of expenses. Keep these costs in mind:

>> **Premiums:** Many plans charge a *premium,* or a monthly fee, that varies depending on the plan sponsor and the amount of coverage. Generally speaking, the more coverage under the plan, the higher the premium. The median monthly premium has been around $40 in recent years. As with other plans and policies, don't choose a policy primarily based on the monthly premium. Consider all your potential out-of-pocket costs.

You have several options for the way you pay your premiums. You can use one of the following:

- Automatic drafts from a checking or savings account
- Automatic charges to a credit or debit card
- Monthly billing statements
- Deductions from Social Security benefits

You'll pay a higher premium as your income rises. As with the Medicare Part B premium, your income from two years earlier is used to determine your premium. Table 3-2 shows the additional premiums for 2015.

TABLE 3-2 **Part D Premiums and Monthly Adjustments According to MAGI**

You Pay	If Your MAGI Is	
	Single	Married Couples
The plan premium	$85,000 or less	$170,000 or less
$13.30 plus the plan premium	$85,001–$107,000	$170,001–$214,000
$34.20 plus the plan premium	$107,001–$160,000	$214,001–$320,000
$55.20 plus the plan premium	$160,001–$214,000	$320,001–$428,000
$76.20 plus the plan premium	Above $214,000	Above $428,000

The following list outlines the different costs associated with Part D plans. As with other medical expense plans, make sure you estimate your total out-of-pocket costs when comparing prescription drug plans. With Part D plans, this means comparing several possible types.

>> **Deductibles:** The *deductible* is the annual amount you have to pay before insurance kicks in. You pay all prescription drug costs up to the deductible each year. After you incur the deductible, the plan coverage kicks in. The deductible often is around $250.

>> **Copayments or coinsurance:** On prescriptions covered by the policy, you may have to pay part of the cost of each prescription. Often this copayment or coinsurance is a relatively small amount, such as $5 per prescription. A copayment is a flat dollar amount per prescription, and coinsurance is a percentage of each prescription. The difference is important, especially if you're prescribed an expensive drug. With a copayment, you pay the same amount regardless of the cost of the drug. With coinsurance, you pay a percentage of the cost, so the more expensive the drug, the more you pay.

REMEMBER

This factor is important because of the doughnut hole or coverage gap we discuss next. If you aren't responsible for a copayment or coinsurance for most prescriptions, it's unlikely you'll spend enough to reach the coverage gap.

» **Doughnut hole or coverage gap:** This facet of Part D is undergoing changes through 2020. Part D was set up as a catastrophic coverage plan. That means the bulk of its coverage kicks in only after your out-of-pocket payments exceed several thousand dollars. Policyholders are expected to make a significant contribution to the cost of their medicines to that point, and then the coverage pays most of the costs. That's why Part D has a provision often known as the *coverage gap* or *doughnut hole.* After your total prescription costs for the year equals a floor amount, you pay all the prescription costs between that amount and the top of the coverage gap (unless your income is less than a minimal level, which changes each year). A few plans offer some coverage in the gap. When yours doesn't, you aren't allowed to buy separate insurance to pay for the coverage gap. The levels of the coverage gap are indexed for inflation each year. In 2018, the floor of the gap was $3,750. These levels are likely to change each year.

Once you're in the coverage gap, you pay no more than 35 percent of the plan's cost for brand-name prescription drugs in 2018. You'll also pay 44 percent of the cost of generic drugs in 2018. You pay these percentages until your total out-of-pocket drug spending for the year pushes you above the coverage gap. But for the brand-name drugs, even though you're paying only 35 percent of the price, 85 percent of the price counts toward your out-of-pocket spending.

The coverage gap is being reduced gradually through 2020, when you'll pay only 25 percent of both generic and brand-name prescription drug costs in the coverage gap. Check out www.medicare.gov/part-d/costs/coverage-gap/part-d-coverage-gap.html for updated information on this moving target.

Part D policies are allowed to pay for all or some of the drugs in the coverage gap, but less than one-third do. A plan that offers doughnut hole coverage usually has higher premiums than other plans. For ways to handle the doughnut hole, check out the "Dealing with the doughnut" section later in this chapter.

» **Catastrophic coverage:** After your prescription payouts exceed the limit of the coverage gap for the year (the amount changes with drug costs each year; it is up to $5,000 for 2018), you generally will pay the greater of 5 percent of covered costs above the coverage gap or a maximum amount per prescription, with the dollar amount changing each year.

The costs you pay under a policy are important, but so are other features. We explore these other features in the next section.

Looking at other terms

Out-of-pocket costs may seem low when you examine only the premiums and other costs. However, other policy terms can boost your costs or restrict coverage if you don't examine them closely. When determining which plan is right for you, check out these other policy terms:

>> **The formulary:** The *formulary* is a fancy term for the drugs the policy will cover. A plan doesn't cover all the prescription drugs you order just because it's a prescription drug policy. The plan will pay only for covered drugs. When several brand-name drugs compete, the plan may cover only one of them. And when they're available, sometimes only generic drugs may be covered. New, experimental, or expensive drugs may not be covered or may require you to pay heftier coinsurance or copayments. The plan may exclude certain drugs or drugs in certain categories.

TIP

   If you currently take medication, be sure it's covered under the plan you're looking into. If you aren't taking prescriptions, review the formulary to get an idea of how restrictive the plan is. You can see whether the drugs used by friends or relatives are covered.

>> **Step therapy:** Some plans have a preferred drug in one or more treatment categories. Other competing drugs are covered only if the preferred drug is ineffective for you or you have an adverse reaction to it. A number of plans also may require you to first try a generic drug if one is available.

>> **Authorization:** Your doctor may need to get approval from the plan administrator before a prescription is covered.

>> **Quantity limits:** Some plans limit the quantity of a medicine you can order at one time and the frequency with which you can order. This policy term can be more than inconvenient. If you're charged a copayment for each order, a limit on the quantity of an order means you make more orders and incur more copayments.

>> **Inpatient care:** Often a plan doesn't cover drugs received in an emergency room or in other inpatient situations. These drugs are supposed to be covered under other parts of Medicare. Or your plan may cover them but only after you pay for them out of pocket and seek approval and reimbursement.

>> **Pharmacy restrictions:** Some plans limit the pharmacies from which you can order medications if you want them covered.

>> **Mail order only:** For medications used regularly, many plans require mail order, and usually from a specific pharmacy. Although this term may seem like a limitation, most folks enjoy the convenience and cost savings.

Under some plans, a prescription that isn't covered won't be paid for at all by the plan. You pay the full cost. The plan may only partially cover other drugs, such as by imposing higher copayments on you.

Dealing with the doughnut

A concern of some seniors considering Part D policies is what to do about the coverage gap. This gap is the range of your annual drug expenses in which Medicare or your plan pays a limited share. A few plans cover some or all drugs in the gap. When a plan doesn't offer coverage in the gap, the law prohibits you from buying a separate policy specifically to provide coverage in the gap. You have only a few courses of action available:

>> **Buy a Part D policy that covers the gap.** A minority of Part D policies provide full or partial coverage for expenses in the doughnut hole. Because Medicare reimburses fewer drug expenses in the doughnut hole, the insurer charges higher premiums to offer this coverage. You have to decide whether the higher premiums are worth the coverage. For most people, it's not.

>> **Economize in the gap.** You can take several actions that may reduce medicine expenses. A couple of options are that

- You can buy generic drugs whenever they're available.

- Your doctor can prescribe a 40 milligram pill when you need only a 20 milligram dose. The more potent dose often is cheaper than the less potent dose. Then, you can split the pills in half. Discuss this fully with your doctor, however, because some pills can't be split safely.

>> **Self-insure for the gap.** Congress intended that Part D be primarily for catastrophic, or expensive, prescription drug coverage. Seniors are supposed to save for the bulk of their medicine coverage below the top of the gap. You could do what Congress expects and factor this level of medication expense into your retirement spending plan.

>> **Apply for help.** Medicare has an "Extra Help" or Low-Income Subsidy program for those who are in the coverage and have lower incomes. Details are available on the Medicare website or by calling Medicare.

Comparing plans

Medicare has all the information you need about Part D plans. You can research all this information and compare plans in the following ways:

>> **On Medicare's website:** The site (www.medicare.gov) has a feature listing all the Part D policies available in your area. You can read summary descriptions of each policy to narrow your choices. You can also search by policy features.

Detailed descriptions of any policies that interest you are on the site. A policy comparison feature allows you to compare several policies on one screen.

>> **By calling the helpline:** If you aren't comfortable using computers, keep in mind that Medicare's telephone operators have the same information that's on the website. You may call 800-MEDICARE (800-633-4227) to receive the information you need.

Enrolling in a Part D plan

You can join a Part D Medicare prescription drug plan when you first become eligible for Medicare. If you decide to do so, you can sign up for it during the same period that you can sign up for the rest of Medicare: the three months before the month of your birthday and the three months after the month of your birthday. You can also sign up for a plan in the annual enrollment period from October 15 through December 7. Most plans allow you to enroll over the phone, through the web, or by mail.

The membership period is the same as for Medicare Advantage plans. Your enrollment begins January 1 of the year following the enrollment period (except when you're first eligible for Medicare and it begins soon after you enroll), and you're enrolled in that plan for a year. The exceptions to the one-year enrollment period are when you move out of the coverage area, live in an institution such as a nursing home, or need financial assistance to afford the plan. You can change when any of these events happen, and coverage begins shortly after you complete the paperwork. Medicare will send you a letter stating when the new coverage begins.

WARNING

The Medicare law encourages you to join a Part D plan when you're first eligible. Its encouragement comes in the form of a penalty that increases your premium when you enroll in Part D after the initial enrollment period. The penalty is 1 percent of the national base premium amount for each month you delayed signing up for Part D. The *national base premium amount* basically is the average premium nationwide and usually is around $35 per month. In 2017, the penalty was $0.35 per month for each of the full months you delayed joining. The penalty continues as long as you have a Part D policy and can increase or decrease each year as the base premium changes.

REMEMBER

The main way to avoid the penalty is if the reason you delayed enrolling in Part D was that you had creditable coverage. *Creditable coverage* is prescription drug coverage offered by a current or former employer, a union, or the Department of Veterans Affairs. Plans that offer prescription drug coverage are supposed to send letters to their Medicare-eligible members telling them the coverage is creditable. If you don't have such a letter, ask your plan sponsor for one. Without a letter, assume that you don't have creditable coverage.

This issue is tricky, so don't make assumptions. For example, if you're employed when eligible for Medicare Part D, the employment coverage might not be creditable. Not all coverage is creditable under Medicare. If you don't receive a letter from your plan saying that the coverage is creditable under Medicare, then you should sign up for Part D.

TIP

Here's a simple, low-cost way to deal with the penalty. Suppose you become eligible for Part D and don't have a big need for prescription drugs. But you want to preserve the option to buy a comprehensive Part D policy in a few years without incurring the penalty for waiting. To avoid the penalty, buy the most basic Part D policy that carries the lowest premium. You can always switch to another Part D policy during a future annual enrollment period, and you won't pay the penalty because you bought a basic policy when first eligible.

Eyeing a Medicare Supplement

Parts A and B of Medicare don't pay all your medical expenses. You have to pay for premiums, deductibles, copayments or coinsurance, and care that simply isn't covered. Medicare pays about half the medical expenses of the typical beneficiary, and a beneficiary on average spends around $7,000 or more out-of-pocket on medical care. Some seniors pay much more for medical care and some much less, depending on how healthy they are.

Depending on your financial situation, you may not want the risk that comes with your noncovered medical expenses being close to $10,000 per year. If you're enrolled in Original Medicare, you can buy a Medicare supplement policy, or Medigap policy, from a private insurer. This section analyzes Medicare supplement insurance so you can determine whether it's appropriate for you.

Understanding Medigap policies

Medicare supplement policies, which are often referred to as Medigap policies, are so named because they cover the gaps in Medicare's coverage — the expenses not covered by Medicare. The coverage can include monthly premiums, deductibles, copayments, and care not covered by Medicare.

REMEMBER

You need to be aware of the rules associated with these supplement policies. They're subject to some basic federal rules, but the states also regulate them, and your state may have additional rules. The states also regulate the financial condition of the insurers. Because states can vary so much, and we have only limited space, we concentrate on the federal rules. Questions about state rules and regulations can be answered by the state insurance commissioner. You also may get information from your Area Office on Aging.

A Medicare supplement policy must be clearly identified as Medicare Supplement Insurance. To purchase it, you generally must be enrolled in Parts A and B of Original Medicare (not Part C, Medicare Advantage). The policies are sold by private insurers, and you pay premiums directly to the insurers. The policies aren't reviewed or approved by Medicare. State insurance regulators are the primary regulators of the insurers and the policies.

Standardizing Medigap policies

Medicare law makes comparing Medigap policies somewhat easier than you would expect given the wide range of policy options. A policy must fall into one of the categories defined by Medicare and designated by letters of the alphabet. *Note:* The categories and choices change from time to time. For example, policies E, H, I, and J are no longer available. This section gives you an overview of the plans currently available.

Plan A, the basic plan, covers the fewest items, and coverage items are added on each of the higher-letter categories. Plan F covers the most gaps with G, M, and N leaving some of the gaps uncovered. Plans K and L offer broad benefits but have higher deductibles, but they also have annual out-of-pocket maximums, which none of the other Medigap plans offer. Insurers are also allowed to offer high-deductible versions of Plan F that carry lower premiums in return for requiring you to cover more of your initial expenses before the insurer begins coverage. In 2017, the deductible was $2,200. The deductibles may increase over the life of the policy. The most frequently purchased policies are probably Plans C and F, according to the Medicare Rights Center, because most people seem to like their trade-offs between higher but still affordable premiums and broader coverage.

The following basic benefits must be offered by all the Medigap plans from A through L:

>> Hospital coinsurance coverage.

>> An additional 365 days of full hospital coverage.

>> Payment of the 20 percentage coinsurance under Part B for doctors' charges and other Part B services. Under Plans K and L, this coverage kicks in only after you've met the deductible for the year.

>> First three pints of blood needed for the year (full coverage except for plans K and L).

Table 3-3 summarizes the coverage of the different plans

TABLE 3-3 **Coverage for Medigap Plans**

Coverage Category	Medigap Plan Type									
	A	B	C	D	F	G	K	L	M	N
Part A coinsurance and hospital costs up to an additional 365 days after Medicare benefits are used up	✓	✓	✓	✓	✓	✓	✓	✓	✓	✓
Part B coinsurance or copayment	✓	✓	✓	✓	✓	✓	50%	75%	✓	✓
Blood (first 3 pints)	✓	✓	✓	✓	✓	✓	50%	75%	✓	✓
Part A hospice care coinsurance or copayment	✓	✓	✓	✓	✓	✓	50%	75%	✓	✓
Skilled nursing facility care coinsurance			✓	✓	✓	✓	50%	75%	✓	✓
Part A deductible		✓	✓	✓	✓	✓	50%	75%	50%	✓
Part B deductible			✓		✓					
Part B excess charges					✓	✓				
Foreign travel exchange (up to plan limits)			✓	✓	✓	✓			✓	✓
Out-of-pocket limit							$5,120	$2,560		

* Plan F also offers a high-deductible plan. If you choose this option, this means you must pay for Medicare-covered costs up to the deductible amount of $2,200 (in 2015) before your Medigap plan pays anything.

** After you meet your out-of-pocket yearly limit and your yearly Part B deductible, the Medigap plan pays 100% of covered services for the rest of the calendar year.

*** Plan N pays 100% of the Part B coinsurance, except for a copayment of up to $20 for some office visits and up to a $50 copayment for emergency room visits that don't result in inpatient admission.

REMEMBER

The standardization of these policies forces each insurer to offer essentially the same benefits for competing policies. The insurers compete on price, service, financial stability, and other factors. Studies show that many people overpay for Medigap policies because they don't shop around. (The standardized policies are different in Massachusetts, Minnesota, and Wisconsin.) In some states, Medicare SELECT policies are available that in return for lower premiums require policy-holders to use only select hospitals and doctors to receive coverage.

Choosing a Medigap policy

Selecting a Medigap policy is a four-step process:

1. Decide whether you want a policy to cover Medicare's gaps or whether you want to self-insure for any costs that aren't covered.

Self-insuring is lower cost in the short term. You save the higher premium and keep your money until you actually incur costs. A Medigap policy provides some certainty. You pay the premium and know that if you incur covered expenses, the insurer will pay for them. Your annual fixed costs are higher with a Medigap policy. But if you can afford the higher premiums, you may want the certainty of having additional medical expenses covered.

2. **Narrow the standardized policies to one or two that interest you.**

   Coverage differs under each policy. When you aren't concerned about the cost or probability of incurring an expense, you probably don't want to pay premiums to cover it, For example, you probably don't need emergency care covered while traveling overseas if you don't travel overseas much. Buying an individual policy whenever you make a trip would be cheaper. Of course, when you're trying to hold down premium costs, you would gravitate toward policies with less coverage.

3. **Compare the premiums offered by different insurers for the standardized policies that interest you.**

   These are easily available on the Medicare website or by calling Medicare.

4. **Consider other factors to get the best value.**

   With Medicare's standardized policies, insurers compete on cost, service, history of premium increases, and financial stability. Information on each of these is available from most state insurance departments, and the insurer offering a policy should also have the information.

These factors may help you decide which plan to go with:

» Plans F and G pay the difference when a doctor doesn't accept Medicare's rates. A growing percentage of doctors won't participate in Medicare or accept its reimbursement rates. However, these policies may cover only care from doctors in their networks. Don't assume that the policies will let you see any doctor at Medicare's rates.

» You aren't allowed to have drug coverage under both a Medigap policy and a Part D prescription drug program.

» If you don't travel much outside the United States, a policy covering foreign travel emergencies won't be cost-efficient. Instead, purchase an individual policy when you travel overseas.

TIP

After determining which Medigap plan you want, be sure to shop among insurers. The premiums differ significantly among insurers for the same policies.

Obtaining quotes for Medigap insurance

After selecting a plan you want, the next step is to get premium quotes from insurers. Medicare has details about each plan available, including premiums, on its website or through its toll-free telephone service. The plan comparison feature on the website is a good way to evaluate both features and premiums at the same time.

Be sure to look beyond the quotes for additional details before choosing an insurer. You want to know the history of premium increases for your type of policy from each insurer. Some insurers initially underprice their policies, either to gain market share or because they underestimate costs. An affordable policy today may, through steep future price increases, be unaffordable in a few years.

You also want to know the method used to calculate premiums. Insurers can use three main methods to calculate premiums:

>> **Community rating:** This method charges everyone the same premium regardless of age. With these policies, younger, healthier policyholders essentially are subsidizing older policyholders. The advantage of these policies is that the premium may be more stable over time.

>> **Issue age:** This type of premium is computed based on the insured's age when the policy is issued. After that, premiums are increased based only on increases in medical costs and the insurer's claims and investment experience.

>> **Attained age:** This type of premium is based on the insured's current age. The premium rises as you get older. Premiums using this method are likely to be the lowest when a policy is purchased, but they'll rise the most as you age. This can be an advantage when you first buy the policy, but increases can be steep as the years pass. A policy that was affordable at 65 may be significantly more expensive at 75 or 80.

REMEMBER

Not all states allow all these methods to compute premiums. Some allow only two, and some states require all insurers to use one method. You should find out how the insurer determines premiums to get an idea of how premiums are likely to change over the years. Doing so can help you avoid having the policy become a financial burden in the future.

Resolving Some Sticky Issues

Some issues regularly cause confusion or problems for Medicare beneficiaries. These issues don't have to be a problem for you. Check out the following sections in which we provide some quick pointers to guide you.

Changing plans

Medicare provides a number of choices and flexibility. It also gives you the ability to change your plan choices. Making a change, though, can have unintended consequences if you aren't careful.

REMEMBER

You're allowed to change your Medicare choices during the annual enrollment period from October 15 to December 7. However, doing so can create problems for you if you switch between Original Medicare (Part B) and Medicare Advantage (Part C), especially if you bought Part D prescription drug coverage or a Medigap policy to go with your Original Medicare. Consider these changes and the issues they raise:

» **Start with Part C and purchase a Part D plan:** Prescription drugs are usually covered as part of an Advantage plan under Part C. If you're enrolled in a Part C plan and purchase prescription drug coverage under Part D, Medicare automatically drops you from the Part C plan and enrolls you in Original Medicare. You lose the additional coverage you may have in Part C and also may lose access to doctors who work only under the Part C plan. Your premiums, copayments, and other features also all change.

» **Start with Parts B and D and switch to Part C:** Suppose that you're in Original Medicare with Part D prescription drug coverage. The next year you switch to an Advantage plan with prescription drug coverage. You let the Part D policy lapse, because it duplicates your Advantage coverage. In a subsequent enrollment period, you decide to switch back to Original Medicare. You can purchase a Part D prescription drug policy at that point, but you'll pay the premium penalty on your future Part D premiums. The amount of the penalty will depend on how long you went without a Part D policy.

Switching between Original Medicare and Medicare Advantage can also affect your Medigap policies. In most cases, if you drop a Medigap policy after joining an Advantage plan, you may not be able to get the Medigap policy back. You may get the old Medigap policy back or be able to buy a new one if this is the first time you joined an Advantage plan and you choose to leave the plan within the first 12 months of joining. But the new Medigap policy can't include prescription drug coverage. Under other circumstances, you aren't guaranteed a right to buy a Medigap policy. If the insurers decide you're medically unqualified for a policy, you won't be able to buy one. Your state may offer additional protections, but check it out before you make any changes.

Monitoring changes at work

Changing your employment or your employer medical coverage can cause some confusing situations. Suppose that you're still working when you turn 65, and you plan to continue working. If your employer has a medical plan covering you, you need to ask the employer whether turning 65 changes the plan coverage. Under many employer plans, when an employee turns 65, Medicare becomes the primary plan, and the employer plan only backs it up. In that case, you have to sign up for Part B (Original Medicare) or Medicare Advantage (Part C).

REMEMBER

However, some employer plans in this situation remain the primary health plan. If that describes your plan, you may not have to sign up for Medicare Part B as long as the employer plan is primary and is qualified under Medicare to delay your enrollment period. You won't incur a penalty for waiting to sign up for Part B until after the employer coverage ends.

When you work past age 65, the situation for Part D is different. You incur the penalty for waiting to sign up for Part D unless your current or former employer or union had a prescription drug plan Medicare considers creditable coverage. (Creditable coverage is drug coverage that Medicare considers similar to its own.) You need a letter from your employer stating that the coverage is creditable. Otherwise, when you try to join Part D later, you'll pay a penalty. Don't make assumptions or rely on verbal assurances. If you didn't have creditable coverage and you buy a Part D policy after your initial eligibility period, you'll pay the premium penalty.

Making a foreign move

If you move overseas any time after age 65, you face difficult decisions. Medicare Parts A and B don't cover most care received overseas, whether you're traveling or a resident overseas, though some care received in Canada and Mexico may be covered. A Medigap policy may cover care received when traveling outside the United States, but you aren't eligible to take out a Part D policy when you're a resident overseas.

You could withdraw from Part B while overseas. But if you move back to the United States and re-enroll in Part B, you would owe a re-enrollment penalty that could reach 10 percent for each 12-month period you could have been enrolled but weren't. You may find it cheaper to continue paying Part B premiums while overseas even though Part B won't cover you for any care received there.

TIP

Part D is more generous to overseas residents. After you return to the United States, you can purchase a Part D policy during a special enrollment period and won't owe any penalty. The enrollment period begins when you return to the United States and continues for two months.

Chapter **4**

Introducing the Personal Umbrella Policy

Y ou don't have enough liability insurance. Period. No one does.

Most people are grossly underinsured for injury lawsuits. Common liability limits on auto and home policies are either $100,000 per person or $300,000 per accident. That's not much for a human life — not enough to pay for all the medical expenses of the person you severely injure, plus a possible lifetime of lost wages and compensation for pain and suffering.

TIP

If you don't have nearly enough protection, what can you do? Here's some really good news: You can buy a second layer of liability coverage, called a *personal umbrella policy,* that sits on top of your other personal liability coverages for your car, home, boat, and so on. It defends you and pays legal judgments against you when a covered lawsuit exceeds your primary liability insurance limits.

Best of all, an umbrella policy is amazingly inexpensive — usually about $150 to $200 per year for $1 million of coverage. And about $75 to $100 per year for each additional $1 million of coverage. *Note:* This is not a typo. These costs are truly per *year* — not per month!

Buying an umbrella policy is flat-out the best value in the insurance business. It includes some of the broadest coverage at an incredibly low price. Buying an umbrella policy also satisfies two guiding principles from Book 3, Chapter 1: not risking more than you can afford to lose and not risking a lot for a little.

TIP

Affording an umbrella is easy. You don't even have to increase your insurance bill — just shift dollars away from less important coverages. For example, you can save a few hundred dollars by raising the deductible on your car insurance and homeowners insurance by $500, or by dropping collision coverage on an older car. Use that savings to more than pay for an umbrella policy.

This chapter introduces you to the basics of umbrella policies, fills you in on how an umbrella meshes with your other insurance policies, and helps you determine how much coverage you need.

Discovering the Umbrella Policy's Major Coverage Advantages

If you decide to buy an umbrella policy, you gain more than just higher coverage limits for injuries and property damage you cause — although the higher limits are a great advantage. You also receive

>> Additional coverage for defense costs when the defense coverage under your primary policies runs out

>> Coverage for many types of lawsuits not covered by your other policies (those famous coverage gaps everyone complains about)

Additional coverage to defend yourself

What actually happens when you're sued for a dollar amount greater than your primary liability insurance limits? You receive, from your insurance company, a piece of mail — probably registered mail — that looks something like this:

We Care About You Mutual Insurance Company

Re: Your June 19, 2010 Accident

Dear Mr. Soon-To-Be-Very-Poor:

You are being sued by Mr. James Johnson, the injured party in the above-referenced accident, for $650,000. Your automobile liability insurance limit with us is only $250,000. We will pay your defense costs for the first $250,000 of this lawsuit. You will be responsible for your own defense costs beyond that amount.

We strongly suggest you hire your own attorney right now to protect you for that part of the lawsuit not covered by our policy.

Yours truly,

Grumpy Corporate Attorney

We Care About You Mutual Insurance Company

Why do they send you this letter? Because each of your primary insurance policies defends you only for lawsuit amounts up to your liability policy limit. If you're sued for more than your liability limit, you're personally responsible for the amount of any lawsuit that exceeds your primary liability limit, including the cost of defense for that difference. Those added defense costs often run $75,000 or more. One huge advantage of an umbrella policy is that it pays for those added defense costs.

Gap coverage

Let's say Mike and several of his friends are all turning 50 at about the same time, so they decide it would be fun to have a jumbo group 50th birthday party. They rent a big barn at an empty local fairground and decide to make beer and wine available, at no charge, which adds a potential liability for alcohol related car accidents.

The fairgrounds requires the friends to carry $1 million of liability insurance for the one-day event that also has to include the fairgrounds as an insured party. For Mike, a one-day, special-event policy would cost about $500. But if either of his friends had an umbrella policy, the friend might be covered automatically. Neither one does. Mike signs the contract because he has an umbrella policy that fully covers him for $2 million of liability for this type of rental contract. His umbrella is also broad enough to automatically protect the fairgrounds, as he is contractually agreed to do, and is broad enough to cover the risk of liability for alcohol-related car accidents.

To briefly explore the insurance issues involved in a little more detail, the exposures that Mike faces are as follows:

- Liability for his own actions that cause injuries
- Liability he assumes in the contract, agreeing to be responsible for the actions of everyone else at the event

>> Liability if any partygoer drinks too much and causes an auto accident, resulting in a lawsuit — a lawsuit that any provider of alcohol beverages at a social event may face

>> The costs to defend and protect the fairgrounds for any lawsuit brought against it

>> Liability for damage caused by anyone to the rented barn, such as a fire caused by a guest's carelessly thrown-away cigarette

Many of these risks aren't covered by any other policy, at least not for the amount required by the fairgrounds. Mike's umbrella covers every single risk, automatically. His group saves the $500 cost of a one-day policy that may not have even covered all five risks just listed. He sends the fairgrounds proof of insurance, and everybody's happy!

But one little problem remains: On the remote chance that a lawsuit exceeds Mike's $2 million umbrella policy limit, by contract, Mike would be solely responsible for that excess amount. Therefore, each of his fellow birthday celebrants separately signs a legal agreement to share equally in all losses not covered by the umbrella. (And let's finish the story by saying that the party is a great success.)

What's the point? To illustrate a little-known, major advantage of a good umbrella policy. It not only provides a second layer of liability coverage on top of your other liability policies, but it also fills a lot of the gaps — the gaps between the policies.

REMEMBER

A really good umbrella policy covers many of the lawsuits against you that aren't covered by your auto, home, or other personal policies. In fact, the only real difference between a poor umbrella policy and a great one is how well it covers the cracks.

Coordinating an Umbrella with Your Other Insurance

The coverage under an umbrella policy can be triggered when you're sued for more than your primary liability limits. It also can be triggered when you're sued for something covered only by your umbrella and not by your primary policies (in other words, the gaps). When the latter happens, the umbrella "steps down" and defends and protects you as if it were primary coverage, subject only to a modest deductible, called a *self-insured retention* (SIR) — typically, $250 or $500.

In the fairgrounds story, four of the five risks that Mike assumed — the last four risks — were gaps and were covered only by the umbrella policy. If any of those four risks occurred, Mike would have paid only the $500 umbrella deductible, or SIR.

This section fills you in on how you might need to change your primary insurance to meet umbrella requirements and gives you tips for avoiding gaps between your primary and umbrella coverage.

One reason that umbrella policies are so inexpensive is that they generally don't cover small lawsuits. An umbrella policy requires that your automobile, homeowners, and other personal policy liability limits (also known as *primary liability limits*) meet certain minimum requirements. Depending on the insurance company, the minimums vary from about $100,000 to $500,000. To get an umbrella policy, you must first raise your primary liability limits to these minimums and guarantee that you'll always maintain them. If you violate this guarantee and fail to meet these minimum requirements, *you'll* be personally liable for the difference between what you've guaranteed your coverages will be and what they actually are.

For example, say that the minimum auto liability coverage needed to obtain the umbrella that you have is $500,000, but you've allowed your coverage to slip to $250,000. If you're found liable for $700,000 in damages, the umbrella policy still kicks in after the first $500,000 has been paid — $250,000 by your auto insurance company, and $250,000 by you. (You promised to maintain $500,000 of coverage. You broke that promise by carrying only $250,000. You owe out of your own pocket the $250,000 shortfall.)

REMEMBER

Insurance companies offering umbrella policies are not consistent in the amount of primary liability coverage that they require. Talk to your agent to be sure that your primary coverage always meets your umbrella requirements.

WARNING

Because an umbrella policy requires you to maintain specific primary liability insurance limits, you must be aware of very serious dangers:

>> **Don't let any primary policy cancel for nonpayment.** If you do and you're sued, you'll have to pay the loss out of your own pocket, a loss that otherwise would have been covered.

>> **Pay attention to all notices that come from your umbrella insurer.** They often require you to raise one or more of your primary coverage limits as a condition of keeping the umbrella. If you don't see or don't read the notice and don't raise your limits as required, you'll be personally responsible for the gap.

Determining How Many Millions to Buy

TIP

Here's a bottom-line recommendation: Buy $1 million more umbrella coverage than you think you need. If you think you don't need an umbrella at all, buy a policy with $1 million of coverage; if $1 million sounds right, buy a $2 million policy; and so on.

Most people underestimate the economic value of a serious injury, as determined by a court of law. Also, an extra million of coverage costs very little — around $75 a year. When it comes to catastrophic lawsuits, you're better off erring on the high side. No one ever went bankrupt over a $75 premium.

Reviewing available limits

Personal umbrella policies are sold in million-dollar increments. Most insurers offer a maximum available coverage limit from $2 million to $5 million — several go up to $10 million. Beyond $10 million, the choices are limited, and the cost per million escalates because those buying more than $10 million of umbrella coverage are generally quite wealthy and highly vulnerable to lawsuits.

Assessing how likely you are to be sued

In addition to the seriousness of an injury, several factors influence not only the likelihood of your being sued for more than the amount your policy covers you for but also the dollar amount of the lawsuit.

Your current financial status factor

The size of your current income and/or current assets, particularly liquid assets like investments, affects the probability of your being sued for an amount that's greater than your automobile or homeowners liability limits. If you have a high income and/or a high net worth, congratulations! You're very suable.

WARNING

People who have only one of the two — a high income or a high net worth — often overlook how suable they really are. These are people like new doctors or lawyers in their first year of practice, making almost six figures, but with no money in the bank — yet — and seniors on a modest retirement income but with a large, mostly liquid, portfolio. Both types of people are highly suable and definitely should have an umbrella policy — probably with limits of $2 million or more.

Your future financial status factor

WARNING

If you get a large judgment against you today, for more than your liability insurance limits, it sits out there in limbo waiting for your financial situation to improve. Most people easily overlook their future suability when they're assessing their need for an umbrella policy. If you're a medical student, a law student, a computer engineer — anyone training for a high-paying career — keep this in mind. If you think you may have a lot more money in the future than you have today, you need an umbrella policy to cover your liability risks.

The exceptional risk factor

Lawsuits can occur from either activities (such as hunting, fishing, or playing sports) or exposures (such as cars, homes, boats, and animals). The exceptional risk factor recognizes that one or more of the activities or exposures in your life has a greater potential of causing serious injuries or death and, thus, more substantial lawsuits. Examples include owning a pit bull, operating a day-care center, having a swimming pool (especially one with a diving board), and having a trampoline in your yard.

If you have these or other exceptional risks in your life that have large lawsuit potential, you're a candidate for an umbrella, even if you're only of modest means.

The legal environment factor

The legal climate in your geographic area is definitely a factor in the size of legal judgments and jury awards. In California, where there are a zillion lawsuits for substantial amounts of money, you need a larger umbrella policy limit. In rural Arkansas, where the pace is slow, people don't lock their doors, and lawsuits are rare, you may still need an umbrella, but the legal environment is probably not a factor in how large it needs to be.

Your personal comfort factor

TIP

Insurance is all about peace of mind. When you decide on an umbrella policy limit, do a gut check. If you still feel fearful of possibly not having enough insurance, spend an extra $75 and buy another $1 million of coverage.

Maybe you're a typical middle-class American. Your income, assets, and other factors suggest that a $1 million umbrella policy is about right — but your gut disagrees. You'd feel a lot better getting $2 million of coverage, especially when the extra million costs you only $5 a month.

Your moral responsibility factor

Some people live by that golden rule about caring for your fellow men and women. They're often of modest means and not necessarily very suable. They may not really need an umbrella. Their agent may suggest a liability limit on their automobile, homeowners, and other policies — say, $300,000 — and they'll say, "Oh, no, I want more than that. If I seriously hurt someone, I want to make sure he's fully cared for — that I can provide for him by paying all his medical bills, all his lost wages, and pay him something extra for all the pain and suffering I put him through. I can't undo the hurt I've caused in his life. But at least I can help take care of his financial burden." Such people are rare and wonderful.

Setting your limits: Recommendations

So you've thought long and hard about your own lifestyle, considered all the factors that go into deciding to buy an umbrella policy, and now you just want a dollar figure. Here are recommendations for umbrella policies:

>> Buy a personal umbrella policy of at least $1 million.

>> Buy at least $2 million in coverage if you have some affluence.

>> Buy at least $5 to $10 million in coverage, or more, if you're very affluent.

>> Buy $1 million more than you think you need.

>> Buy a policy that covers the major liability gaps in your primary insurance program.

4
Handling Budgets and Investments

Contents at a Glance

Chapter **1**

Protecting Your Employment Income

During your working years, especially your earlier working years, your future income earning ability is probably your most valuable asset. Consider that the typical person in his 20s and 30s has many years (decades, in fact) ahead of him to earn money to feed and clothe himself and make other expenditures (for example, transportation, taxes, medical bills, and vacations) and save for the future. Unless you're independently wealthy (or have a deep-pocketed relative ready to provide long-term care for you if you hit hard times), you should carry the proper types and amounts of insurance to protect yourself and your family if something occurs to you that would affect your ability to earn a living. In this chapter, the focus is on protecting income you're earning while employed.

Insurance isn't free, of course. Like other companies, insurance companies are in business to turn a profit. So you want to make sure you obtain proper insurance protection at a competitive price and buy only the coverage you need.

This chapter dives into the details regarding life and disability insurance you may need. It also discusses your employment income and how best to protect it. And it covers the importance of making the most of your health to minimize the chances of future insurance claims. If your health isn't good as you enter retirement, you're going to have more issues to face than just those dealing with your personal finances. So getting your health in order is important.

Assessing Your Need for Life Insurance

Needing insurance is kind of like needing a parachute: If you don't have it the first time you need it, chances are you won't need it again. Regarding your need for life insurance, of course, you don't get second chances (unless you're considering near-death experiences, and the life insurer doesn't pay out for those). So if you "need" life insurance, you should get it as soon as possible.

The following sections explain what life insurance can do for you. We also help you determine whether you need insurance, and if you do, how much you should consider buying.

Understanding the purpose of life insurance

The primary reason to consider buying life insurance is to provide financially for those who are dependent on your employment income. However, just because you have a job, earn employment income, and have dependents (children, a spouse, and so on) doesn't mean that you need life insurance.

How do you know whether you need life insurance coverage? Your current financial situation is an important factor in determining your need. If you haven't already assessed your retirement plan and tallied your assets and liabilities, be sure to read Book 1, Chapter 6.

REMEMBER

If you're still working, aren't financially independent, and need your current and future employment income to keep up your current lifestyle — and you're saving toward your financial goals — life insurance probably is a good choice. If others depend on your employment income, you generally should get term life insurance coverage (discussed in the later section "Figuring out what type to buy").

On the other hand, you may find that even though you're still working, you've achieved financial independence. In other words, you've accumulated enough assets to be able to actually retire and no longer need to earn employment income.

For example, consider one extreme: Microsoft founder Bill Gates has dependents and he doesn't need life insurance to protect his current income. That's because he has billions in investments and other assets to provide for his dependents. Of course, the rest of us aren't Bill Gates! But the crucial point is that if you've accumulated significant enough assets compared to your annual living expenses, you may not need life insurance.

Determining your life insurance need

Each person's circumstances vary tremendously, so this section doesn't tell you specifically how much life insurance to get. Instead, it shows you the factors you need to look at to determine that amount. You're not about to get a bunch of general rules like getting ten times your annual income in coverage, especially for those approaching or already in their senior years. The reason? Each person's circumstances can vary tremendously among many factors, such as

>> **Your assets:** Generally speaking, the more you have relative to your income and obligations, the less life insurance you need.

>> **Your debts:** Of course, not all debts are created equal. Debts on real estate or small businesses tend to have lower interest rates, and the interest is often tax-deductible. But the more of this type of debt you have, the more life insurance you may need. On the other hand, consumer debt — such as credit card and auto loan debt — tends to be at higher interest rates, and the interest generally isn't tax-deductible. But again, the more of this debt you have, the more life insurance you're likely to need.

>> **Your health and the health of your family members:** If you have major medical problems or have a family member who's ill or who has special needs, you may need more coverage.

>> **The number of children you need to put through college:** A four-year college education, especially at private schools, is a major expense. So if you have kids to put through school — and they may attend costly schools — you could be talking some really big bucks. And you face even bigger bucks if you want to help them through graduate or professional school after college.

>> **Whether you'll have elderly parents to assist:** Of course, this factor is difficult to predict, but you should have some sense of your parents' physical and financial health. If you don't, try to broach the topic in a sensitive fashion with them.

REMEMBER

After completing your retirement planning (see Book 1, Chapter 6), you should have the current financial information you need to begin your calculations for how much life insurance you need. Here's a quick and simple way to determine how much life insurance to consider buying:

1. **Determine your annual after-tax income (from working, not investments).**

You can find this number on your tax return or W-2 form from the past year. (The reason you work with after-tax income is because life insurance death benefit payouts aren't taxed.)

2. **Determine the amount of money you need to replace your income for the appropriate number of years.**

   You can find this amount by simply using the information in Table 1-1.

3. **Consider your overall financial situation and whether you need to replace all your income over the time period you chose in Step 2.**

   High-income earners who live well beneath their means may not want or need to replace all their income. If you're in this category and determine that you don't need to replace all your income, apply an appropriate percentage.

TABLE 1-1   ## Calculating Your Life Insurance Needs

To Replace Your Income for This Many Years	Multiply Your Annual After-Tax Income by
5 years	5
10 years	9
15 years	12
20 years	15
25 years	17
30 years	19

Assessing your current life coverage

Before you rush out to buy life insurance, make sure you first assess how much coverage you may have through your employer and through Social Security. The amount of coverage you have could reduce the amount you need to purchase independently. Employer-based life insurance coverage is an easier issue to deal with compared to Social Security survivor's benefits.

Employer-based life insurance

Some employers offer life insurance coverage. If it's free, by all means factor it into your calculations for how much additional coverage you may need. (Refer to the preceding section, "Determining your life insurance need," for more on calculating the coverage you need.)

For example, if your employer gives you $50,000 in life insurance without cost — and using Table 1-1 you calculated you should have $300,000 of coverage — simply subtract the $50,000 your employer provides to come up with $250,000 of life insurance you need to get on your own.

Keep in mind, however, if you leave the employer, you'll most likely lose the provided insurance coverage. At that time, if your needs haven't changed, you'll need to replace the employer coverage.

TIP

If you have to pay out of your own pocket for employer-based life insurance, you can probably pay less elsewhere. That's because group life plans tend to cost more than the least expensive individual life insurance plans.

REMEMBER

Here's one important caveat: You must be in good health to get life insurance on your own (at a competitive price, if at all). If you have health problems, group coverage may be your best bet.

Social Security survivor's benefits

Social Security can provide survivor's benefits to your spouse and children. However, if your surviving spouse is working and earning even a modest amount of money, she's going to receive few to no survivor's benefits.

Prior to reaching Social Security's full retirement age, or FRA, your survivor's benefits get reduced by $1 for every $2 you earn above $16,920 (the limit for 2017). This income threshold is higher if you reach FRA during the year. For example, for those reaching FRA during 2015, their Social Security benefits are reduced by $1 for each $3 they earn above $44,880 until the month in which they reach FRA. (Check out Book 4, Chapter 4 for more on FRA and Social Security benefits.)

If you or your spouse anticipate earning a low enough income to qualify for Social Security survivor's benefits, you may want to factor them into the amount of life insurance you calculate in Table 1-1. For example, suppose that your annual after-tax income is $30,000 and Social Security provides a survivor's benefit of $12,000 annually. You calculate the annual amount of life insurance needed to replace like this: $30,000 − $12,000 = $18,000.

TIP

Contact the Social Security Administration (SSA) to request Form 7004, which gives you an estimate of your Social Security benefits. To contact the SSA, call 800-772-1213 or visit www.ssa.gov. You also can set up a "my Social Security" account on the Social Security website that lets you obtain updated benefits estimates, verify your earnings, and take other actions.

Figuring out what type to buy

When looking to buy life insurance, you basically have two choices: term life insurance and cash-value insurance. The following sections outline these two options and their differences and help you determine which may be better for your circumstance.

Protecting Your
Employment Income

Term life insurance

Term life insurance is pure life insurance protection. It's 100 percent life insurance protection with nothing else, and, frankly, in our opinion, it's the way to go for the vast majority of people. Agents typically sell term life insurance as temporary coverage.

Remember that the cost of life insurance increases as you get older. You can purchase term life insurance so that your premium steps up annually or after 5, 10, 15, or 20 years. The less frequently your premium adjusts, the higher the initial premium and its incremental increases will be.

The advantage of a premium that locks in for, say, 10 or 20 years is that you have the security of knowing how much you'll be paying over that time period. You also don't need to go through medical evaluations as frequently to qualify for the lowest rate possible. Policies that adjust the premium every five to ten years offer a happy medium between price and predictability.

WARNING

The disadvantage of a term life insurance policy with a long-term rate lock is that you pay more in the early years than you do on a policy that adjusts more frequently. Also, your life insurance needs are likely to change over time. So you may throw money away when you dump a policy with a long-term premium guarantee before its rate is set to change.

REMEMBER

Be sure that you get a policy that's guaranteed renewable. This feature assures that the policy can't be canceled because of poor health. Unless you expect that your life insurance needs will disappear when the policy is up for renewal, be sure to buy a life insurance policy with the guaranteed renewable feature.

Permanent coverage

Whole life insurance combines life insurance protection with a guaranteed rate of return backed by the insurance company, and usually pays dividends based on the profits of the insurance company. *Variable life insurance* combines a life insurance policy with an underlying investment account. For a given level of coverage, permanent coverage costs substantially more than term coverage, and some of this extra money goes into a low-interest investment account for you. This coverage appeals to people who don't like to feel that they're wasting money on an insurance policy they hope to never use.

The reality is that people who buy term insurance generally hold it as long as they have people financially dependent on them (which usually isn't a permanent situation). People who buy permanent insurance are more likely to hold onto their coverage until they die.

TIP

Check out `www.lifehappens.org/insurance-overview/life-insurance/life-insurance-options/` for a lot more information on different types of life insurance.

WARNING

Insurance agents often pitch cash-value life insurance over term life insurance. Cash-value life insurance costs much more and provides fatter profits for insurance companies and commissions to the agents who sell it. So don't be swayed to purchase this type unless you really need it.

Cash-value life insurance can serve a purpose if you have a substantial net worth that would cause you to be subject to estate taxes. Under current tax law (which could, of course, change), in 2017, you can leave up to $5.49 million — free of federal estate taxes — to your heirs. Buying a cash-value policy and placing it in an irrevocable life insurance trust allows the policy's death benefits to pass to your heirs free of federal estate taxes.

Choosing where to buy life insurance

If you're going to purchase life insurance, you need to know where to go. You can look at the following two places:

>> **Your local insurance agent's office:** Many local insurance agents sell life insurance, and you certainly can obtain quotes and a policy through them. As with any major purchase, it's a good idea to shop around. Don't get quotes from just one agent. Contact at least three. It costs you nothing to ask for a quote, and you'll probably be surprised at the differences in premiums.

REMEMBER

As discussed earlier in this chapter, many agents prefer to sell cash-value policies because of the fatter commissions on those policies. So don't be persuaded to purchase that type of policy if you don't really think it's right for you.

>> **An insurance agency quote service:** The best of these services provide proposals from the highest-rated, lowest-cost companies available. Like other agencies, the services receive a commission if you buy a policy from them, but you're under no obligation to do so.

To get a quote, these services ask you your date of birth, whether you smoke, some basic health questions, and how much coverage you want. Services that are worth considering include

- **AccuQuote:** `www.accuquote.com`; 800-442-9899

- **ReliaQuote:** `www.reliaquote.com`; 800-940-3002

- **SelectQuote:** `www.selectquote.com`; 800-963-8688

- **Term4Sale:** `www.term4sale.com`; 888-798-3488

Protecting Your
Employment Income

CHAPTER 1 **Protecting Your Employment Income**   253

Protecting Your Employment Income: Disability Insurance

Long-term disability (LTD) insurance replaces a portion of your lost income in the event that a disability prevents you from working either permanently or temporarily for an extended period of time. For example, you may be in an accident or develop a medical condition that keeps you from working for six months or longer. During your working years, your future income earning ability is likely your most valuable asset — far more valuable than a car or even your home. Your ability to produce income should be protected or insured.

REMEMBER

Even if you don't have dependents, you probably still need disability coverage. After all, aren't *you* dependent on your income?

The following sections point out why you should have disability insurance and help you determine the type of coverage you need to protect your income.

Why most people lack disability insurance and why you need it

Most folks lack long-term disability insurance. The two main reasons people don't obtain this important type of insurance are as follows:

>> **Their company doesn't offer it.** Just three in ten workers are offered access to an LTD plan. Only 19 percent of those working for smaller employers — those employers with fewer than 100 employees — have access to an LTD plan. And just 6 percent of part-time workers have access to LTD insurance.

>> **They don't enroll.** Even among those in the minority who have access to LTD, many people don't enroll. A common reason folks bypass coverage is that they believe their chances of disability are rare. Another perception is that only old people become disabled. Both of these perceptions are wrong.

REMEMBER

Why should you spend money and buy LTD? The answers are simple. If you want to protect your future employment income, an LTD plan is one of the best ways to do so. Here are some reasons you should get LTD:

>> **Life is uncertain.** You can't know when and what type of disability you may suffer. That's because many disabilities are caused by medical problems (arthritis, cerebral palsy, diabetes, glaucoma, multiple sclerosis, muscular dystrophy, stroke, and so on) and accidents (head injuries, spinal injury, loss of

limb, and so on). Although older folks are at greater risk for more severe medical problems, plenty of people in their 20s, 30s, and 40s suffer accidents or major medical problems leading to disability.

>> **Most applicants for Social Security disability benefits coverage are turned down.** You can receive payments only if your disability will result in death or if you aren't able to perform any substantial, gainful activity for more than a year.

>> **Even if you do qualify, your state's disability plan and Social Security insurance programs won't provide you with sufficient coverage.** Many people are mistaken in thinking that their state's disability plan and the Social Security disability insurance program will take care of them if they become disabled. Unfortunately, those programs don't provide adequate coverage. State programs typically pay benefits for only one year or less, which isn't going to cut it if you truly suffer a long-term disability that lasts for years. Although one year of coverage is better than none, the premiums for such short-term coverage often are higher per dollar of benefit than through the best private insurer programs.

Similarly, although Social Security disability benefits can be paid long term, remember that these payments are intended to provide for only basic subsistence living expenses. Those earning more than $20,000 per year find that less than half of their income is replaced by Social Security disability payments. Basically, the higher your annual income was while working, the smaller the percentage of that number will be made up by your Social Security benefits.

>> **Workers' compensation, if you have coverage through your employer, won't pay benefits at all if you get injured or become sick away from your job.** Such narrow coverage that pays benefits only under a limited set of circumstances isn't the comprehensive insurance you need.

Identifying needed disability coverage

Unless you're already financially independent, you need long-term disability insurance during your working years. Generally speaking, you should have LTD coverage that provides a benefit of approximately 60 percent of your gross income. Because disability benefits payments are tax-free if you pay the premium, they should replace your current after-tax earnings.

TIP

If you earn a high income and spend far less than that, you may be fine purchasing a monthly benefit amount less than 60 percent of your income.

We recommend that your disability policy contain the following:

>> **An "own occupation" definition of disability:** This definition allows you to collect benefits if you can't perform your regular occupation. For example, if you work as an accountant, your disability policy shouldn't require you to take a job as a brick layer or retail worker if you no longer can perform the duties of an accountant.

>> **A noncancelable and guaranteed renewable clause:** This clause guarantees that your policy can't be canceled if you develop health problems. If you purchase a policy that requires periodic physical exams, you could lose your coverage when you're most likely to need it.

>> **A financially appropriate benefit period:** Obtain a policy that pays benefits until an age at which you would become financially self-sufficient. For most people, that would require obtaining a policy that pays benefits to age 65 or 67 (when Social Security retirement benefits begin).

If you're close to being financially independent and expect to accomplish that or retire before your mid-60s, consider a policy that pays benefits for five years.

>> **A high deductible/waiting period:** The *waiting period* is the "deductible" on disability insurance. It's the time between your disability and when you can begin collecting benefits. It's recommended that you take the longest waiting period that your financial circumstances allow, because doing so will greatly reduce your policy's premiums. A waiting period of at least 90 or 180 days is recommended.

>> **Residual benefits:** This feature pays you a partial benefit if you have a disability that prevents you from working full time.

>> **Cost-of-living adjustments:** This provision automatically increases your benefit payment after you're disabled by a set percentage or in step with inflation.

Shopping for disability coverage

After you understand the importance of having good disability insurance, hopefully you'll be motivated to close the deal and buy it. Here are some ways to shop and compare so you end up with good coverage at a competitive price:

>> **Check with your employer.** Group disability plans can greatly accelerate your shopping process and generally offer decent value. Unlike with life insurance plans, group disability plans tend to offer more bang for your buck.

>> **Peruse professional associations.** For many self-employed people, if you find the associations that exist for your occupation or profession, you may well discover a fine disability plan. Just be sure to compare their offerings to whatever individual policy proposals you find.

>> **Avail yourself of agents.** Get referrals to insurance agents in your area who specialize in disability insurance. Using the policy guidelines in the preceding section, "Identifying needed disability coverage," solicit and evaluate proposals.

FINDING A CAREER YOU LOVE

Most folks spend decades working. And getting caught up in the financial end of your career is easy and tempting. Of course, all other things being equal, you should earn more rather than less money! However, you should manage your career with an eye toward protecting and enhancing your earnings *and* your happiness.

We know folks who have been doing the same type of work for decades and love what they do. But they are the exception, not the norm.

A survey conducted by the Society for Human Resource Management found that when employees are younger (35 and under), their primary concerns are compensation and benefits. Older workers (over the age of 55) are more concerned with issues like job security, feeling safe at work, having the opportunity to use their skills and abilities, enjoying the work itself, and communication between employees and management. So the financial aspects of work become less important for most workers as they get older.

Remember, you live only once. Take advantage of the opportunity to dream about alternative careers. Go back to school, take some continuing education classes, or go to an interesting seminar. For example, an insurance agent dissatisfied with the sales aspect of his job may move into public school teaching and then become a school administrator.

To brainstorm about your career options, including buying or starting your own small business, check out these books:

- *Starting a Business All-In-One For Dummies* (Wiley, 2015)

- *What Color Is Your Parachute? A Practical Manual for Job-Hunters and Career-Changers*, by Richard N. Bolles (Ten Speed Press, 2018)

Protecting Your
Employment Income

The insurance company you choose should have strong financial health with the leading credit rating agencies.

Investing In and Protecting Your Health

Your health is one of the most important components of a quality life. So as you enter your senior years, if you're not healthy, squaring away your personal finances can be much more difficult. After all, if you're facing serious health issues and costly doctor and hospital bills, your finances probably won't be as healthy either.

To make wise choices about your health — so you're in good shape to deal with your finances during your senior years — you need to make sure you're informed. The good news is that knowledge and information about healthy living is readily available so you can make smart, health-conscious choices.

The following sections give you an overview and pointers about what you can do to ensure that your health is in order now and in the years ahead. With your good health in check, you can then enjoy retirement and be in a better financial situation. These sections rely on Dr. Mehmet Oz and Dr. Michael Roizen for some help. They've coauthored numerous personal health books that are helpful for seniors.

Take care of your ticker

One of the most important aspects of healthy living is ensuring that your heart is in tiptop shape. You can start by choosing to eat the following foods, which have heart-healthy and anti-inflammatory properties:

>> **Alcohol:** You must be careful with the amount (and type) of alcohol you drink. Women can drink one drink per day while men can partake of two. The benefits of alcohol? It raises levels of healthy HDL cholesterol and also helps you to wind down so your blood pressure can do the same. (Just be sure not to drink too close to bedtime, because alcohol can disrupt sleep in some folks.) The best alcohol to choose is red wine with its abundant antioxidants.

>> **Dark chocolate:** Eating dark (not milk) chocolate may lower blood pressure, increase good HDL cholesterol, and lower nasty LDL cholesterol. Interesting fact: The Kuna Indians (who live near Panama) drink more than five cups of flavonoid-rich cocoa a day. They have little age-related hypertension.

- >> **Extra-virgin olive oil:** Extra-virgin olive oil contains healthy phytonutrients and monounsaturated fats, which boost good HDL cholesterol. The docs recommend that about 25 percent of your diet come from healthy fats (for example, olive oil, avocados, and nuts).

- >> **Fish:** Fatty fish, such as mahi-mahi, catfish, flounder, tilapia, whitefish, and wild, line caught salmon, are rich in omega-3 fatty acids that reduce triglycerides in your blood. High triglycerides can cause plaque buildup in your arteries. Omega-3s also help reduce the risk of *arrhythmia* (irregular heartbeat) after a heart attack, decrease blood pressure, and make platelets less sticky, which reduces clotting. The docs recommend three portions of fatty fish per week.

- >> **Fruits and veggies:** Many fruits and vegetables — for example, red grapes, cranberries, tomatoes, and onions — contain powerful antioxidants called *flavonoids* and *carotenoids*.

- >> **Garlic:** A clove a day is believed to be beneficial to help thin your blood and lower blood pressure. You can take 400 milligrams in pill form (called *allicin*) if you don't care for the taste of garlic or its effects on your breath.

- >> **Magnesium-rich foods:** Whole-grain breads and cereals, soybeans, lima beans, avocado, beets, and raisins help lower blood pressure and reduce arrhythmias by expanding the arteries. Strive to get 400 milligrams of magnesium each day from your food.

Exercise (and sweat)

Exercise makes you feel (and look) better. To keep your heart healthy, try to walk about 30 minutes daily and get at least one hour of sweaty activity, such as an aerobics class (ideally you'd break that hour into three 20-minute sessions).You should get your heart pumping up to about 80 percent of its age-adjusted maximum (220 minus your age) for extended periods of time, according to the docs.

REMEMBER

If you like to jog, keep the following pointer in mind: Besides having to dodge SUV-driving lunatics yammering on cellphones, running on hard asphalt isn't good for your body. The older you get, the more careful you should be about the stresses and strains you're placing on your joints. You should go for low-impact activities, such as swimming, cycling, or using an elliptical trainer to elevate your heart rate without stressing your joints.

Exercise also has other benefits. As you age, your sense of (and ability to) balance slowly declines. Falls are one of the leading causes of injury and death among the elderly. More than one in three adults age 65 and older fall each year in the United States. Among older adults, falls are the leading cause of injury deaths.

They're also the most common cause of nonfatal injuries and traumatic hospital admissions.

Naturally, many people who fall develop a fear of falling. This fear may cause them to limit their activities, leading to reduced mobility and physical fitness and increased risk of falling.

To improve your balance and develop some strength, try the following activities:

>> **Crunches:** Performing crunches on an unstable surface, such as on a stability ball, forces your body to balance.

>> **Light weight lifting:** Use dumbbells instead of weight machines, because dumbbells force you to balance the weights better.

>> **Standing exercises on one leg at a time:** Doing these exercises helps you develop better balance.

>> **Step-type moves:** Activities such as lunges or step-up moves require you to balance your weight.

Hydrate with good-quality H$_2$O

You want to drink plenty of water to realize a variety of health benefits, especially for your digestion and intestines. Drinking water, preferably filtered, lubricates everything, allowing food to more easily slide through your system. It also quells hunger and fights bad breath. Furthermore, you need to regularly drink water as you age because your body's ability to detect thirst weakens as you get older.

TIP

The more active and larger you are, the more water you'll need to drink. The best indicator for whether you're drinking enough water is the color of your urine; drink enough water that your urine is light yellow. (*Note:* If you take vitamins, they may turn your urine bright yellow even if you are drinking enough water.)

For Dummies author Eric Tyson's website (www.erictyson.com) has a summary of research on bottled water quality and demonstrates how most bottled waters are a waste of money. Your most effective and healthy avenue is to install a water filtration system at home to improve the virtually free tap water you're already receiving.

Include fiber in your diet

If you're eating healthy foods like fruits, vegetables, whole grains, oats, and beans, you'll also be eating valuable fiber. (Some cereals have a decent amount of fiber as well.) The combination of fiber and water helps move food easily through your system without putting too much pressure on your intestines. Doctors recommend that men get 35 grams a day and women 25 grams.

REMEMBER

The other often-overlooked benefit of eating fiber-rich foods and being well hydrated is that the combination makes you feel full. Eating too much in general and eating too much of the wrong foods leads to obesity, heart disease, diabetes, and a variety of related problems.

Manage your stress

Stress does horrible things to your body. You can't eliminate all stress, of course (and, besides, doing so would make life dull). However, you can do plenty to minimize it and turn it to your advantage. You can make the following health-conscious choices to keep stress under control:

>> **Identify the sources of your stress.** You can't manage stress if you're not clear on the real sources.

>> **Focus on the moment.** Spend time every day thinking about the here and now and not brooding over yesterday or worrying about tomorrow. Also, notice the things that most people tend to ignore — like breathing, bodily sensations, and emotions.

>> **Take good care of your health.** Make sure you have the other aspects of your life in order, such as getting enough sleep, eating well, and exercising. When you don't, you're more vulnerable to the stress.

>> **Get moving.** Exercise is one of the best stress (and depression) busters ever invented. See the earlier section "Exercise (and sweat)" for more information.

>> **Do the opposite.** Whenever people feel negative emotions, such as fear or anxiety, they tend to avoid them and withdraw. If you try experiencing the opposite emotions, you can start to feel better. So, for example, if you're upset with someone, try to be empathetic instead of lashing out.

>> **Focus on and relax your muscles.** Tense and then relax the muscles in one part of your body (such as your legs, your arms, your face, and so on) at a time. Doing so reduces stress that you're storing in your body.

>> **Take some deep breaths.** Take ten deep breaths in the morning and another ten at night — and as many as needed in between for stress relief. Find a position that helps you relax. For example, lie on the floor, flat on your back, with one hand on your chest, and another on your stomach. Breathe in deeply and slowly, picturing your lungs filling with air. When your lungs feel full, slowly breathe out.

Protecting Your Employment Income

Get your calcium

Most people don't get enough calcium for optimal bone density. Most folks need about 1,500 milligrams daily from foods or supplements. So to reach your optimal health, make sure you're taking in calcium. Foods plentiful in calcium include whole grains, leafy green vegetables, and nuts. It's also often helpful to get some calcium from chewable calcium-citrate tablets.

REMEMBER

Along with your calcium, take 1,000 international units (1,200 for women over age 65) of vitamin D daily. Doing so helps your body absorb the calcium you take in. In addition, if you aren't getting it in your diet, you want to add 400 milligrams of magnesium daily to prevent the constipation that calcium can cause. See the list of foods that are particularly high in magnesium in the earlier section "Take care of your ticker."

Chapter **2**

Managing Budgets and Expenses

By the time most people reach their retirement years, they've been managing money for several decades. That's a good thing. Between the knowledge acquired over time and the valuable lessons learned in the school of hard knocks, people enter retirement a lot wiser and more money-savvy than they were as young adults.

Making the most of your senior years and your money requires you to plan ahead and be prepared for some surprises. At the same time, you can learn from others' experiences and put many worries to rest. This chapter looks at some potential fears you may have about entering retirement and helps you manage your expenses and spending throughout your retirement to make the transition as easy as possible.

Pointing Out Some Retirement Worries You May Have

What are the worries and fears of retirees and senior citizens? Thanks to research and studies, we know what folks are concerned about, and this section discusses everything you need to know. Being aware of this information helps you plan ahead and prepare. The challenge for most people is this: Retirement is financially unlike any other period in their lives because retirees generally are

>> **Working less (or not at all):** Retirees have more free time in which to spend money and less earned income coming their way.

>> **Living off investments and monthly benefit checks:** During most wage earners' working years, their income exceeds their spending, and psychologically they get used to that. For many retirees, on the other hand, spending exceeds income.

>> **Using more medical services:** Retirees use more medical services even if they have comparably good health within their peer group. They need more medical tests, spend more on prescription and over-the-counter drugs, and have more medical problems.

Many seniors and near-seniors understand these changes, which is why they worry about money and other retirement issues. Many fears revolve around concerns about running out of money. The following sections go over these specific anxieties, why they exist, and what you can do to address them.

Running out of money

One worry far exceeds all others: the fear of running out of money. Even people who possess what seems to most folks like plenty of money, worry about having enough. This section enumerates the sources of this fear and suggests what you can do about it.

REMEMBER

One way some seniors deal with the problem of running out of money is that they continue to work during retirement. You may need to make some slight adjustments and work part time during retirement or even start a small business to help make ends meet.

Supporting others

For sure, plenty of seniors are concerned about making ends meet for the duration of their retirement. But seniors aren't egocentrically focused on their own finances. In fact, to the contrary. They're also concerned about other family members that they're taking care of financially. More than four in ten (44 percent) retired Americans support one or more people living outside their home. Among those receiving support are

>> Adult children (53 percent)

>> Grandchildren (37 percent)

>> Elderly parents (12 percent)

Before hitting retirement, plenty of near-seniors get "sandwiched" providing for their own children and helping their aging parents. How can near-seniors who then end up retiring accomplish all of this? Consider the following reasons (and try applying them to your own life if you're in a pickle and being sandwiched):

>> **They continue to be frugal.** Folks who saved and invested during their working years generally continue their frugality in retirement. The best savers often have trouble learning to live off their money in retirement. In those types of cases, retirees may need to understand that it's okay to spend a little more!

>> **They have a desire to help loved ones.** Most seniors adore their offspring (not always and not all the time, of course). And nothing makes most seniors happier than helping their kids, grandkids, and extended families. Sometimes you also have to help your aging parents.

>> **They have fears about outliving their available funds and becoming a burden to others.** There's great uncertainty about how long any one person or couple will live as well as what will happen to their personal health. So most people assume that they'll live longer and perhaps need extensive medical care later in life, and as a result they keep more money saved. However, retirees often overlook the fact that Social Security and monthly pensions keep paying benefits as long as you live. Money left invested will also continue compounding and growing over the long term — as long as it's invested intelligently (see Book 4, Chapter 3 for details).

>> **They spend less on many things later in retirement.** Qualitatively, as soon as folks cut back on work, they spend a lot less on work-related expenses — from clothing to commuting to buying fewer services — compared with when they had far greater demands on their time. Even among active seniors, as mobility is reduced later in retirement, travel and shopping are also reduced. Yes, people may spend more on some things (like healthcare) as they age, but in general, they spend less, which leads to folks having more of their money last longer than they may have guessed. Check out the section "How Spending Really Changes in Retirement," later in this chapter, for the specifics of retiree spending patterns and behavior.

>> **They live in a wealthy country with an economic bounty.** Notwithstanding the severe recession of the late 2000s and the associated financial market turmoil, America is still a wealthy nation and provides a relatively high standard of living for the vast majority of people. Yes, in the years and decades ahead, the United States will likely be sharing its economic superpower status with some other emerging, higher-growth economies, but its economy should continue to grow.

Addressing your worries

Dr. Frank Luntz, author of *What Americans Really Want . . . Really* (Hyperion), is a prolific pollster and focus-group organizer who has studied retirees through focus groups and research surveys. He developed "The Seven Most Frequently Asked Questions About Retirement," a list of questions asked by people age 60 and older.

The first six of these seven items deal with a senior's ability to manage his cash flow and match up his income to his expenses. And the last item on the list — concerning maintaining independence and mobility — is partly related to income and expenses, too. Here are Dr. Luntz's questions, along with easy-to-understand explanations:

>> **Will I be able to afford healthcare when I get too old to work? Am I one medical emergency away from bankruptcy and ruin?** Yes, you should be able to afford healthcare in retirement, and, no, a medical emergency or major illness doesn't have to bankrupt you. As discussed in Book 3, Chapter 3, Medicare is a pretty comprehensive major medical insurance plan that can include prescription drug coverage. You can also buy long-term care insurance and a Medicare supplement.

>> **Is Social Security going to be there for me?** Yes, it should be. Book 4, Chapter 4 discusses this worry at length and shows you why you shouldn't be worried about it.

>> **Will prescription drugs be so expensive that I'll be forced to choose between medications and food?** No. The vast majority of prescription drugs have been in the market for many years and have competition from generics, which keeps costs down. You can also purchase prescription drug coverage through Medicare. Copayments, however, have been increasing over time, and the price of new drugs (such as those for treating cancer) can be quite costly.

>> **Will I run out of money before I run out of years?** No. Social Security benefits, which increase annually with inflation, continue for your life. The same is true for company pension benefits, if you elected the lifetime payment option. To ensure that your invested dollars stretch for as long as

possible, be sure to follow our investing advice in Book 4, Chapter 3. Finally, if you're a homeowner, equity in your home provides another financial safety net in case you need additional resources later in your retirement.

>> **Will I be a financial and physical burden on my spouse or my children? Will I lose my independence and mobility?** These last two questions are the hardest to answer and address. Financially, you should be fine in the long term with the advice provided in this book. However, you can't predict your health. As you age later in your elderly years, you'll experience an inevitable reduction in mobility and ability to do some things you've historically been able to do. You can make the most of your health for as many years as possible by taking sensible steps to maintain your good health. See Book 4, Chapter 1 for details.

Spending Your Nest Egg

A day will come when you have to consider how much of your retirement nest egg you can spend each year. For some retirees, that day happens right when they retire; for others, it occurs years into retirement. And for a small minority, they actually never tap into their nest egg in retirement. The following sections discuss important considerations as you decide when and how to spend your nest egg.

Considering the 4 percent rule

The vast majority of retirees need to live off at least a portion of their investment portfolio's returns. If you're in this majority, a logical concern you may have is determining how much of your portfolio and its returns you can use each year, while still having some reasonable expectation that your portfolio will last throughout your retirement. That's where the 4 percent rule comes into play.

REMEMBER

Analyses and studies have found that if you withdraw about 4 percent of your nest egg in the first year of retirement and then bump that amount up by a few percent per year for increases in the cost of living, your portfolio should last at least 30 years.

Here's an example to illustrate: Suppose that you retire with about $500,000 invested in a balanced portfolio of stocks and bonds. The 4 percent rule would suggest that you plan on taking about $20,000 from this retirement nest egg in your first year of retirement. If you assume a 3 percent rate of inflation, in the second year you could take $20,600.

Naming the factors affecting your use of retirement assets

The preceding section explains that 4 percent withdrawals are a starting point to consider for typical folks planning retirement and expecting to maintain a balanced portfolio. However, 4 percent may not be the ideal number for you based on the amount of money you have in savings. For example, if you want to ensure that your money lasts even longer, you could try 3 percent withdrawals rather than 4 percent withdrawals.

Here are some important factors affecting whether you should use 4 percent or a slightly different number:

>> **Actual expenses relative to your income:** You may find early in your retirement that you don't need 4 percent from your financial assets to make ends meet. This occurs perhaps because you still have some employment income coming in or your monthly checks from Social Security and pensions are sufficient for your spending needs. If that's the case and you can delay tapping into your investment returns or income, then by all means do so.

One challenge of planning ahead is that you can't predict unexpectedly large expenses; you can make only intelligent guesses. Be sure to see our discussion later in the chapter for which types of expenses may give your budget some stress in the years ahead.

>> **Health and life expectancy:** If you come from a family where folks routinely live a long time, you want to ensure that your money lasts as long as you do. You may have to use an investment withdrawal rate of less than 4 percent, such as 3 to 3.5 percent.

>> **Investment performance:** If you're an investor who's less willing to be reasonably aggressive with asset allocation (say a 50/50 mix between growth investments like stocks and real estate and lending investments like bonds), consider using a retirement withdrawal figure of less than 4 percent. Conversely, if you're willing to be more aggressive, you could use 4.5 to 5 percent. However, be aware of the potential downside of the financial markets producing lower-than-expected returns over a number of years.

>> **Risk tolerance:** How comfortable are you with taking risk? If you're a nervous wreck about putting even a small portion of your money in something other than bank accounts or Treasury bonds, using 4 percent withdrawals is too high a number.

How Spending Really Changes in Retirement

Seeing how much other retirees spend can help you plan your own retirement better. Our fine federal government actually collects and collates consumer spending data that can be sliced and diced many ways. With this information, how people's spending habits change after age 65, an age by which many people retire or are close to retiring, can be analyzed.

The average number of people in the "consumer unit" (household) changes over time:

Age	Average Number of People in Household
55–64	2.1
65–74	1.8
75+	1.5

The primary reason for the decline in the average number of people in a household after ages 65 and 75 is because of the passing of an elderly spouse. So you have to make adjustments for changes in the number of people in the household to make better sense of some of the numbers. For example, you would expect a smaller number of people to eat less food.

The first column in Table 2-1 shows the average expenditures for households that fall into the 55-to-64-year-old age bracket. Of course, these are national averages and may differ greatly from how much and where you spend your own money. (*Remember:* Taxes weren't accurately captured by this survey and thus are omitted, although they're discussed briefly later.)

TABLE 2-1 Per Person Changes in Expenditures by Age Group

Expenditure	Age 55–64	Age 65–74	Age 75+
Total expenditures	$54,783	–11.8%	–19.0%
Housing	$17,611	–8.3%	–4.3%
Transportation	$9,377	–16.1%	–34.4%
Food	$6,357	–2.0%	–13.3%
At home	$3,711	7.6%	0.6%
Out	$2,646	–15.5%	–32.9%

(continued)

TABLE 2-3 *(continued)*

Expenditure	Age 55-64	Age 65-74	Age 75+
Healthcare	$3,825	45.8%	61.5%
Entertainment	$3,036	–7.1%	–37.8%
Cash contributions (to loved ones and charities)	$2,163	9.6%	48.3%
Apparel	$1,622	–0.7%	–34.8%

REMEMBER

Here are the highlights of what's shown in the data from Table 2-1:

>> Overall expenses per person decline significantly as do the vast majority of the individual expense categories, which are ranked in order of their overall amounts (at age 55–64).

>> Note how expenses drop even more later in retirement (age 75+). This decrease makes sense given that many folks downsize their housing and become less mobile. Notice the big drops in transportation and entertainment as well.

>> Later in retirement, apparel expenses drop. That's because most older retirees shop less and are more content to wear what they have rather than to keep buying more.

>> Spending on food declines due to eating out less. Spending on food consumed at home rises a little.

>> Healthcare spending per person goes up significantly, which is no big surprise.

>> Cash donations went up, too, especially at age 75+. This makes sense, because as folks with excess money approach the end of their lives, they become more interested and motivated to give away money to loved ones and favorite charities.

It's also useful to look at the household level changes in expenditures (see Table 2-2) that aren't adjusted for changes in household size, because they reflect an average or typical household's changes in expenditures over the retirement years.

TABLE 2-2   ## Household Changes in Expenditures by Age Group

Expenditures	Age 55-64	Age 65-74	Age 75+
Total expenditures	$54,783	–24.4%	–42.1%
Housing	$17,611	–21.4%	–31.7%
Transportation	$9,377	–28.1%	–53.2%

Expenditures	Age 55-64	Age 65-74	Age 75+
Food	$6,357	–16.0%	–38.1%
At home	$3,711	–7.8%	–28.1%
Out	$2,646	–27.5%	–52.1%
Health care	$3,825	24.9%	15.4%
Entertainment	$3,036	–20.4%	–55.6%
Cash Contributions	$2,163	–6.0%	5.9%
Apparel	$1,622	–14.9%	–53.4%

REMEMBER

Consider these highlights from the data in Table 2-2:

>> Large, overall reductions occur in total expenditures and in most of the individual expense categories. These reductions raise an interesting issue for your planning purposes as a couple and for consideration of how your individual health and expected longevity affects your household's spending. If both you and your spouse have and expect to maintain excellent health, you should probably use the per person changes in spending from Table 2-1.

>> Note the bigger declines in housing expenses. Unlike food costs, for example, which are driven by the number of people in a consumer unit, housing costs are more fixed, so these bigger declines would be more typical of what an average retiree experiences. To realize these housing cost reductions, though, older retirees downsize their homes or take advantage of property tax breaks available through many towns and cities.

>> Although taxes weren't accurately captured in this survey, they clearly would have shown a significant reduction in the retirement years when most people earn far less income and are also paying much less in Social Security and Medicare taxes, which applies only to employment earnings.

Managing Your Expenses

Most folks do a decent job managing their expenses in retirement. After all, by the time people reach retirement, they have decades of experience managing their finances and spending. That said, people make mistakes and worry about things they shouldn't worry about while overlooking issues that they should have paid closer attention to. That's what this section is all about.

Bigger-picture issues

Before digging into specific expenditures, let's consider some overarching retirement spending issues and concerns. Here are the important points to keep in mind:

>> **After you retire and stop earning employment income, one of the cash outflows that should go away is saving more money.** Some folks early in retirement continue to effectively save by not using all the money coming in (for example, from Social Security, pensions, and so on). They scrimp and save and do without when they don't need to. If your retirement analysis shows that you don't need to save anymore, then don't!

>> **Throughout your retirement, you need to consider inflation.** When you examine your spending now or next year, remember that you're examining a snapshot or point in time. Over the years, most (but not all) items increase in price (3 percent per year is a good average to use, because that is what consumer price inflation in the U.S. has averaged over many years). So plan accordingly by considering not just your current spending but also your spending in the years and decades ahead.

>> **Remain optimistic about your retirement.** One study from a large accounting firm ominously warned that about 60 percent of middle-class retirees would probably run out of money if they maintained their preretirement lifestyles. Technically, that may be true, but an important detail the study failed to mention is that the vast majority of retirees spend less — in some cases quite a bit less — when they retire in comparison to their preretirement spending.

The sections that follow go through important expense categories, discuss what typically happens to retirees regarding those expenses, and offer money-saving opportunities.

Taxes

One fringe benefit of ceasing work and getting over the financial impact of losing that income is the associated and often dramatic reduction in income taxes — both federal and state — as well as in FICA (Social Security and Medicare) taxes and possibly local taxes. However, even though you're retired, some of your taxes may actually increase or stay the same. So keep close tabs on the following taxes:

>> **Taxes on Social Security benefits:** One tax issue worth paying close attention to in retirement is the triggering of taxes on Social Security benefits if your income exceeds particular thresholds. You also may get socked with

higher taxes if you begin collecting Social Security benefits before full retirement age and you're still earning income above a specific threshold. If you can reduce your income below the thresholds, you can save a lot on taxes. These issues are covered fully in Book 4, Chapter 4.

If you're working part time in retirement, you may want to consider contributing to a retirement account to reduce your taxable income. You can establish a Keogh plan to allow contributions from self-employment income.

TIP

When investing your money, be sure to pay close attention to your tax situation and select investments that match your tax status.

REMEMBER

>> **Property taxes:** If you're a homeowner, these taxes are a significant item. Many communities offer some seniors the ability to postpone property tax payments and offer reduced tax rates for lower-income seniors. To qualify, you typically have to present a copy of your completed Internal Revenue Service (IRS) Form 1040 each year. Here are the options of one town's property-tax assistance program for homeowners age 65 and older:

- **Abatement (reduction):** This option is available for those with annual household incomes of less than $49,000 (which consists of all income, including Social Security benefits and investment income) and a net worth of no more than $1 million, including equity in your home. This particular town abates 75 percent of a senior's property tax on the first $400,000 of assessed housing value for those with incomes of less than $32,000 annually and abates 60 percent for those with incomes between $32,000 and $49,000.

- **Deferment:** Those with incomes of less than $125,000 per year may defer property taxes (on the first $400,000 of assessed value) for up to 15 years. Each year, the taxes deferred as well as the interest at a reasonable rate (recently 4 percent) accumulate as a lien on the property.

- **Freeze:** To take advantage of this option, you must be a town resident for 10 years and have an annual income of less than $100,000. This option of the program allows for an interest-free deferral for up to 15 years on future increases in the property taxes on as much as $800,000 of assessed property value. A lien is placed against the property for the amount owed. The amount of taxes paid in the year prior to application must still be paid annually after the freeze.

Housing

Many retirees are able to enjoy and benefit from the fact that they no longer have mortgage payments in retirement. To manage and even reduce your housing expenses during retirement, you have several options (check out Book 6, Chapter 1 for more in-depth discussion about your options for housing during retirement):

TIP

>> **You may choose to downsize or move to a lower-cost area.** If you live in a high-cost urban or suburban area, after the kids are grown and out in the world, you may choose not to pay higher property taxes and have so much money tied up in a home.

Before you call the moving company, don't resign yourself to being forced to move for financial reasons. If you want to stay in your current home because you like the community, neighbors, local service providers, and area amenities, see what property tax reduction/deferment programs your town or city offers to seniors.

>> **You may reduce household expenditures for services.** With more free time in retirement, you may be able to reduce some expenditures for services such as a gardener, housekeeper, and household maintenance and repair worker.

WARNING

Don't underestimate the expertise or physical demands of particular jobs. Servicing your furnace unit may not sound like rocket science, but you can damage the unit or hurt yourself if you don't know what you're doing. Likewise, climbing up a ladder to clean out your gutters may sound like an easy way to save some money until you fall off and break some bones.

>> **You may consider taking on a tenant to bring in rental income.** A tenant can help you reduce some of your housing expense burdens. Bringing in a tenant is easier and less intrusive if the proposed rental quarters have a separate entrance and are completely separate from the rest of your living quarters.

REMEMBER

It may be worth making a modest investment to configure your living space to allow for such a rental unit. Just be sure not to undermine the property's value by changing it in such a way that makes the home unappealing to potential buyers. Consult some local real estate agents on your proposed project. Also, be sure to check local zoning laws, building codes, and community association rules for limits on renting part of your home.

Renters and owners with mortgages face different issues, unless the renters have a rent-controlled apartment they're able and willing to stay in for the long term. The long-term downside to renting is that your rent is exposed to inflation. Don't allow the late 2000s real estate market softness and decline fool you — rents do rise over the years and decades. Here are some strategies for reducing your housing costs as a long-term renter in retirement:

>> **Consider shared housing.** Living with others can improve your social life and reduce your costs. Check with your local senior center or senior's group for information, ideas, and contacts.

>> **If you're a lower-income senior, explore rent-subsidized senior housing.** The government gives funding directly to apartment owners who lower the rents they charge to low-income tenants. The U.S. Department of Housing and Urban Development can help you in your search for a rent-subsidized apartment and with understanding the income restrictions to qualify. (Visit www.hud.gov/apps/section8 for more information.) Low-rent apartments are available for senior citizens and people with disabilities as well as for families and individuals. Your state or locality may also have additional programs providing affordable housing to seniors. Many localities have an Area Office on Aging to help seniors identify programs for which they're eligible.

Utilities and communication

When energy prices seemed to be spiraling out of control and were ever higher in the mid– to late 2000s, folks on relatively low, fixed incomes — as some seniors are — really felt the pinch. Thankfully and predictably, that bubble broke and prices came back down.

TIP

Changing the energy and communication sources you're using in your home or car isn't a simple matter, of course, for everyone. However, that doesn't mean you're powerless to reduce your utility bills. Here are some steps you can take:

>> **Get an energy audit of your home.** Especially if you've lived in your home for many years, odds are it's not as energy efficient as it could be. Contact your local utility company for an energy audit, which you generally can have done for free. Many local utilities offer special incentive programs for energy upgrades.

>> **Improve your home's insulation.** If you own an old home, you probably can improve its insulation at a modest cost.

>> **Take advantage of tax credits.** A number of state-specific and federal tax credits are available for energy-efficiency improvements. For up-to-date information, check out the Database of State Incentives for Renewables & Efficiency website (www.dsireusa.org), which includes links to all state-based and federal incentives.

>> **Upgrade energy-wasting appliances.** You'll have to spend some money on these upgrades, but the payback from energy savings can be quite rapid for the worst energy-guzzling appliances.

>> **Reduce your garbage bill.** You may be able to reduce the money you spend on garbage services. By recycling more of your household's trash at your local recycling center and creating a compost pile for biodegradable trash, you may be able to reduce your garbage bill. Comparison shop for sanitation services.

>> **Slim your water bill.** Unless you have a well on your property, you have a water bill that you can lower. Consider taking water-saving actions, such as installing water flow regulators in shower heads and faucets. If you buy bottled water or have it delivered, consider instead installing a water purification system.

>> **Address telephone costs.** Over the years and decades, phone service costs have declined. However, some folks can get carried away with the increasing numbers of communication devices, including cellphones and smartphones. Be careful about dropping your home phone service and simply going with cellphone service. Cellphone service tends to have less reliable connections and may not be as easily referenced by local emergency responders when you call 911. Landline service immediately communicates your physical location when you place a 911 call.

For sure, having a simple and easy-to-use cellphone can be helpful when you're out and about. To minimize cellphone costs, consider one of the increasing numbers of service providers that charge you only for the calls you make and receive as opposed to a monthly fixed-rate plan that offers a large number of calling minutes you may not come close to using.

>> **Try to bundle your television and Internet with your phone bill.** Most folks find that service providers in their area offer both of these services along with others like phone service. Bundling with one provider can lead to the best deals and pricing. Just be careful not to get locked into a long-term plan you may not be happy with or that has hefty early-termination fees.

Food

During retirement, you want to manage how much you spend on food. To avoid spending too much, try the following suggestions to help you save money:

>> **Prepare more meals at home.** With the extra free time afforded by leaving behind full-time work, some folks find that they have the time and energy to prepare more meals at home. An added benefit of eating at home is that you can eat healthier and plan ahead. For example, you can cook a casserole and then eat the leftovers for a couple of meals.

>> **Buy store brands.** The quality and ingredients of store brands are often the same as higher-cost name brands at a much lower price.

>> **Eat out for lunch.** Prices usually are less expensive than for dinner.

>> **Eat out early for dinner.** If you eat dinner earlier, you can qualify for early-bird dinner specials.

» **When you eat out, make two meals out of your purchase.** Most regular servings in restaurants are large enough that you can eat the leftovers at home. Ask the server to put half of your meal in a take-out container; you can eat it for lunch or dinner the next day.

» **Order off the seniors menu.** Some restaurants offer a discounted seniors menu wlth smaller portions.

» **Split your meal with a friend.** Some restaurants serve gigantean portions, so ask your server for an additional plate and split your meal with a friend or loved one.

» **Order take-out.** If you enjoy someone else preparing your food without spending a fortune, pick up your meal from your favorite local restaurants.

Transportation

Another benefit of leaving the workforce and retiring is the elimination of work-related transportation expenses. You no longer have a commute and the associated expenses, including gasoline, maintenance, tolls and public transit fees, parking charges, and so on. Your car should last longer, too, because you likely won't drive as much.

You can further reduce your expenses related to transportation by possibly reducing the number of cars you own. Because you no longer have the burden of daily commutes, you may even be able to make do without a car at all and rely on public transportation. When you need a car for a weekend or other excursion, you can just rent one. Some areas also have rent-by-the-hour car rental services for local driving. Getting rid of your car also reduces your auto insurance expenses.

Personal care and fashion

Spending on clothing, shoes, jewelry, dry cleaning, and other amenities also takes a tumble when folks retire from jobs, especially those who worked in more formal office settings. You'll also likely spend less on haircuts and salon treatments.

TIP

Don't skimp on taking care of your health and being physically active. Consider joining a health club or gym that's user friendly for folks of your age and interests. Of course, you don't need a gym membership to be active. Walking, hiking, and other outdoor activities are low cost and generally healthy. Just be careful about falls, which become increasingly common as we age.

Travel and fun

One aspect of retirement you may be looking forward to is the opportunity to travel more. However, be aware that traveling and entertainment aren't cheap. Consider what type of person you are and how your recreation desires may change once you retire.

You may end up spending a bit more on travel and entertainment during your early retirement years compared with later in your retirement years. Most folks don't travel much later in retirement due to reduced mobility and increased health issues. Keep that in mind in the earlier years of retirement and be sure to take advantage of your mobility and money while you're able.

TIP

During your retirement years, you can save money on entertainment and travel expenses in a couple of easy ways:

>> **Travel during off-peak times.** You probably have more flexibility as a retiree, so you can travel during the nonbusy times and take advantage of cheaper airfares, hotel rooms, and car rental fees.

>> **Benefit from reduced senior prices.** You can usually find discounted senior rates at movie theaters, hotels, public golf courses, and other venues. Don't be shy about asking for a senior discount. If you'd rather not inquire when you're at a venue, call in advance and ask about senior rates and who qualifies.

Healthcare

Most people end up spending more on healthcare during retirement. The average American over the age of 65 spends about $7,000 per year, and costs keep rising faster than the overall rate of inflation. In your elderly years, even if you remain in good health, you'll probably visit the doctor more and undergo more frequent routine and preventative testing. You also may be unpleasantly surprised at the increase in how much you spend on prescription drugs and dental and vision care visits and procedures.

Insurance

Being able to retire financially is a major milestone. The fact that you're sufficiently financially independent should enable you to reduce and eliminate some insurance, including life and disability insurance. *Note:* One insurance you may need more of is umbrella or excess liability coverage (see Book 3, Chapter 4 for more). As your net worth has grown over the years, your need for this coverage grows, too. This insurance protects your assets against lawsuits and other liability claims arising from your home and cars.

Subscriptions

Make sure you review all your subscriptions to magazines, newspapers, cable TV and radio, music- and video-streaming apps, and any other kinds of subscription-based services you may have signed up for. You should review these at least quarterly and make sure you're still actually using them and that you still find them worth the expense.

Children and grandchildren

Having kids grow up and move out of the nest dramatically reduces expenditures related to your kids. Think about all the money parents spend on diapers, day care, toys, sports, music lessons, activities, braces, and so on. If you had kids later in life, or have a special needs child, you may still have some expenses into your senior years. The same may hold true with helping to pay off your kid's student loans. So factor these expenses into your financial plan.

REMEMBER

Your grown children and their offspring (your grandkids) may need or want your financial assistance sometime during your retirement years. If you can afford to help them, consider doing so. But be mindful of keeping them from taking responsibility for their own lives; if they learn that they can always get more money from the First Bank of Mom and Dad, they'll always come around.

Chapter **3**

Guiding Investments and Distributions in Retirement

As you approach and enter retirement, you'll have plenty of decisions and issues to deal with regarding your investments. Although some of these are straightforward, others can be quite complex and stressful because you're making decisions that are irrevocable and have long-term consequences.

This chapter should help you minimize that stress and maximize the financial results from these important decisions. This chapter explains how to adjust your investment mix over the years, estimate your investment income, keep your portfolio in balance, assess what roles annuities should play in your retirement plans, choose among your pension options, and plot your retirement account withdrawal strategies.

Guiding Your Investments through Retirement

As you approach retirement, you'll likely need to assess how to live off your investments, such as by receiving the investment income from your portfolio. To help you figure out how to manage your allocations and figure out how much you need to live comfortably, the following sections come to the rescue.

Estimating your Investment Income

Most near-retirees are at least a little frightened at the prospect of losing their employment income and having to live off their investments and monthly benefit checks (such as Social Security and their pension, if they're lucky to have one). Even if you don't have to withdraw money from your financial assets at the beginning of your retirement, you may need to later.

REMEMBER

Be careful to understand that your investment income may vary. For example, in a severe economic downturn (like the one in the late 2000s), stock dividends and bond interest may be reduced, so give yourself some wiggle room.

Making the calculations

When estimating your investment income, make sure you examine your current investment holdings to determine about how much annual income (not capital gains distributions) those investments are throwing off. Tally that income with your other income to see whether you'll have enough to meet your anticipated annual spending desires or needs. *Note:* Most folks don't feel comfortable tapping into their investment principal, so they seek to use the income from their investments. If you have sufficient assets and those assets are properly diversified, you may be able leave your investment principal intact.

The good news: You can figure out all the numbers and estimate how much money you have by using the relatively simple guidelines, such as the 4 percent rule, discussed in Book 4, Chapter 2. These guidelines can help you determine how much of your assets you can safely use each year and have confidence that your money will last as long as you do.

Determining whether to modify your investments to earn more income now

WARNING

Some folks are so opposed to using their investment principal that they're willing to dramatically overhaul their portfolios to be able to live off the income for a significant number of years. Generally, this isn't a good idea.

Consider, for example, the case of a couple who are insistent that they live off investment income. To be able to do so, their portfolio would have to produce about 8.5 percent investment income per year. Consistently achieving that level of income would require them to invest nearly everything in junk bond funds. Doing that would enable them to meet their income objectives in the short term, but over the long term, their portfolio would have no real growth potential.

You may, however, want to modify your holdings if you're coming close to realizing your investment income desires. For example, suppose that you have about 65 percent in stocks and 35 percent in bonds. You crunch some numbers and realize that a 50/50 mix will boost your investment income enough to close the gap. As long as that mix makes sense given your overall goals and situation, making a modest shift like this may be a good idea. But the trade-off is that reaching for more current income will likely reduce the longer-term appreciation potential of your portfolio.

Rebalancing your investments

Rebalancing is a rather clever system that disciplines you to buy low and sell high. It forces you to get your portfolio's asset allocation back to where it should be. For example, suppose that you had a 50/50 mix between stocks and bonds. And then suppose that stocks do poorly while bonds do well, so now you've got a 40/60 mix with bonds now in the majority. Rebalancing would have you sell enough bonds and buy more stocks to get back to the original 50/50 mix. The following sections show you why balancing is so beneficial and then illustrate its success with an example.

Understanding the benefits of rebalancing

Now, you may ask why anyone would take money from an investment that's doing well (bonds) and put some of that into an investment that's doing poorly (stocks). The reasons are twofold:

» **It helps get your investment plan back on track.** You developed an asset allocation plan and should stick to it unless you have a compelling reason — such as a change in your personal situation — to alter your plan.

» **It allows you to take advantage of the inevitable rebound that stocks should eventually enjoy.** Asset classes like stocks that suffer setbacks don't stay down forever.

Here are some important tips to make the most of and be smart about rebalancing:

» **Beware of tax consequences.** If you're selling investments outside retirement accounts and those sales trigger realized profits, you'll owe taxes on those profits. That's why rebalancing is best done with money inside retirement accounts where you don't need to be concerned with tax consequences on transactions.

>> **Beware of transaction costs.** When you buy and sell certain investments, such as individual stocks and bonds, you may incur fees.

With most exchange-traded funds and no-load mutual funds, this isn't an issue, but it will cost you to trade most other investments. That doesn't mean you shouldn't rebalance if you have to pay some transaction costs; it simply means you should fully understand trading fees before you take action. You may want to rebalance a little less frequently than you would if no transaction costs are involved.

>> **Find ways to rebalance by not making unnecessary trades.** You can avoid transaction and tax costs through rebalancing with distributed investment income (interest and dividends), new contributions, and planned withdrawals.

>> **Select a sensible rebalancing period/trigger.** Numerous studies have shown that the benefits don't outweigh the costs when rebalancing is done frequently — such as monthly and quarterly. Those studies suggest that the best approach is to review your portfolio at least one or two times per year and rebalance if your investment allocations have moved off base by at least 5 percent. Say, for example, that you have 60 percent in stocks and 40 percent in bonds. If the stock allocation gets to 55 or 65 percent or the bond allocation gets to 35 or 45 percent, you should rebalance.

Taking a look at a rebalancing example

Consider the following example that shows rebalancing in action: Suppose that you currently have $100,000 invested for your retirement in an asset allocation of 60 percent stocks and 40 percent bonds. And further suppose that over the next two years the stocks drop 50 percent in value while your bonds produce a total return of 10 percent. Table 3-1 shows what will happen to your asset allocation in the absence of any changes from you.

TABLE 3-1   ## Allocation Changes

	Starting Mix	Mix after Two Years
Stocks	$60,000	$30,000
Bonds	$40,000	$44,000

As you can see from Table 3-1, after two years, instead of having 60 percent in stocks and 40 percent in bonds, you now have about 41 percent in stocks and about 59 percent in bonds. To return to your original chosen allocation, you would need to move about $14,400 out of bonds and into stocks. See Table 3-2 to see what the numbers would look like after the rebalance.

TABLE 3-2

Allocations after Rebalancing

	Starting Mix	Mix after Two Years	Mix after Rebalancing
Stocks	$60,000	$30,000	$44,400
Bonds	$40,000	$44,000	$29,600

Looking Closer at Annuities

As discussed in Book 1, Chapter 7, you can channel contributions into numerous types of retirement accounts. By directing money into such accounts, you may derive significant tax benefits.

Annuities provide an additional vehicle for saving and investing money in a tax-sheltered fashion. And compared with traditional retirement accounts like IRAs and 401(k)s, annuities offer a unique way of tapping the money within them through *annuitizing* (receiving monthly payments).

Annuities: A cross between a retirement account and insurance

Annuities are a bit of a quirky investment vehicle in that they have similarities to some retirement accounts but also have some elements of insurance. Although annuities don't offer upfront tax breaks for contributions, the investment earnings accumulate without taxation, as they do in retirement accounts, until withdrawn.

REMEMBER

This is how the insurance feature of an annuity works: If the annuity holder passes away and the annuity account value is lower than the original amount invested, the beneficiaries of the annuity get back the original investment amount.

Here's an example to illustrate: Suppose that Alan invested $100,000 in 2007 in a variable annuity (discussed in the following section) and directed much of the money into stock mutual funds. His stock fund investments dropped significantly along with the rest of the global stock markets during the late 2000s recession and bear market. When his investments were beginning to bounce back in 2010, Alan died. His annuity's account value was $85,000, or $15,000 less than he invested. In this case, his beneficiaries get $100,000 from the annuity, not just $85,000.

Contributing in your working years

If you've maximized contributions to retirement accounts through your employer and an IRA, and you want to put away more money to compound without taxation during your working years, you can consider an annuity. You have several options when investing in annuities:

>> **Variable annuity:** With this type, you may invest in mutual funds inside the annuity.

>> **Fixed indexed annuity:** This type of annuity credits interest to the account annually, but the interest is determined by the return of one or more investment indexes, such as a major stock market index.

>> **Fixed annuity:** This type of annuity pays you a set rate of interest, which is typically adjusted annually at the discretion of the annuity issuer.

People who have been comfortable with investing in mutual funds should be fine using a variable annuity. On the other hand, if you prefer knowing your return in advance and are willing to accept a likely lower long-term return in exchange for eliminating the downside risk, consider a fixed annuity. A fixed indexed annuity is sort of a hybrid of the two. It has the potential to earn more than a fixed annuity when the market indexes you selected have a good year, and it won't lose value as a variable annuity will when the indexes do poorly. Your account will have a 0 percent return when the indexes do poorly. In other words, you're giving up some of the upside to eliminate some of the downside.

WARNING

During your working years, be careful not to assume that contributing more money into annuities is always better. Some folks contribute more to their retirement accounts than makes good financial and tax sense. For example, it may not make sense for a taxpayer who's temporarily in a low tax bracket (or owing no tax at all) to contribute to retirement accounts. That person could end up paying a much higher tax rate when receiving the investment earnings in retirement. Similarly, folks who already have a large estate and have significant money inside retirement accounts that could get walloped by estate and income taxes upon their passing should be cautious about investing in an annuity. Few people, of course, have this perhaps enviable "problem."

TIP

When in doubt, especially if you have reason to believe you should scale back on retirement account contributions, consult with a competent financial or tax adviser who works for an hourly fee and doesn't sell products or manage money. You can also refer to the latest edition of Eric Tyson's *Personal Finance For Dummies* (Wiley) for more details.

Annuitizing in your retirement years

With fixed, fixed indexed, or variable annuities, you can *annuitize* the assets. In other words, you can convert them into a monthly income stream during your retirement years. When you annuitize, you're entering into an agreement to receive monthly payments in exchange for the total balance in the account.

Under this agreement, you receive monthly payments in one of the following ways:

>> **Variable payments:** The monthly income you receive varies with the performance of the investments.

>> **Fixed payments:** Under this option, you receive the same amount per month for a certain period of time.

>> **A combination:** With this option, a portion of your payment is fixed and a portion can be variable.

A few annuities offer monthly payments that are indexed for inflation. The trade-off with an inflation adjusted payment is that the initial payment is much lower than for a fixed payment annuity.

TIP

If you currently don't have money in an annuity and are approaching retirement, you can immediately put funds into a *lifetime income annuity,* also called an *immediate annuity.* In other words, with your contribution, you immediately annuitize and begin receiving monthly payments. As with annuitizing an existing annuity, lifetime income annuities can provide fixed, variable, or inflation-adjusted monthly income. The choice is up to you.

REMEMBER

When you annuitize, you generally have a lot of payment options. The options may vary a bit by annuity provider and by state, but the following are the most common:

>> **Period certain:** In this case, you choose a certain number of years (for example, a minimum of 5 years to a maximum of 30 years) over which you're guaranteed to receive monthly payments. Obviously, the longer the period over which you want to get payments, the lower those payments will be. In the

event that you pass away before the end of the designated period, your beneficiary receives your remaining payments.

>> **Lifetime annuity:** With this option, you receive a monthly check for the rest of your life. Payments cease when you pass away.

>> **Lifetime annuity with period certain:** This option provides payments for life, but you're also guaranteed payments for a particular period of time (for example, between 5 and 30 years). If you pass away before the completion of the period of certain payments, your designated beneficiary receives your remaining payments.

>> **Joint and survivor annuity:** In this case, monthly payments continue as long as you or your designated annuitant (for example, your spouse) are alive. You have options for the survivor's payments. You may continue payments at 100 percent, 75 percent, or 50 percent of your amount. The higher the percentage you desire, the lower your initial payments will be, however.

Examining the newest annuity

The newest type of annuity is the *longevity annuity,* also known as the *deferred income annuity.* A variation of it is the *qualified longevity annuity contract (QLAC).*

In a longevity annuity, you give a lump sum to an insurer today, and the insurer promises at some point in the future to pay you a fixed annual stream of income for life, no matter how long you live. You're told when you make the deposit exactly the amount of the annual lifetime payments.

In a typical longevity annuity, you make a deposit with the insurer at age 60 or 65. You decide not to begin receiving income payments until years later, perhaps 70, 75, or even 80. Or you can make the deposit at age 50 and have the income begin at 65 or 70.

Some people like longevity annuities, because having one means you never can outlive your income. They also provide a form of inflation protection. When your pension or regular annuity isn't indexed for inflation, it loses its purchasing power over the years. The longevity annuity can kick in and restore your purchasing power. With the longevity annuity, your financial risks of just earning low investment returns and living a long life are transferred to the insurer instead of resting with you. Of course, you pay for this risk transfer "insurance."

In a standard longevity annuity, if you pass away before the income payments begin or you receive enough income to recover your initial investment, your estate or heirs don't receive anything additional from the insurer. You can avoid this disadvantage by selecting a return of premium feature, but doing so reduces your annual income payments.

A QLAC is a variation of a longevity annuity. In 2014, the IRS issued rules that said when computing the required minimum distributions from Individual Retirement Accounts (discussed in Book 1, Chapter 7), QLACs aren't included in the IRA balance. The total QLACs that qualify for this treatment can't exceed the lower of $125,000 or 20 percent of your IRA balances.

Choosing Your Pension Options

A *pension plan* certainly simplifies the process of saving for retirement. With such a plan, the employer puts away money on your behalf and invests it on your behalf. Couldn't get much easier than that, could it?

Some employees, especially those who work for larger organizations, earn pension benefits. Slowly but surely, however, such plans are being phased out and replaced by plans like 401(k)s where the employee must elect to save their own money from their paycheck and direct the investment of it over the years. Head to Book 1, Chapter 7 for more on 401(k)s.

REMEMBER

If you're fortunate enough to have a pension plan, you want to make the right decisions to receive distributions during your senior years. With pension plans, you typically face two important decisions:

>> You have to decide whether to take the pension as a monthly retirement payment or a lump sum distribution.

>> Those who opt for the monthly pension payment usually have a second decision among several payment plan options.

Let's start with the first and biggest issue: lump sum or monthly payments.

Selecting between a lump sum or monthly payments

The first question you should contemplate when considering your pension options is whether to take a lump sum payment or monthly payments. With a *lump sum payment*, you get one large payment, and with *monthly payments,* you get a set amount per month over an extended period of time. (Some pensions increase the monthly payments for inflation; this increase is known as a *cost of living allowance*, or COLA.)

Like the sticker price on a house, a lump sum sounds like a big number. However, pension plans offering a lump sum option are generally structured to provide about the same expected value to employees. That's why it's usually difficult to decide based on financial factors; the decision hinges more on qualitative considerations — for example, your desire to control and invest the money yourself and have money left over for heirs should you pass away prematurely in retirement.

WARNING

In making this important decision, beware of financial planners' and brokers' advice when they aren't paid hourly or with a fixed fee. If you take a monthly pension, there's no lump sum for them to manage.

Taking stock of your situation

When making the decision between a lump sum and a monthly payment, start by surveying your progress with retirement planning and determining how much risk you can take with your pension money. Prospective retirees should conduct a retirement analysis to determine how the standard of living likely to be provided by their assets compares with their expected retirement expenses.

As an example, consider the case of Walter and Susan. Walter was 56 years old and ready to retire from his employer of the past 27 years. He had to decide whether to take a $20,000 annual pension, with no cost-of-living allowance (COLA) and a 50 percent survivor's annuity, or a lump sum of $265,000.

The couple surveyed their finances, and they seemed to have quite a bit of money earmarked for retirement already. They had expected Social Security benefits totaling $2,650 per month at age 62, Susan's pension of $1,500 monthly (with a COLA), and their traditional retirement savings plans — his was worth $255,000 and she had about $70,000 in hers. However, the standard of living that these assets could provide was only about 50 percent of their current annual combined salaries of $130,000.

Walter did an analysis through the investment company managing his firm's 401(k), and the results suggested that they had enough to retire. However, this presumed that he worked to age 60, and Walter didn't recall specific numbers detailing how much wiggle room he might have. Because he was trying to call it quits by age 56, he needed to update the analysis.

The bottom line was that the income from Walter's pension was of great importance. If they took the lump sum and managed it badly or simply had bad investment luck, it would affect their living standard. The good news: They didn't live lavishly. Their modest ranch home had no mortgage, and Walter's long and costly commute would vanish when he retired.

Walter's $20,000 annual pension payment is greater than the expected income from the lump sum would be for about the first 18 years of Walter's retirement (when he reached age 74). So they determined that the monthly payments would make more sense for their situation.

Considering key issues regarding your pension decision

REMEMBER

After you take stock of your financial situation, you have a few additional key considerations to think about when weighing a pension versus a lump sum. Keep these in mind as you make your decision:

>> **How adept are you with managing money?** A major benefit of a pension is that the investment responsibility rests with professional pension managers who are far less likely to make dramatic moves. The best way to answer this question is to reflect on your past experience managing money. If your track record is problematic or you simply lack such experience, lean toward the monthly pension and steer clear of the lump sum.

Walter's investment management history (see the preceding section) showed evidence of being emotionally driven. He sold most of his stock holdings when he was worried about the economy and gas prices. He also admitted to getting jumpy the closer he got to retiring.

>> **What's your health situation and family longevity record?** If you have a major medical problem or reason to believe that your genes destine you to fewer golden years, one advantage of the lump sum is that you get all the money to use and use sooner if you choose — and you can leave the remainder to your heirs. A monthly pension lasts only as long as you do (with reduced benefits as long as your spouse survives after you).

>> **How comfortable will you be tapping into principal?** Many retirees are fine with living off investment income, but it's psychologically difficult for most to use principal. Thus, pension checks, which are more comfortably spent, can indeed provide a higher standard of living.

>> **What's the safety of your pension benefits?** Retirees often fear that a pension benefit also may last only as long as a company does. But you don't have to worry; pensions are backed by the Pension Benefit Guaranty Corporation (PBGC), an independent government agency.

Table 3-3 shows the 2018 annual and monthly maximum PBGC benefit guarantees for retirees from age 75 to 45. The maximum amount is lower for benefits commencing at ages below 65, reflecting the fact that younger retirees receive more monthly pension checks over a longer expected remaining life span. The maximum amount is higher for benefits commencing at ages above 65, reflecting the fact that older retirees receive fewer monthly pension checks over their expected remaining life spans.

TABLE 3-3   ## Maximum PBGC Benefit Guarantees

Age	Monthly Maximum	Monthly Joint and 50% Survivor Maximum
45	$1,355.11	$1,219.60
46	$1,463.52	$1,317.17
47	$1,571.93	$1,414.74
48	$1,680.34	$1,512.31
49	$1,788.75	$1,609.88
50	$1,897.16	$1,707.44
51	$2,005.57	$1,805.01
52	$2,113.98	$1,902.58
53	$2,222.38	$2,000.14
54	$2,330.79	$2,097.71
55	$2,439.20	$2,195.28
56	$2,656.02	$2,390.42
57	$2,872.84	$2,585.56
58	$3,089.66	$2,780.69
59	$3,306.47	$2,975.82
60	$3,523.29	$3,170.96
61	$3,902.72	$3,512.45
62	$4,282.16	$3,853.94
63	$4,661.59	$4,195.43
64	$5,041.02	$4,536.92
65	$5,420.45	$4,878.41
66	$5,962.50	$5,366.25

Age	Monthly Maximum	Monthly Joint and 50% Survivor Maximum*
67	$6,558.74	$5,902.87
68	$7,263.40	$6,537.06
69	$8,076.47	$7,268.82
70	$8,997.95	$8,098.16
71	$10,493.99	$9,444.59
72	$11,990.04	$10,791.04
73	$13,486.08	$12,137.47
74	$14,982.12	$13,483.91
75	$16,478.17	$14,830.35

Both spouses the same age.

As you can see from the table, Walter (from the preceding section's example) is covered. His $20,000 annual pension payments are safe under the PBGC. However, pessimists who feel the PBGC is woefully underfunded would argue that he may take a haircut should his employer fail in the years ahead.

TECHNICAL STUFF

PBGC is a federal corporation created under the Employee Retirement Income Security Act (ERISA). It currently guarantees payment of basic pension benefits earned by 44 million American workers and retirees participating in over 26,000 private-sector defined-benefit pension plans. The agency receives no funds from general tax revenues. Operations are financed largely by insurance premiums paid by companies that sponsor pension plans and investment returns.

Deciding among monthly payment options

If you opt for a monthly check, some plans offer different options that basically differ from one another the way that investments do in terms of risk and return.

REMEMBER

Here's a rundown of the most common options:

>> **The 100 percent joint and survivor option:** The "safest" option, with the lowest payment, is the *100 percent joint and survivor option*. This payment continues as long as either the pensioner or his or her spouse is still living. This option makes sense for risk-averse retirees who are dependent on the pension check (and perhaps aren't in the best of health) and whose spouses are also dependent on that pension check.

>> **The two-thirds joint and survivor plan:** The *two-thirds joint and survivor plan* is intermediate in risk and payment amount. With this plan, after the death of the pensioner, the survivor receives two-thirds of the pension amount paid to the pensioner before his or her passing.

>> **The single-life option:** The riskiest option but the one that maximizes payments now is the *single-life option.* This option makes payments only as long as the pensioner is living. You should select this option only if you're in good health, have plenty of assets, and your spouse could afford to live without the pension check.

TIP

After you decide you want a monthly check instead of a lump sum, don't automatically take the pension offered by your employer. You may find a better deal from an insurance company annuity. For instance, you can take the lump sum from your employer and use the funds to buy an annuity. Find out the monthly check you would receive from some insurance annuities purchased with the lump sum that you're eligible for. Compare those with the monthly payments offered by your employer. Before opting for an insurance annuity, however, keep financial security in mind. An insurance annuity is backed only by the insurer and perhaps a limited guarantee from a state insurance fund. Your employer annuity is backed by both the pension fund and the PBGC.

Eyeing Withdrawal Strategies for Your Investment Accounts

To make the most of your money, you should understand the rules and your options regarding withdrawing money from various accounts, both retirement and regular, in your golden years. This section provides some suggestions and tips for you to keep in mind regarding your investment accounts.

If you haven't already done so, be sure to read Book 1, Chapter 7, which discusses the rules, early withdrawal penalties, and required distributions that apply to retirement accounts. Book 4, Chapter 2 covers issues pertaining to how much of your nest egg you could spend annually.

Here are some additional and general tips to keep in mind regarding tapping your investment accounts:

>> **Tap nonretirement account money first.** All other things being equal, it's generally better to tap your nonretirement holdings first — if you'll experience less of a tax bite by doing so. However, don't assume that you'll pay more taxes

to tap money inside retirement accounts. That may not be the case if some of that money already has been taxed and if selling nonretirement assets would trigger a big tax bill.

REMEMBER

An exception is when your nonretirement accounts are invested to earn much higher returns than your retirement accounts, especially when the returns in the nonretirement accounts will be taxed at favorable long-term capital gains rates. When the nonretirement accounts earn 4 percent or more annually than the retirement accounts, it's better to tap the retirement accounts first.

» **Let tax-free accounts, such as Roth IRAs, compound as long as possible.** Spend from your other accounts before tapping a Roth IRA. You'll maximize your long-term returns by keeping more money in accounts that provide for tax-free accumulation and withdrawal of money.

» **Tap your nonretirement accounts efficiently.** Sell investments with *paper losses* (those that have gone down in value versus their purchase price) first. Next, sell assets that will incur the lowest tax bill as a percentage of their value. These steps defer taxes as long as possible and maximize the amount of after-tax wealth available during retirement.

» **Understand bigger-picture tax issues.** In addition to income taxes, you may have estate tax issues to consider regarding which of your assets you should use. Spend the money to consult with a competent tax adviser as needed.

» **Use your money!** Too often, retirees who were good savers during their working years have great difficulty enjoying and using their money in retirement. See the discussion in Book 4, Chapter 2 to calm your fears and worries about possibly running out of money.

Chapter **4**

Making Your Best Choices under Social Security

Social Security is one of the least understood components of senior Americans' personal finances. Traditionally, income during retirement comes from a combination of three sources, often referred to as legs of a three-legged stool. The three legs are employer pensions, personal savings, and Social Security. Many Americans generally take the Social Security leg for granted and don't give it much thought.

However, this leg is quite important as you attempt to get a firm grasp on your personal finances. Too few people take the time to understand their options and the effects of their decisions about Social Security. And most financial advisers don't know enough about Social Security retirement benefits.

That's why this chapter is here: to help you get a better grasp of how Social Security can affect your finances. This chapter focuses on the important decisions involving Social Security retirement benefits and how you can make them. It explains how benefits are calculated, how to determine the best age at which to begin taking benefits, and how having a spouse may affect that decision. Although the benefits were once tax-free, an increasing number of beneficiaries pay taxes on their benefits each year. So this chapter talks about how to minimize income taxes on your Social Security benefits as well. You can also review how working while receiving Social Security benefits may cause your benefits to be reduced.

We also consider the financial condition of Social Security in this chapter. A number of people say they don't include Social Security benefits in their planning because they don't expect to receive any benefits. This chapter takes a look at the program's solvency and asks whether that's a reasonable way to view Social Security benefits and plan your retirement finances.

REMEMBER

Although the Social Security program also offers disability and survivor benefits, this chapter focuses primarily on retirement benefits with some attention paid to the survivor benefits of a spouse.

The Lowdown on Social Security

Most Americans think that Social Security simply is an automatic payment that begins at retirement and that they have little or no influence over the amount of the payment. In truth, Social Security is a fairly broad and complex program that provides retirement, survivor, and disability benefits. Retirement benefits are not automatic. You choose when they begin, and the choice affects the amount of benefits you receive. The amount of benefits you receive can also depend on your spouse's benefits. You may even be able to change your mind after starting to receive benefits.

The original intent of Social Security's retirement benefits was to provide a basic minimum income for retired workers. The lower your working years' income was, the greater the percentage of that income Social Security would replace. However in recent years, Social Security has undergone some changes, and employers are steadily eliminating *defined benefit pension plans* (those that guarantee a fixed monthly retirement payment for life), shifting the risk of saving and investing to employees. As a result, for many people, Social Security retirement benefits are the only source of retirement income that's both guaranteed and indexed for inflation.

EYEING THE OTHER SOCIAL SECURITY BENEFITS

Of the total amount of Social Security benefits paid each year, just over 60 percent are retirement benefits. The rest of the payments are for disability and survivor benefits.

To qualify for disability benefits, the worker must be completely disabled and unable to engage in any kind of employment. If a worker dies, the spouse or children may be eligible to receive survivor benefits. Children under age 18 (or 19, if full-time high-school students) generally are eligible for a monthly survivor benefit of up to 50 percent of the deceased's benefits. This chapter doesn't discuss these benefits — just be aware that these benefits are part of what you receive for your Social Security taxes.

REMEMBER

When you decide to begin receiving Social Security benefits determines the amount of the benefits. Other issues also decide the amount of your benefits. The key issues that determine the amount of benefits you receive are

>> The age at which you (and your spouse, if you're married) begin receiving retirement benefits

>> Whether your benefit payments are based on your work record or your spouse's

>> Whether you should change from receiving benefits based on your spouse's earnings record to benefits based on your earnings record, or even change the age at which you begin receiving benefits

>> Whether your marital status changed over the years — which could lead to additional choices

You (and other beneficiaries) have several opportunities to make choices about your retirement benefits, and the choices greatly influence the amount of payments you'll receive. Because Social Security continues for life, the choices you make can alter lifetime income by tens of thousands of dollars or more. The decisions you make also affect the amount of survivor benefits received by your spouse. Your financial security is enhanced if you search for ways to increase the guaranteed income from Social Security retirement benefits.

Many people believe decisions about Social Security retirement benefits are final, but that's not the case. You can change your mind and restart benefits in at least two situations (explored in this chapter). See the later sections "Understanding the choices for spousal benefits" and "Ensuring spouses are taken care of: Survivor's benefits."

Determining When You're Eligible for Benefits

You're eligible for Social Security retirement benefits after earning 40 work credits. You earn a *work credit* for each quarter year (three months) in which your earned income, subject to the Social Security tax, exceeded a minimum level. The minimum income level is indexed for inflation and was $1,120 for 2010. Therefore, you're entitled to retirement benefits if you work a total of at least 40 quarters (ten full years) during your lifetime in which you earn more than the minimum amount of income covered by Social Security.

After you know you're eligible to receive benefits, determining the level of benefits you use isn't quite as clear. The benefits are based on the highest 35 years of earnings before beginning benefits. The earnings from prior years are indexed for wage inflation as part of the computation. The result is a figure called *average indexed monthly earnings,* which is used to determine your benefits. This computation is quite technical, but this chapter covers the essentials. If you're interested in more of the fine details, go to the Social Security website (www.ssa.gov).

REMEMBER

What you need to know is that, in general, the higher the income you post for your highest 35 years of working, the higher your benefits will be. However, remember that there's a limit on the amount of income subject to Social Security taxes during your earning years. The benefit computation doesn't include income earned above that limit.

Even though higher income earners receive more benefits than lower income earners, the benefits for higher income earners replace a smaller proportion of earnings than for lower income earners. In other words, individuals with lower lifetime earnings have a higher replacement ratio than those with higher incomes. The *replacement ratio* is the percentage of working income that's paid in retirement benefits. Lower income retirees can receive Social Security benefits equal to about 90 percent of their preretirement income. The benefits of high income retirees are about 15 percent of preretirement income.

So how can you figure out when you can start receiving distributions from Social Security and what the benefits would be at different ages? The following two sections can help you make those determinations. If you're not at retirement age yet, your first resource is the annual earnings history report you receive from the Social Security Administration (SSA) or can find on the Social Security website. You also need to know what Uncle Sam has defined as the age you can retire to receive your full benefits.

Reviewing your earnings history

The SSA used to send everyone over age 24 with an earnings history an annual statement of estimated benefits a few months before his or her birthday. That practice was stopped as a cost-saving measure in 2011. In 2014, the SSA said it would mail statements to workers 25 or older in years when they attain ages that end in "0" or "5" (25, 30, 35, and so on). You can obtain a statement of your earnings online anytime by establishing a personal account at www.ssa.gov/myaccount. SSA is encouraging people to open online accounts and hopes to phase out paper statements and forms. The statement shows the earnings history in Social Security's records and estimates the retirement benefits that would be received if benefits were to begin at ages 62, 70, and full retirement age (which for most people still working is around age 66 or 67). Other information and estimates are also included.

REMEMBER

The earnings history in SSA's records is critical. If the history is incorrect, the benefits eventually paid to you will be incorrect. You have three years to correct an error in a year's earnings amount. You should at least review the recent earnings history every couple of years and decide whether it needs to be corrected. If you do need to correct it, you can contact SSA online or call the SSA at 800-772-1213 from 7 a.m. to 7 p.m. EST every business day. Or you can take your records to your local SSA office. To correct your earnings record, you need to give your name, Social Security number, the year or years which contain erroneous earnings, and the business name and address of your employer in those years. Helpful items to have are your W-2 forms (or tax returns if you're self-employed) for the years with incorrect earnings history.

REMEMBER

An examination of the earnings history can provide you with useful information to decide what may be a good age for you to retire. Most people have low earnings during the early years of their careers and mostly steadily rising earnings after that. Workers suffering extended layoffs, however, may have low income earning years at other times in their work histories. Remember that the benefits calculation uses only your highest 35 years of earnings, so working a few extra years could remove the lowest earning years from your "high 35" and ultimately increase your Social Security retirement benefits. And keep in mind that an increase in the benefits means a higher payment every month for the rest of your life, so it could amount to a large sum over time.

Defining when you can retire

The federal government has set the benchmark for retirement benefits, called *full retirement age* (FRA), or *normal retirement age*. If you begin retirement benefits at this age, you receive *full retirement benefits* (FRB), also known as *normal retirement benefits*. Begin benefits earlier, and you receive lower monthly benefits. Delay receiving benefits after FRA, and you receive a higher annual payment.

For many decades, FRA was 65. The reforms of 1983 phased in a higher FRA for anyone born after 1937 (anyone who turns 65 after 2002). When fully phased in, the schedule creates a new FRA of 67 for anyone born after 1959. Check out Table 4-1 for a schedule of FRAs to see where you fall.

TABLE 4-1 ## Age to Receive Full Social Security Benefits

Year of Birth	Full Retirement Age (FRA)
1937 or earlier	65
1938	65 and 2 months
1939	65 and 4 months
1940	65 and 6 months
1941	65 and 8 months
1942	65 and 10 months
1943–1954	66
1955	66 and 2 months
1956	66 and 4 months
1957	66 and 6 months
1958	66 and 8 months
1959	66 and 10 months
1960 and later	67

Note: If you were born on January 1 of any year, you should refer to the previous year. If you qualify for benefits as a survivor, your full retirement age may be different.

An annual limit exists on the amount of retirement benefits, regardless of preretirement income. The limit is indexed for inflation. So, for example, someone retiring at full retirement age in 2017 received no more than $2,687 monthly regardless of how high her lifetime earnings were. Someone retiring at age 70 in 2017 had a maximum monthly benefit of $3,538. (For comparison, the average monthly retirement benefit paid in 2009 was $1,328.)

REMEMBER

You can begin receiving Social Security retirement benefits as early as age 62, and you don't have to be retired from work to receive them. You can choose the starting date. However, note that if you begin the benefits before FRA, the amount of benefits will be reduced below the FRB. The benefit is reduced by a percentage for each month you begin benefits before FRA. The amount of the reduction depends on the year of your birth. The reduction in benefits for early retirement is a little complicated. The beneficiary loses a percentage of the full benefit for each month of the first 36 months before FRA, and a percentage of the full benefit for each additional month before FRA that benefits begin. We discuss this penalty in the later section "Noting How Working Reduces Benefits." Table 4-2 shows the reduced benefit for taking benefits at 62 for each age group.

TABLE 4-2   ## Full Retirement and Age 62 Benefit by Year of Birth

Year of Birth	Full (Normal) Retirement Age	Months between Age 62 and Full Retirement Age	At Age 62			
			A $1,000 Retirement Benefit Would Be Reduced to	The Retirement Benefit Is Reduced By	A $500 Spouse's Benefit Would Be Reduced to	The Spouse's Benefit Is Reduced By
1937 or earlier	65	36	$800	20.00%	$375	25.00%
1938	65 and 2 months	38	$791	20.83%	$370	25.83%
1939	65 and 4 months	40	$783	21.67%	$366	26.67%
1940	65 and 6 months	42	$775	22.50%	$362	27.50%
1941	65 and 8 months	44	$766	23.33%	$358	28.33%
1942	65 and 10 months	46	$758	24.17%	$354	29.17
1943–1954	66	48	$750	25.00%	$350	30.00
1955	66 and 2 months	50	$741	25.83%	$345	30.83%
1956	66 and 4 months	52	$733	26.67%	$341	31.67%
1957	66 and 6 months	54	$725	27.50%	$337	32.50%
1958	66 and 8 months	56	$716	28.33%	$333	33.33%
1959	66 and 10 months	58	$708	29.17%	$329	34.17%
1960 and later	67	60	$700	30.00%	$325	35.00%

Note: *If you were born on January 1, you will be treated as if born the previous year. If you were born on the first of the month, the benefit is figured as if your birthday was in the previous month. You must be at least 62 for the entire month to receive benefits. Percentages are approximate due to rounding. The maximum benefit for the spouse is 50% of the benefit the worker would receive at full retirement age. The % reduction for the spouse should be applied after the automatic 50% reduction. Percentages are approximate due to rounding.*

The law provides an incentive, known as *delayed retirement credits,* to delay receiving benefits after FRA. The credits are a rate of increase in your benefits for each month you postpone receiving benefits, and the rate of increase depends on the year you were born. So your age and the number of months you delay receiving benefits determine how much benefits increase when you wait. A third factor is the salary you receive if you continue to work before receiving benefits. Because your highest 35 years of earnings are used to calculate benefits, working more years may increase your FRB if later higher-earning years push lower-earning years out of the top 35. Table 4-3 shows the rate at which FRA increases. There are no increases for delaying benefits past age 70.

TABLE 4-3   ## How Much Will Delayed Retirement Increase My Benefits?

Year of Birth	Yearly Rate of Increase	Monthly Rate of Increase
1930	4.5%	of 1%
1931–1932	5.0%	of 1%
1933–1934	5.5%	of 1%
1935–1936	6%	of 1%
1937–1938	6.5%	of 1%
1939–1940	7%	of 1%
1941–1942	7.5%	of 1%
1943 or later	8%	of 1%

Taking a Closer Look at Spouses' and Survivor Benefits

Many seniors consider more than themselves in financial decisions. They also have spouses to be concerned about, and benefits for a spouse are among the least understood aspects of the Social Security program. Here are the two dimensions to incorporating a spouse in decisions on Social Security benefits:

>> A married person receives either *spousal benefits* based on the other spouse's earnings record or *retirement benefits* based on his own work record, whichever results in higher benefits.

>> A surviving spouse can receive either *survivor benefits* based on the earnings record of the deceased spouse or retirement benefits based on his own work

record, whichever results in high benefits. Keep in mind that the decision of when to begin receiving your own benefits can affect the amount of survivor benefits received by your spouse.

REMEMBER

Note the important difference between the spousal benefit and survivor benefit: While the higher-earning spouse is alive, the lower-earning spouse's retirement benefit is half of the higher-earning spouse's benefit at FRA (or his own retirement benefit, whichever is higher), regardless of when the higher-earning spouse decided to begin benefits. But after the higher-earning spouse passes away, the lower-earning spouse's survivor benefit is equal to the retirement benefit that the higher-earning spouse was receiving. The amount of the survivor benefit depends on the age when the higher-earning spouse chose to begin benefits. If the higher-earning spouse began receiving benefits before FRA, the surviving spouse will receive less than the FRB as a survivor benefit, and that reduction will continue for the rest of the surviving spouse's life.

The age at which you decide to begin benefits affects the benefits received by a spouse, a surviving spouse, and even by an ex-spouse. If you're not married and have never been married, you can skip this section. We begin with some simple strategies and build to some more sophisticated strategies.

Understanding the choices for spousal benefits

One way you can enhance your personal finances as a senior is to take advantage of the spousal benefit. The *spousal benefit* is the amount of retirement benefits a married person is entitled to based on the earnings record of the other spouse. This benefit is different from the *retirement benefit* you're entitled to based on your own earnings history. You may receive either the spousal benefit or the retirement benefit, but not both.

TIP

The Social Security Administration is supposed to automatically compare the spousal benefit to the earned retirement benefit and automatically pay the higher of the two. No action is supposed to be required by a beneficiary to receive the higher benefit. But mistakes can be made, so you should know the benefit you're entitled to and be sure that is what you're receiving. If you aren't, contact the SSA.

If you're the lower-earning spouse, you can start receiving spousal benefits when your higher-earning spouse begins receiving retirement benefits. The two of you have some important decisions to make before the lower-earning spouse takes benefits, however. *Note:* To help you grasp what you and your spouse can do, this discussion assumes that one spouse has higher lifetime earnings than the other, hence, the *higher-earning spouse* and the *lower-earning spouse.*

REMEMBER

In general, the spousal benefit is one-half of the benefit at FRA earned by the other spouse, if the lower-earning spouse doesn't begin receiving benefits until her own FRA or later. But note that it doesn't matter whether the higher-earning spouse begins benefits at age 62, age 70, or somewhere in between. The spousal benefit is one-half the benefit that the higher-earning spouse would receive by beginning benefits at FRA. Also, when the lower-earning spouse receives the spousal benefit, it doesn't affect the amount of benefits received by the higher-earning spouse.

So what choices does the lower-earning income spouse have? The following sections explain your options along with some examples.

Choice No. 1: Lower-earning spouse retires first, takes own benefits

When the higher-earning spouse hasn't begun receiving retirement benefits, the lower-earning spouse's only option is to begin receiving retirement benefits based on her earnings history. A spousal benefit can't begin until the higher-earning spouse actually begins receiving benefits. If the lower-earning spouse wants to begin benefits but the higher-earning spouse is delaying benefits, the lower-earning spouse's only option at that point is to receive benefits based on her own earnings record. After the higher-earning spouse begins receiving benefits, the lower-earning spouse can shift to the spousal benefit.

Choice No. 2: Higher-earning spouse retires, boosts lower-earning spouse's benefits

After the higher-earning spouse begins retirement benefits, the lower-earning spouse can choose either a spousal benefit or his own retirement benefit. When the lower-earning spouse already is receiving benefits based on his own earnings history, he can switch to the spousal benefit after the higher-earning spouse begins retirement benefits.

If a lower-earning spouse decides to take benefits based on the higher-earning spouse's earnings record, the lower-earning spouse receives half of the higher-earning spouse's FRB, but only if the lower-earning spouse waits until his own FRA to begin any benefits. If the lower-earning spouse decides to begin benefits (whether his own retirement benefit or a spousal benefit) before his own FRA, the spousal benefit will be less than half of the higher-earning spouse's FRA. The benefit will be reduced on a sliding scale just the same as if the person began receiving his own benefits before FRA. If the lower-earning spouse selects age 62, he will receive a benefit that's 35 percent of the higher-earning spouse's FRA benefit.

For example, say that each spouse is age 62. The lower-earning spouse's earned retirement benefit is $900 monthly at FRA or $500 at 62. The higher-earning spouse is entitled to $1,900 monthly at FRA. The lower-earning spouse wants to begin receiving benefits now. The higher-earning spouse continues to work and delays benefits. The lower-earning spouse begins receiving $500 at 62. The higher-earning spouse finally begins receiving benefits at FRA of $1,900. The lower-earning spouse now can switch to receive half of the higher-earning spouse's benefit. Normally, the spousal benefit would be $950 (half of the higher-earning spouse's FRB), but because the lower-earning spouse began receiving benefits at 62, the benefits are reduced by 35 percent. By beginning his own retirement benefits early, the lower-earning spouse permanently reduces monthly benefits, even if he later switches to the spousal benefit.

REMEMBER

If the lower-earning spouse begins retirement benefits before FRA based on his earnings record and later shifts to spousal benefits, the spousal benefit will be reduced based on the age at which the lower-earning spouse began receiving the retirement benefits based on his earnings record.

Choice No. 3: Claim and suspend

You have a third option as a lower-earning spouse. Social Security allows a person to file for retirement benefits and then suspend receipt of them. The suspension is treated as though the person never applied for benefits during the suspension period. The monthly reductions for claiming benefits before FRA aren't applied, and delayed retirement credits accumulate during the suspension period. When a beneficiary suspends benefits, he can have the benefits resume at any time. Benefits can be suspended only at FRA or later. If the benefits are applied for at FRA, say at age 66, but suspended until age 70, the maximum benefit may be received at 70.

WHAT IF I'M DIVORCED?

If a prior marriage of yours lasted 10 years or longer, you may be able to receive benefits on your ex-spouse's record. You need to be at least 62, divorced, and currently unmarried. Your ex-spouse must be entitled to retirement or disability benefits — and those benefits need to be bigger than the ones you're entitled to based on your own work.

As an ex-spouse, your benefit equals half of your ex-spouse's full retirement amount or disability benefit if you start receiving benefits at your full retirement age. If you remarry, you can't collect benefits on your former spouse's record unless your marriage ends. You can find a lot more details about how this works at www.ssa.gov/planners/retire/divspouse.html.

This is known as the *claim-and-suspend strategy*. The claim-and-suspend strategy can be used to allow the lower-earning spouse to begin receiving a spousal benefit now while the higher-earning spouse effectively delays receipt of benefits and receives higher benefits in the future. The higher-earning spouse files for benefits at FRA and then immediately files to suspend the benefits. Then the lower-earning spouse can begin receiving one-half of the high-earning spouse's benefits at FRA.

Ensuring spouses are taken care of: Survivor's benefits

If you're the higher-earning spouse, you want to make sure your lower-earning spouse is taken care of. In that case, you, the higher-earning spouse, need to consider survivor's benefits when deciding the age to begin retirement benefits. A Social Security *survivor's benefit* is the benefit payable to a surviving spouse after the other spouse passes away. The survivor's benefit is 100 percent of the benefit the deceased spouse was receiving. A surviving spouse can begin survivor's benefits as early as age 60 but will receive a lower benefit. This section identifies some strategies you can use to ensure that your spouse receives the maximum benefits after you're gone.

REMEMBER

As the higher-earning spouse, you have to figure out how your decision regarding taking benefits affects your lower-earning spouse. Your goal should be to maximize the lifetime income of your spouse.

Strategy No. 1: Delay retirement benefits

You can increase the lifetime income of your lower-earning spouse if you delay retirement benefits, but only if you, the higher-earning spouse, die first. Delaying benefits is a form of free life insurance that provides extra income to the lower-earning spouse.

REMEMBER

When both spouses are alive, the lower-earning spouse can receive the higher amount of his earned benefit or 50 percent of the higher-earning spouse's benefit at FRA. When the higher-earning spouse dies, the lower-earning spouse can't receive retirement benefits and a survivor's benefit. When someone is eligible for both types of benefits, he receives only the higher of the two types of benefits. If the higher-earning spouse passes away, the surviving spouse either continues to receive his own earned benefit or receives 100 percent of the benefit that the higher-earning spouse was receiving before passing away. In other words, when both spouses were receiving benefits and one passes away, the household's income will be reduced by the lower of the two benefits the spouses were receiving.

The survivor's benefits rules should influence the age at which a higher-earning spouse decides to begin retirement benefits. For example, say the higher-earning spouse is eligible for $1,800 monthly at FRA, while the lower-earning spouse is eligible for an earned benefit of $700. (Assume both are at FRA.) If the lower-earning spouse chooses to take the spouse's benefit while the other spouse is still alive, he will receive $900 monthly, half of the higher-earning spouse's FRA benefit. The amount received by the higher-earning spouse (and the lower-earning spouse) will depend on the age her benefits began. Suppose she delayed benefits past FRA and receives $2,200 monthly. If the higher-earning spouse passes away first, the lower-earning spouse would then receive $2,200 monthly as a survivor's benefit. If the lower-earning spouse passes away first, the higher-earning spouse continues to receive only her earned benefit. Suppose instead the higher-earning spouse began benefits before FRA and was receiving $1,500 monthly. If the higher-earning spouse passes away first, the surviving spouse will receive $1,500 monthly.

Strategy No. 2: Begin benefits twice

The Social Security law allows married couples to use a strategy that could be called "beginning your benefits twice," which can increase lifetime benefits. With this strategy, a spouse initially begins benefits, either his own earned benefit or a spousal benefit. After a few years, he switches to the other benefit. The strategy can maximize lifetime benefits, depending on which spouse earned more income and when each begins receiving earned retirement benefits.

For instance, consider the example in the earlier section "Understanding the choices for spousal benefits," where the lower-earning spouse began benefits based on his own earnings record because the higher-earning spouse hadn't yet begun receiving benefits. After the higher-earning spouse began benefits, the lower-earning spouse switched to spousal benefits based on the higher-earning spouse's earned benefit at FRA. In this case, the lower-earning spouse began benefits twice.

Similarly, a high-earning spouse can choose to receive spousal benefits based on the lower-earning spouse's benefits — even if that results in a lower monthly benefit — and then later switch to a benefit based on her own earnings record.

Suppose, for example, the lower-earning spouse would be entitled to $1,000 monthly at FRA and the higher-earning spouse would receive $2,000 at FRA. They're both 62 years old. The lower-earning spouse begins benefits now, receiving $750 monthly. The higher-earning spouse wants to delay retirement benefits until age 70 to maximize lifetime benefits and also the survivor's benefit. To generate cash flow before then, at her FRA, the higher-earning spouse applies for only spousal benefits equal to one-half the lower-earning spouse's earned benefits at FRA, or $500. Then at age 70, the higher-earning spouse can apply for retirement benefits and begin receiving about $2,600 monthly.

REMEMBER

A higher-earning spouse who opts to receive spousal benefits based on her lower-earning spouse's benefits doesn't receive a reduction in her retirement benefits, because retirement benefits weren't applied for early. At the earlier age, only spousal benefits were applied for — and only at her FRA or later.

TECHNICAL STUFF

The rule that allows this strategy states that a married person who has reached FRA is eligible for a benefit based on either his earnings record or the spouse's earnings record. If both retirement and spousal benefits are applied for, the higher benefit automatically is paid. But the person has the option to apply for only spousal benefits. If the application isn't made until after FRA, beginning spousal benefits at that age doesn't reduce the eventual retirement benefits. If a person applies for benefits before FRA, he'll be treated as applying for both spousal and retirement benefits. Beginning the benefits will trigger a reduction based on the person's age, and that reduction will be permanent.

Either spouse or both spouses can use this strategy. If both spouses wanted to use the strategy, each would receive half of the other's FRA benefit until choosing to begin retirement benefits based on his or her own earnings record. For example, say a husband and wife are the same age and have reached FRA. The higher-earning spouse is entitled to $2,000 monthly and the lower-earning spouse to $900 monthly on their own earnings records. The higher-earning spouse applies for spousal benefits, receiving $450 monthly. The lower-earning spouse applies for retirement benefits, receiving $900 monthly. At age 70, the higher-earning spouse applies for retirement benefits, which now are $2,700. The lower-earning spouse applies for the higher of retirement benefits and spousal benefits. The spousal benefit is half of what the higher-earning spouse was entitled to at FRA, $1,000 monthly, and is likely to be the higher benefit.

REMEMBER

Only one spouse at a time can receive spousal benefits. One spouse must have filed for retirement benefits for the other to be receiving spousal benefits.

Identifying When You May Need to Receive Benefits

Social Security is an asset. It's a stream of income the government owes you. Like any asset, you need to manage Social Security to maximize lifetime income in a way that's consistent with your other goals and needs. When considering the time to begin drawing benefits, answer the questions in the following sections, which cover both a case of an individual deciding when to take benefits and a case when a spouse is involved. The situation with a couple is a little more complicated. The couple can decide either to maximize lifetime benefits or to ensure that the lower-earning spouse receives the highest possible benefits if he survives the other spouse.

What are your cash flow needs?

If you need access to your benefits to pay expenses before you're eligible for full benefits, you probably have no choice but to begin receiving benefits early. If you've left the workforce — whether through choice or circumstances — you may have limited sources of income. You may need to begin Social Security retirement benefits to pay living expenses as early as 62. Someone who is still in the workforce but on a part-time basis or at a reduced income may also need to begin benefits to meet expenses. If, however, you can continue to work and have investments or pensions that generate enough income to support your standard of living, you can afford to hold off on receiving benefits until your FRA or later.

Will waiting pay off?

When you don't have immediate need for retirement benefits before FRA, you may want to receive benefits based on the age that will generate the largest lifetime income. You can estimate this age by considering a simple trade-off: Begin retirement benefits early and you receive benefits for a longer period of time. Delay benefits and you receive a higher benefit. At some point, waiting to receive the large benefit is worthwhile.

So how do you really know when you've reached this point? A simple way to decide is to calculate the rough *break-even point.* The break-even point is the year when the total lifetime benefits received from beginning benefits at a time other than FRA equals the benefits that would be received from beginning benefits at FRA.

For example, say your benefit at FRA (age 66) is $1,400 per month. If you start benefits at 62, the benefit is reduced by 25 percent to $1,050, or $350 less per month. But you receive the benefits for an extra 48 months. The total benefits received between 62 and FRA would be $50,400. Divide that by $350, and the result is 144. That's the number of months you would have to live beyond FRA to receive the same lifetime benefits as would be received by starting benefits at age 62. If you divide 144 by 12, you get 12 years. You would have to live to age 78 to reach the break-even point. If you live longer than the break-even point age of 78, you would come out ahead by $1,050 for each additional month lived by waiting to receive benefits.

Now, consider yourself in the same position but drawing benefits later. The benefit at age 70 would be $1,820 monthly, or 130 percent of the FRA benefit. Beginning benefits at 66 means receiving benefits for 48 extra months for a total of

$67,200 of benefits received by age 70. Waiting until age 70 would result in an extra $420 per month. Divide the total benefits that would be received between ages 66 and 70 by the extra amount received by waiting until age 70. The result is 160. So it would take 160 months after age 70 for the lifetime payments received by beginning benefits at 70 to equal those received by beginning benefits at 66. If you divide 160 by 12, the result is 13.33 years. That means you would have to live another 13.33 years (until age 83 and a third) to reach the break-even point of receiving the same amount of lifetime benefits. If you live longer than 13.33 years, the lifetime benefits are higher by waiting.

After you calculate the break-even point, review the later section "What's your life expectancy?" Doing so can give you a good idea of the probability you'll reach the break-even point should you choose to delay benefits.

REMEMBER

In either of the preceding cases, you come out ahead by waiting to receive benefits if you live past the break-even point. If you pass away earlier, your lifetime benefits would be higher by taking benefits early.

The break-even calculation is very simple. It can be made more complicated and precise by considering alternative uses of money and investment options as we discuss briefly in the next section.

What other income do you have?

If you have an investment portfolio or other income capable of paying living expenses, you have discretion over when to begin Social Security retirement benefits. By beginning benefits early, you have the option of leaving money invested instead of taking it out to pay expenses. Or you can invest the Social Security benefits as received and continue spending the other sources of income.

Under either scenario, you have an investment *side fund* that compounds until it's needed. You can assume an after-tax rate of return on this fund and estimate whether the fund would compound enough to justify taking lower benefits early instead of waiting for the higher benefits. If your side investment fund does well, the break-even point from waiting to begin benefits is pushed further into the future. (Refer to the preceding section "Will waiting pay off?" for more on break-even points.)

WARNING

The problem with considering the results of an investing side fund is the uncertainty of investment returns. You can't assume a long-term average rate of return, because you won't be investing for the long term. The projections of how well the side fund would perform would depend on your assumptions about investment returns and taxes. This area is where consulting with your accountant or financial planner can be helpful.

Do you want to continue to work?

Another factor to consider is any penalty for earned income received while receiving Social Security benefits. If you won't be working when receiving benefits, this isn't an issue for you. It also isn't an issue after FRA. But if you plan to work full- or part-time before FRA, you may earn so much that your benefits are reduced. In that case, it may not make sense to begin receiving benefits before FRA or until you stop working. Check out the section "Noting How Working Reduces Benefits," later in this chapter for more details.

What are the potential income taxes on benefits?

You need to consider income taxes when deciding your beginning date for benefits. The general rule is that Social Security benefits are excluded from gross income when computing federal income taxes. But as income rises, a portion of the benefits may be included in your gross income. If your income is high enough to trigger taxes on the benefits after 62 but the income is likely to decline later, it may make sense to delay benefits until a smaller portion of them are taxed. See the later section "Being Aware of Potential Income Taxes on Your Benefits" for more info on the income taxation of Social Security benefits.

What's your life expectancy?

The key to choosing the best date to begin Social Security retirement benefits is to estimate how long you'll live. The benefit levels for different ages were calculated so a person who lives to life expectancy receives the same lifetime benefits regardless of when the benefits were begun. Life expectancy for an age group means half the people in the group will live longer and half will live shorter lives.

Of course, you don't have a crystal ball you can rub to tell how long you will live (and you may not want to know either). But here are a couple of factors you can keep in mind when considering the issue:

>> **Your personal health:** If you have a strong probability of living less than life expectancy (for example, you know that you have a chronic disease that will shorten your life), receiving benefits as early as possible makes sense. Otherwise, you may want to assume you'll be in the group that lives to life expectancy or longer.

>> **Your family history:** If your family has a history of long life spans and you're in good health, you may consider delaying benefits to maximize lifetime payments.

TIP

The good news for you: The schedule used for determining life expectancies is outdated, and life expectancies have increased. About half of men turning age 65 today will live beyond age 85. More than half of women age 65 today will live beyond 85. The bonus for delaying benefits probably is higher than it should be under current life expectancies. So more than half of an age group is likely to live beyond the life expectancy used in the benefit calculations, and more people will benefit from delaying benefits. Of course, if personal or family history raises doubts about living to life expectancy, you should consider taking benefits early.

Noting How Working Reduces Benefits

If you receive Social Security retirement benefits from age 62 to your FRA, you face a limit on the amount of income you can earn while receiving those benefits. The limit and amount of the penalty for earning more than the limit depend on your age. You can check out the limits on the Social Security Administration website at www.socialsecurity.gov. *Note:* The limit is applied monthly and applies until you reach FRA.

Earned income is income from a job or self-employment. It includes most sources of income from providing personal services or selling goods or services. Earned income doesn't include investment income and passive income such as interest, dividends, capital gains, pensions, and IRA distributions. Self-employment income is *net self-employment income,* which is gross income from the business minus business-related expenses.

Taking the penalty for exceeding the annual income limit

If you're still working, you tell the SSA before the start of each year how much income you expect to earn for the year. When your estimated income will exceed the earned income limit, the SSA then computes the penalty and withholds the appropriate amount from your benefits check each month. If your earned income changes in either direction, you must notify the SSA so it can adjust the withholding.

Between age 62 and the year FRA will be reached, benefits are reduced $1 for every $2 earned over the limit. The limit was $16,920 for 2017 and is indexed for inflation each year. For example, 62-year-old Sally is due $7,200 in benefits, but because she's earning $35,000 in 2015 she would lose all Social Security benefits for the year. If Sally actually earned only $20,000 that year, only $1,540 of her benefits would be withheld. (The income of $20,000 minus the limit of $16,920 shows an excess income of $3,080. Divide the excess by two, and she loses $1,540 of benefits.) The SSA would withhold her January through April benefits. The $600 monthly benefits would be paid May through December. In January 2018, Sally would be paid the $440 that was withheld in April 2017.

In the year you reach FRA, retirement benefits are reduced $1 for every $3 earned over a dollar limit. The limit, which is indexed for inflation, is $44,880 in 2017. The limit applies on a monthly basis until the month you reach FRA. Beginning with that month, full retirement benefits are received no matter how much income is earned.

For example, say that Bobby Beneficiary hasn't yet met FRA at the beginning of 2017, but he reaches it in November 2017. The retirement benefits are $600 per month, or $7,200 for the year. Bobby earned $46,200 in the ten months from January through October. The SSA would withhold $440 ($1 for every $3 earned above the $44,880 limit). To implement the limit, the SSA would withhold the January check of $600. Beginning in February 2017, Bobby would receive the $600 benefit monthly, and this amount would be paid each month for the remainder of the year. The SSA would pay Bobby the remaining $160 from his January 2017 check in January 2018.

Determining the penalty on a monthly basis

When someone begins Social Security benefits during a calendar year (versus at the beginning of the year), income earned before the benefit beginning date doesn't count in applying the penalty. Instead, the annual earnings limit is computed on a monthly basis, and only the monthly earnings after the date retirement benefits begin count toward the penalty. For example, in 2017, the monthly earnings limit for someone younger than FRA is $1,410 ($16,920 divided by 12).

Imagine a man begins retirement benefits at age 62 on October 30, 2017. He had $45,000 of earned income through October. He leaves that job and takes a part-time job beginning in November earning $500 per month. His earnings for the year substantially exceed the limit of $16,920, but only the monthly earnings after October count. Because each month after October he will earn less than $1,310, he won't experience any reduction in benefits in November and December. Beginning in 2018, only the annual limit will apply for this beneficiary if he continues to work the entire year.

REMEMBER

Special rules apply to the self-employed. In addition to the net income, the SSA looks at the amount of time spent on the business. In general, if someone works more than 45 hours a month in self-employment, that person isn't considered retired and will lose all or some of her benefits. Someone who works less than

15 hours a month is considered retired and faces no penalty. Someone who works between 15 and 45 hours a month isn't considered retired if the job requires a lot of skill or the person is managing a sizeable business.

The penalty isn't always bad

The loss of benefits from the earned income limit may not be permanent. After FRA is reached, benefits will be recomputed to give you credit for the lost benefits. But credit is allowed only for the months when the entire benefit was withheld.

Continuing to work may actually increase your benefits after FRA. Your highest-earning 35 years will be used to determine the benefits. Each year, the SSA reviews the records of beneficiaries who receive earned income. If the most recent year is one of the top 35 earnings years, the benefits are automatically recalculated. The higher benefit should begin in December of the year after the earnings year. For example, suppose your 2017 earnings would result in a recalculation of benefits during 2018. The additional benefits would be retroactive to January 2018 and would be paid in a lump sum in December 2018.

Preserving Your Benefits

You may be able to plan and manage your income to avoid losing Social Security retirement benefits before reaching FRA. But you also need to be wary of any strategies that people suggest, because if the Social Security Administration doesn't like what it sees, your strategy could be a mistake that costs you money. If someone recommends a strategy to you, check it out with a knowledgeable, objective adviser or contact the SSA. The good news: This section looks at a few ways you may be able to earn some income legally without having your Social Security retirement benefits reduced.

TIP

The rules for earned income have many nuances and technical terms, and a lot of misinformation and fraudulent strategies, sometimes recommended by unscrupulous individuals, are floating around. So if your earned income and Social Security benefits are high enough to merit the investment, before choosing a strategy, get the advice of an attorney, accountant, or financial adviser who's familiar with the rules.

Deferring income

One strategy you may be able to take to preserve your Social Security retirement benefits is to defer some of your income. *Income deferral* means you perform services this year but payment for the services is not due until a future year. The classic case of income deferral is a pension. You work for 30 years or more and part of your earnings are not paid until you retire. Income can be deferred for shorter periods, even from one year to the next, and you can defer income outside of a retirement plan.

In most c~~ ~~gainst the limit in the year it's earned, ~~ ~~l the earnings limit simply by agreeing ~~ ~~r. If you have the legal right to receive ~~ ~~ed income for Social Security purposes

~~ ~~ome that help you avoid the earned

~~ ~~mployer contributions aren't
~~ ~~s are paid into a retirement
~~ ~~ons aren't considered earned
~~ ~~don't have a legal right

~~ ~~d earn retirement benefits
~~ ~~hough the money deferred
~~ ~~ed in earned income to

~~ ~~tion plan. This type of
~~ ~~ avoid having the money
~~ ~~ a risk that you would
~~ ~~y can't be payable to
~~ ~~ the money in a trust
~~ ~~nployee's name. If the
~~ ~~atus of a general
~~ ~~ay the income.

~~ ~~nced lawyer to
~~ ~~worth the amount

If you o~~ ~~to use the corporation to ~~ ~~fits. You set your
salary so ~~

WARNING

Be careful. There's a right way and a wrong way to do this, and corporate owners often get caught doing it the wrong way. You really shouldn't try to use this strategy without the advice of a tax expert who knows this area of the law. You can't simply cut your salary the year Social Security benefits begin, especially if you take the same amount of cash out of the business through dividends and other distributions that don't qualify as salary or bonus. Both the IRS and the SSA state a salary must be reasonable in light of the work done and qualifications of the employee. If the salary is set at an artificially low level, the SSA considers it fraud. Both the IRS and SSA have litigated and won cases against corporate owners who set unreasonably low salaries to avoid either payroll taxes or the earned income limit.

TIP

To successfully avoid the earned income limit, you have to establish the new salary as reasonable for the work done and your level of expertise. If your salary declines sharply the year benefits begin, your hours worked also should change. The corporate minutes should document why the salary level is reasonable. Some advisers believe you also should transfer voting control of the corporation or set up an independent board or committee that sets the salary.

Considering exempt income

When trying to preserve your Social Security benefits, you may want to take a closer look at ways to earn exempt income. *Exempt income* is income that doesn't count toward the earnings limit. As a general rule, compensation that's tax-free under the tax code isn't counted as wages or earned income for purposes of the Social Security earnings limit.

FINDING ADDITIONAL INFORMATION

The Social Security Administration (SSA) website has a great deal of information about the different aspects of retirement benefits, and the search function usually makes it easy to find answers. In addition, you can estimate retirement benefits at different ages using the calculators on the website. The calculators allow you to change different assumptions and factor a spouse into the estimates. The site also enables you to download or view SSA publications.

The SSA website allows you to conduct many transactions online. You can apply for benefits, change your address or telephone number, check your information or benefits, start or change direct deposit, and more. You can visit the site at www.socialsecurity.gov.

You can also visit a local SSA office or call the SSA toll-free number at 800-772-1213 for information.

For example, you may be able to work with your employer to maximize medical expense coverage and other tax-free benefits and minimize cash compensation. Your employer, for example, may be able to restructure things so it pays more of your insurance premiums and out-of-pocket expenses. These generally are exempt income. In return, the employer reduces your cash compensation. You should check with the SSA to verify that a form of compensation doesn't count toward the earnings limit.

Relying on special income

To preserve your Social Security benefits, you can rely on other types of income that are taxable but that the SSA doesn't consider earned income. Examples of special income include the following:

>> Employer reimbursements for travel or moving expenses

>> Jury duty pay

>> Lottery and prize winnings

>> Pension and IRA distributions

>> Rental income

>> Unemployment compensation

>> Worker's compensation

More details about how different payments are classified are available in the Social Security Handbook (free from local SSA offices), on the SSA website, and through the SSA telephone assistance hotline at 800-772-1213.

Being Aware of Potential Income Taxes on Your Benefits

Originally, Social Security retirement benefits were exempt from federal income taxes. However, in 1986, Congress made some benefits subject to income taxes. In 1993, more of the benefits paid to higher-income beneficiaries became subject to federal income taxes. The result is that the *marginal tax rate* (the tax rate on the last dollar of income earned) for some Social Security beneficiaries can be 70 percent or higher. Lower-income beneficiaries still receive all their benefits tax-free, but higher-income beneficiaries can have up to 85 percent of benefits included in gross income.

As a result, you need to know when your Social Security retirement benefits may be subject to income taxes. This section explains how the taxes are calculated on your benefits and what you can do to lower yours.

Understanding how modified adjusted gross income works

The level of taxation of Social Security benefits depends on your *modified adjusted gross income,* or MAGI. MAGI is *adjusted gross income* (AGI) from your income tax return (before considering taxable Social Security benefits) plus one half of your Social Security benefits and some types of exempt income (such as interest from tax-exempt bonds).

Your AGI is the amount left after subtracting from gross income deductions such as IRA contributions, self-employed health insurance premiums, and a few other expenses. Itemized expenses (such as mortgage interest and charitable contributions) and the standard deduction aren't subtracted to arrive at AGI. (*Tip:* You can find your AGI on the bottom of the first pages of Forms 1040 and 1040A and line 4 of Form 1040EZ.)

The main type of excluded income that's added back is *tax-exempt interest income.* This type of income is interest earned on debt issued by states and localities. Other types of exempt income to add back are interest from qualified U.S. savings bonds, employer-provided adoption benefits, foreign-earned income or foreign housing assistance, and income earned by bona fide residents of American Samoa or Puerto Rico.

So if you're married and filing a joint return, Social Security benefits are taxed as follows:

>> Up to 50 percent of benefits are included in gross income when MAGI is between $32,000 and $44,000.

>> Up to 85 percent of benefits are included in gross income when MAGI is more than $44,000.

If you're unmarried, Social Security benefits are taxed as follows:

>> Up to 50 percent of benefits are included in gross income when MAGI is between $25,000 and $34,000.

>> Up to 85 percent of benefits are included in gross income when MAGI is more than $34,000.

Benefits are included in gross income on a sliding scale. In other words, if you're married and filing jointly and your MAGI is $33,000, you don't include a full 50 percent of benefits in gross income. You include a portion of the benefits in income, but 50 percent of benefits isn't included in gross income until your MAGI equals $44,000.

Unlike other parts of the tax code and Social Security, the levels at which Social Security benefits are taxable aren't indexed for inflation. That means more and more people are paying taxes on their Social Security benefits each year.

IRS Publication 915, "Social Security and Equivalent Railroad Retirement Benefits," contains details about the taxation of benefits. It also has examples and worksheets to help you estimate the amount of benefits that are taxable. The publication is available for free on the IRS website (www.irs.gov).

The SSA doesn't withhold income taxes on your benefits. You must make quarterly estimated tax payments to avoid incurring a penalty for underpayment of estimated taxes. You can find details of how much to pay and how to pay estimated taxes in Publication 505, "Tax Withholding and Estimated Tax," which also is available for free on the IRS website. However, if you're taking IRA distributions or receiving a pension, you can request that the payer withhold income taxes. If enough is withheld, you'll avoid penalties for underpayment of income taxes without having to make quarterly estimated tax payments.

You also need to check with your state department of taxation or your tax adviser about how your state taxes Social Security benefits. Some states completely exempt Social Security benefits. Others piggyback on the federal system or tax the benefits at a different rate.

Reducing taxes on benefits

If your MAGI is in the range at which some of your benefits will be included in gross income, you may be able to take steps to reduce the taxes on your benefits.

Be careful: You may encounter financial gurus and other people recommending strategies that don't comply with the tax law. If you're advised to use a strategy not recommended here, you should have it verified by an objective, experienced tax adviser.

For a married couple, the amount of benefits included in gross income is determined by the joint MAGI. The tax on benefits isn't avoided or reduced by filing separate returns. In fact, for married couples filing separately, the benefits will be included in gross income when MAGI exceeds $0. On a joint return, it's the joint MAGI that determines the level of benefits taxed. The taxes aren't computed separately on the benefits of each spouse. The joint income can cause benefits to be taxed even if only one spouse is receiving them.

If MAGI is significantly above the threshold at which benefits are taxed, planning strategies probably won't reduce the amount of benefits included in gross income. The changes would have to dramatically reduce MAGI to bring it close to or below the threshold.

Strategies to reduce taxes on your benefits

Almost all regular tax planning strategies that reduce MAGI can be used to reduce the amount of benefits included in gross income. These strategies include reducing gross income and increasing deductions for AGI. Remember that increasing itemized deductions, such as mortgage interest and charitable contributions, doesn't reduce MAGI. Here are strategies that are most likely to be valuable to you when reducing the taxes on your benefits:

>> **Minimize distributions from IRAs, pensions, and annuities.** Don't take money from one of these vehicles unless you need it. Every dollar distributed to you is included in gross income and AGI. Consider tapping other sources, such as taxable investment accounts first. If you have scheduled regular distributions from one of these vehicles, determine whether you can reduce the distributions. After age 70½, when required minimum distributions from IRAs and pensions are imposed, this strategy is more difficult. Before then, limiting distributions to those needed to pay expenses may reduce the amount of benefits that are taxed.

>> **Change investment strategies in taxable accounts to minimize gross income.** Reduce trading in the account so capital gains are recognized less frequently. When gains are realized, sell investments in which you have losses to offset the gains. If the accounts hold mutual funds that frequently have high annual distributions, consider switching to funds with lower distributions.

>> **Consider using taxable accounts to purchase deferred annuities.** Income earned within an annuity is tax deferred; it won't increase MAGI as long as it remains in the annuity. In addition, annuities aren't subject to the required minimum distribution rules. For more information on annuities, see Book 4, Chapter 3.

This strategy probably isn't worth using simply to avoid taxes on benefits. You need to consider a wide range of issues (such as whether an annuity fits with the rest of your portfolio and helps you meet your investment goals) before deciding an annuity is appropriate for you. Furthermore, if you do decide to go this route, many different types of annuities are available, so make sure you know what you're getting.

>> **Switch from taxable bonds to tax-exempt bonds.** This move doesn't directly reduce the amount of Social Security benefits that are taxed. Tax-exempt interest is added back to AGI to reach MAGI. But the switch may indirectly reduce the tax on benefits, because tax-exempt bonds usually, though not always, pay lower interest rates than taxable bonds. When the tax-exempt interest is added back to AGI, it results in a lower MAGI than if the investments were still in higher-yielding taxable bonds.

>> **Shift income to family members other than your spouse.** You don't want to shift assets that are needed to maintain your standard of living. But when assets and the income from them exceed your needs, consider transferring income-producing investments to other family members. This transferring should be done only as part of a comprehensive estate planning strategy with the reduction in taxes on Social Security benefits a side advantage.

Reducing your MAGI: Deduction strategies

The list in the preceding section includes ways you can reduce income and reduce MAGI. You can also take some deductions from gross income that can reduce MAGI. Even though itemized deductions (such as mortgage interest and charitable contributions) don't reduce taxes on Social Security benefits, the following deduction strategies may help:

>> **Sell capital assets that have paper losses.** Many investors don't like to sell losing investments because the sale locks in the losses. A capital loss, however, can be used to your advantage. One advantage is that the loss reduces MAGI and therefore the amount of Social Security benefits included in gross income. Capital losses first are deducted against capital gains dollar for dollar. Each dollar of loss offsets a dollar of gains and reduces MAGI by a dollar. If the losses exceed the gains for the year, up to $3,000 of the losses are deducted against ordinary income. If you still have excess losses, they're carried forward to be used in future years in the same way.

>> **Examine your portfolio for investments with paper losses.** Sell those investments and make the losses deductible. If you still like the long-term prospects for the investments, you can repurchase them. If they're securities (stocks, bonds, mutual funds), you have to wait more than 30 days to repurchase the same or substantially identical investments. If you don't wait, the loss deductions are deferred. If you don't want to wait to be back in the market, you can purchase investments that are similar but not substantially identical.

>> **Look for deductions for business losses.** Eligible losses include those from partnerships, S corporations, and proprietorships. It may be possible to turn a hobby into a business that generates deductible losses. The losses are deductible if a profit is made in at least any three out of the last five consecutive years. The losses can also be deducted if the operation never earns a profit but is managed in a professional manner with the intention of making a profit. *Remember:* The rules for deducting business losses can be complicated, so you want to study the rules or receive qualified advice before deducting them.

Changing Your Mind: A Do-Over

Social Security benefit decisions are generally permanent, but some exceptions do exist. For example, a spouse can switch from retirement benefits to spousal benefits or vice versa under some circumstances. You can also switch to survivor's benefits after a spouse dies. You can begin retirement benefits and then suspend them as well (as discussed earlier in this chapter).

Finally, you can change your mind with your Social Security benefits in one other way — when you realize you may have made a mistake. Suppose that you are already receiving Social Security retirement benefits and decide you should have waited to a later age to begin benefits. Believe it or not, you may get a "do-over." You may be able to change the beginning date of your benefits.

Unfortunately, SSA greatly restricted the availability of the do-over. You used to be able to implement a do-over at any time. Now, the do-over is allowed only within 12 months after you begin receiving retirement benefits.

Deciding whether you should take a do-over

So how do you know whether you should consider changing your benefits with a do-over? You may find yourself in one of the following situations:

>> **You elected to receive benefits without much thought and then realized you didn't need them.** This scenario is probably the most typical. You then believe your spouse would be better off if your benefits had a later starting date. You have enough in your investment portfolio to repay the benefits. At this time, you may decide to file the do-over and pay back the benefits.

>> **Changed circumstances or a fresh review indicate later benefits are better.** You thought you would need the benefits to meet expenses, but your cash flow changes. For example, you may receive an inheritance or an unexpected job offer.

Doing the do-over

To complete a Social Security do-over, just follow these steps:

1. **Complete Social Security Form 521, "Request for Withdrawal of Application."**

   Filling out this form is simple. You can find a copy of the form at any Social Security office or online at www.socialsecurity.gov.

2. **Submit the form with repayment of all the benefits paid to date.**

   Repaying may seem like a stiff price for a change, but keep in mind that no interest is charged. You return only the amount received. In return, after repaying the benefits, you can change the start date of your benefits so you receive higher benefits every month for the rest of your life. Your spouse may receive higher survivor's benefits as well.

Looking at What the Future Holds for Social Security

Each year, usually in May, the trustees of Social Security and Medicare issue reports on the financial status of the programs. The reports have worsened over the years. As the Baby Boom generation approaches normal retirement age (the first Boomers turned 65 in 2011), the financial strain on the system is expected to increase because the Boomers aren't being replaced in the workforce at the same rate they're expected to retire.

The 2015 report estimates that after 2019 the Department of the Treasury will redeem trust fund assets to the extent that the program's costs exceed tax revenue and interest earnings. The trust fund reserves are estimated to be depleted in 2033. Although this may paint an unhappy picture, it doesn't mean you should write off Social Security and assume no benefits will be available to you. If you're already a senior, the government is likely to find a way to pay you the full benefits you expected. It would be difficult politically to reduce promised benefits to a large, financially vulnerable and politically powerful part of the population.

Most people overlook one positive factor from the report. Each year, the trustees estimate that annual Social Security tax revenues will finance 70 to 75 percent of scheduled benefits almost indefinitely. This means that Social Security will be able to pay most of the promised benefits for many years. Congress will make changes, but those changes won't include a complete cessation or dramatic reduction of benefits. Instead of eliminating Social Security retirement benefits, Congress is likely to take a combination of the following actions:

>> **Further means-testing of benefits:** Benefits may be reduced or eliminated for higher-income seniors. Another form of means-testing is to include more Social Security benefits in gross income. What's unknown at this point is the income level at which means-testing may be imposed.

>> **A change in the replacement ratio:** The *replacement ratio* is the percentage of your working years' income received in Social Security benefits. For example, someone earning less than $20,000 is likely to receive Social Security benefits equal to 90 percent or more of that income. The replacement ratio declines as income rises. The formula may be changed so that those with higher incomes in their working years have their replacement ratios reduced. It's possible that people at some income levels will receive no Social Security retirement benefits.

>> **A change in the index to determine initial benefits:** The initial benefit payment is determined by taking a worker's lifetime wages earned and inflating them based on average U.S. wage growth over the worker's career. Historically, the Consumer Price Index (CPI) has risen at a lower rate than wages. In the future, the inflation adjustment may be based on increases in the CPI or a fixed rate instead of the growth in wages. This would lower initial benefits, but few people would notice and no one would see an actual reduction in benefits already being received. The change could also apply only to those age 50 and younger.

>> **A change in the formula that indexes the benefits for inflation:** Beneficiaries could receive less than full inflation indexing on their benefits.

>> **A rise in payroll taxes:** Those still working would pay more to fund their own benefits and the benefits of those already retired. The tax increase wouldn't have to be across the board. Instead, the earnings limit on which Social Security taxes are imposed ($127,200 in 2017) could be raised or eliminated, as was done for Medicare.

Social Security's solvency may also be improved by actions of beneficiaries. If fewer Baby Boomers are financially prepared for retirement, they may work longer and delay benefits. Because they would pay more taxes into the program during those additional working years, the financial condition of the program would improve. The improvement isn't likely to be enough to prevent any future changes to the program, but it would extend its life for some years and allow other changes, such as higher taxes and reduced benefits, to be less extreme. The program's financial health could also be improved if the young working population increases faster than expected.

Although the elimination or dramatic reduction of Social Security benefits isn't expected, you should make plans for possible changes in benefits. Those with higher retirement incomes should leave a cushion in their retirement budgets to accommodate possible means-testing. Those not already retired should plan for the possibility of lower retirement benefits than currently promised and higher taxes at some point during their working years.

5

Planning Your Estate

Contents at a Glance

IN THIS CHAPTER

» Understanding what your estate is

» Knowing why you need to plan your estate

» Realizing that your estate-planning goals are different from others'

» Understanding the critical path method to planning your estate

» Finding the right people to help with your estate planning

Chapter **1**

Yes, You Have an Estate

T *he protection and control that you need.*

No, that phrase isn't the marketing slogan for a new deodorant. Rather, it expresses the two most important reasons for you to spend time and effort on your estate planning. The two reasons are these:

» After you die, the government will try to take as much of your estate as possible, so you want to protect your estate from the government to the greatest extent that you can.

» For the portion of your estate that you are able to protect from the government, you want to have as much control as possible over how your estate is divided up. Basically, you want to decide what will happen to your estate rather than have a jumbled set of complicated laws dictate who will get what.

Before you can plan your estate, you need to understand what your estate really is. Many people think that for the average nonbillionaire, estate planning involves only two steps:

>> Preparing a will

>> Trying to figure out which inheritance and estate taxes — the so-called "death taxes" — apply (and if so, then how much money will go to the state and federal governments)

But even though wills and the death taxes are certainly important considerations for you, chances are your own estate planning will involve much, much more.

This chapter presents the basics of estate planning that you need to get started on this often-overlooked topic of your personal financial planning. In this chapter (and book), you also discover that estate planning is every bit as important as saving for your child's college education or putting money away for your retirement.

What Is an Estate?

In the most casual sense, your estate is your *stuff* or all your possessions. However, even if your only familiarity with estate planning comes from watching a movie or television show where someone's will is read, you no doubt realize that you aren't very likely to hear words like "I leave all of my stuff to. . . ." Therefore, a bit more detail and formality is in order.

The basics: Definitions and terminology

"All my property."

Think of that phrase when you plan your estate.

What's that, you say? You don't own a house or any other real estate, so you think you don't have any property? Not so fast! In a legal sense, all kinds of items are considered to be your property, not just real estate (more formally known as *real property*, as discussed later in the "Property types" section), but also your

>> Cash, checking account, and savings account

>> Certificates of deposit (CDs)

>> Stocks, bonds, and mutual funds

>> Retirement savings in your Individual Retirement Account (IRA), 401(k), and other special accounts

>> Household furniture (including antiques)

>> Clothes

>> Vehicles

>> Life insurance

>> Annuities

>> Business interests

>> Jewelry, baseball card collection, autographed first edition of *Catcher in the Rye,* and all the rest of your collectibles

As discussed in the "Property types" section, your estate consists of all the preceding types of items — and even more — divided into several different categories. (For estate-planning purposes, these categories are often treated differently from each other; that distinction is covered later.)

The types of property listed almost always have a *positive balance*, meaning that they are worth something even if "something" is only a very small amount. Of course, an exception may be your overdrawn checking account, which then is actually property with a negative balance. In the case of an overdrawn checking account, the "property" is the amount that you actually owe a person or company (your bank, in this case). So your estate also includes *negative-value* property such as

>> The outstanding balance of the mortgage you owe on your house or a vacation home

>> The outstanding balances on your credit card accounts

>> Taxes you owe to the government

>> Any IOUs to people that you haven't paid off yet

REMEMBER

Basically, all debts you have are as much a part of your estate as all the positive-balance items.

In addition to understanding what your estate is, you also need to know what your estate is worth. You calculate your estate's value as follows:

1. Add up the value of all the positive-balance items in your estate (again, your banking accounts, investments, collectibles, real estate, and so on).

2. Subtract the total value of all of the negative-balance items (remaining balance of the mortgage on your home, how much you still owe on your credit cards, and so on) from the total of all the positive-balance items.

The result is the value of your estate. In most cases, the result is a positive number, meaning that what you have is worth more than what you owe.

(If calculating a *net value* by subtracting the total of what you owe from the total of what you have seems familiar, you're right. In the simplest sense, calculating the value of your estate involves essentially the same steps that you follow when you apply for many different types of loans: mortgage, automobile, educational assistance, and so on.)

WARNING

However, in many cases — including perhaps your own — determining what the parts of your estate are, and what they are worth, can be a bit more complicated than simply creating two columns on a sheet of paper or in your computer's spreadsheet program and doing basic arithmetic. If you are a farmer, for example, you need to figure out the value of your crops or livestock. If you own a small one-person business, you need to calculate what your business is worth. Or perhaps you and six other people are joint owners of a complicated real estate investment partnership; if so, what is your share worth?

Book 5, Chapter 2 goes over more technical and sometimes more complicated ways to determine your estate's value. (*Note:* For estate planning and estate tax purposes, more is not always better.)

For now, another point to keep in mind is that in addition to what you have right now, your estate may also include other items that you don't have in your possession but, at some point in the future, you will have, such as the following:

» Any future payments you expect to receive, such as an insurance settlement or the remaining 18 annual payments from that $35 million lottery jackpot that you won a couple of years ago

» Future inheritances

» A loan you made to your sister to help get her business started and when she plans to repay you

If you're familiar with the business and accounting term *accounts receivable* — what people or businesses owe to you — you need to include your own personal accounts receivable along with your banking accounts and home when figuring out what your estate contains and what your estate is worth.

One final term to cover is estate planning. By definition, *estate planning* means to plan your estate. (Duh.) More precisely, you need to follow a disciplined (as contrasted with haphazard) set of steps talked about later in this chapter. Why? Referring back to the opening slogan of this chapter, you want to protect as much of your estate as possible from being taken away and you (not the government or a scheming family member) want to control what happens to your estate after you die.

Your estate plan typically includes the following:

» Your will

» Documents that substitute for your will

» Trusts

» Tax considerations, with the idea of minimizing the overall amount of taxes you have to pay

» Various types of insurance

» Items related to your own particular circumstances, such as protecting your business or setting aside money to pay for your healthcare or a nursing home in your later years

All these aspects of estate planning are discussed in this book. If this collection of estate-planning activities seems a bit overwhelming, think of estate planning as a parallel to how you plan your personal finances and investments. Your investment portfolio may be made up of individual stocks, bonds, and mutual funds, along with bank CDs or other savings-related investments. And then, within each type of investment, you have further categories (for example, different types of mutual funds) that you may want to use.

Your investment objective is to sort through this menu of choices and put together just the right collection for your needs. You must also do the same with your estate plan. You need to have the right will and insurance coverage, possibly accompanied by trusts if they make sense for you and your family (see Book 5, Chapter 4). Furthermore, you may need additional estate-planning activities and strategies particular to your own needs.

Property types

You can have several types of property within your estate. Make a distinction between these types of property because various aspects of your estate planning treat each type differently. For example, in your will (see Book 2, Chapter 4) you can use different legal language when referring to various types of property, so remember to keep these definitions and distinctions straight.

Real property refers to various types of real estate:

>> Your home (house, condominium, co-op apartment, or some other type of primary residence that you own)

>> A second home, such as vacation property on a lake or near a ski resort

>> A "piece" of a vacation home, such as a timeshare

>> Any kind of vacant land, such as a building lot in a suburban development or even agricultural land you may own next to your "main" farm

>> Any investment real property that you either own directly yourself or with anyone else, such as a house you rent out or your share of an apartment building

TECHNICAL
STUFF

In addition to the actual real property itself, your estate also includes any improvements that you can't even see. For example, if you and three of your friends bought 200 acres of land with the intention of turning that land into a subdivision and you have spent loads of money on infrastructure — water lines and hookups, sewer lines and hookups, in-ground electricity and cable, and so on — then those improvements (or, more accurately, your share of those improvements) are also considered to be part of your estate along with the original real property itself.

In addition to real property, your estate also contains imaginary property.

No, not really. Just kidding. Your estate has no such thing as "imaginary property," unless some years back you got tripped up by some investment scam such as an oil or gas well that didn't really exist, or stock in some company that turned out to exist only on paper. (And if that's the case, don't even think about leaving that worthless swampland or your share of the Brooklyn Bridge to one of your children in your will, unless you want that "lucky" person to curse your name for all eternity.)

Actually, the other type of property in your estate in addition to real property is called *personal property,* which is further divided into two different categories:

>> Tangible personal property

>> Intangible personal property

Your *tangible personal property* includes possessions that you can touch, such as your car, jewelry, furniture, paintings and artwork, and collectibles (baseball cards, autographed first-edition novels, and so on).

REMEMBER

Your house is considered to be real property, not tangible personal property, even though you can touch it. Why? Because your house is permanently attached to (and thus made a part of) the land upon which it is built.

Your *intangible personal property* consists of financially oriented assets such as your bank accounts, stocks, mutual funds, bonds, and IRA. Of course, you can hold a stock certificate or mutual fund statement in your hand, but the stocks or mutual funds are still considered intangible personal property.

TECHNICAL STUFF

Technically, that stock certificate or mutual fund statement isn't actually what you own; it represents your portion of the ownership of some company (in the case of the stock certificate) or your portion of that mutual fund in the companies' stocks in which it invests. Sound confusing? Don't worry; just keep in mind that financially oriented paper assets are typically intangible personal property, while actual possessions are tangible personal property. If you have any doubt as to what category any particular item of your possessions falls, just ask one of your estate-planning team members mentioned later in this chapter.

Types of property interest

For each of the three types of property in your estate — real, tangible personal, and intangible personal — you also need to understand what your interest is.

"Of course I'm interested in my property," you may be thinking. "After all, it's my property, isn't it?"

In the world of estate planning, *interest* has a somewhat different definition than how that word is used in everyday language, or even as the word is often used in the financial world (interest that you earn on a certificate of deposit or pay on your mortgage loan). And more importantly, the specific type of interest in any given property determines what you specifically need to be concerned about for your estate planning.

Property interest is an essential part of almost all your estate planning, from the words that you put in your will (Book 2, Chapter 4) to how you may set up a trust (Book 5, Chapter 4), for two very important reasons:

>> You need to clearly understand what type of interest you have in your property so you can make accurate decisions about how to handle your property when you plan your estate.

>> As you decide what to write in your will and perhaps also set up trusts as part of your estate plan, you need to make decisions about what type of interest in each property that you want to set up for your children, your spouse, other family members, or institutions such as charities.

The two main types of property interest are as follows:

>> Legal interest

>> Beneficial interest

If you have only a *legal interest* in a property, you have the right to transfer or manage that property, but you don't have the right to use the property yourself. For example, trusts may be an essential part of your estate planning. By way of a very brief introduction to that topic, when you set up a trust, you name a *trustee* who is a person who manages the trust.

Suppose you set up a trust for your eldest son, Robert, as part of your estate plan, and you name your brother-in-law, Charlie, as the trustee. Charlie isn't allowed to use Robert's trust for his (Charlie's) own benefit, such as withdrawing $10,000 for a trip to Paris. That's called "Uncle Charlie goes to jail for stealing." Assuming Charlie does what he is supposed to do — and, more importantly, doesn't do what he's not supposed to do — Charlie has a legal interest in your son's trust as the trustee.

Unlike his Uncle Charlie, Robert has the other type of property interest in his trust: a *beneficial interest*, meaning that he does benefit from that trust. Basically, you set up that trust to benefit Robert.

Now, to complicate matters a bit more, two "subtypes" of beneficial interest exist:

>> Present interest

>> Future interest

If you have a *present interest* (remember that means "present beneficial interest"), you have the right to use the property immediately. So if Robert has a present interest in his trust that is managed by his uncle Charlie, Robert may receive payments of some specified amount — say $30,000 every three months for this example — from the trust. After Robert receives the money, he can do whatever he wants with it; the money is his to use, no strings attached.

The other type of beneficial interest — *future interest* — comes into play when someone with a beneficial interest (that person is allowed to benefit from that property) can't benefit right now but instead must wait for some date in the future.

For example, you can set up the trust described to benefit not only your eldest son but also your other two sons, Chip and Ernest. But you decide to take care of your three sons differently within that same trust. Suppose that after Robert receives his quarterly $30,000 payments for five years, his payments will then stop and Chip and Ernest each begin receiving $30,000 quarterly payments at that point. Essentially, Chip and Ernest have a future interest in the property (the trust) because they can't benefit right now, but rather they benefit in the future.

Complicating factors just a bit more, someone with a future interest in property can actually have one of two different types of future interest:

>> Vested interest

>> Contingent interest

If you have a *vested interest,* you have the right to use and enjoy what you will get from that property at some point in the future, with no strings attached.

TECHNICAL STUFF

In the world of estate planning, the word *vested* means basically the same as it does in the world of retirement plans, stock options, and other financial assets. After you are vested in your company's retirement plan, you have the right to receive retirement benefits according to the particulars of your company's plan, even if you leave your job. (Unless you worked at Enron, but that's another story. . . .) Similarly, if you have stock options that have vested, you have the right to "exercise" those options and buy your company's stock at your "strike price." Furthermore, if you want, you can immediately sell those shares for a quick profit if your company's stock price has gone way up. (Unless you worked at Enron, but that's basically the same story. . . .)

However, if you have the other type of future beneficial interest — *contingent* — then you have to deal with some "strings attached" other than the simple passage of time. For example, you may set up that trust for your three sons in such a way that for Chip and Ernest to *realize* that future benefit, each must graduate from college and spend two years in the Peace Corps.

(Or you may set up the trust so that Chip receives his future benefit only if he marries and his wife gives birth to a set of triplets — in keeping with the theme of this example, which references, as you may have already realized, the old television show *My Three Sons.*)

Why You Need to Plan Your Estate

You can, of course, decide to leave what happens to your estate after you die totally up to chance (or, more accurately, the complicated set of state laws that will apply if you haven't done the estate planning that you need to do). But because you're reading this chapter, chances are that the two fundamental goals of estate planning at the beginning of this chapter — protection and control — are uppermost in your mind.

But going beyond the general idea of protecting your possessions and being in control, you have some very specific objectives that you're trying to accomplish with your estate planning, such as these:

>> **Providing for your loved ones:** You have people like your spouse or significant other, children, grandchildren, and parents who may rely on you for financial support. What will happen to that financial support if you were to die tomorrow?

Even if you have a "traditional" family (that is, the kind of family typically shown in a 1950s TV show), financial and other support for family members after you die can get very complicated if your estate isn't in order. But if your family is one that may be described as (quoting Nicholas Cage in the movie *Raising Arizona*) "Well, it ain't *Ozzie and Harriet*," then you absolutely need to pay attention to all the little details of protecting your family members if you die. Specifically, if your loved ones include former spouses, children living in another household, stepchildren, adopted children, divorced and remarried parents, or an unmarried partner, then you have a lot of decisions to make with regards to your estate about who gets what.

>> **Minimizing what your estate will have to pay in estate taxes:** Yes, we know that we said that estate planning involves much more than the inheritance and estate (death) taxes, but make no mistake about it, death taxes are certainly a consideration. Why pay more than you have to? You can take several steps — such as giving gifts while you're still alive — to reduce the value of your estate and therefore reduce the amount of death taxes that will have to be paid.

>> **Protecting your business:** Politicians love to talk about the small business owner or the family farmer when describing how they are "a friend to the little guy," but the fact remains that if you own a small- or medium-scale business, such as a retail store or a farm, that business can be turned topsy-turvy if you die without a solid estate plan in place. (So actually, you want to make sure that if you're a farmer, your farm is protected after you've "bought the farm.")

Sure, it's human nature to just let things happen. You're very busy with your career and your family. And after all, do you really want to dwell on morbid thoughts such as your own death?

But as The Beatles sang in "The Ballad of John and Yoko": "Oh boy, when you're dead, you don't take nothing with you but your soul. Think!" And because you really can't take any of your property with you, you do leave behind people and institutions (charities, foundations, and so on) that you care about along with all of your possessions. Why wouldn't you want to take the time to appropriately match up your property with those people and institutions?

Besides, estate planning is as much (if not more) about what you do during your life to manage your estate than what happens after you die. Sure, it makes good theater to have a deathbed scene where the aged family patriarch or matriarch dictates what will happen to the vast family fortune, but the place to begin your estate planning isn't on your deathbed. That last-minute approach usually opens up the probability of one or more disgruntled family members trying to overturn your dying words. More than likely, due to the result of your lack of estate planning, your estate will dwindle away through legal fees and taxes in excess of what should have been paid.

(And not to be morbid, but if you were to die suddenly and unexpectedly, you may not even have the "opportunity" for that dramatic deathbed scene. If you haven't done your estate planning, then chances are nobody in your family will have any idea of what you want to happen to your estate.)

Need more? How about the game Congress is playing with the federal estate tax? As part of the estate tax laws, you have an *exemption* — an amount that you may leave behind that is free of the federal estate tax. (The estate tax doesn't kick in until your estate exceeds the exemption amount).

Currently, the federal estate tax exemption in 2017 is $5.49 million. That will rise to $5.6 million in 2018. Always bear in mind that Congress can keep messing with that thing, which can affect your estate planning. The main point for now is that for federal estate tax purposes, your estate planning is actually a moving target.

TIP

Another reason to plan your estate deals with a mistake that many married couples make with their respective estates. Regardless of the federal estate tax and varying exemption amounts already discussed, you can leave an unlimited amount of your estate to your spouse free of federal estate taxes.

WARNING

However, sometimes you are better off not leaving your entire estate to your spouse, especially if your spouse also has a sizable estate (not only property jointly owned with you, but personal property that only your spouse owns). Why? Because then your spouse (assuming you die first) now has an even larger estate, which is then subject to a potentially larger tax liability than if you had done something else with your estate. Basically, your children or whomever else you and your spouse are leaving your respective estates to will likely be stuck with paying more in federal estate taxes just because you decided to take the easy step with your estate and leave it all to your spouse.

Many states also impose inheritance and estate taxes, which your estate pays in addition to federal estate taxes.

The answer? You need to proactively conduct your estate planning, take all of the matters in this section into consideration, and create a personalized estate plan.

Why Your Estate-Planning Goals Are Different from Your Neighbors'

You are a unique individual. That's why you need to take time to create an individualized estate plan for your own situation.

Many people finally and grudgingly acknowledge that they need to worry about their estate plans but then take a haphazard, lackadaisical approach to estate planning: a generic fill-in-the-blank will purchased in a stationery store, a cursory review of active insurance policies, and checking to see whose names are listed as beneficiaries on the retirement plan at work. But that's all; everything else will fall into place, right?

And besides, is it really worth putting any more time and effort beyond those basic tasks? After all, you're the one who will be dead. Why make all that effort for a series of events that will take place after you've died?

However, consider all the factors that make up many different aspects of your life, including the following:

>> Your marital status: married, divorced, separated, single, widowed (or "widowered"), or maybe unmarried but living with someone

>> Your age

>> Your health (not to be excessively morbid, but if you know that you have a potentially fatal condition or illness, or are in generally poor health, time is of the essence for your estate planning)

>> Your *financial profile*, such as the property (real and personal) you have and what that property is worth

>> Any potentially complicated business or financial situations you have, such as investment partnerships

>> Any money you expect to receive — particularly large sums — such as an inheritance, lawsuit settlement, or severance pay from a job you are leaving

>> What insurance policies you have, the types (see the chapters in Book 3), and the value of each

>> If any of your assets are particularly risky, such as stock or stock options in a start-up company that on paper is worth millions of dollars, but you can't do anything with those assets for some reason (such as your stock options haven't fully vested)

>> If you have any children and if so, how many, their ages, their respective financial states, and their respective marital statuses

>> If you have any grandchildren and if so, if you want to explicitly take care of them as part of your estate planning or, alternatively, leave it to your children to take care of their own children as part of their own estate planning

>> If your parents are still alive and if so, whether they are still married to each other, if either may have remarried, their financial status (together or, if divorced, separately) and if you need to take care of them

>> Your siblings (brothers and sisters) and if you want or need to take care of them as part of your estate planning

>> Any other family members (cousins, aunts, uncles, and so on) or even friends that you want to include in your estate planning

>> Charities and foundations that you support

Just considering the items in that list — not to mention dozens of others that you can probably think of — you'll realize how unique your situation is. Sure, somewhere in the United States, you can probably find someone else with more or less the same profile as yours, but the point is that no estate plan is a one-size-fits-all plan that you can effortlessly adapt to your situation.

Additionally, even a canned plan that seems to be suitable for your situation may actually be a poor choice after you really dig into the details. Think of the man's suit or woman's evening dress that looks great in a magazine advertisement or even on a store mannequin — one that seems to be bodily proportional to your own — but when you try that suit or dress on, something just doesn't look or feel right.

REMEMBER

Make your credo for estate planning be: "No shortcuts allowed!" The time and effort, and even expense, that you put into developing a solid, comprehensive estate plan will be well rewarded. True, you won't necessarily be alive to fully see the benefits of your efforts, but those people that you care about enough to include in your estate plan likely will be grateful.

The Critical Path Method to Planning Your Estate

Estate planning is a process that can be further divided into multiple steps or activities (or, for your computer and business types, *subprocesses*). In business, building computer applications, or even life itself (weddings, for example), most processes tend to take days, weeks, months, or even years from start to finish; rarely does any process happen overnight.

You need to treat your estate planning activities as a process. The process includes a disciplined method created from a set of steps that lead you from a state of *estate-planning nothingness* (that is, you have no estate plan at all) to the point where you have a well-thought-out estate plan in place. This is called the *critical path method* to planning your estate.

TECHNICAL STUFF

If you have taken a college business class in operations research, quantitative methods, or a similar topic, you may already be familiar with the critical path method, which is defined as "the most effective way through a series of steps to reach your objectives." In other words, even when you have a seemingly infinite number of possible paths in front of you, you can find one particular path that is the most effective and efficient of all of those alternatives.

In estate planning, you're often faced with many side roads when working on your will or setting up a trust. Before you know it, the side road has turned into a detour and your estate plan is up to its lug nuts in mud.

TIP

If the terms *operations research* and *quantitative methods* cause you to flinch, then simply think of the critical path method as a map. If you're standing on a corner in Winslow, Arizona, and you want to go to Phoenix, Arizona, you can get in your car and, after checking a map, drive approximately 190 miles of interstate highway. Or you could head to Los Angeles, then drive up to San Francisco, then maybe go over to Chicago, back to Denver, and then drive to Phoenix.

Anyway, the critical path method is fairly straightforward and includes the following steps:

1. **Define your goals.**

   Before you begin your estate planning, decide what you're trying to achieve. Are you trying to make sure that your spouse has enough income for some period of time (say, five years, or maybe longer) if you were to die suddenly? Are you trying to make sure that your children have enough money for college after you're gone? Is your estate worth upwards of $10 million, and are you trying to protect as much as possible from the eventual federal estate tax bite?

As mentioned earlier in this chapter, your estate-planning goals are almost certainly different from anyone else's that you know, so make sure that you take the time to define exactly what those goals are.

TIP

Write down your goals; don't just think about them. Often by actually writing your goals rather than just visualizing them, you get a better handle on how your goals relate to one another, and you make sure that you haven't forgotten anything.

2. **Determine which estate-planning professionals you want to work with.**

Financial planners, insurance agents, attorneys, and accountants (all of whom are discussed in the next section) can provide valuable guidance and service to you. You need to determine which professionals best help you meet your goals. For example, have an attorney work with you on your will to be sure you meet all of your own state's requirements for the will to be legally binding. You may also decide to work with other professionals depending on the complexity of your estate and the particular goals you defined in the previous step.

3. **Gather information.**

Whether you work with professionals or not (more on this particular decision point in the next section), you need to have as much available information as possible so that you know where you are currently in your estate-planning process:

- Do you have a will right now, and, if so, when did you prepare that will?

- What in your life has changed since you created that will?

- What insurance policies do you currently have?

- Have any insurance policies expired?

- Perhaps most importantly, what property is in your estate and what is the value of that property?

4. **Develop your action plan.**

Basically, get ready to do the many different activities discussed in this book: Work on your will. (Create your will if you don't have one, or perhaps update your will if the will is out of date — see Book 2, Chapter 4.) Decide whether trusts make sense for you, and, if so, choose which ones. Figure out what you need to do to protect your business, and so on.

5. **Actually conduct your action plan.**

People often trip up on this step during their estate planning (or anything else they like to procrastinate on). Take the plans that you developed in Step 4 and actually do them. If you die without a will, complications may arise even if someone in your family finds a sheet of paper on your desk that reads "Step 4: Prepare my will."

6. Monitor your action plan.

You may like going through all the previous estate-planning steps, finishing them, and then just forgetting about them all. But in estate planning, you never really finish. You periodically need to resynchronize your estate plan with any major changes in your life. For example, have you gotten divorced and remarried? You had better get cracking on those updates. Even less dramatic changes in your life can trigger changes, so your best bet is to double-check everything in your estate plan once each year so you can make sure that all changes to your life, great and small, are reflected in your estate planning in a timely fashion. You can even tie your "checkup" to an annual occurrence, like your birthday, or the beginning or end of daylight saving time, or to some other occasion that you won't easily forget.

By following these steps and staying on the critical path, you greatly reduce the chances of taking all kinds of unnecessary and potentially serious detours with your estate planning and can typically get through the tasks with a minimum amount of stress.

TIP

Take the initiative to meet with each member of your estate-planning team annually. Or ask someone on the team to remind you annually to review your estate plans — the way your dentist reminds you to come in for a checkup.

Getting Help with Your Estate Planning

You can do all your estate planning by yourself, but you don't have to, and even more importantly, we don't recommend that approach. But can you turn to someone with a job title along the lines of professional estate planner for help?

Not exactly. As mentioned several times in this chapter, estate planning actually consists of several different specialties or disciplines, and if you want, you can work with one or more people in each of those specialties as part of your estate planning.

The number of people you work with largely depends on two main factors:

>> How comfortable you are with the overall concepts and mechanics of estate planning

>> How complicated your estate is

The material covered in this book can go a long way toward helping you with the first of those two factors. But even if you thoroughly understand little nuances of the clauses to include in your will or the basic types of trusts, you may still want to tap into a network of professionals if your estate is particularly complicated. Sure, you'll spend a bit more money on fees, but in the long run, you're more likely to avoid a horrendously costly mistake (financially, emotionally, or both), particularly if your estate is rather complicated.

How to make sure your team of advisers is "FAIL" safe

So who do you work with? Here's an acronym to help you remember whom you need to think about for your estate-planning team: FAIL, which stands for

>> Financial planner

>> Accountant

>> Insurance agent

>> Lawyer

TIP

You don't necessarily need a full slate of estate-planning professionals on your team. You may, for example, work with your attorney and accountant. But if you've decided that insurance is only a minimal part of your overall estate plan, then you may not need to work with an insurance agent. Or if you are well versed in investments and financial planning, then you can handle that aspect of your estate plan by yourself and work with team members from the other specialization areas.

STRAIGHT TALK

You need to talk candidly and honestly about personal and sometimes sensitive — or even painful — matters with your estate-planning team. The last thing you want is for your insurance agent to recommend a certain type of insurance policy that the issuing insurance company could invalidate because you hid some important fact that was later found out. And your attorney needs to thoroughly understand all aspects of your relationships with your family to help you create a will that accurately reflects your wishes. For example, if you really want to cut someone out of your will and leave that person nothing at all, make sure your attorney knows that so your will can be constructed appropriately.

WARNING

The best professionals sometimes set things into motion that can have unintentional and less-than-desirable consequences if another member of your estate-planning team isn't aware of what was done. For example, you need to be certain that you understand all the tax implications — federal income, state income, gift, estate, and so on — of a trust that your financial planner recommends and that your attorney sets up. Therefore, your accountant needs to work side by side with your attorney and your financial planner before the trust is created to be certain that no unpleasant tax surprises pop up.

Working with financial planning professionals

Because a significant portion of your estate is likely to involve your investments and savings, consider working with some type of financial planning professional. You can work with a financial planning professional solely on an advisory basis. If you want, you can make your own decisions about your investments and savings, after consulting with a professional. Your financial planning professional can also play a much more active role, such as making major decisions for your financial life (with your consent, of course).

WARNING

All financial planning professionals aren't created equal, nor do they necessarily have the same background and qualifications. In the following paragraphs, we provide a brief overview, and you can also find a very candid, no-holds-barred discussion of financial planners in the latest edition of *Personal Finance For Dummies*, by Eric Tyson (Wiley).

Before you decide to work with any financial planning professional, you need to understand just who these people are, what type of formal training and credentials they have, and how using them relates to your estate planning.

Certified Financial Planners (CFPs) provide financial planning services and general financial advice on a wide range of topics from investments to taxes and from estate planning to retirement planning. CFPs are required to pass college-level courses in a broad range of financial subjects and then a two-day, ten-hour examination. CFPs must also either have a bachelor's degree and at least three years of professional experience working with financial planning clients or, without a degree, have at least five years of experience doing financial planning.

TIP

You can check with the Financial Planning Association at www.fpanet.org or search for planners by state, city, or zip code or call 404-845-0011 (toll-free 800-322-4237). You can find financial planners who have the CFP credentials. You can then verify a planner's CFP status with the CFP Board of Standards at www.cfp-board.org. You can regularly check *Money Magazine, Smart Money,* and other personal finance publications for the latest information and even problems and scandals in the profession.

OTHER FINANCIAL PLANNING PROFESSIONALS

If your financial life is particularly complicated, you may need to work with several types of financial planning professionals in addition to a basic financial planner (who may or may not be a CFP).

Another type of financial planning professional is the *Investment Adviser* (IA) or the *Registered Investment Adviser* (RIA). IAs and RIAs specifically advise their clients about securities (stocks, bonds, and so on). Any IA who manages at least $25 million in assets must register with the Securities and Exchange Commission (SEC), and you can check this information out at www.adviserinfo.sec.gov.

Chartered Financial Analysts (CFAs) are typically portfolio managers or analysts for banks, mutual funds, or other institutional clients (in Wall Street lingo), but some CFAs also advise wealthy individuals and families who have particularly complicated investment situations. CFAs take a series of examinations covering portfolio management, accounting, equity analysis, and other subjects and must have at least three years of professional experience in investments. CFAs are also required to sign an ethics pledge every year.

A *Certified Investment Management Consultant* (CIMC) works with the wealthiest of the wealthy — high-net-worth private clients. A variety of examinations and continuing education plus at least three years of professional experience are required.

A *Certified Fund Specialist* (CFS) works with clients on mutual funds. (Some CFSs also provide general financial planning services.) Examinations and continuing education are required to retain CFS status.

WARNING

Make sure you clearly understand how your financial planning professional — CFP or otherwise — gets paid. Some financial planning professionals get paid on a "fee-only" basis, meaning that they don't receive any commissions for selling you financial products. They are compensated only for advice (basically, they're consultants).

Fee-based financial planning professionals earn fees not only from the advice they give you but also from commissions for selling you financial products, while commission-based financial planning professionals make money only from the products they sell you.

You can certainly find both ethical and unethical people (not to mention competent and incompetent) in any of these three categories. However, always pay particular attention to recommendations from fee-based or commission-based financial planning professionals. Perhaps those investment choices are the perfect match for you, but you need to make that decision, not your financial planning professional who stands to benefit financially from selling you some type of product.

Knowing what to expect from your accountant for your estate planning

Your accountant can do a lot more for you than fill out your tax returns for the year where you do. Besides tax return preparation, for planning purposes, trying to alter what happens in the future for tax purposes by doing certain steps today. Plan on working with an accountant on your estate planning for those very same reasons, even if you do your own income taxes and haven't really worked with an accountant before.

Make sure the accountant on your estate-planning team presents you with scenarios of what can likely happen, based on recommendations from other members of your estate-planning team. If your CFP recommends certain investments or insurance products, then what are the tax implications when you die? What are the tax implications if you die tomorrow versus dying ten years from now?

Your accountant can also have a more active role in your estate planning, suggesting certain tactics with an eye toward reducing your overall estate tax burden, giving gifts in particular.

WARNING

Never do any financial gift giving (as contrasted with birthday gift giving or holiday gift giving) without consulting with an accountant for all the tax implications.

Seek out an accountant who is a Certified Public Accountant (CPA), meaning that the accountant has passed the American Institute of Certified Public Accountants (AICPA) examination.

TIP

You may also consider combining two of the roles on your estate-planning team — the financial planning and accounting specialists — by working with someone who is a Certified Public Accountant/Personal Financial Specialist (CPA/PFS), in other words, a CPA who also provides overall financial planning and has passed the PFS exam. Check out www.cpapfs.org.

Your insurance agent and your estate

Depending on your particular estate-planning needs, various forms of insurance (life, disability, liability, and other types discussed in Book 3) may play a key role.

Most people who have dependents (particularly a spouse and children) wind up working insurance into their estate plan to meet the "protection" objective of estate planning.

Therefore, consider your insurance agent a part of your estate-planning team. For example, when you discuss life insurance and make decisions between different types of life insurance policies, make sure your insurance agent is aware of any estate-planning strategies, such as trusts, so you can make sure that your policy beneficiaries are listed correctly.

TIP

Some insurance companies are *agentless,* meaning that unlike traditional insurance companies where you have an assigned insurance agent, your contact with the company is through any one of hundreds or even thousands of customer service representatives, almost always over the phone or the Internet. In these situations, ask one of the customer service representatives whether you can speak with or even work with anyone at the company on estate-planning matters. Chances are the representative will say yes, so even though you don't technically have an insurance agent, you may still have access to short-term estate-planning assistance when you need it.

Working with your attorney

Even though your attorney is last on the list of the members of your estate-planning team (courtesy of the "L for Lawyer" used in the FAIL acronym), he or she could quite possibly be the most important member for one simple reason: Your attorney keeps you from inadvertently making very serious mistakes.

All kinds of problems can trip you up and cause serious headaches in the future, if not headaches for you because you've already died, then headaches for someone else. For example:

>> How should your will read to make sure that your significant other (to whom you are not married) receives what you want out of your estate?

>> How should the deed to your home be written to make sure that your unmarried significant other isn't forced to move if you die first?

>> If you have an elderly parent who needs to go into a nursing home, what are the implications to your parent's estate and your own?

Basically, think of your attorney as your "scenario-planning specialist." Your attorney takes all kinds of information about you and your estate into consideration. He or she then presents you with options, based on various scenarios, such as you dying suddenly next week (morbid, but definitely an eye-opener for many people when first doing their estate planning) versus you dying at the ripe old age of 134 (courtesy of advanced biotechnology), having outlived everyone else in your family.

Beyond the scenario planning, make your attorney your primary adviser for your will, trusts, legal implications for your business, and pretty much any other legal matter that directly or indirectly relates to your estate planning.

IN THIS CHAPTER

» Determining the value of your real and personal property

» Including your debts in your estate's value

» Reducing and controlling your estate's value through gift giving

» Figuring out adjustments in your estate's value after your life changes

Chapter **2**

Bean Counting: Figuring Out What You're Worth

Quick: How much are you worth?

You may think you have a pretty good idea of what your estate is worth — within 5 to 10 percent, give or take — but you may be very surprised when you actually sit down and start taking stock of your assets.

If you've ever filled out a loan application for a new car or a home mortgage, chances are that when you began listing your assets, you thought of several items beyond your savings accounts and mutual funds that turned out to be quite valuable. What about that wardrobe of $2,000 custom suits? And how about all those antiques from trips to Europe? Even families with more modest tastes usually have the family silverware, jewelry, household furniture, and several other items that add up to a decent amount of money.

Therefore, to be accurate in your estate planning, you need to know how much all your estate is really worth. And if you're like most people, you need to dig beneath the surface and beyond the obvious — factoring in your debts and the future, too. This chapter tells you how.

Calculating the Value of Your Real Property

Your *real* property (your home and other real estate–related investments) may very well be the most valuable part of your estate. You need to carefully determine the value of all real property, especially if your estate plans call for dividing the value of that real property among more than one beneficiary. You want to be fair, and you want to have a good idea of what each beneficiary will receive, particularly if some beneficiaries will get other (non-real property) parts of your estate and you're trying to divide your overall estate as equally as possible.

Your home on the range

If you recently purchased your home (say within the last year or two), you have a pretty good idea of your home's worth, even if you live in an area where real estate prices are rapidly going up.

However, if you purchased your home a long time ago, you may have no idea of your property's value. For example, maybe you never purchased your home at all — perhaps you're living in the family's ancestral home that's been in your family since the early 1900s.

Either way, you need to get an official idea of your home's value, and you can do so in one of two ways:

>> You can hire a real estate appraiser who does nothing but determine property value. A paid appraiser is likely to give you the most thorough and accurate idea of your home's value because you pay for that service.

>> If you don't want to pay an appraiser, you can do what real estate professionals call "checking comparables." You can find the sale price of a comparable property in or near your neighborhood with the same floor plan, the same exterior design, roughly the same lot size, and other characteristics nearly identical to your home.

WARNING

In most suburban settings, prices and values for nearly identical properties can vary widely depending on what neighborhood the house is in, even if those neighborhoods are right next to each other. So make sure that if you decide to determine your home's value based on comparable properties yourself, you understand the differences in property values between popular, highly coveted neighborhoods and others not quite so prestigious.

If you live in a home that's unique in any way — a farmhouse set on hundreds of acres or a two-centuries-old brownstone in a downtown neighborhood, for example — then you should definitely hire an appraiser. Otherwise, you can be way off in determining what your home is worth.

That time-share in Timbuktu and other hideaways

If you own a second home of any kind, from a beachfront bungalow to a condominium at the foot of a prestigious ski resort (or even a part of a second home, such as a time-share), you can figure out what that property is worth in much the same way as you do your primary home.

Your investments as a landlord

If you have any investment real property, such as a rental duplex or a share of an apartment building or office complex, then you probably have some background in how to value residential or commercial real estate. (At least you should, because you had to decide whether the investment you were considering making was a good deal or not.)

TIP

If you do your own finances for your real estate investments, you're familiar with terms like *net operating income* and *capitalization rate,* which are used to calculate how much your investment is worth. But if you don't do your own finances for your real estate investments, don't worry. Whoever manages your investment for you does know these terms, so just ask your investment manager how much your investment is worth. If, however, you invested $50,000 ten years ago in rental property because your brother-in-law told you it was a good idea and you have no idea about operating expenses and cap rates, then take the easy way out: Contact a commercial real estate appraiser and get your investment property appraised.

TIP

If you hire an appraiser for commercial investment property, make sure the appraiser is experienced in valuing the type of property you have. (Don't hire a residential home appraiser to tell you what your 20 percent of a commercial farming operation is worth.)

Your real estate partnerships

You may have an investment in real property that isn't a direct investment but rather is an investment in a Limited Liability Company (LLC) or Limited Liability Partnership (LLP). (LLCs and LLPs are just methods of ownership that have gained favor over the past years primarily because of their tax advantages.)

TECHNICAL STUFF

The value of some LLCs and LLPs can vary greatly from year to year. Additionally, you usually have restrictions on how you can sell or otherwise transfer control of your ownership portion of an LLC or LLP. Those restrictions often result in a *valuation discount,* meaning that your portion of an LLC or LLP is actually worth less than you would calculate using your share of the income minus your share of the expenses. Consequently, you need to keep current — usually through regular statements you receive from the LLC or LLP — and adjust the value of your estate accordingly.

For example, if you have an investment in a shopping center through an LLP, the shopping center's value can be dramatically affected if an anchor (main) tenant files for bankruptcy and shuts down the location at your shopping center. The property's revenue decreases, which in turn decreases the net operating income, ultimately decreasing the shopping center's value when you divide the net operating income by the cap rate.

You typically use LLCs and LLPs to own shares of more valuable investment real properties (such as large office complexes or an apartment complex with hundreds of apartments) rather than shares of properties you invest in directly (such as smaller office buildings or a duplex residential site). Therefore, the value of LLCs and LLPs is likely to fluctuate more than any direct real estate investments you have. Monitor them closely, not only for estate-planning purposes but also for personal investment purposes.

Calculating the Value of Everything Else: Your Personal Property

Get out the notepad or the spreadsheet program, and get ready for some long lists of your tangible and intangible personal property. You need to be as thorough as possible so that you can accurately figure out what your estate is worth.

Tangible personal property — items you can touch

You will likely see an interesting paradox with regards to your *tangible personal property* (cars, jewelry, and other household items). You probably have far more individual items of tangible personal property that you need to catalog and value than the other types of property in your estate (real property and intangible personal property). However, for most people, tangible personal property has the smallest overall value.

Some of your personal property may be almost (or even totally) worthless in a financial sense, but you still need to catalog those items and decide what you want to happen to them after you die. For example, who do you want to get the lucky Liberty nickel that your grandfather carried over on the boat when he came to the United States in 1898, the one that was handed down to your father and then to you? Maybe the nickel isn't worth much more than a nickel even though it's more than 100 years old, but it still carries great family sentimental value. So which of your four children will you leave that nickel to, and what other sentimental goodies will you leave to the others?

You could, of course, let your children, grandchildren, and other family members "put in a claim" on some or all your "trinkets" while you're still alive — sort of a grab-bag approach to giving away part of your estate. But even if you decide to take that approach, you need to have everyone's "wish lists" and make sure that your will reflects all those who-gets-what decisions.

But even leaving aside small-value personal property, the rest of your tangible personal property can add up. Just take a look around your living room at the furniture and antiques, or in your den at that autographed 1927 New York Yankees' baseball and your collection of first-edition Hemingway novels.

So get cracking. You need to figure out what your property is worth, after you first figure out what you have. Overwhelmed at the thought? Here are a few tips to help:

TIP

>> Combine your estate planning-related valuation of your tangible personal property with the same activities for Insurance purposes. Most homeowner or renter's insurance policies require you to provide a list of your jewelry, collectibles, and antiques to be included beyond your basic coverage (often more than a certain dollar amount, or for certain types of items). If you need to spend the time cataloging those items and determining what they're worth for your insurance company, use those efforts for your estate planning as well!

>> Cataloging hundreds of items can be tedious, and even if you aren't prone to procrastinating, you can often find some way to stretch out the process as long as possible. But if you have a video camera, you can take a guided tour through your home (as well as your second home, if you have one) and narrate the tour into the camera's microphone: "Here is that first-edition *Batman* that my idiot husband insisted be framed and hung over the sofa in the living room instead of the painting that I wanted to put there; it's worth . . ."

>> Appraisal fees can really add up, especially for hundreds of items. You can get a pretty good idea of what your tangible personal property is worth by using eBay or another online auction service for research. Look for the identical

item (or one close enough and in more or less the same condition) that you have and check the final winning bid of recently closed (completed) auctions, or current bids of active auctions about to close.

Intangible personal property — bank accounts, stocks and bonds

Your *intangible personal property* — your paper financial assets, such as your bank accounts, stocks, mutual funds, annuities, and so on — may make up a substantial portion of your estate, particularly if you've invested your money wisely and diversified your assets.

Fortunately, figuring out what most types of your intangible personal property are worth is fairly straightforward. (More about what's not so straightforward in a moment.) You can

>> Check your bank statements for the value of your checking accounts, savings accounts, certificates of deposit (CDs), Individual Retirement Accounts (IRAs), and so on.

>> Consult an interest payment schedule to get the current value of savings bonds.

>> Look up the current prices of your stocks in the newspaper or check any of the many online financial websites that give you stock prices, and multiply that price by the number of shares you own.

>> Read the paper each morning and find the *net asset value* (NAV, a mutual fund term meaning the actual value of each share) of the mutual funds you own, and multiply the NAV by the number of shares you own.

>> Ask your broker for the value of your government or corporate bonds, or more complicated investments like call-and-put options and commodities futures.

TIP

If you use a computer program to track your portfolio's value, you probably already have the information described at your fingertips; just consult the program you use to figure out the value of those investments.

You may have some intangible personal property that is a bit more complicated when it comes to figuring out its value. For example, you may have *stock options* from your employer. (Stock options give you the right to purchase shares of your company's stock at some point in the future at a guaranteed price per share, no matter how much higher — you hope, anyway — your company's stock price goes.)

If you're one of the "Head Honchos" at work and have a sizable stock option package, consult with an experienced investment professional to help figure out what your options are worth.

TECHNICAL STUFF

Valuing your stock options may be complicated, particularly if your company hasn't gone public yet. If your company hasn't gone public, you can't look up your company's stock price in the newspaper or online because your company isn't yet publicly traded. And even if your company has gone public, the real value of your stock options isn't quite as simple as if you actually owned those shares of your company's stock covered by those options, where you simply multiply the number of shares by the price per share. To calculate the precise value of stock options, investment professionals use complicated factors and terms, such as *intrinsic value* and the Black-Scholes Model. Sound confusing? If you want to find out more about valuing stock options, you can check out *Trading Options For Dummies*, 3rd Edition, by Joe Duarte (Wiley, 2017).

Dead Reckoning: Subtracting Your Debts from Your Assets

Book 5, Chapter 1 mentions that in addition to your *positive balance* assets — real property, tangible personal property, and intangible personal property — your estate's value must also include *negative balance* (amounts that you owe).

After you figure out the value of your assets, you simply add up all the debts you owe and subtract that total from your assets to give you the net worth of your estate. These debts include the outstanding balances on

>> Any real estate–related loans, including the first mortgage on your home, any second mortgage you may have, the unpaid balance on a home equity loan, the mortgage(s) on a second home, and so on

>> Your student loans

>> Your credit cards

>> Any automobile loans or loans on other vehicles, boats, airplanes, and so on

>> Any personal loans, whether from a bank or a person

>> Department store loans or other retailer charge accounts

>> Any margin loans with your stockbroker

>> Future debts you're sure to incur, such as paying for your children's college education

TECHNICAL
STUFF

If you have any kind of credit-related life insurance — mortgage insurance, credit card insurance, and so forth — that will pay off the balance of a particular debt, then that life insurance effectively cancels out the debt for purposes of calculating your estate. So don't forget to consider any credit-related life insurance when you're adding up all your property and debts. However, credit-related life insurance isn't a particularly good idea if you can get life insurance elsewhere. Book 3, Chapter 2 talks more about life insurance.

Giving Gifts throughout Your Life to Reduce Your Estate's Value

You've probably seen the expression that was popular on bumper stickers and posters in the mid-1990s: "He who dies with the most toys wins."

Well, not when it comes to estate planning and, specifically, death taxes. The more your estate is worth when you die, the bigger the tax bite. So part of your estate-planning strategy may be to *give away* some of those toys while you're still alive, effectively transferring those assets from your estate to someone else's estate.

WARNING

You need to remain aware of many complications with gift giving, such as annual limits on the value of gifts, lifetime asset transfer limits, strategies where you and your spouse coordinate your respective gift giving, and tax implications.

For now, though, realize that as you tally up all the property in your estate and the property's value, you need to work with your estate-planning team to figure out whether gift giving makes sense for you and, if so, how to get started on a sensible, tax-managed gift plan.

TIP

You also need to consider gift giving even if financial and tax reasons don't come into play. For example, you may want to give certain items of sentimental value to a family member or friend, or perhaps a charity or foundation instead of waiting until your estate is settled (and you're no longer alive). Even in these sentimentally based situations, consult with your accountant to determine any tax implications.

Calculating Adjustments in Your Estate's Value Due to Life Changes

Like pretty much everything else related to estate planning, you need to be very vigilant about keeping up-to-date with the change in your estate's value over time.

Changes in your life can dramatically alter your estate's value and, in turn, cause you to rethink your overall estate planning and how you want your estate divided after you die.

For example, if you get divorced, your estate's value will likely change dramatically as a result of the divorce settlement. Or, on a more uplifting note, if you win the lottery or have the value of your stock portfolio go way up, your estate's value also increases and you may want to rethink your estate plan.

WARNING

If you ignore dramatic changes in your estate's value, you run the risk of having an out-of-date estate plan that doesn't come close to reflecting what your original intentions had been.

For example, suppose you have two children, and in your estate you have $200,000 in various certificates of deposit and treasury bills, plus $200,000 worth of stock in an Internet company called NeverShouldHaveGonePublic.com that you purchased in early 1999. When you finally got around to preparing your will later that year, fearing that the Y2K computer bugs would cause widespread chaos and who knows what else, you decided to leave the $200,000 in CDs and T-bills to your daughter and the NeverShouldHaveGonePublic.com stock to your son.

By early 2002, NeverShouldHaveGonePublic.com had joined the dot.com graveyard and the stock was totally worthless. If you die before you update your will, your daughter will get the current value of the CDs and T-bills (now a little bit more than $200,000 because of interest earned since 1999), but your son will get a whole bunch of worthless stock. Therefore, if your intention had been to divide your estate equally between your two children, you first need to realize that your estate's value has changed, and then you need to update your will to reflect those changes and a new strategy of who gets what.

(As discussed in Book 2, Chapters 2 and 3, if your intention had been to leave each of your children equal shares of your estate, you could have — and should have — divided those assets equally between your daughter and your son. If you had done so, you would not have to update your will simply because of the dramatic change in your estate's value.)

IN THIS CHAPTER

» **Understanding how probate works**

» **Revealing the good, the bad, and the ugly of probate**

» **Selecting or being a personal representative: What you need to know**

» **Grasping the basics of will substitutes**

» **Exploring the different types of will substitutes**

Chapter **3**

Probate and How to Dodge It

Dealing with *probate* may sound like you've just been sprung from jail and have to walk a straight and narrow path for a while. Actually, that's *probation*, a word that also means "to prove," like when you call Officer Krupke and reassure him that you've left your criminal past behind.

Probate, on the other hand, happens after you die — specifically what happens to your estate. Like probation, probate works through the legal system and is probably the most misunderstood aspect of estate planning.

Fear not. This chapter covers the probate process, including both positive and negative aspects of probate, as well as alternative forms of probate. It also suggests a sensible process for selecting your *personal representative*, the person you name in your will who takes charge of your affairs after you've left the scene.

Probing Probate: What You Should Know

Probate is a term that is used in several different ways. Probate can refer to the act of presenting a will to a court officer for filing — such as, to "probate" a will. But in a more general sense, probate refers to the method by which your estate is administered and processed through the legal system after you die.

The probate process helps you transfer your estate in an orderly and supervised manner. Your estate must be dispersed in a certain manner, as outlined in this chapter (your debts and taxes paid before your beneficiaries receive their inheritance, for example). Think of the probate process as the "script" that guides the orderly transfer of your estate according to the rules.

Many people think that probate applies to you only if you have a will. Wrong! Your estate will be probated whether or not you have a will:

>> **With a valid will:** If you have a valid will, then your will determines how your estate is transferred during probate and to whom.

>> **Without a valid will:** If you don't have a will, or if you die *partially intestate*, where only part of your estate is covered by a valid will (see Book 2, Chapter 4), the laws where you live specify who gets what parts of your estate.

So read on for a few important points about probate that you need to know.

The probate process

Even though you won't be around when your estate goes through probate (after all, you'll be dead), you need to understand how the probate process works. At the most basic levels, the probate process involves two steps:

>> Pays debts you owe

>> Transfers assets to your beneficiaries

A state court called the *probate court* oversees the probate process. Because probate courts are state courts and not federal courts, the processes they follow may vary from one state to another. Yet despite their differences, these courts all pretty much follow the same basic processes and steps, which typically include

>> Swearing in your personal representative

>> Notifying heirs, creditors, and the public that you are, indeed, dead

>> Inventorying your property

>> Distributing your estate (including paying bills and any taxes)

Swearing in your personal representative

In your will, you name who you want to be your personal representative — that is, the person in charge of your estate after you die. However, the court determines the personal representative for your estate if

>> You die without a will.

>> You have a will but for some reason didn't specify who you want to be your personal representative.

>> The person you selected has died or for some reason can't serve   and you didn't "bring in someone from the bullpen" to replace your original choice.

A family member, such as your spouse or an adult child, can request that the court appoint him or her as the personal representative for your estate. Regardless of who is finally selected, the court gives your personal representative official rights to handle your estate's affairs. As evidence that this person has the authority to act on behalf of your estate, the court gives your personal representative a certified document called the *Letters of Administration* or *Letters Testamentary.*

In either case, the personal representative named in your will or determined by the court has to first be formally appointed by the court before officially entering into office (the term that's used). Usually this involves that the personal representative take an oath of office, after which he or she will then receive the official documentation showing his or her status (the *Letters of Administration* or *Letters Testamentary* just mentioned).

Your personal representative files a document called a *Petition for Probate of Will and Appointment of Personal Representative* with the probate court. This petition begins the probate process. If you have a will, the probate court issues an order admitting your will to probate. Basically, the court acknowledges your will's validity.

Notifying creditors and the public

Some state laws require your personal representative to publish a death notice in your local paper. The death notice serves as a public notice of your estate's probate and enables people who think they have an interest in your estate (such as creditors) to file a claim against your estate within a specified time period.

The notice is part of the process to make the matters of your estate part of the public record. Some people view the general public's ability to review your private estate matters as one of probate's disadvantages, as discussed later in this chapter.

Inventorying your property

The personal representative must inventory the different types of property — real and personal — that make up your estate so that your estate value can be determined. This inventory is important for a couple of reasons:

>> **To make sure you left enough to cover your debts and distributions to beneficiaries:** If your estate doesn't meet the monetary obligations of both your estate creditors and your property transfers to your beneficiaries, it's subject to *abatement statutes,* meaning that one or more beneficiaries may receive less than you had wanted or even nothing at all.

>> **To ensure that all property is accounted for:** Your personal representative is in charge of collecting and inventorying your estate's assets to make sure that all property is available for distributing at the end of the probate process. (Your beneficiaries, of course, will want to know what assets are in your estate.) If property is missing or not in your ownership at the time of your death, *ademption statutes* become relevant. These statutes determine whether a replacement asset or cash equivalent should replace the missing property intended for your beneficiary.

TIP

You should already have a pretty good idea of what your estate is worth (see Book 5, Chapter 2 for details) so that you can make intelligent choices for your estate plan. Obviously, your personal representative needs to know this information, too. So make sure that your personal representative has easy access to the list that shows what your estate includes and what your assets are worth. Even a slightly out-of-date list can serve as a starting point so that your personal representative doesn't have to create an inventory from scratch.

Distributing the estate

The final step in the probate process is the distribution of your estate property. In other words, everyone (ideally) — both your creditors and your heirs — gets what's coming to them.

Creditors that have a valid claim are likely to be paid in the following order (though the order varies from state to state):

1. Estate administration costs (legal advertising, appraisal fees, and so on)

2. Family allowances

3. Funeral expenses

4. Taxes and debt

5. All remaining claims

Whatever's left after your creditors get their money is distributed to your heirs or to the beneficiaries you named in your will. If you died without a will, the laws in your state determine how your property is distributed.

If probate proceeds according to plan and all notices and communications are properly handled, your personal representative is usually protected against any subsequent, late-arriving claims. Your personal representative will be protected after some specified time period expires.

Some complicating factors to the probate process

Some probate processes can be relatively straightforward, while others can be particularly complicated depending on how complicated an estate is. The following sections describe some of the more common complicating factors about probate that you'll likely encounter.

What's probated where: Differences between states

All states have probate, and all the types of property that make up your estate — real and personal — may be part of your estate's probate. Tangible and intangible personal property, like your collectibles and your stock portfolio, are probated in the state where you live, but your real property (your primary home and other real estate, as discussed in Book 5, Chapter 1) is probated where the property is actually located. So if you live on a farm in Pennsylvania and also have a vacation condo in Florida, you'll have two probates: Pennsylvania probate for your farm and your personal property, and Florida probate for your condo.

If you have more than one probate, the additional probate is called an *ancillary probate*. Ancillary probate can be costly because your personal representative usually needs to hire an attorney in the state where the real property is located to handle the ancillary administration of probate.

Here's some good news, though: In many cases, the second state's courts will legally recognize your personal representative's authority, and he or she can act on your estate's behalf in the second state without the necessity of a duplicate probate proceeding.

Probate or not: Differences between types of property

Another common misconception is that probate applies to all of your estate. Actually, probate handles the processing of all assets in your *probate estate.* Your probate estate is made up of all the property that's distributed through probate; the remaining property is called *nonprobate property.*

TECHNICAL STUFF

In a general sense, probate assets are those you own alone, while you own nonprobate assets jointly with others and to whom those assets will pass automatically upon your death. Nonprobate assets also include assets that pass to a named beneficiary: a life insurance policy, for example. Because these nonprobate assets pass to someone automatically, there is no need for probate.

Nonprobate property is your estate's way of saying, "No, thank you, Mr. Probate. I can handle this part myself!" Nonprobate property includes *will substitutes,* such as joint tenancy with right of survivorship and living trusts (discussed later in this chapter). Other assets, such as life insurance proceeds, qualified retirement plan benefits, and individual retirement accounts (IRAs) with named beneficiaries are also included.

Knowing the Good, the Bad, and the Ugly of Probate

Be aware of both the positive and negative aspects of probate. Know the pros and cons when you're planning your estate. You need to determine which assets will require probate and which assets should be nonprobate assets and pass to others through a will substitute.

Probate: The good side

The positive aspects of the probate process include the following:

>> Fairness

>> Defined procedures

>> Protection

>> Potential tax savings

Life isn't fair, but probate is

The probate court's independent role allows for an objective processing of your estate. The probate court regulates all parties involved in the process to make sure that everyone is treated fairly.

For example, the fees paid to attorneys, appraisers, or any other outside parties must be fair and reasonable before they can be paid from your estate.

Defined procedures

The probate process provides an orderly administration of your estate. The probate process guarantees that the probate court will correctly transfer your estate's property.

Here to protect you

The probate process allows creditors that have valid claims to receive what they are rightfully owed from your estate by proving the validity of their claims. If mechanisms weren't in place requiring creditors to prove the validity of their claims, your estate could be subject to fraudulent claims.

Imagine a sleazy finance company calling a grieving surviving spouse two days after a funeral and claiming that a loan payment of $5,000 is now two days overdue, but if the payment is made that day by certified check, no late charges will be applied. By requiring creditors to go through the probate process, your estate is mostly protected from these types of fraudulent claims.

Potential tax savings (cha-ching!)

If your estate is in a lower income tax bracket than the beneficiaries who receive the property transfers, tax savings may occur from lower income tax rates. Income tax savings are dependent on current tax rates and thus may not always be advantageous.

TIP

Don't forget that many probate costs are tax deductible and therefore may also reduce death taxes.

Probate: The bad and downright ugly side

Although the positive aspects present a good case for probate, several offsetting negative aspects can make probate an unpleasant process. The negative aspects of probate include the following:

>> A complicated process

>> A lack of privacy

>> Costs

>> An often-lengthy process

Talk about complicated!

The probate process can cause almost anyone to throw his or her hands toward the heavens and yell "Noooooo!" Multiple, often complicated steps are required before your property transfers can occur. The process often requires numerous hearings and professional assistance — for example, from appraisers to determine value and attorneys simply to get through the process.

Privacy? Forget it

Probate and privacy are polar opposites — the only thing in common is that both begin with *p*. Privacy typically doesn't exist in the probate process because after your will is probated, your will then becomes a part of the public record. Additionally, your estate's inventory and inheritance tax return (if applicable) also becomes parts of the public record. Anyone then can see what your will and estate contain. ("Wow! I didn't know John had so much money! Let's try to sell his widow all kinds of shady investments!") However, some states may offer additional means of privacy for the probate process, so check with your own attorney to understand what your estate will go through some day.

Many people consider their own financial situation, including what their estate contains, to be a private matter. On the other hand, you may not be a private person or you may figure that after you're dead, you really don't care about the lack of privacy. In this case, the negative aspect of lack of privacy becomes irrelevant.

Costs can be significant

Everything in life comes with a price. And this old adage applies even in death: Even after you're gone, the probate process is going to cost your family (or beneficiaries).

Your personal representative is entitled to reasonable compensation that typically ranges between 2 and 5 percent of your gross estate.

TIP

Your personal representative also has the option of waiving the fee, and may wish to do so for income tax reasons. You may consider a family member or trusted friend as your personal representative if you know that person will waive the fee, as long as you feel that person is qualified to serve.

Attorneys are also entitled to a reasonable fee that also may range between 2 and 5 percent of the gross estate but may vary depending on factors, such as the complexity of the estate, the attorney's time spent settling the estate, the attorney's experience, and other factors. If you add other costs like ancillary probate costs for real property located in another state, the costs of probate add up quickly.

Your beneficiaries need to be patient

Probate may be an orderly and defined process, but it's anything but fast. The probate process for an uncontested will — meaning no one comes forward to say they have an issue with your will — can easily take between 6 and 24 months. And if your will is contested, the process can be even longer, often years longer.

WARNING

Typically, your beneficiaries can't receive any property transfers until all the valid creditors' claims and taxes have been paid (see "An early payout" sidebar). While your beneficiaries await the completion of your estate's probate, your estate's value may decline — maybe even significantly (think bear market and declining stock prices) — leaving your beneficiaries with a lot less than they would have received if the probate process was faster.

Streamlining the Probate Process

The legal system hasn't failed to notice the negative aspects of probate. Probate courts and personal representatives everywhere face the costly, timely, lengthy, and complicated process again and again.

In response to the drawbacks of the probate process, several alternatives may be available for smaller estates. Some states have attempted to simplify the process with streamlined versions of probate. Remember, you can't avoid probate with your will, but these alternatives attempt to improve the process. (Hey, every little bit helps!)

TECHNICAL STUFF

In your state, you may come across terms such as *probate affidavit, summary probate,* or *small estate affidavit* that describe your state's alternatives to its formal probate process. Some of these probate alternatives have a cutoff amount that your estate would need to be under (that is, worth less than the specified dollar amount cutoff) for your estate to be eligible to use that particular alternative. Your attorney can advise you what alternatives are available in your state, whether your estate qualifies for one or more of those alternatives, and whether or not one of those alternatives makes sense for your estate.

Appointing Your Person in Charge

Choose carefully — your personal representative plays the central role in your estate's administration.

The appointment of your personal representative (and a contingent personal representative as a backup person) is one of the most important actions in your will. Your estate represents your lifetime of work. You, basically, are your own personal representative while you're alive, but after your death, you need to have some-one watch over your estate and make sure that your wishes are carried out. Your personal representative performs this function.

If you don't designate a personal representative, the probate court may appoint someone for you one way or another. So whether you have a will or not, someone is appointed to handle your estate administration.

Identifying your personal representative's role

Before you choose someone as your personal representative, double-check that the person understands his or her responsibilities. For that matter, you need to be aware of your personal representative's responsibilities so that you can select the most appropriate person.

The personal representative follows a *critical path method* — a road map of the most efficient way to proceed — in the administering of your estate. The steps of the critical path are as follows:

>> Collecting and inventorying estate property

>> Managing estate property

>> Processing creditors' claims

>> Filing tax returns and paying taxes

>> Distributing estate property

Collecting estate assets

Your personal representative first must locate your assets and see what you have in your estate for distribution. Think of this part of your personal representative's responsibilities as the same as the objective of an Easter egg hunt: to find the eggs and put them in a basket, or in this case, find and gather together all your property.

When collecting and inventorying your assets, your personal representative must notify banks and companies where you have investments of your death, change the address of record on your accounts, and make sure all future communication is through the personal representative. Additionally, your personal representative may need to hire an appraiser to determine your property's fair market value.

Your personal representative also serves as your accounts receivable coordinator. He or she collects all amounts owed to you, such as your final paycheck, rent from an investment property, or payments from a note or loan. If your estate is still responsible for what you owe to others after you died, you certainly want to make sure that all amounts owed to you will still come into your estate. You're not letting anyone off the hook for what is owed to you.

Your personal representative also collects payments you're due and entitled to receive from Social Security (but must also return any inadvertent payments from Social Security after your death) and any life insurance proceeds, if the proceeds are payable to your estate.

Your personal representative must transfer all receivables and any other *liquid* part of your estate (liquid is a financial term that means readily available assets, such as cash on hand or amounts contained in your bank accounts) to an account in which he or she controls. Through this account, your personal representative pays valid creditors' claims, fees, taxes, and cash bequests to your beneficiaries after being approved by the probate court.

Your personal representative needs to be careful not to commingle estate assets with his or her own, so he or she must use a separate bank account.

Managing estate property

Because probate doesn't happen overnight and can drag on for months (or even years in the worst-case scenario), your personal representative manages your estate during the entire probate process. He or she keeps an eye on your estate and its contents until the assets are transferred to your heirs or beneficiaries. Managing your estate includes

>> Supervising property

>> Maintaining property

>> Insuring property

>> Securing property

For example, if your estate has income-producing investment property, such as a rental house or apartment, the personal representative must manage the property or retain a property management company.

The personal representative needs to insure both real property and tangible personal property, such as jewelry and household furnishings, against loss until the property is transferred to your beneficiaries. Some of your estate property likely had sentimental value to you and to the beneficiary you intended to receive the property. In addition to insurance, your personal representative should physically secure your property to prevent any theft or damage.

Processing creditors' claims

One of your personal representative's major tasks is the processing of creditors' claims. Typically creditors have a specified period (varying from state to state) to file their claims or they lose their ability to receive a part of the estate. Because creditors must typically be paid before any property transfers can occur to beneficiaries, processing creditors' claims is an important function of the personal representative to keep an already lengthy process moving along.

The personal representative provides notice to creditors of your death by delivering specific notices to the creditors or by general public notice through the newspaper. The notice includes information such as

» Case or file number assigned by probate court

» Probate court's location

» Personal representative's contact information

» Due date for filing a claim

» Documentation needed to process the claim

The personal representative must determine which creditors' claims are valid — sort of like being one of the celebrity panelists on the old game show *To Tell the Truth*. If a creditor's claim is valid and filed within the required time period, the personal representative pays the claim from estate assets. (In fact, sometimes the personal representative must turn to the court to decide whether or not a claim is valid.)

Paying taxes and filing returns

Your personal representative must pay all taxes associated with your estate. Taxes can include any of the following that apply to your estate:

» Federal estate taxes

» State inheritance and estate taxes

» Federal, state, and local income taxes

» Gift tax

» Generation-skipping tax

TIP

Feeling overwhelmed and a little bit guilty about what you're leaving your personal representative to do? Don't. Typically, one of your estate-planning team members — your accountant — actually prepares and files all the tax returns. But your personal representative is ultimately responsible to make sure all taxes are paid.

Many of the tax returns have filing date deadlines that are triggered by your date of death. Your personal representative needs to keep track of these deadlines, which means he or she must be organized. The important characteristics to look for when choosing your personal representative are discussed in the section "Deciding who's eligible to be your personal representative," later in this chapter.

Distributing estate assets

The final step for your personal representative is your estate's actual distribution. If you have a will (and hopefully you do), your assets are distributed to your beneficiaries. If you don't have a will or your will lacks a *residuary clause* (the clause in your will to deal with whatever property you don't specifically mention in a giving clause) so that some of your assets don't have a beneficiary named, your personal representative distributes the assets in accordance with your state's intestate succession laws.

Even if you have a will, your estate distribution can be affected by other statutes. Your personal representative follows the statutes' requirements when distributing your estate assets, such as spousal elective shares, homestead statutes, and exempt property awards.

Real property is transferred to your beneficiaries by a deed evidencing legal ownership. Personal property is transferred by either an assignment document to the beneficiary or by a certificate of title if appropriate (for example, a vehicle). For cash distribution, the personal representative provides a check on the estate account payable to your named beneficiary. The property transfers complete the role of your personal representative. The heirs or beneficiaries generally provide receipts as evidence of the distributions, thus releasing the estate and personal representative.

Deciding who's eligible to be your personal representative

Now you know what your personal representative does in administering your estate. So who can be your personal representative? Practically anyone, but usually it's one of the following:

>> Family member

>> Friend

>> Business associate

>> Attorney

>> Corporate executor (from a bank, for example)

You have a relationship with all these people. The corporate executor is typically a financial institution that you have a financial relationship with, like the trust department of a bank.

Now, whom do you choose? You know their responsibilities as your personal representative. The person — or institution — you select must possess certain characteristics that are needed to perform their duty, such as

>> Trustworthiness

>> Honesty

>> Dependability

>> Good organization

>> Common-sense judgment

>> Fairness

>> Geographical proximity to the probate court and your property

Your personal representative needs these characteristics to properly administer your estate. For example, your personal representative needs to be fair because one of the hats the personal representative wears is often as a referee to settle disputes that can arise in your estate.

Geographical proximity to your estate property and the probate court is helpful in your estate's administration. (Long-distance relationships are difficult enough when you're alive and even more complicated when you're dead.)

Okay, so you look around and see many choices. (On the other hand, you may think: "If these are my choices, I'm in trouble!") Many people choose their spouse as their personal representative. After all, you have just spent a lifetime (or it may just feel like a lifetime) with your spouse, and who knows you better? Besides, your spouse most likely is receiving the largest part of your estate.

But the job is time-consuming and tedious. Make sure your spouse and anyone else you are considering understands what is expected. If you have a somewhat complex estate that involves numerous beneficiaries and creditors, inform your personal representative.

Avoiding the pitfalls

WARNING

You need to be aware of several potential pitfalls when selecting your personal representative, including

>> Being perceived as favoring one family member over another

>> Keeping your business going (if applicable to your situation)

If you have three adult children, all about the same age and equally well off financially, you run the risk of slighting two of those children if you select the other as your personal representative. Never mind that pretty much anyone who has ever served as a personal representative agrees that the job is basically one of dealing with details and complications — and plenty of aggravation — for months on end. The other children may conceivably think that the child selected as your personal representative is somehow favored, and this can cause all kinds of family strife and hard feelings for years to come.

If you find that you're in a similar situation, you may be tempted to designate two or more of your children as co-personal representatives of your estate. Think carefully! You open your estate up to unnecessary disputes and complications if two or more people share that role and then start to use your estate as a battleground for disputes between themselves. As Abe Lincoln (or, for *Seinfeld* fans, George Costanza) may have put it, "A personal representative divided against itself can't stand!"

A better alternative than co-personal representatives is to ask your attorney or perhaps your lifelong best friend (hopefully a trustworthy one — remember the key characteristics) to be your personal representative.

WARNING

If you own your own business, or are one of the handful of owners (along with several partners of a closely held business), you need to pay special attention to whom you designate as your personal representative. Your personal representative may have to keep your business going. But if that person has no experience in your business, or doesn't have the time to devote to your business, a significant portion of your estate's value may go down the drain if your business collapses. Therefore, if you own a small business, you need to either select a personal representative who can represent your interests and keep your business going, or make other business continuity arrangements separate from the usual personal representative responsibilities.

Paying your personal representative

Now that your personal representative has done all this work, what does he or she get? You really can't personally say, "Thanks for a job well done," because you're dead. Your personal representative is typically entitled to receive a *personal representative fee.* The fee varies among states, and the probate court approves the personal representative fee. Your personal representative receives payment at or near the end of the probate process.

Thinking Things Through When Someone Asks You to Be a Personal Rep

What if your brother asks you to become his personal representative? Suddenly the tables are turned and you have to decide whether to take on that role. You now know what responsibilities are expected of you if you say yes.

But what factors do you consider in making your decision? If you accept the role as a personal representative, are you personally liable for anything to do with the estate? Well, the answer is no — most of the time. You aren't personally liable for any claims, lawsuits, or other monetary obligations of the estate itself as a personal representative.

TECHNICAL STUFF

Traditionally a personal representative is held to a standard regarding investment responsibilities and liabilities known as the *Prudent Person Rule.* In many states, the Prudent Person Rule has been recently replaced by the similarly sounding — but functionally different — *Prudent Investor Rule.* The difference between the two relates to the personal representative's investment focus. The newer Prudent Investor Rule imposes significant new duties on the personal representative for how investments are managed, with resulting increases in potential liability if those duties aren't properly performed. Make sure you completely understand the specific rules and obligations that govern how you serve as a personal representative, should you find yourself in that role.

As a personal representative, you're entitled to receive a fee for your services. The fee is typically a percentage of the probate estate. Many times personal representatives waive their fee for a family member or good friend. Be aware that if you do accept the personal representative fee, the payment you receive is taxed as ordinary income. Compare tax rates between ordinary income and estate-related taxes to see if receiving payment or property is the most tax advantageous for you.

TIP

If you're also an heir or beneficiary of an estate for which you're serving as a personal representative, the distribution you receive is free of income tax (any applicable estate tax is usually taken before you get your share). If you're both a personal representative and beneficiary of the same estate, you should consider waiving the taxable personal representative fee in exchange for a tax-free larger distribution.

Despite the hassles and occasional aggravation, the vast majority of personal representatives find the job to be at least a little bit personally rewarding. You have a feeling of helping a friend or family member complete his or her final wishes and intentions. But again, as with anything in life, make sure you know what you're getting into before you agree to become someone's personal representative.

Understanding Will Substitutes

So far, you've been pointed toward two main objectives of estate planning: protecting your property and controlling it as long as possible after you die. Your will is your No.1 legal weapon, of course.

But you have other ways to reach your goals of maintaining protection and control — various types of contracts, agreements, and legal documents that are called *will substitutes.* For many, having a substitute conjures up memories of school days. When you heard that a sub was coming in for the regular teacher, you wanted to know whether the stand-in was harder or easier than your regular teacher.

As with substitute teachers, you're wise to be prepared and do your homework about various types of will substitutes and figure out which ones, if any, make sense for your estate planning. Some will substitutes (like some substitute teachers) can give you peace of mind by filling in the gaps and working hand in hand with what you've specified in your will. Other will substitutes (like the occasional nasty substitute teacher who for some reason seemed to pick on you) may actually have very little benefit for you, other than wasting some of your money and triggering unpleasant down-the-road consequences.

REMEMBER

In your will, you specify your instructions for what you want to happen to your property after you die. You can specifically mention various items and who will get those items, or you can use your will's residuary clause to instruct how anything you haven't specifically mentioned should be distributed and to whom. If you forget to include a residuary clause in your will, or if you die without a valid will, your state's intestate laws come into play and "write a will for you" that determine who gets what.

However, the covered-in-your-will-or-not distinction has a little wrinkle, and that's where will substitutes come in. Will substitutes treat property transfers by designating who receives the property at your death through *operation of law*. The same way that certain *statutes* can interpret and may override what your will says, will substitutes can take precedence over both your will and your state's intestate laws.

Why would you want to use a will substitute rather than your will for certain property? One word, and you can probably guess what it is by now: probate. Actually, make that three words: outside of probate. Property covered by a will substitute is transferred *outside of probate*, which may provide you with some significant advantages, including the following:

>> **Time:** As you know from earlier in this chapter, the probate process can be lengthy (especially if you have a complicated estate), and the actual transfer of property typically doesn't occur until probate is mostly or totally completed. With will substitutes, however, property is typically transferred immediately upon your death, even if other parts of your estate are just beginning what may be a lengthy probate process.

>> **Money:** Will substitutes may save you and your estate some money, depending on whether or not your state's version of the Estate Recovery Act applies to your estate after you die. For purposes of discussing will substitutes, remember that your state's version of the Estate Recovery Act may apply only to your probate estate. As noted earlier, by definition, your probate estate includes only your property that is passing through probate, and certain property — including what is covered by various forms of will substitutes — isn't part of your probate estate. Therefore, if the government is trying to grab part of your estate after you die under provisions of its Estate Recovery Act, you may be able to protect property from the government's grasp by using will substitutes rather than your will.

WARNING

If the resulting transfer of nonprobate property results in a death tax — whether state, federal, or any other tax — the taxes must still be paid. Will substitutes only help you do an end run around probate; applicable death taxes must still be paid. However, in many cases, will substitutes may reduce your taxes, so work with your accountant and attorney to coordinate your tax strategy with what you plan to do for will substitutes.

Sorting through the List of Will Substitutes

You can hold property in a variety of will substitute types, including perhaps the two most important:

>> Joint tenancy

>> Living trusts

The following sections discuss each of those in detail. Additionally, you should try to have at least a passing familiarity with some other will substitutes, including

>> Tenancy by the entirety

>> Payable on death accounts (PODs)

>> IRAs, life insurance annuities, and other assets paid to named beneficiaries

Will substitutes predetermine who gets your property upon your death by one of two ways:

>> Right of survivorship

>> Beneficiary designation

Joint tenancy, tenancy by the entirety, and payable on death accounts use right of survivorship, whereas the other will substitute types use beneficiary designations.

Figuring out joint tenancy

Joint tenancy means that you and others have an equal and undivided ownership of some property. Basically, each joint tenant has the same right to use whatever property the joint tenancy agreement applies to. Joint tenants must own an equal percentage of the property. If two people hold interest in property as joint tenants, each owns one-half of the property; if three people hold interest, then each owns one-third; four people, each owns one-fourth, and so on.

The distinguishing characteristic of joint tenancy as a will substitute is the *right of survivorship.* In fact, joint tenancy is usually referred to as *joint tenancy with right of survivorship,* sometimes abbreviated JTWROS. The key feature of joint tenancy is that when you die, the other co-owner (or co-owners) receives your share of the property by *right of survivorship.* Whether you have a will or not is immaterial to the property transfer. If you have a will, the property transfers outside of your will. If you don't have a will, the property transfers outside of intestate succession laws. The surviving joint tenant(s) receive(s) the property.

Family members often create joint tenancy to automatically leave property to the surviving joint tenant family member. However, as discussed later, joint tenancy has some significant disadvantages, so work with your attorney to figure out whether joint tenancy, or perhaps some other form of a will substitute (such as living trust) best suits your needs.

For example, Tom and Meghan own a house and hold title to the property as joint tenants with right of survivorship. At Tom's death, Meghan automatically receives Tom's share of the house because of the right of survivorship feature as joint tenants.

Now, suppose Tom, Meghan, and Avery — three people now instead of two — own the house as joint tenants with right of survivorship, meaning that each of them owns one-third of the house. Again, Tom dies. In this case, Tom's share of the house is split equally between Meghan and Avery, who now each have a one-half interest in the house as joint tenants with right of survivorship. Later, upon one of their deaths, the surviving joint tenant will own the house.

In most states, during his or her lifetime a joint tenant can sever the joint tenancy without the consent or notification to the other joint tenants. The joint tenant who severs the joint tenancy then owns the property as a tenant in common with the other former joint tenant. But if more than one joint tenant remain, they still own their share of the property as joint tenants between themselves.

What? An example clarifies the preceding confusing scenario. Suppose Tom, Meghan, and Avery still own the house as joint tenants from the previous example. But Tom decides to *deed* (basically, to give) his interest to Sandra, thereby breaking his joint tenancy with the other co-owners. Now, the property is owned as follows: Sandra owns a one-third interest as a tenant in common, and Meghan and Avery own two-thirds interest as joint tenants between themselves.

Remember, Meghan and Avery still own the property as joint tenants so they have retained the right of survivorship with each other for their portion of the property. If Avery dies, Meghan receives Avery's share of the property by right of survivorship and would then own two-thirds of the property as a tenant in common with Sandra.

Later, if Sandra dies before Meghan, her share of the property goes to her heirs or beneficiaries and not to Meghan as the other co-owner, because at that point, Sandra and Meghan own the property together as tenants in common. No right of survivorship feature exists because long ago, Tom (the original one-third owner who had deeded his interest to Sandra) broke his side of the joint tenancy relationship. Likewise, because Meghan no longer has a co-joint-tenant, her interest also passes to her heirs or beneficiaries at her death and not automatically to Sandra.

Advantages of joint tenancy

Why should you consider joint tenancy specifically as a will substitute? As an alternative to probate, joint tenancy provides you with several advantages:

>> **Cost savings:** The formation and eventual termination of joint tenancy is inexpensive. Unlike other forms of will substitutes, such as a living trust that an attorney should at least review and ideally prepare, you may save money by not necessarily needing to use an attorney to create a joint tenancy. (However, as with all other aspects of your estate planning, you need to work with your attorney as you plan your strategy and figure out what techniques best apply to you.)

>> **Clear title transfer:** Because joint tenancy is based on right of survivorship, joint tenancy allows for a clear transfer of title to the surviving joint tenant. No questions exist about the intent of who is to receive the property upon the death of one of the joint tenants. (To be certain that no question about intent exists, some states require that the wording "as tenants with rights of survivorship and not as tenants in common" be added.)

>> **Creditors claim reductions:** One of the main steps in the probate process is the payment of valid creditors' claims. Before any of your beneficiaries can receive property transfers after you die, your personal representative must first pay any valid creditors' claims. If your estate doesn't have enough cash or cash equivalents to satisfy the creditors' claims, your estate may be forced to sell property to pay the claims. However, because property held as joint tenants isn't part of the probate process, creditors don't have ready access to property held as joint tenants. Thus the amount of creditors' claims may be reduced.

If the court can prove that you transferred title of property to joint tenants to hide from creditors, your creditors may still make a claim against part of your joint tenancy property.

» **Convenient and fast:** You can easily create and ultimately dissolve ownership as you craft and later refine your estate plan. Furthermore, by not having to deal with complex legal documents — wills, trusts, and living trusts — you can use joint tenancy without worrying about the legality and hassles of the wording in these documents. Just a few simple words added to the property title and you're done. In estate planning, you can't get any faster than that! Beware, though: Even though you can dissolve the joint tenancy after it's created, you can't turn back the clock to the way things were before you created the joint tenancy without the permission of the other joint tenant or tenants.

» **Private:** If you value your privacy, even after you've died, joint tenancy offers you a better alternative than probate, where your will and estate become part of the public record. Note, however, if your state has an inheritance or estate tax, you may be required to file a tax return and pay a tax on the decedent's share of the jointly owned property. Because the tax return is usually a matter of public record, your wishes for privacy will be defeated.

Work out the tax scenarios with your accountant as part of your overall estate planning before you put joint tenancy wording on any property titles.

Disadvantages of joint tenancy

So far, so good with joint tenancy. The concept seems straightforward and the advantages sound pretty good. So why hold property any other way? Well, you know the old saying: If it sounds too good to be true, it must be an estate-planning concept. Holding property as joint tenants has significant limitations and disadvantages that you need to be aware of, including

» **Forced disposition:** The surviving joint tenant(s) receive(s) your share of the property. Period. You can't decide to leave a portion of that property to your joint tenant and another portion to someone else; the law forces you to leave your share to your joint tenant. So depending on the property in question and what you want done with that property after you die, joint tenancy may not be the right estate-planning tactic.

» **Lack of control in property transfer:** The right of survivorship feature may not control the final transfer of property under joint tenancy. The death of the next-to-last joint tenant leaves the property to the surviving joint tenant as sole property; no right of survivorship exists when you own something by yourself. So unless other arrangements are made (even creating a brand new joint tenancy with other people), the property may ultimately become a part of the sole surviving joint tenant's estate.

>> **Undesirable property transfers:** After the next-to-last joint tenant has died, the surviving joint tenant can dispose of the property in any way he or she wants, even if the disposal is contrary to the intentions of any other joint tenants who have died earlier. In effect, if you're involved in a joint tenancy, you have to let go of any desires you have for the ultimate disposal of the property beyond the other joint tenants.

For example, suppose Kathy and Greg, who aren't married and have no children, own a house as joint tenants. They discuss their intentions to leave the house upon their deaths to their favorite local charity. But after Kathy dies, Greg owns the house as the surviving joint tenant and can direct the property transfer to anyone he chooses at his death. Suppose Greg changes his mind and decides that instead of the charity, his sister — who didn't get along with Kathy — gets the house at his death. So Greg's sister receives the house and Kathy's intentions for the property are out the window. (If the property was named in a will or held in a trust, they may have set up a chain of property transfers. The will could state that the survivor had use of the house while he or she was alive and upon his or her death, the charity is guaranteed to receive the house. In effect, choosing joint tenancy prevented Kathy from achieving her ultimate objective for the property.)

>> **Exposure to other joint tenant's creditors:** Joint tenancy may protect property from your creditors' claims after you die, but what about protection from creditors' claims against your joint tenant? For example, if your joint tenant loses a court battle and has a large judgment against him, the property you hold as joint tenants can potentially be subject to the judgment resulting in a forced sale of the property.

>> **Numerous tax disadvantages:** Perhaps the biggest disadvantage of joint tenancy is in the area of taxes. A tax disadvantage? Didn't you just read that a potential income tax savings from joint tenancy by the surviving joint tenant in a lower tax bracket may occur? Well, yes, but taxes are funny: In estate planning, what often saves you money in one tax area increases your taxes (sometimes significantly) in another tax area. In this case, the savings in income tax may be more than offset by the increase in estate tax.

TECHNICAL STUFF

For example, if you're the surviving joint tenant from a property that you once held with two others as joint tenants, this property may inadvertently cause a payment of a larger estate tax. Furthermore, if your estate is large enough to be in a federal estate tax bracket, joint ownership and particularly a joint tenancy (or a tenancy by the entirety between husband and wife, as discussed later in this chapter) may preclude the ability to save or reduce federal estate taxes. For now, think of joint tenancy as having potential tax disadvantages when compared with wills or other will substitutes, such as living trusts.

JOINT TENANCY AND UNMARRIED COUPLES

Many unmarried couples (either same sex or opposite sex) use joint tenancy with right of survivorship as a way to transfer their respective ownership shares to their partner. Most estate-planning laws are oriented toward "traditional" families (a married couple, 2.53 children, and so on). If you're in an unmarried relationship and you co-own your home with your partner, joint tenancy with right of survivorship may be an ideal way to protect your partner's right to stay in the home after you die (and vice versa), even though the law doesn't recognize your relationship in the same way as — and with the same rights of — a married couple.

Setting up a living trust

Book 5, Chapter 4 examines trusts in-depth, but here we look at the popular living trust as a will substitute form. A *living trust* is created while you're alive (thus, the word *living*), unlike a *testamentary* trust, which is created at your death through your will. (Technically, a testamentary trust is similar to a will because it provides for property transfers at your death.)

You place certain property called *trust principal* into a living trust. (You may also see the word *corpus* referring to the property used to fund the trust, which often makes people nervous, considering how similar that word sounds to corpse — makes sense because both corpus and corpse come from the same root meaning "body.")

When you create a revocable living trust, you can be in charge of your own living trust. When you die, the revocable living trust becomes *irrevocable* (meaning you can't "undo" the trust — more on that in Book 5, Chapter 4) — and the trust principal (again, the property that you have placed into the trust) then passes to your beneficiaries without having to go through probate.

By making a trust revocable, you can dissolve the trust at any time up until death or until the trust document makes the trust irrevocable (such as in the event of your incapacity).

Roles for everyone!

TECHNICAL
STUFF

The best way to examine a living trust is to look at the parties and roles involved. Living trusts involve the following roles (note that one person can play more than one role, as explained later in this chapter):

>> Trustor (or settlor)

>> Trustee

>> Successor trustee

>> Income beneficiaries (or current beneficiaries)

>> Remainderman (a "special class" of beneficiary)

>> Designated person managing minor beneficiaries

Don't panic at the legal jargon. In a typical trust, the *trustor* (or *settlor*) creates the trust, and the *trustee* has the legal interest in managing the trust for the *income beneficiaries* who will have beneficial interest or right to use the trust property. After the beneficiaries receive their portion of trust, the remainderman is the trust beneficiary who receives the remainder or what is left over.

Book 5, Chapter 1 discusses two main types of property interest: *legal,* the right to manage property, and *beneficial,* or the right to benefit from the property. Trustees have the legal interest to transfer and manage property in the trust while beneficiaries have the right to use the property.

The *successor trustee* is the person you name to become trustee when you die (or become incapacitated) if you're currently the named trustee. Think of your successor trustee as the personal representative of your trust. Look for a successor trustee who has the same attributes recommended for a personal representative earlier in this chapter. Typically, people name a spouse, child, or trusted friend as successor trustees.

You need to appoint someone (usually referred to as a guardian or a custodian) to manage the property of *minor beneficiaries* — those beneficiaries who aren't of legal age.

The paperwork — ugh!

The actual living trust document varies just as wills do. (Work with your attorney to make sure you get all the necessary information correctly on paper.) The variations may include

>> Designating the trustor and the initial trustee

>> Defining trust property

>> Naming a successor trustee

>> Defining ways to revoke or amend the trust

>> Administering trust by trustee during trustor's lifetime

>> Administering trust by the successor trustee after trustor's death or incapacity

>> Defining trustee's power

>> Restricting beneficiary assignments *(spendthrift clause)*

The trust sets forth in detail how the trustor must handle the trust after you've died.

Advantages of living trusts

So why the frenzy over living trusts? Living trusts are a convenient way to avoid additional probates if you have real property like a house, vacation home, or income-producing investment property located in more than one state.

Real property must be probated in the state where the property is located. More than likely, your entire probate process will be slowed down because of the need to administer more than one probate and the increases in fees and costs.

TIP

Some states consider real property held in a living trust to be intangible personal property, enabling your estate to avoid ancillary probate. If you have real property in more than one state, check to see how your state views real property held in a trust.

Privacy (as compared with probate) is another advantage of a living trust. As with other will substitute forms, your trust is a private agreement — a contract between the trustee and trustor. However, some county recorder offices require the filing of trusts as part of the public record.

To retain the privacy of trusts, your attorney can draft a separate document called a *memorandum of trust,* which identifies the most basic information of the trust. Therefore, your trust usually doesn't become public record as your will does in probate.

WARNING

However, if your state has an inheritance tax, the trust's details may be required to be filed with the state through an inheritance tax return or other document. You may need to include the amount of trust principal and the identification of beneficiaries or remainderman.

The real attraction of living trusts stems from the advantages offered beyond the typical will substitute form advantages. Living trusts offer unique advantages:

>> Better planning

>> Better protection from probate

>> Better prediction of the future

>> Ability to name alternate beneficiaries

>> Ability to name guardianships

In preparing a trust, you place property into the trust (called *funding the trust*), and that property is thereafter known as your *trust principal.* By thinking through what property to include in your trust principal, you examine what property you have.

REMEMBER

Unlike joint tenancy, where ultimately the last surviving joint tenant holds the property that can become part of the probate estate, living trusts provide you with better assurance of avoiding probate. In the earlier example, if Tom and Meghan own a house as joint tenants and Tom dies, Meghan, as the surviving joint tenant, now owns the house individually, making the house part of her probate property.

But instead of joint tenancy, suppose Tom and Meghan use a living trust to hold title as co-trustors and co-trustees to the house for both of their lifetimes. If Tom dies, Meghan still owns the house in trust, and the house is not part of the probate estate. Upon Meghan's death, the house passes from the trust to the designated beneficiaries without being subjected to probate.

And what does predicting the future have to do with living trusts? Plenty, sort of. A living trust provides you with a peek into your estate's future and how it will be handled. If you establish a trust as the trustor and name someone other than yourself as the trustee to manage your trust, you can preview how he or she handles the management of the trust property and determine if adjustments in your estate need to be made. No need for guesswork on how he or she will perform when you're dead, when you can't make any changes (for obvious reasons). You can preview the future now.

If your trust is set up to make distributions while you're alive, you have the opportunity to see how both your trustee and beneficiaries may handle the trust principal distributions, affording you the opportunity to make adjustments if needed.

A living trust also allows you to name alternate beneficiaries if something happens to your primary beneficiary. You can't name an alternate with other will substitute forms like joint tenancy or, as discussed later, payable on death accounts.

A living trust can also be set up to provide for you in case you become incapacitated and unable to care for your own affairs. This advantage is part of the reason living trusts are touted for the elderly. In such a case, you can avoid the necessity of a court-appointed guardian or conservator, or at least assist those persons in carrying out their duties.

Another method of avoiding guardianship or conservatorship is by the popular *durable power of attorney,* usually in addition to a living will.

Disadvantages of living trusts

Keep this adage in mind when you're planning your estate: No good will substitute goes unpunished. Disadvantages exist no matter what road you choose, even with living trusts. These disadvantages include

>> Funding

>> Ongoing maintenance

>> Longer creditor claims period

The upfront funding of the living trust is a deterrent to many people. Remember, to hold title as joint tenancy, all you have to do is change the title to property with the appropriate wording. It's not so simple with living trusts.

Living trusts require you to execute a trust document. But beyond the paperwork, the next step in the process is the trust's actual funding. You as trustor must transfer your property's title to the trust. So what's the problem? Every time you acquire property — from stocks to real estate — you must transfer title of the property into the trust. For active investors, transferring your property's title to the trust can become a hassle. (Then think about other property, such as cars, furniture, collectibles, and so on, which can be even more of a hassle!)

WARNING

If you forget to put property in your trust, the property is treated as if it was never part of the trust and is handled through probate if you have a will, or intestate succession laws if you don't have a will. For example, if you're the beneficiary of someone's life insurance or if you receive property that was formerly held as part of a joint tenancy — and you forget to take care of this property for living trust purposes — then that property isn't part of the living trust.

Trusts require monitoring to make sure that everything is proceeding in accordance with the terms of the trust. Don't just sign a trust document and put it away. The only way to achieve the advantage of previewing the future is to monitor the trust on an ongoing basis, which takes time and may not be for everyone.

Another living trust disadvantage is the potentially longer period for creditors' claims. Why? In some states, trusts don't protect property from being subject to creditors' claims. Consequently, trustees may delay distributions to beneficiaries and remainderman until they're certain all claims have been paid. Remember, no probate for trust principal exists, so consequently no probate process exists for the controlled processing of creditors' claims.

If a trustee doesn't perform certain required duties after the trustor's death, he or she can have substantial personal liability. This reason is why trustees often delay property transfers until they're certain all creditors have been paid.

Focusing on the costs of living trusts

You may have noticed that the costs of living trusts haven't been mentioned as either an advantage or disadvantage. Why? Because the costs to set up a living trust can vary greatly. As with your will, you can prepare a basic living trust with preprinted legal forms or, alternatively, with an attorney.

Accordingly, the costs can range from a few dollars if you go the do-it-yourself route to more than $1,500 for each living trust that an attorney prepares. Because a living trust is considered a contract between the trustor and trustee, you shouldn't mess around with a contract that may contain glitches. A living trust requires careful preparation and thinking. So just like with your will, if you decide to try to create a living trust on your own (which, again, we don't recommend), at least have an attorney review it before execution.

Interestingly, the promotion and marketing of living trusts as part of estate planning has been anything but subtle. Some financial advisers hype living trusts especially to older citizens — giving sales pitches on how living trusts are the solution to all the world's ills, and bombarding them with offers of expensive how-to seminars, workshops, and books on living trusts. Before exploring any of these options, make sure you understand what is being offered and what it will cost you. Although these preparations are touted as cost-saving, you'll probably find it less expensive to work one on one with an attorney on your living trust instead of buying an expensive, boilerplate sales pitch.

Identifying Some Less Common but Worthy Will Substitutes

Beyond joint tenancy and revocable living trusts, you have some other options for will substitutes available. Although not as common as the first two methods, the ones discussed here still provide you with the opportunity to use will substitutes in your estate planning.

Tenancy by the entirety — the spouse's option

Tenancy by the entirety — also called *interests by the entirety* — is related to joint tenancy. Similar to joint tenancy, the property's co-owners have a right of survivorship feature that enables property to automatically transfer at the death of a co-owner to the surviving co-owner. Different states have different rules for tenancy by the entirety, so make sure your attorney advises you as you consider this type of will substitute.

There is one distinguishing characteristic of this form of will substitute: Only spouses can use it. Unlike joint tenancy, which can have any number of unrelated parties, a husband and wife are the only persons eligible to hold property as tenancy by the entirety. The surviving spouse becomes the sole property owner.

Tenancy by the entirety follows general guidelines for marital life. Always tell your spouse what you're doing. Accordingly, one spouse can't transfer his or her interest in the property without the consent of or notification to the other spouse. (Remember, a joint tenant can transfer his or her share to another person without the consent or notification of the other joint tenants.)

WARNING
Some states don't allow property to be held as tenancy by the entirety. Specifically, tenancy by the entirety isn't recognized in most community property states (Arizona, California, Idaho, Louisiana, Nevada, New Mexico, Texas, Washington, and Wisconsin), and even some common law states don't allow it. Where tenancy by the entirety is available, a divorce changes property ownership from tenancy by the entirety to tenants in common. If you decide to explore using this will substitute form, check with an attorney to see if your state recognizes it.

Joint tenancy bank accounts

A joint tenancy bank account is a form of joint tenancy where two or more people take title to property — in this case, a bank account — with the surviving joint tenant receiving the proceeds from the account.

With joint tenancy, a joint tenant can sever the joint tenancy without the consent or notification to the other joint tenants. Here, the bank account joint tenant can sever the relationship by withdrawing funds from the joint account.

WARNING
Gift taxes may come into play with joint tenancy bank accounts. Before you use this will substitute form, talk to your accountant and attorney to understand the implications. Don't just ask the person at the bank who helps you fill out the forms.

Savings bonds

Yes, the same savings bonds that, along with green stamps, Hula-Hoops, and first-run shows of *Leave it to Beaver,* are often thought of as icons of days long ago. But savings bonds actually are a form of will substitute.

Savings bonds can be issued in two ways:

» Alternative payee

» Beneficiary payee

When you use the *alternative payee* option on a savings bond, payment of the bond can go to either co-owner of the bond (you or your alternative) similar to the joint tenancy provision of right of survivorship. After one of you dies, the surviving payee is the bond's sole owner.

By using the other option — a *beneficiary payee* — you and another person have a similar relationship to a beneficiary named in your will. If the savings bond is yours, the beneficiary you have named receives the bond's proceeds after your death.

TIP

If you have a stash of savings bonds locked away in your safe deposit box or some other safekeeping place, double-check to see what the estate-planning impact is of each individual bond when you're inventorying the contents of and determining your estate's value (see Book 5, Chapter 2).

PODs — payable on death accounts

They may sound rather morbid, but *payable on death accounts* (PODs) are a simple will substitute form that keeps personal property out of probate. You fill out a form at your financial institutions and designate your account beneficiary. After your death, your beneficiary provides the financial institution with a copy of the death certificate and proof of identity and then collects what is in the account. (Doesn't get much simpler than that.)

TIP

Because your beneficiary receives the account proceeds at your death, periodically review the accounts for two reasons. First, verify that the named beneficiary is still who you want to receive the proceeds. Remember you can change your mind at any time while you're alive. Second, some accounts may also grow faster than others, causing disproportionate proceeds to different beneficiaries that you may not be aware of without reviewing the account.

Your beneficiary doesn't have beneficial interest in the account and thus can't withdraw money from the account until your death. You have the flexibility to change your mind and name a different beneficiary, or you can even decide that you want to use the funds in the account. Easy come, easy go!

Deeds

For real property like your house, a deed is a weapon in your will substitutes arsenal available for your use.

TECHNICAL STUFF

A *deed* is the legal evidence of real estate ownership. Deeds, like wills, have several legal requirements to be valid, including being in writing with an accurate legal description of the property.

You can write wording into a deed to create a will substitute for your real property. Work with your attorney to make sure the wording in your deed accurately reflects the type of will substitute you want to set up.

WARNING

If the deed is used only as a property transfer mechanism at the grantor's death, the deed may not be considered a valid will substitute form and is subject to probate. Check with your attorney about state laws to find out what requirements are needed for a deed to be considered a will substitute form.

IRAs and your other retirement accounts

Even if you're just beginning your estate-planning efforts, you may already have will substitutes as part of your estate and not even know it.

Most of your retirement savings accounts — your IRA, 401(k) or 403(b) plan, your Roth IRA, and other retirement-oriented investments — are forms of will substitutes. For example, for a 401(k), the spouse is automatically listed as the beneficiary.

A TIP ABOUT ESTATE-PLANNING LEGAL-SPEAK

You may have noticed a pattern in legal terminology. Words ending in *-or,* like trustor and grantor, are always the person in control of the property. Conversely, words ending in *-ee,* like trustee or grantee, are always the person receiving something from the *-or.* An easy way to remember this is that *-ee* receives something from *-or*. Put it together as *ee-or* and you have Winnie the Pooh's buddy.

Chapter **4**

Understanding Trusts

Y ou can use a trust to save on estate taxes, to protect property in your estate, and to avoid probate. You can even use a trust to get dents out of your car and clean the toughest stains in your carpet. Okay, the last two items are fake, but various types of trusts may be the secret weapons in your estate planning. Beware, though: Trusts are also the most overhyped part of estate planning.

This chapter helps you make sense of the extremely complicated topic of trusts: what they are and why you may want to consider trusts for your estate plan. Before you seriously start considering trusts, you must understand the basics covered in this chapter so you can make informed decisions about what does — and doesn't — make sense for you.

Defining Trusts, Avoiding Hype

WARNING

Trusts can be difficult to understand when you hear some estate-planning professionals talk about them. But those people may be more interested in selling you expensive investment vehicles than they are in making sure you understand enough about trusts to make wise and informed decisions yourself.

Don't worry. This chapter helps you get a handle on trusts — with three definitions:

>> An incredibly oversimplified definition

>> A slightly more complicated definition but still using plain language

>> An "official" definition that uses just enough legalese but still won't cause your head to start spinning

Shazam! An oversimplified definition of trusts

In many comic books and related movies and TV shows, an ordinary person goes into a "special place" and comes out a superhero with a new identity and, very often, with superpowers. Bruce Wayne goes into the Batcave and comes out as Batman. Clark Kent goes into a phone booth and comes out as Superman. Billy Batson says "Shazam!" and turns into Captain Marvel.

Think of a trust as a special place in which ordinary property from your estate goes in and, as the result of some type of transformation that occurs, takes on a sort of new identity and often is bestowed with superpowers: immunity from estate taxes, resistance to probate, and so on.

So in many ways, a trust is your own personal Batcave — a place to go when you want to change the identity of some of your estate's property. And even though Batman doesn't have any superpowers, he does pick up that nifty utility belt with all kinds of weapons while he's in the Batcave. Similarly, when property is in your trust, it can "pick up its own utility belt" and do things that aren't possible outside of the trust.

Adding a bit of complexity with an ingredient list

Suppose you want to set up a trust. Just like with a cooking recipe or building something in your garage workshop, you need to make sure you have everything you need before you start. To cook up a trust, you need these seven basic ingredients:

>> The person setting up the trust (that's you)

>> The reason you want to set up the trust and certain objectives you want to achieve

>> The trust document itself

>> The property that you decide you're going to place into the trust

>> The trust's beneficiary (or beneficiaries, if more than one), whether that beneficiary is a person (your oldest daughter, for example) or an institution, such as a charity

>> Someone to watch over and manage the trust and the property that is now in the trust

>> A set of rules that tells the person watching over and managing the trust what he or she can and can't do

All the items in the preceding list come together, and when everything is done properly — Shazam! — you now have a trust.

Adding some lawyer talk to the definition

If you're comfortable with a little bit of legalese, here's a somewhat more "official" description than comic book analogies and simple recipe–style lists. Here, we add a tiny bit of attorney talk to the seven basic elements:

>> **Person setting up the trust:** The person is commonly known as the *trustor*, though you may sometimes see the terms *settlor* or *grantor*.

>> **Objective of the trust:** You use different types of trusts to achieve a variety of specific estate-planning objectives. You can use some trusts for a single estate-planning objective, while others help you achieve more than one goal. Some of the most common estate-planning objectives for trusts (discussed later in this chapter in more detail) are to reduce the amount of estate tax liability, to protect property in your estate, and to avoid probate for certain property. Before you decide whether you need one type of trust or another, you must think about what you're trying to accomplish in the first place.

>> **Specific kind of trust:** As discussed later in this chapter, trusts come in many different varieties. And just like ice cream, yogurt, or pudding, you find different colors and flavors, some of which you may like and others which just don't do it for you. Regardless, when you're setting up a trust, you need to decide what type of trust you want and make sure that you follow all the rules for that particular type of trust to make sure that it's proper and legal, and carries out your intentions.

>> **Property:** After you place property into a trust, that property is formally known as *trust property* — that is, just like with the Batcave analogy, the property now has a different identity and, in one way or another, isn't quite the same as it was before you placed it into trust.

>> **Beneficiary:** As with other aspects of your estate plan (your will, for example), a trust's *beneficiary* (or, if more than one, *beneficiaries*) benefits from the trust in some way, usually because the person or institution will eventually receive some or all of the property that was placed into trust.

>> **Trustee:** The person in charge of the trust is known as the *trustee*. The trustee needs to clearly understand the rules for the type of trust he or she is managing to make sure everything in the trust stays in working order.

>> **Rules:** Finally, some of the rules that must be followed are inherently part of the type of trust used, whereas other rules depend on what is specified in the trust agreement. You'll find still more rules in state and federal law.

Putting all the preceding information together, the trust agreement is a document that spells out the rules that you — the trustor — want followed for the property that you've placed into the trust to benefit the beneficiary (or beneficiaries) of the trust, as managed by the trustee. (Got all of that? If not, keep rereading until it makes sense, checking back with the list to help clear up the parts that seem difficult.)

Consider the following simple example. You decide to put $300,000 in a trust for your two twin 10-year-old daughters, and you want your sister to oversee the trust. You specify that neither daughter is allowed to receive anything other than interest on the property in that trust before reaching the age of 25, and then they can receive a maximum of only $10,000 each year on their birthday until the age of 35, at which time the remaining money in the trust (which hopefully has been growing along the way because of your sister's wise investment choices) will be split 50-50 between the two of them.

In this example, you are the trustor, your twin daughters are the beneficiaries, and your sister is the trustee. The conditions about when your daughters can start receiving money, how much, and until when are part of the terms of the trust agreement.

But what kind of trust can you set up? Aha! That is often the $64,000 question (or $300,000 question, or $1 million question, or perhaps the $5,000 question . . . all depending on the value of the property you place in the trust). You can use different trusts to achieve different objectives, and we discuss the major categories briefly later in this chapter.

Attaching all the bells and whistles to a trust

Beyond the basic definition (or, in this case, multiple definitions) of what a trust is, you need to be aware of several little tidbits about trusts. When Batman enters the Batcave, he needs to know where his utility belt is, whether the Batmobile has enough fuel, and where he's headed as soon as he gets outside. Otherwise, he may be in big trouble.

The same is true for trusts, which is why you need to work with your estate-planning team — particularly your attorney — to make sure that before that trust goes into effect, you have everything in order and haven't set yourself up for the estate-planning equivalent of an ambush by the Joker.

TECHNICAL STUFF

The following list may seem a bit nitpicky, but you can use the items in this list when you work with your attorney to avoid any problems. For example:

>> **Make sure the trust agreement is in writing.** Although an oral trust may be considered valid, just like an oral (nuncupative) will can be, certain trusts, such as those dealing with real estate, must be in writing. Therefore, just like with your will, you should put the trust agreement in writing instead of relying on word of mouth so misunderstandings or other problems don't arise.

>> A trust must provide duties and obligations for the trustee (again, the person in charge of the trust). Typical duties and obligations include how and when to make payments from the trust, or how to manage or oversee the property in the trust (such as paying property taxes on real estate in the trust, renewing certificates of deposit in the trust, and so on). In legalese, a trust that adequately features such duties and responsibilities is known as an *active trust*.

WARNING

>> If the trust doesn't adequately include trustee duties and obligations, a court may consider it to be a *passive trust*. Watch out! The court may deem it as "no trust at all." Furthermore, the law automatically transfers the trust's property to the beneficiary or beneficiaries, and everyone loses out on whatever the objective of the trust was, such as tax savings. So make sure that when you (or, more accurately, your attorney) set up a trust that the trustee's role is well defined so you won't have any problems down the road.

>> The wording of the trust agreement must clearly specify that you're actually setting up a trust and indicate what property you're placing in the trust (or intend to place in the trust at some future date).

>> The trust agreement must clearly identify the beneficiary or beneficiaries — the person or people by name and other identifying characteristics ("my daughter Ellie Mae Clampett," for example) or an institution ("The Meow Cat Shelter of Tucson, Arizona").

Understanding Trusts

>> Don't take the process of deciding on and appointing a trustee lightly. Make sure that whoever you select as a trustee has the right background — education or profession, for example — for the job at hand. If you want someone to manage a trust containing lots of money, make sure that the trustee understands and has adequate experience in portfolio management, diversification strategies, and other investment management techniques. But just as important (maybe even more important) than education and professional background is that your trustee has the honesty, character, and integrity to fulfill the responsibilities. Sometimes being in charge of lots of money intended for someone else (the trust's beneficiary or beneficiaries) can be, shall we say, a bit too tempting.

A trustee may have a *legal interest* in the property in a trust but doesn't have a *beneficial interest.* The trustee is responsible for managing the trust's property, but he or she can't benefit from the trust other than receiving the agreed-to trustee compensation (fees and costs) for taking on this job.

REMEMBER

Designate a *successor trustee* — a pinch hitter to step in if the primary trustee can't serve or continue to serve for some reason — when you set up a trust. Otherwise, the court that has jurisdiction may appoint a successor trustee, and that may not be someone whom you want.

Trust Power — Making Your Beneficiaries Smile

You're probably thinking: "Why should I care about trusts?"

In a very general sense, the primary reason you set up a trust is to benefit a person or institution more than if you didn't set up the trust. After all, trusts are often complex, can be time-consuming to set up and oversee, and cost you some amount of money (a modest amount for a straightforward trust, or perhaps a lot of money for a very complex setup involving multiple trusts, different jurisdictions' laws, and so on). So you should have a good reason to go to all this trouble.

Here are some examples of benefiting a person or institution better:

>> You have some part of your estate or your overall personal financial situation, such as a life insurance policy, that under applicable law is likely to cost your estate some amount of money in estate taxes. But by setting up a trust, your estate can avoid paying some or all taxes, meaning that more money is left over for your trust's beneficiaries.

>> As described in Book 5, Chapter 3, the probate process can cause problems for your estate, anywhere from minor annoyances and delays to major costs and inconvenience. However, you can use trusts for certain property that you absolutely, positively don't want to be subjected to the problems and delays of probate. Your beneficiary may gain ownership and use of that property more quickly if you had set up a trust than if you used the regular method of having that property as part of your probate estate.

The following sections look at the most significant objectives you likely want to achieve by using trusts.

Avoiding taxes

Some trusts have the "special power" (or maybe that's "superpower") to avoid estate-related taxes that otherwise may apply. One of the most common tax-saving trusts is an *irrevocable life insurance trust.* The proceeds from your life insurance policy (the death benefit amount) are added back into your estate, often turning an estate that isn't subject to federal estate taxes into an estate that needs to write a substantial check to the IRS.

However, an irrevocable life insurance trust is one of several ways you can shelter life insurance death benefit proceeds from estate taxes. After setting up the trust, you still have life insurance, and your beneficiary or beneficiaries still receive the proceeds from your policy upon your death. But now, estate taxes may not be a problem.

Avoiding probate

Book 5, Chapter 3 discusses *living trusts* as a form of will substitute to help you avoid probate. By keeping certain property out of your *probate estate* — the part of your estate that is subject to probate — you may be able to avoid many of the hassles, costs, and concerns about privacy that are related to probate.

TIP

You have a number of other means at your disposal to avoid probate for other property — joint tenancy with right of survivorship, payable on death (POD) accounts, and others discussed in Book 5, Chapter 3 — so work with your estate-planning team to figure out what the best probate-avoidance tactic may be for each type of property in your estate. For some, the costs of a trust may make sense, particularly if you're not only trying to avoid probate but also trying to accomplish one of the other goals talked about in this section (avoiding estate taxes, protecting your estate, and so on). For other property, a simpler, less costly way to avoid probate, such as joint tenancy, may be a better choice for you.

Protecting your estate

One of the primary uses of trusts is to protect your estate — not only while the estate is yours but also when your estate becomes someone else's estate (and so on).

For example, suppose you want to leave $500,000 to your only son, but you're concerned that if you were to die while your son is still relatively young (say, under 30), he won't be responsible or mature enough to adequately manage a large amount of money. Before you can say, "sail around the world," you're afraid he will have spent the entire half million.

You can use a trust in the manner described in the previous paragraph to parcel out the money to your son as you see fit. The trust can give him a little bit each year for some duration and then a final lump sum at some age when you think he'll be mature enough to protect the money as if he had actually earned it himself. Or you can add conditions to how the money in the trust is dispersed, such as your son receives a little bit of money until a certain age, and then he gets the rest only if he graduates college or meets some other criteria you determine when you set up the trust.

TIP

Trusts are an important part of your estate plan when you want to leave money to your minor children and make sure that

>> The money is available to them when they reach certain ages.

>> The money is set aside (think "officially reserved" meaning that nobody else can touch it) for your children and managed by a trustee, instead of just leaving it to your brother-in-law and saying, "Please don't spend this money on a Rolls Royce; make sure you keep it safe for my kids."

Providing funds for educational purposes

Another common use for trusts is to make money available to your children, grandchildren, other relatives, or even nonrelatives (your employees' children, for example) for educational purposes, such as college tuition and living expenses.

You can set up and fund trusts that parcel out money for educational purposes, but that also come with the restriction of "no school, then no money!"

Benefiting charities and institutions

You can help out charities in many ways: through gift giving or by leaving money or other property to one or more institutions as part of your will.

Alternatively, you can set up some type of *charitable trust* that may, for example, annually give money to the charity while you're still alive, give a larger amount upon your death, and then from what is left in the trust after you die, continue to make regular payments to the charity. You can even set up a charitable trust to make regular payments to the charity for some amount of time but eventually "give back" whatever is left to you or, if you've died, to someone else in your family. Alternatively, you can set up a charitable trust to work the other way — pay you while you're still alive, and upon your death, the remaining amount in the trust goes to the charity.

Sorting Out Trusts — from Here to Eternity

In general, there are two different ways of categorizing trusts:

>> Those trusts that are in effect while you're still alive versus those that take effect upon your death

>> Trusts you can change your mind on versus those that are absolutely, positively, unchangeable

Trusts for when you're alive versus when you're gone

TECHNICAL STUFF

An *intervivos trust* is a trust that you set up and that is in effect while you're still alive. In contrast, if you set up a trust under your will and that trust doesn't take effect until your death, you're using a *testamentary trust.*

Here's a quick example to emphasize the distinction between these two categories. Suppose you want to help out your favorite charity and, after consulting with your estate-planning team, you decide that a trust is the best way to go. If you set up a particular type of charitable trust that makes annual payments to the charity while you're still alive, then that trust is an intervivos trust. If, however, you set up a trust under the terms of your will to become effective (and start making payments) after your death, you've set up a testamentary trust.

The following sections look at both of these categories of trust in more detail.

Selecting intervivos trusts for your estate plan

If your primary objective of creating a trust is to provide an economic benefit (cash payments, transfer of real property that is currently in your estate, and so on) to specific people or institutions (again, your children, your favorite nephew, your favorite charity, and so forth) in the future, then you should strongly consider setting up some type of intervivos trust.

With an intervivos trust, payments and other types of property transfers may begin while you're still alive instead of waiting until your death (in this case, "sooner" is better than "later" when it comes to money). Furthermore, you usually have a better handle on the amount and value of your property with which you fund an intervivos trust than with a testamentary trust, as we discuss in the next section.

With an intervivos trust, you know what your estate is worth and how much is available to fund such a trust. Essentially, you have a higher degree of control with an intervivos trust than with a testamentary trust. When you set up an intervivos trust, you can initially fund the trust with certain property from your estate, add more property throughout your lifetime, and even make arrangements for additional property to be added to the trust upon your death. For example, if you initially fund an intervivos trust with stock, you can always add more later to cover any shortfalls if the shares you used for the trust have decreased in value. Or if your portfolio has skyrocketed — including the stock you used to fund the trust — and you're feeling particularly generous, you can increase the trust's value.

Choosing testamentary trusts for your estate plan

If you aren't particularly concerned about providing economic benefit to a trust beneficiary while you're still alive, you can still set up an intervivos trust, or you can hold off on creating the trust until after your death and instead, create a testamentary trust under your will.

So how exactly do you set up a testamentary trust if you're already dead? Actually, you lay the groundwork for a testamentary trust in your will while you're still alive, which means the following:

>> Along with all the other contents of your will discussed in Book 2, Chapter 4, you include appropriate language to set up a testamentary trust that, just like everything else in your will, doesn't actually "come alive" until your death. (Ironic, huh?)

>> Your will goes through probate and must be in compliance with various will statutes. Your testamentary trust also needs to be in compliance because it's technically part of your will. If you make any goofs in the language you use relating to the trust (or trusts) you want to establish, all kinds of complications set in, just as with any other part of your will.

TECHNICAL STUFF

>> Unlike a testamentary trust, an intervivos trust generally doesn't have to go through probate, but the probate court still has jurisdiction over an intervivos trust if any controversy or problems arise, just as it does for a testamentary trust.

>> The funding of a testamentary trust can often be up in the air because the actual funding doesn't take place until your death. As with other parts of your will, if your circumstances have changed and property you had anticipated using for the trust no longer is in your estate or is worth far less than it once was, you and the trust's beneficiaries may be out of luck because, quite simply, the necessary funds aren't available.

TIP

To help prevent unpleasant surprises, such as an underfunded or even unfunded testamentary trust, review all aspects of your trust when you do your annual review of your will. (After all, the provisions for a testamentary trust are contained in your will, so doing so is only logical.) If the property you had planned to use to fund the trust is no longer worth enough to accomplish your goals, then you can look for additional property in your estate and adjust your will accordingly, change the details of the trust to reflect a reduced value, or in the worst case, cancel your plans for the testamentary trust.

Deciding whether an intervivos or testamentary trust is better

Which is better for your estate plan: an intervivos trust or a testamentary trust? The favorite answer of estate-planning professionals comes into play here: *It all depends.* As with most other aspects of estate planning, you and your estate-planning team need to carefully look at many different factors to put strategies and instruments in place that are specific to your needs.

Intervivos trusts, together with plain old gift giving, are a good way to reduce your estate's value and reduce or negate the effect of federal estate taxes. And, as mentioned earlier in this section, you can give early and give often with an intervivos trust, benefiting people or institutions sooner than if they had to wait for your death.

On the other hand, suppose that you want a trust to come alive only if you die before a certain age and you want to make provisions for your minor children's care, education, and so on. You can use a testamentary trust as part of your will. If you live long enough so that your children are no longer minors and are out on their own and don't need to have money protected and, you can revise your will and eliminate the testamentary trust provisions.

TIP

If you do a good job at outlining your objectives for setting up a trust in the first place, the most appropriate category of trust — intervivos or testamentary — should become fairly obvious.

Changing your mind: Revocable and irrevocable trusts

An intervivos trust — again, a trust you set up that goes into effect while you're still alive — can be either

>> *Revocable,* meaning that you can change your mind

>> *Irrevocable,* meaning, sorry, what's done is done

Irrevocable trusts are the easier of the two to understand. After you place property into an irrevocable trust, you can't retrieve the property. For all intents and purposes, that property now belongs to the trust, not to you.

With a revocable trust, however, you can place property into the trust and at some point in the future, undo the transfer by removing the property and terminating the trust.

TECHNICAL
STUFF

Very often, if you die or become incompetent, the provisions of a revocable trust call for the trust to become an irrevocable trust. Consider a revocable *burial trust* as an example, which you can terminate at any time, usually before death or incompetency. However, if the burial trust is still in existence when you die (or become incompetent), the trust becomes irrevocable and the money is used for your funeral expenses.

The most significant distinctions between revocable and irrevocable trusts are the estate tax considerations. Property that you place in an irrevocable trust is no longer considered part of your estate, meaning that the property typically isn't included in your estate's value when it comes to determining if you owe death taxes and, if so, how much. However, you still own property that you place into a revocable trust, and therefore that property is still subject to death taxes. (Which is very logical, if you think about it. If you can change your mind about the trust and retrieve the property from the trust at any time while you're still alive, the property is really yours and should be considered part of your estate).

LOOKING CLOSELY AT REVOCABLE TRUSTS

Estate-planning advisers often point to revocable trusts — particularly living trusts, discussed in Book 5, Chapter 3 — as "the perfect way to totally avoid probate." Put all your property into revocable trusts and you can have control over that property, the pitch goes, and because none of your property is now in your probate estate (that is, it's all held in trust), your estate doesn't have to go through the probate process because your probate estate is "empty!" And, by avoiding probate, you avoid the costs of probate, the lack of privacy, and the other disadvantages to the probate process discussed in Book 5, Chapter 3.

Not so fast. True, you can avoid probate costs, but do you really think setting up and maintaining trusts is free? No way! Your costs to set up a revocable trust vary depending on attorney fees and other costs, but be prepared to pay to have your trust managed.

You also need to make sure that everything you own is held in trust form. If you fail to include any part of your estate in your trust(s), then you have a probate estate that is subject to the probate process. So every time you buy a new home, open a new brokerage account, or make any changes to your estate's inventory, you need to make sure that you transfer that property into your trust(s). And that can be a pain.

Remember also that probate isn't always bad, either. The probate court, which has the responsibility of making sure that property in your probate estate is disposed of properly with no behind-the-scenes funny games, supervises your probate estate. Without the probate court's supervision, part or all of your estate that is held in trust or other nonprobate form (joint tenancy with right of survivorship, for example) can be in for problems if someone close to you in a position of authority has, shall we say, a lack of ethics. Eventually, all the beneficiary problems may get straightened out but quite possibly because of prolonged, costly legal battles.

Also keep in mind that you may be required to file state or federal estate or inheritance tax returns, even though you have no "probate estate" (or "probate assets"). At the state level, at least, those returns are usually considered to be public records. Therefore, if privacy concerns are important to you, your desire for privacy may be defeated.

You most likely have gift tax consequences when you establish an intervivos irrevocable trust, so make sure your accountant is "in the loop," along with your attorney. Also, certain transfers within certain time periods prior to your death can be included in your estate as "gifts in contemplation of death" under both state and federal statutes. So watch out for possible death tax implications.

If you get a break on estate taxes only with an irrevocable trust, why would anyone want to use a revocable trust without the estate tax break? Estate tax savings is only one of the reasons you may consider including a trust in your estate planning. If your estate's value is nowhere near the federal estate tax exemption amount magic number, then you really don't need to be concerned about federal estate-tax-saving tactics — for now, anyway. Your motivation for setting up a trust may have more to do with estate protection or helping out a charity, but you also may want a safety valve that allows you to pull money out of a trust if circumstances change in some way.

Make sure to work with your accountant to understand any and all tax implications — gift, federal estate, and state inheritance or estate — for property transfers to both irrevocable and revocable trusts. He or she can help you set up the right provisions and avoid unpleasant tax-related surprises from the government because of some provision of the tax code you didn't know about.

Chapter **5**

Minimizing Estate-Related Taxes

I f you enjoy games and puzzles like chess and the good ol' Rubik's Cube, then you may feel at home when it comes to planning for estate-related taxes. But if you always lose at chess and were never able to solve a Rubik's Cube, and if you prefer a jigsaw puzzle that comes with a label that states "suitable for ages five and up," then don't worry. This chapter boils down the steps you need to take for estate-related tax planning into a concise, comprehensive action plan.

Notice the phrase *estate-related taxes,* and not estate tax, *federal estate tax,* or even the slang term *death tax.* Just as you do when you play your annual income tax fun and games, you likely find yourself dealing with more than one type of tax. You run into the federal income tax, state income taxes, local income taxes, property taxes, as well as state inheritance and estate taxes. As a result, when dealing with estate planning, you need to think about *estate-related* taxes, not just the federal estate tax.

This chapter helps you to focus on the estate-related taxes that will most likely impact your estate — and to not worry about taxes that don't.

Figuring Out Where You Are Today

Your first step in minimizing your estate-related taxes is to conduct a snapshot analysis of your current situation. Ask yourself: "Would I have any estate-related tax liability if I died today?"

To determine your estate-related tax liability, you need to perform the following activities:

>> Determine your estate's value

>> Conduct an inventory of what estate-planning steps you've already taken.

>> Consult the appropriate tables and charts to understand preliminary federal and state tax liability.

>> Look for tax traps that may unnecessarily cost you money.

After completing the preceding list of activities (this section shows you how), you'll have a good idea which of the following categories you fall into with regards to estate-related taxes:

>> Significant tax-related concerns, which means you have a lot of work to do with your estate-planning team

>> Modest tax-related concerns, meaning you have some exposure, but with some fairly simple tactics, you can minimize your estate-related tax liability — or perhaps make that liability disappear altogether

>> No tax-related concerns, meaning your estate's value is so far below the tax radar and you live in a state without any estate or inheritance taxes that you don't need to worry at all about estate-related taxes

Determining your estate's value

Book 5, Chapter 2 describes how you need to have a good idea of your estate's value and gives you the tasks and steps you need to assess that value. So if you haven't completed this estate valuation activity, get to it! This section, purely for example, assumes that your estate right now is worth $900,000 after subtracting out liabilities, such as the remaining mortgage on your home, an automobile loan, and credit card debt.

Totaling your gifts to date

The federal estate tax and gift tax are part of a unified tax system. In that system, you have a set of magic numbers that you can use in a mix-and-match manner to transfer property from your estate to others. Beyond nontaxable gifts, such as those with amounts lower than the annual exclusion amount or that are otherwise free of gift tax, your taxable gifts reduce the amount of property that you can leave to others free of federal estate taxes after you die.

You need to compile a comprehensive list of any gift giving as well as the tax impact of those gifts. Take that amount and set it aside (you use it in the next section). Also, write down your estate's value. You use the two figures to get an idea of estate-related tax liability if you were to die today.

For example, suppose you're generous and have given $250,000 worth of taxable gifts through the years and haven't paid gift taxes along the way. Instead of paying the gift taxes, you filed your gift tax returns as required and are holding off on gift taxes until those amounts are settled up against federal estate taxes after you die.

Checking the tax tables

Assume, God forbid, that you were to die today. You want to compare the exemption amount magic numbers for this year (that is, the year in which you're doing your estate-related tax planning) with the answers to the questions you've asked according to the steps in the "Figuring Out Where You Are Today" section ("How much is my estate worth?" and "What have I done so far?").

TIP

Make sure you use official tax table sources, such as those available on the Internal Revenue Service website at www.irs.gov and the tax-related pages you find on the website for your state.

The federal estate tax exemption magic number for 2018 is $5.6 million. But suppose, for the sake of simplicity, that the exemption amount magic number is a nice, round $1 million, as it was in 2003. From the previous example, if your estate is worth $900,000, then you don't have to worry about federal estate taxes, right?

Wrong! Because (again, according to the previous example) you've already used up $250,000 of your exemption amount through taxable gift giving. Therefore, you have a potential federal tax liability. Specifically, you may have to pay estate taxes on $150,000, calculated as follows:

1. **Take the $1 million exemption amount.**

2. **Subtract out the $250,000 you've already used up through gift giving.**

   You have $750,000 left.

3. **Take the $900,000 value of your estate and subtract the $750,000, leaving approximately $150,000 of your estate that may be subject to federal estate taxes.**

Why "approximately"? Well, you have several available deductions to further reduce your estate's value when it comes to tax liability, such as probate costs, funeral expenses, and appraisal fees. So that $150,000 figure may be further reduced before applying any tax rate calculations.

Even more importantly, regardless of your estate's value, you can make two deductions that enable you to avoid having to pay any federal estate taxes. Specifically, you can use the marital deduction and charitable deduction to transfer significant amounts of property to your spouse or your favorite charities free of taxes. So if you leave most or all of your estate to your spouse or to one or more charities, then at least from a federal estate tax perspective, you don't have any concerns right now.

WARNING

Even rather modestly valued estates that are way beneath the amounts at which federal estate taxes become applicable may face significant tax liability in certain states that have fairly high estate or inheritance tax rates. So don't forget to check your state's tax rates.

In some states, the estate and inheritance tax system has different rates that apply to different people to whom you leave property. Those rates vary by the relationship of those people to you: a relatively low rate for your children, for example, but a fairly high rate for someone unrelated to you. Additionally, your state may have various rates that increase the more your estate is worth (in technical terms, a *graduated* tax system).

Therefore, you need to take a look at the answer to yet one more question — "Who gets what?" — as you've specified in your will and as set up in various will substitutes (see Book 5, Chapter 3), such as joint tenancy with right of survivorship, or payable on death bank accounts. The answer to this "who-gets-what?" question, in concert with "What is my estate worth?" and "What have I done so far?" helps you obtain an accurate picture of your total estate-related tax liability if you were to die today.

Looking out for tax traps

To assess your current estate-related tax liability, look for tax traps in how your estate is structured. One of the most common tax traps that can whack even the most modest estate with unanticipated and unnecessary tax liability is your life insurance policy.

TECHNICAL STUFF

Depending on how you've structured your life insurance — specifically, who owns your life insurance policy — the insurance's death benefit (that is, the amount of money that will be paid to one or more beneficiaries upon your death) may be added on top of your estate's value for federal estate tax calculation purposes.

For example, suppose your estate is valued at $500,000 and you live in a state that has neither an estate nor inheritance tax, and you've never given any taxable gifts before. Most likely, you have no estate-related tax liabilities — or so you hope. But suppose the following three items occur:

>> You have a term life insurance policy (see Book 3, Chapters 1 and 2 for more on life insurance) with a death benefit of $2 million.

>> You haven't taken steps to negate the federal estate tax bite, such as setting up a *life insurance trust.*

>> You die in a year when the federal exemption amount for estate taxes is $1 million.

WARNING

Guess what. You essentially have died with $1.5 million subject to federal estate taxes (the $500,000 value of your estate plus the $2 million life insurance death benefit minus the $1 million exemption amount) — even though your estate is really only worth $500,000 until you die!

So make sure that as you inventory your estate to determine its value, you work with your estate-planning team to look for tax traps in the following areas:

>> Life insurance (the previous example being a painful case in point)

>> Pensions, particularly any guaranteed future amounts that may be considered part of your estate even if you don't have the right to take distributions right now

>> Other guaranteed future payments that may be considered part of your estate, such as future payments on deferred compensation, royalties, patents, monthly payments and balloon payments on money you've loaned out, and so on

Fortune-Telling: Picturing the Future as Best You Can

Taking a snapshot of where you are today is fairly easy if you follow the suggestions given earlier in the chapter. But most estate planning is based on some future scene — your circumstances in 5, 10, 20, 50, or even 100 more years. Impossible, you say? Far-out tax planning is much more possible than you may imagine if you take care to do the following:

>> Predict (as best you can) your estate's future value when you die.

>> Cross-reference your life span possibilities (that is, various scenarios on how much longer you may live) against future estate-related tax liability, paying special attention to the exclusion (or exemption) amount magic numbers.

>> Understand the tax impact of estate-planning strategies you already have in place.

>> Consider the tax impact of likely or inevitable changes to your family situation.

>> Make your best guess at future estate-related tax exposure.

Predicting the future

No, you didn't suddenly wind up at the state or county fair, walking down the midway and finding yourself beckoned over to the palm-reading booth. But *estate planning* does involve making some educated guesses about what may happen in the future.

Specifically, you need to make a rough guess about how much your estate will be worth when you die. Of course, few people know when they'll die, other than those who have a terminal illness and who have received a medical opinion as to how much longer they have to live.

For most other people, the best course of action is to look ahead to whatever an average life span is and how many years are left between now and then. For example, suppose you're a 35-year-old female, in fairly good health, and with a family medical history that doesn't have a lot of your relatives dying at relatively young ages. You may reasonably expect to live until 75, 80, or maybe even older, meaning that you can predict the future and settle on one particular target age — say 80 years old.

Hopefully, you already have a general-purpose financial plan (and if you don't, please consult with your accountant to develop one) that takes into account factors, such as

>> Your property's value

>> Your property's expected future earnings, such as interest on your bank accounts and growth in your stocks, annuities, and mutual funds

>> Your current and anticipated future income

>> Anticipated significant future family expenses, such as your children's college education or weddings for your three daughters

- Additional expenses that are likely, such as caring for your own aging parents and your own anticipated medical expenses (as well as those of your spouse, if applicable)

- The age at which you plan to retire

- Some rough idea of ordinary living expenses during your retirement years, based on the lifestyle you anticipate and your retirement-versus-estate philosophy. (Do you specifically want to leave certain amounts of property behind for your children, grandchildren, or charities, or do you plan to spend as much of your money as possible during your retirement years?)

If you're looking at a span of 30, 40, or more years between now and the age at which you're trying to predict your estate's value, your calculations may be way off. But that's okay, because all you're trying to do is get a rough idea of whether your future estate may be worth, say, $1 million or $10 million when it comes to estate-related tax planning.

If, however, you're close to retirement age — or maybe already in your retirement years — and you have a fairly accurate idea of how much of your estate you already are or soon will be spending during your retirement, then you can predict whether your estate's value will be

- About the same as it currently is

- More than it currently is (you're earning more in interest and retirement-years income than you're spending, meaning that your estate continues to grow in value)

- Less than it currently is because you're gradually drawing down your estate's value to provide retirement-years living expenses

Regardless of your current age and your particular situation, you need to have some idea of your estate's future value so you can perform the next step — tax liability analysis — with some degree of accuracy.

Looking at several scenarios for the federal estate tax

The 2001 tax law made tax planning the financial equivalent of skeet shooting. The exemption amount magic number changed frequently between 2002 and 2009, disappeared along with the estate tax in 2010, and then came back at a lower amount in 2011. It's been climbing ever since. How can you possibly do any tax planning in such a volatile environment?

You should set up three different comparison numbers that feed into the steps that follow. Specifically, you want to look at

>> The best-case scenario

>> The in-between scenario

>> The worst-case scenario

The best-case scenario

You can hope that the federal estate tax is repealed, meaning that no matter how much your estate is worth, you won't have any federal estate tax liability. So if that's the case, why do any tax planning at all?

WARNING

Don't get complacent. Your *state* may still have estate or inheritance taxes that don't go away, either temporarily or permanently. Or Congress may decide to keep the federal estate tax repealed but still apply the gift tax and generation skipping transfer tax (GSTT). Another concern: If you receive certain government-provided medical care, your estate may get whacked for big dollars under the Estate Recovery Act.

So in the best-case scenario, you can put a big fat zero in the column titled "federal estate tax I may owe" because you won't have an estate tax or an exemption amount. But don't forget to consider other estate-related taxes and any related exemption amount magic numbers and other details.

The in-between scenario

The second scenario to consider — the in-between scenario — is one in which the federal estate tax hovers right around where it is now: around five and a half million dollars. Under the in-between scenario, you may find yourself having to worry about federal estate taxes, but only if your estate is worth more than that.

WARNING

Again, as with the best-case scenario that has no federal estate tax, don't forget to check your state's estate-related taxes.

The worst-case scenario

The last scenario to consider is that the federal estate tax exemption amount will be lowered back to $1 million, meaning that if your taxable estate's value exceeds that amount, say hello to federal estate taxes.

You should use the worst-case scenario because many people may find themselves susceptible to federal estate taxes, simply because of the possibly low exemption amount.

Blending your present strategies into the future

So far, from the preceding steps in this chapter, you have some key pieces of information with regards to estate tax planning and your future. Those keys are

>> Your future estate's likely (or at least possible) value

>> Some raw data with regards to three different taxation scenarios that you can cross-reference against your estate's value to predict future tax liability

Chances are, though, that if you're not a newcomer to estate planning, you are already using some of the strategies discussed in this book, such as

>> Below the radar tax-free gift giving

>> Various types of trusts

>> The marital deduction for property you leave behind for your spouse, if doing so makes financial and tax sense

After looking at the items just listed and noting which ones are already part of your estate-planning strategy, you can come up with a revised figure — call it an *adjusted future estate value* — that more accurately represents what your estate is likely to be worth in the future, regardless of what it's worth now.

The *adjusted future estate value* figure you come up with is what you use as you move forward to the next few steps as you try to predict future estate-related tax liability.

Considering the impact of death, divorce, and other bum breaks

Significant changes in your life, such as divorce or your spouse's death, can dramatically affect your estate's value.

For example, if your spouse is terminally ill and will almost certainly die before you do, and if your spouse plans to leave his or her property to you under the marital deduction, then your estate's value will increase, perhaps significantly, after your spouse dies.

Similarly, if you expect a significant inheritance in the near future from an elderly relative who is in poor health, factor that inheritance into your calculations.

Or if a divorce is on your horizon, your estate's value will likely be lower if you expect that a significant portion of your estate will be lost as a result of the divorce settlement.

The important point to note is that when you try to figure out your estate's value in the future, you need to look at more than just the regular financially oriented factors, such as income, expenses, earnings on your investments, and so on, plus estate-planning strategies you already have in place. All factors are complicated enough when you look out more than a year or two. To complicate matters, you need to look at significant life changes and try to understand as best you can how they may affect your estate's value.

Carefully comparing then betting the house and rolling the dice

You now have all the numbers you need: your estate's future value when you die as well as three sets of tax-related data from the best-case, in-between case, and worst-case scenarios. Now you need to compare the three.

>> First, look at the best-case scenario: no federal estate tax at all but possible state inheritance or estate taxes and possibly other liability, such as Estate Recovery Act considerations. Based on what you think your estate will be worth, are you still looking at significant tax liability? Moderate tax liability? No tax liability?

>> Now look at the in-between scenario: a federal estate tax exemption amount that stays at $5.6 million. Now do the same comparisons, looking to see whether you have significant tax liability, moderate tax liability, or no tax liability.

>> Finally, as shampoo labels say, "lather, rinse, repeat": Do the same comparisons and come up with the same significant/moderate/none answer for tax liability under the worst-case scenario of the federal estate tax exemption amount being at $1 million when you die.

The three answers you get for the three possible scenarios tell you how much estate-related tax-planning work you have ahead of you. If, for example, your answer under all three scenarios is "no tax liability," then your estate-planning job is done! (Well, for tax purposes anyway; don't forget you still need to worry about your will, probate, insurance, and so on.)

On the flip side, if your answer under all three scenarios is "significant tax liability," then you have lots of work ahead. You specifically need to spend time with your estate-planning team looking at different tax-saving strategies.

If your answers are somewhere in between — for example, you have significant tax liability only if the federal estate tax exemption amount is $1 million, but otherwise you have either moderate or no tax liability — then you still need to consult with your estate-planning team. More likely, the basic trade-offs discussed in the next section will be enough to reduce or eliminate estate-related taxes.

TIP

Whatever answers you come up with under the three scenarios, run your results past your estate-planning team at least once just as if you were still in grade school and asking one of your parents to double-check your homework. Certainly, do most of the planning work on your own but also get a professional opinion.

Hmmm . . . Deciding on Strategies and Trade-Offs

Good news: Most of the basic tax-savings strategies you can employ as part of your estate planning are very straightforward and simple and require very little effort and expense on your part.

WARNING

Bad news: If you don't plan carefully, you can really mess up your estate planning and wind up with a larger tax bill. And if you really mess up, your beneficiaries may get stuck paying more taxes.

So use the following list as a starting point of tax strategies. Realize that each point has several alternatives available to you and, depending on various circumstances, may or may not be advantageous to you. Also, you need to plan ahead beyond the most immediate tax consequences and consider down-the-road tax consequences as well. The most common estate tax-related strategies available to you include

» Whether you should give property to someone as a gift or leave that property in your will

» Whether you should leave all your property to your spouse

» How to structure your life insurance policy or policies

» Whether you should use gifts below the exclusion amount

» How to use double dipping on tax savings from charitable gifts

Make sure you structure your life insurance policy or policies to avoid an unpleasant surprise from the estate tax agents.

Gifting versus leaving property as part of your estate

Suppose you and your spouse have a vacation home that you purchased 20 years ago for $50,000. It was a real fixer-upper. Over the past 20 years, you've put about $100,000 in renovations into the home, and — even better — property values in that area have gone way up. In fact, your vacation home is now valued at $500,000, according to the most recent appraisal.

(For the sake of this example, the home is entirely in your name rather than jointly owned with your spouse, meaning that the $500,000 value is entirely within your estate.)

You decide to give the house to your oldest daughter — a freelance writer who wants to live in a secluded location. You have two options available. You can

>> Give the home to your daughter as a gift (being the generous parent you are).

>> Leave the home to your daughter in your will as part of your estate or through a trust.

Suppose you decide to give the home as a taxable gift. The home's value — $500,000 — becomes the starting point for figuring out any gift tax liability. Starting in 2018, you have a $15,000 annual exclusion on gifts that reduces the taxable amount to $485,000 ($500,000 minus $15,000).

If, however, you decide to hang onto the home and leave it to you daughter as part of your will, the entire $500,000 would potentially be subject to federal estate taxes.

TECHNICAL STUFF

But forget about the $15,000 difference because that's not the point. Assume your estate isn't subjected to any federal estate taxes at all because in the year you die, your estate's value is far below that year's exemption amount. In fact, the value is far enough below that even if you had given the home to your daughter as a taxable gift and therefore used up part of your combined gift-and-estate exemption amount and unified credit, you still don't have to worry about federal estate taxes.

For purposes of your estate, either giving the home to your daughter as a gift or leaving the home to her as part of your estate has the same tax impact on your estate: zero. But from your daughter's perspective, receiving the home as part of your estate likely will cost her much less in eventual taxes if she ever decides to sell that home than if she had received the home as a gift.

Why? The answer lies in how the tax basis of the home is calculated and how for estate purposes — but not for gifting purposes — that tax basis is "stepped up" to the current value of the home at the time it was transferred.

Don't panic. We go through it step by step. You may recognize the first part of this puzzle — calculating the tax basis — if you've ever owned and sold a home. To overgeneralize a bit, the *tax basis* of any property (not just real property like a house but any property, even including your stocks and mutual funds) is usually calculated as the price you paid for that property, plus any improvements you've made. (In the case of stocks and mutual funds, those improvements include dividends and capital gains that you reinvest.) In this example, the tax basis of your vacation home is $150,000: your original $50,000 purchase price plus the $100,000 in renovations you put into the home.

As noted earlier, if you leave property to someone upon your death as part of your estate, the value of that property is stepped up to the current value. Now, your daughter inherits a home worth $500,000, and that same $500,000 figure is her tax basis in that property. Assume that she doesn't make any further improvements, and ten years later she sells that home for $700,000; she would potentially have a taxable gain of $200,000 (the $700,000 she receives minus her $500,000 tax basis).

If, however, you give the home to your daughter as a gift, she doesn't receive a stepped-up basis and instead receives the same tax basis in the property as you had: $150,000. So if she were to someday sell that home for $700,000, her gain is now a whopping $550,000 ($700,000 minus her $150,000 tax basis) rather than the $200,000 if she had received the property from your estate upon your death.

Depending on the tax laws governing the sale of primary residences, your daughter may never owe any capital gains tax, regardless of the home's value or how low the tax basis is. So for a house, as in this example, the gift-versus-estate consideration may be different than for stock or anything else that doesn't qualify for the primary residence tax break. However, this tax break, the rules for rolling over gains, and the amount of the final tax break have changed occasionally in recent years. As with pretty much everything else in tax planning, you need to look ahead, make some educated guesses, and consult with your estate-planning team.

REMEMBER

The two key points to keep in mind are

>> For purposes of your estate, the federal tax impact of giving property as a gift is more or less the same as leaving that property as part of your estate.

>> For the person to whom you give or leave the property, the down-the-road tax impact can be very different depending on which choice you make.

Imagining the ups and downs of leaving your estate to your spouse

Many married people automatically set up their wills and their overall estate plans to leave their entire estate to their surviving spouses. But they could be walking into a trap.

Suppose you and your spouse each have estates that are slightly below the federal estate tax exemption amount. Suppose you die before your spouse does, and you leave all your property to your spouse. Now suppose that your spouse dies shortly after you do, with most of the property that was once yours still unspent and part of your spouse's estate. Guess what? Federal estate taxes probably come into the picture because by leaving your estate to your spouse, you have created a situation where estate taxes kick in. Now your spouse's new, larger estate is higher than the exemption amount.

TIP

When deciding whether to leave property to your spouse, you need to look ahead and understand whether you're creating a tax liability that you can avoid. (You can leave your property to your children or someone else, or place your property into a trust for your spouse.)

Using gifts below the exclusion amount

You can give gifts to anyone up to the exclusion amount (currently $15,000, and later adjusted annually for inflation) without having any tax impact at all or even using up your unified credit against down-the-road estate taxes.

If you have cash, investments, or other property that you're certain you'll leave to certain people — your children, for example — and if your estate is valuable enough that federal estate taxes will apply, then why not transfer that property now as gifts in small-enough chunks to stay below the gift tax radar and therefore lower the value of your taxable estate?

Why not indeed? Go to it!

Double dipping on tax savings from charitable gifts

The charitable deduction for gifts allows you to give gifts to qualified charities without worrying about gift taxes.

But guess what? You can double dip on the tax savings front and also take an itemized deduction on your federal income taxes for those same gifts. So you're not only skipping out on gift taxes and reducing the amount of future estate taxes, but you're also saving more money on your federal income taxes. And, if your state allows you to itemize deductions on your state income tax and to include charitable deductions, you can save even more.

So why not get two — or even three — tax deductions out of the same charitable gift?

Putting Together a Comprehensive Estate-Related Tax Plan

What's that? You're still a bit uncertain about where to start? Just follow this section, and before you know it, the tax portion of your estate planning will be well within your control.

Fixing the holes

You've identified the problem areas in your estate plan that can possibly cause your estate to get hit with unnecessary taxes, so do something about those problems — right now. If, for example, your life insurance is poorly structured so the death benefit amount causes an otherwise nontaxable estate (for federal estate tax purposes) to be taxed, then create a life insurance trust or otherwise change your life insurance policy's ownership.

Starting on that gift giving

Remember that one way or another, the ownership of every single piece of property in your estate is eventually transferred to someone else, in some way: through your will, through your state's intestacy laws, through a will substitute, such as joint tenancy, through a trust, or through a gift. Because you really can't take your property with you, and if you've already given serious consideration to the many beneficiary decisions when you prepare your will, why not give certain property away now or in the near future instead of waiting until after your death for that property to be transferred? You can not only smooth out the property transfers in your estate by regularly giving gifts, but you can also keep a substantial amount of the overall property transfer tax-free by keeping the gifts below the annual exclusion amounts.

TIP

You can take the complete inventory of your estate that you created (see Book 5, Chapter 2, as well as the discussion earlier in this chapter) and divide the list into three columns:

>> Identify the intended recipient (person, charity, foundation, and so on) for that property.

>> Indicate whether you want to give that property as a gift rather than wait for it to be transferred as part of your estate.

>> Specify the year or years in which you want to make the gift.

You can also split up certain property to keep the gift amounts below the annual exclusion amounts and further reduce any potential tax exposure. For example, if you have 1,000 shares of a stock that's relatively stable in price, and the current price per share is $50 — meaning that you have $50,000 worth of stock — you may decide that you want your oldest daughter to receive that stock to start her own portfolio. Rather than give her the entire 1,000 shares in a single year, which means that part of the gift is taxable, you can give her just enough shares this year, next year, and also the following year (and so on) to stay beneath the annual exclusion radar of $15,000 (or whatever the figure adjusts to each year along with inflation).

Setting up trusts if necessary

Book 5, Chapter 4 discusses types of trusts, many of which you can use to reduce or eliminate tax liability on your estate. Don't go overboard — that is, don't set up all kinds of trusts (and pay lots of fees to your attorney or financial planner) if you don't really need to do so. By all means, set up the trusts you need to help prevent an unnecessary tax bite.

Planning ahead for property transfers upon your death

How much should you plan ahead if you leave all your estate to your spouse? How about part of your estate? Or maybe none of your estate to your spouse? Should your spouse leave his or her estate to you?

Part of your beneficiary decisions you specify in your will or through various types of will substitutes must include estimating the tax impact. If your state has an estate or inheritance tax, pay particular attention, because chances are that even if you can sidestep the federal tax bite, your estate may get hit hard by your state. So the key, just as with every other aspect of estate planning, is to plan ahead.

REMEMBER

Schedule a meeting with you estate-planning team to discuss what tax-planning ideas may make sense for you, the pros and cons, and potential pitfalls.

Minimizing
Estate-Related Taxes

6

Tapping Into Your Home's Value

Contents at a Glance

Chapter **1**

Making Important Housing Decisions

Your housing needs change during your life, but they can really change in your retirement years. Life changes — such as ceasing work, kids growing up and moving out, divorce, death of a spouse, and so on — can have a dramatic impact on your housing wants and requirements and ability to afford housing.

In particular, you face significant housing choices during your golden years. Most retirees grapple with moving, possibly downsizing, and moving into retirement communities that may offer healthcare. This chapter addresses the decisions you have to make and how the choices you make can potentially affect your finances. Additionally, it covers the key tax issues you need to understand to make the most of your housing decisions. Finally, it introduces an emerging area: reverse mortgages as a way to partly finance your retirement. Book 6, Chapter 2 covers reverse mortgages in detail.

Analyzing Moving

When Laura and Rick Idealists (a real couple but obviously not their real names) were in their middle-aged years and still working, they imagined a slower-paced life in a less-crowded and lower-cost area for their retirement. Like many folks dreaming about and envisioning retirement, the Idealists believed that once unchained from needing to work, they would have much better choices for places to live.

As they neared and finally entered retirement, the Idealists didn't move. Upon reflection, they better realized and appreciated the joy brought to them by their local friends, favorite restaurants, and service providers (including their medical providers). When confronted with the reality of moving from their local area, they realized that they'd lose a lot of personal connections that meant so much to them.

Some folks who move when they retire are motivated largely or in part by the attraction of reducing their expenses. Some do lower their living costs, and some don't. Their happiness varies with their new locations as well. This section discusses the appeal and realities of moving and the issues to weigh and contemplate.

Considering the pros and cons of moving

Although many folks are content to and prefer to stay put when they retire, others wish to move. Among the primary motivations for retirees moving are the following:

>> **Being closer to family and good friends:** Because jobs and careers take folks to locations that may not be their first or even second or third choices location-wise, it's no surprise that some retirees find themselves geographically isolated from their closest relatives and even best friends. Especially if you have adult children and possibly grandchildren living elsewhere, the pull to move closer to them can be strong.

Clearly, moving closer to family and friends may have little or nothing to do with your finances, but that doesn't mean you should take the decision lightly. At a minimum, you should discuss your feelings and possible plans with the folks to whom you'd be moving near. Also, consider the possibility that someday these relatives may need or want to move somewhere else.

>> **Living in a better climate:** With all the free time that retirement generally entails, climate escalates in importance for some people. Many older people prefer more temperate climates — that is, fewer days of extreme heat or cold. Think locales near Santa Barbara and San Diego rather than Houston or Minneapolis. Some folks with particular health conditions such as allergies or asthma find that moving to a temperate climate helps improve their symptoms and health.

>> **Reducing their cost of living:** During their working years, many people live in more congested urban or near-urban areas with pricey housing and property taxes. If you have kids, you're probably also paying a premium to live in an

area with better public schools. No longer constrained by where work is located or the need for access to good schools, you can consider moving to lower-cost areas.

>> **Selecting housing that's user friendly for the elderly:** As people age, their mobility and coordination inevitably decline, albeit at different rates for different people. So the housing you choose to live in during your younger years may no longer make sense. Steep driveways, stairways to the house and in the house, and other design issues may be decidedly unfriendly and potentially dangerous to your aging body.

WARNING

Moving does have its downsides. And people often overlook them in the excitement and allure of believing the grass is greener elsewhere. Check out these downsides to moving:

>> **Living costs may not decrease enough or at all.** The mistake all too many folks make is that they assume their overall living costs will be lower after a move to an area that attracts them with, for example, lower-cost housing. You must and should examine all your living expenses and how they may change with a proposed move.

>> **You may introduce other negatives.** You may be successful in reducing your living costs with a move, but you also may find yourself in an area with other problems — more crime, traffic congestion, higher insurance costs on your home and car, and so on. Minimize your chances for disappointment by doing sufficient research before you make a decision to move.

>> **Moving is costly.** Although you may be able to save money after your move is complete, be sure to make realistic estimates of your likely moving costs and how many years it will take to recoup them. The biggest expenses include real estate transaction costs and moving company costs.

REMEMBER

Here's the bottom line: To make an informed decision, do all your homework and research concerning the topics discussed in this section. Don't focus on one reason to move. And don't make assumptions, such as your living costs will be lower because housing costs less in a new community. Get the facts on how all your living costs will change with a move. The best sources are people you know who already live there. You can consult official sources, such as chambers of commerce and realtors, but they may not be objective.

Eyeing the options for where you can move

Traditional retirement living and housing choices are changing. New generations of retirees are looking for new living experiences, and developers are obliging, giving older Americans more choices for living arrangements than ever before.

These new choices involve more than simply relocating outside the traditional retirement Sunbelt havens like Florida and Arizona. They also involve different types of housing and living arrangements and different types of activities in the communities.

One reason for the new senior living choices is that people are retiring earlier. At some adult communities, about one-third of residents are under age 65. Those under age 55 can make up 10 percent or more of the residents in some communities.

Another reason for the changes is that today's longer retirements have more stages than in the past, generally up to three stages. Each stage has a range of living choices. And, of course, not everyone goes through all these stages or even any of them. The following sections identify some specific choices you have if you decide to move during retirement.

REMEMBER

Retirement housing decisions are more complicated than ever because you have more choices. Review all your options so you'll be happy with the choice you make until you're ready to move to the next stage.

Stage No. 1: Downsizing

When folks downsize — that is, move to a smaller home — the goal is usually to maintain the same contacts and activities while shedding the labor and costs of maintaining a larger home. When you hit this stage, you've decided it's time to stop mowing the lawn, raking leaves, checking the gutters, and maintaining the mechanical systems. You also don't want to pay for rooms you aren't using.

REMEMBER

You have several options for downsizing. You can move to a smaller house, townhouse, or condominium in a regular development. In this case, your neighbors will consist of those from all the age groups. Or you can move to a planned senior community (or age-restricted community) where people are similar in age, such as those discussed in the next section.

Stage No. 2: Looking at retirement communities

You may consider moving into a retirement community after you retire. Oftentimes, these communities are in warmer locations, such as sunny Florida or Arizona. If you're considering moving into a retirement community, make sure you look at the following factors:

>> **The demographics of the community and how that appeals to you:** Some seniors prefer to be around people their own age; others prefer more diversity. If you're a young retiree, you may want to check the average age in a senior community, because in some the average age is 75 or older. An adult community also may make you feel isolated from your family and friends, though you do

have the opportunity to make new friends. A community that includes all ages may be noisier, less well kept, and keep later hours. You may want to visit at different times of the day and week to get a good flavor of the lifestyle.

» **The types of activities offered on-site and in the surrounding community:** Each type of community will have its own activities plus the activities in the surrounding community. A development built for seniors may provide services that are helpful to seniors, such as laundry, housecleaning, and on-grounds restaurants. Many newer senior communities also have amenities such as spas, golf courses, health clubs, and Internet centers. They can be more like resorts or country clubs than traditional adult communities or regular developments. Also, be sure to consider how your current activities would be affected.

TIP

The adult communities outside Florida and Arizona tend to have younger residents than those in the traditional retirement states. Some university towns are also courting retirees and seniors. You may have more variety in your lifestyle by choosing a senior community located in an area that isn't a traditional senior haven. Newer communities also have up-to-date features such as wiring for high-speed Internet.

Stage No. 3: Housing that's near family and has healthcare

The third stage of retirement often involves moving near friends and family, especially grandchildren, and moving into traditional senior housing with some healthcare facilities on premises. This stage has four basic choices when it comes to housing:

» **Independent living:** This essentially entails living in an apartment or condo complex for seniors. As part of your monthly rental, you get some basic services, such as housekeeping, transportation, activities, and some meals.

» **Assisted living:** This type of housing offers additional services and is for someone who needs help with two or more of the basic activities of daily living (bathing, dressing, walking, and so on). You may be able to avoid or delay this option by having in-home care at your existing residence.

» **Nursing home:** This option is for someone who needs daily medical care help.

» **Continuing care retirement community (CCRC):** This option bundles all the preceding living arrangements into one. You can start in independent living or assisted living, and then as your needs change, you're guaranteed a place in the other types of care. You only have to move to another location in the same community instead of having to look for a different facility and moving there. CCRCs are becoming very popular and are being built all over the country.

REMEMBER

There's no one right answer in terms of housing. Each person's situation and preferences are unique, so explore your options and select the choice that feels right for your situation. Your doctor or other medical professional may direct you to one of the options. You also may find objective advice from your local Area Office on Aging or other local government sources.

Tapping Your Home's Equity: Reverse Mortgages

If you own the same home during most of the decades of your adult life, you'll probably have some decent equity accumulated in it. You may want to tap that equity to supplement your retirement income. For example, you can sell your home, buy a smaller, less costly property, and use the profit you make to finance your retirement.

Another way to tap into your equity is through a *reverse mortgage,* also known as a *home equity conversion mortgage* (HECM), which enables you through a loan to receive tax-free income on your home's equity while still living in the home.

Reverse mortgages fill a void and are just beginning to tap into growing demand. The first reverse mortgage was actually done generations ago — in 1961 to be exact. Clearly, it took many years for them to really begin to take hold, but now more than 100,000 are done on an annual basis.

The following sections outline the specifics of reverse mortgages, including how they work and how to determine whether one is right for you. This is just to whet your appetite. Book 6, Chapter 2 covers reverse mortgages in much more detail.

Defining terms and costs

With a reverse mortgage, the lender pays you (via lump sum, monthly payments, or a credit line), and the accumulated loan balance and interest is paid off when your home is sold or you pass away. The typical borrower is a widow who's 70 years old or older and running out of money, wants to stay in her home, and needs money for basic living expenses or for important home-maintenance projects such as replacing a leaky roof.

REMEMBER

So are you wondering whether you qualify? Here are the basic standards of eligibility:

>> You, the homeowner, must be at least 62 years of age.

>> You must use the home as your principal residence.

>> You must have any outstanding debt against the home paid in full. (Co-op apartments generally aren't eligible for a reverse mortgage.)

Retirees who have taken a reverse mortgage generally say it has been a good experience for them. They often cite that the extra income has allowed them to keep up a home's maintenance, pay medical and other costs, avoid having to scrimp so much on things like eating out sometimes, and gain peace of mind not having to make house payments.

You can use a reverse mortgage in several ways. You can take a lump sum and use it to pay medical bills or other debt, make needed repairs on the home, or pay other expenses. You can also set it up to pay you a fixed amount each month. Or you can set up a line of credit that you tap only when you need cash, such as when an unexpected or larger expense comes up. You can also tap the line of credit when investment markets take a tumble and you don't want to draw from your investment accounts until they recover at least some of the losses. The nice thing about the home equity line of credit (also called the *Standby HECM*) is that you can pay it down and restore the full line of credit.

Reverse mortgages aren't free of their downsides. Keep the following in mind:

>> **The effective interest rate can vary greatly.** With their high upfront costs, the *effective interest rate* (which factors in all the fees and interest you pay relative to the number of years you actually keep the loan) on most reverse mortgages easily jumps into the double-digit realm if you stay only a few years into the loan.

>> **They can be complicated to understand and compare.** Your effective interest rate varies greatly depending on how long you're in the home and using the loan, the timing and size of payments you receive, and your home's value over time. One unknown that you can't control is if an extended nursing home stay keeps you out of your home for 12 months and forces the sale of your home. In such a situation, at least the proceeds from the sale could be used toward the nursing home.

On the flip side, some aspects to qualifying for and having a reverse mortgage are actually easier than with a traditional mortgage. Consider the following:

>> **You don't need to have any income.** Income isn't important because you're not making any payments. The loan balance is accumulating against the value of your home, and it gets paid when the home is sold.

>> **You don't need good credit.** You're not borrowing money, so your credit score doesn't matter.

>> **You can't lose your home for failing to make payments, because there are none.** Reverse mortgages are *nonrecourse loans,* which means that the lender can't take your home if you default on the loan.

Determining whether a reverse mortgage is right for you

To consider whether a reverse mortgage may make sense for you, consider the following:

>> **Start with nonfinancial considerations.** Do you want to keep your current home and neighborhood? What's your comfort level with the size of your home and the associated upkeep? Consider whether you want to stay in your home for the foreseeable future or would rather tap into your home's equity by moving and downsizing to a smaller home or by simply renting.

>> **Discuss your explorations and concerns with your family.** Make sure everyone is aware of the range of options. Discussion and brainstorming may lead you to a better solution.

» **Understand what a reverse mortgage can do for you compared to a home equity loan.** Part of the appeal of a reverse mortgage is the lack of attractive alternatives if you want to stay in your home. For example, with a home equity loan, the big challenges are qualifying for a loan when you have limited income and making the required payments when you do get a loan. Home equity loans are *recourse loans,* which means that if you're unable to keep up with payments later in retirement, the lender can foreclose.

Also know that any money invested generating investment income would be taxed. Most seniors don't like taking risks with their investments, so invested home equity money would be unlikely to generate high enough returns to cover the loan's interest costs.

Searching for more information on reverse mortgages

Turn to Book 6, Chapter 2 for much more on reverse mortgages. If you're seriously considering a reverse mortgage, you may have more particular questions about the specifics that aren't covered in either chapter. If so, visit the AARP website at `www.aarp.org/revmort` for lots of helpful information; for referrals to free independent reverse mortgage counselors, call them at 800-209-8085.

Looking at Tax Issues Regarding Your Housing Decisions

Whenever you approach the decision as to what to do with your home, you should explore your options and be aware of important tax issues that come into play. That's what this section is about.

Being aware of capital gains exclusion rules

When you sell your home, you may be able to shelter a substantial amount of *capital gains* (the difference between your home's selling price and what you paid for it plus improvements over the years) that you have in the property.

How much? You can avoid capital gains taxes on up to $250,000 of profit if you own the property as a single person and up to $500,000 for married couples who file their taxes jointly. Profits that exceed these amounts are taxed at the relatively low long-term capital gains tax rates, which max out at 20 percent at the federal level. The Affordable Care Act (commonly known as Obamacare) can add another 3.8 percent to this for high-income earners. You may use this tax exclusion once every two years. And you must have used the home as your principal residence for at least two of the previous five years for it to qualify.

Converting your home to a rental: Yes or no?

Selling your home may take longer than you expected, particularly if you try to sell during a slumping real estate market as many parts of the country experienced in the late 2000s. If you overprice your home, you also may experience some delay in selling your home.

To help improve their cash flow if their house is sitting vacant, some home sellers rent the home while trying to sell it. Tread lightly here, because this tactic can cause you major tax trouble.

WARNING

If you stop trying to sell your home and continue renting it, the Internal Revenue Service (IRS) considers that you've converted your home into a rental property. If you then sell the property, it will no longer be eligible for the home ownership capital gains tax exclusion (see the previous section) when it wasn't your principal residence during at least two of the five years preceding the sale. In this case, your profit from the sale will be taxable.

TIP

You may be able to shelter your rental property sale profits from capital gains taxation. You need to do a so-called *like-kind, 1031 Starker exchange.* Check out the latest edition of Eric Tyson's book *Real Estate Investing For Dummies* (Wiley, 2015) for more details, and be sure to consult a competent tax advisor as well.

Chapter **2**

Reverse Mortgages for Retirement Income

A s touched on in Book 6, Chapter 1, if you own a home, a reverse mortgage allows you to tap into its *equity* (the difference between the market value of your home and the mortgage debt owed on it) to supplement your retirement income — while you still live in your home. Because these mortgages are so different from what most people expect, it generally takes a while for the most basic information about them to make sense. Even experienced financial professionals are often surprised to learn how these loans really work, how different their costs and benefits can be, and what you have to look out for.

Are you full of questions about these types of mortgages perhaps for yourself or for an elderly relative? If so, this chapter gives you the lowdown on reverse mortgages and helps you figure out whether they're right for you.

Grasping the Reverse Mortgage Basics

A *reverse mortgage* is a loan against your home that you don't have to repay as long as you live there. In a regular, or so-called *forward* mortgage (the kind you likely had when you bought your home), your monthly loan repayments make your debt go down over time until you've paid it all off. Meanwhile, your equity is rising as you repay your mortgage and as your property value appreciates.

With a reverse mortgage, by contrast, the lender sends *you* money, and your debt grows larger and larger as you keep getting cash advances (usually monthly), make no repayment, and interest is added to the *loan balance* (the amount you owe). That's why reverse mortgages are called *rising debt, falling equity* loans. As your *debt* (the amount you owe) grows larger, your *equity* (that is, your home's value minus any debt against it) generally gets smaller. However, your equity could still increase if you're in a strong housing market where home values are rising nicely.

TIP

If your financial goal is to preserve the equity in your home, you may be able to conservatively structure your reverse mortgage so you limit the amount of equity you pull out of your property to the estimated increase in home values anticipated over future years. Of course, predicting future real estate appreciation is definitely an inexact science. But real estate values do generally rise over time, and you may find that if you're modest in the amount of money you receive from the lender, you won't erode your home equity as much as you thought.

As mentioned in Book 6, Chapter 1, reverse mortgages differ from regular home mortgages in two important respects:

>> To qualify for most loans, the lender checks your income to see how much you can afford to pay back each month. But with a reverse mortgage, you don't have to make monthly repayments. Thus, your income generally has nothing to do with getting a reverse mortgage or determining the amount of the loan.

>> With a regular mortgage, you can lose your home if you fail to make your monthly repayments. With a reverse mortgage, you can't lose your home by failing to make monthly loan payments — because you don't have any to make!

TIP

A reverse mortgage merits your consideration if it fits your circumstances. Reverse mortgages may allow you to cost-effectively tap your home's equity and enhance your retirement income. If you have bills to pay, want to buy some new carpeting, need to paint your home, or simply feel like eating out and traveling more, a good reverse mortgage may be your salvation.

This section focuses on the ABCs of reverse mortgages and helps clarify any confusion you may have.

Considering common objections

Most older homeowners contemplating a reverse mortgage have worked hard for many years to eliminate their home's mortgage so that they own their home free and clear. After what they've gone through, the thought of reversing that process and rebuilding the debt owed on their home is troubling. Furthermore, reverse mortgages are a relatively new type of loan that few people understand. And most of today's reverse mortgage borrowers are low-income, single seniors who have run out of other money for living expenses. Some people think reverse mortgages are only a last resort, but that isn't true. The following sections answer some of the most common questions about reverse mortgages.

Can you lose your home?

It's not too surprising that folks who don't fully understand reverse mortgages often have preconceived notions, mostly negative, about how they work. Seniors with home equity often erroneously think that taking a reverse mortgage may lead to being forced out of their homes or ending up owing more than the house is worth.

Seniors taking out a reverse mortgage won't be forced out of their home. Nor will they (or their heirs) end up owing more than their house is worth. Federal law defines reverse mortgages to be *nonrecourse loans,* which simply means that the home's value is the only asset that can be tapped to pay the reverse mortgage debt balance. In the rare case when a home's value does drop below the amount owed on the reverse mortgage, the borrower isn't on the hook for the extra debt. The lender assumes that risk.

WARNING

As detailed later in this chapter (see the section "When do you pay the money back?"), not keeping current with your property taxes and homeowners insurance can trigger your reverse mortgage going into default and requiring payoff. When a loan is called due and payable, the reverse mortgage borrower or the borrower's estate needs to repay only the lesser of either the loan balance or 95 percent of the home's appraised value at that time.

Would a home equity loan or second mortgage work better?

Some people who are intimidated by having to understand reverse mortgages wonder whether it would be simpler to get a home equity loan or a new mortgage that allows them to take some equity out of their home. The problem with this strategy is that you have to begin paying traditional mortgage loans back soon after taking them out.

For example, suppose you own a home worth $200,000, with no mortgage debt. You decide to take out a $100,000, 15-year mortgage at 7 percent interest. Although you'll receive $100,000, you'll have to begin making monthly payments of $899. No problem, you may think; you'll just invest your $100,000 and come out ahead. Wrong!

Most seniors gravitate toward safe bonds, which traditionally may yield in the neighborhood of 5 percent — a mere $416 of monthly income — an amount far short of your monthly mortgage payments. If you invest in stocks and earn the generous average return of 10 percent per year, which is by no means guaranteed, your returns would amount to more — $833 per month — but still not enough to cover your monthly mortgage payment. (Also note that most income from stocks and bonds is taxable at both the federal and state level. By contrast, reverse mortgage payments you receive aren't taxable.) Advantage: reverse mortgage.

Here's another big drawback of taking out a traditional mortgage to supplement your retirement income. The longer you live in the house, the more likely you are to run out of money and begin missing loan payments, because you drain your principal to supplement inadequate investment returns and cover your monthly loan payment. If that happens, unlike with a reverse mortgage, the lending institution may foreclose on your loan, and you can lose your home.

Who can get a reverse mortgage?

Of course, reverse mortgages aren't for everyone. As discussed later in this chapter (see the section "Deciding Whether You Want a Reverse Mortgage"), alternatives may better accomplish your goal. And not everyone qualifies to take out a reverse mortgage. Specifically, to be eligible for a reverse mortgage, the following must be true:

>> You must own your home. In the early years of reverse mortgages, as a rule, all the owners had to be at least 62 years old. Now, for a couple, you may qualify for a reverse mortgage if one person is at least 62 years of age and the other person is younger than that. However, such a couple will qualify for less reverse mortgage money due to the younger spouse because "life expectancy" is part of the calculation.

>> Your home generally must be your *principal residence* — which means you must live in it more than half the year.

>> For the federally insured *Home Equity Conversion Mortgage* (HECM), your home must be a single-family property, a two- to four-unit building, or a federally approved condominium or planned-unit development (PUD). Reverse mortgage programs will lend on mobile homes with foundations that meet the U.S. Department of Housing and Urban Development (HUD) guidelines but won't lend on co-op apartments.

>> If you have any debt against your home, you must either pay it off before getting a reverse mortgage or, as most borrowers do, use an immediate cash advance from the reverse mortgage to pay it off. If you don't pay off the debt beforehand or don't qualify for a large enough immediate cash advance to do so, you can't get a reverse mortgage.

One final and important point about qualifying for a reverse mortgage: Lenders are now required to perform a financial assessment analyzing the prospective borrower's financial situation, including credit history and monthly income and expenses. Lenders pay particular attention to whether borrowers have enough cash flow to pay their property tax and home insurance bills. If borrowers have little wiggle room in their monthly budget, lenders may require a "set aside" fund to ensure payment of property taxes and home insurance, and this "set aside" fund reduces how large a reverse mortgage the borrowers can get. The amount of this "set aside" fund may also vary depending on the age of the reverse mortgage borrowers.

How much money can you get and when?

The whole point of taking out a reverse mortgage on your home is to get money from the equity in your home. How much can you tap? That amount depends mostly on your home's worth, your age, and the interest and other fees a given lender charges. The more your home is worth, the older you are, and the lower the interest rate and other fees your lender charges, the more money you should realize from a reverse mortgage.

>> For all but the most expensive homes, the federally insured Home Equity Conversion Mortgage (HECM) generally provides the most cash and is available in every state.

>> In general, the most cash is available for the oldest borrowers living in the homes of greatest value over current debt (net equity) at a time when interest rates are low. On the other hand, the least cash generally goes to the youngest borrowers living in the homes of lowest value (or with high current debt) at a time when interest rates are high.

The total amount of cash you actually end up getting from a reverse mortgage depends on how it's paid to you plus other factors. You can choose among the following options to receive your reverse mortgage money:

>> **Monthly:** Most people need monthly income to live on. Thus, a commonly selected reverse mortgage option is monthly payments. However, not all monthly payment options are created equal. Some reverse mortgage programs commit to a particular monthly payment for a preset number of years. Other programs make payments as long as you continue living in your home or for life. Not surprisingly, if you select a reverse mortgage program that pays you over a longer period of time, you generally receive less monthly — probably a good deal less — than from a program that pays you for a fixed number of years.

>> **Line of credit:** Instead of receiving a monthly check, you can simply create a line of credit from which you draw money by writing a check whenever you need income. Because interest doesn't start accumulating on a loan until you actually borrow money, the advantage of a credit line is that you pay only for the money you need and use. If you have fluctuating and irregular needs for additional money, a line of credit may be for you. This is also the preferred way to access funds if your financial goal is to limit the equity you pull from your home to its increase in value. The size of the line of credit is either set at the time you close on your reverse mortgage loan, or may increase over time. Generally, during the first 12 months, you can receive up to but no more than 60 percent of the maximum loan allowed.

>> **Lump sum:** The third, and generally least beneficial, type of reverse mortgage is the lump-sum option. When you close on this type of reverse mortgage, you receive a check for the entire amount that you were approved to borrow. Lump-sum payouts usually make sense only when you have an immediate need for a substantial amount of cash for a specific purpose, such as making a major purchase or paying off an existing or delinquent mortgage debt to keep from losing your home to foreclosure. Ironically, but also a blessing, when your financial troubles are caused by falling behind on your mortgage payments, you can get a reverse mortgage to tap the remaining equity in your home to assist in resolving your immediate pending foreclosure.

>> **Mix and match:** Perhaps you need a large chunk of money for some purchases you've been putting off, but you also want the security of a regular monthly income. You can usually put together combinations of the preceding three programs. Some reverse mortgage lenders even allow you to alter the payment structure as time goes on. Not all reverse mortgage programs offer all the combinations, so shop around even more if you're interested in mixing and matching your payment options.

When do you pay the money back?

As mentioned earlier, some reverse mortgage borrowers worry about having to repay their loan balance. Here are the conditions under which you generally have to repay a reverse mortgage:

>> When the last surviving borrower dies, sells the home, or permanently moves away. *Permanently* generally means that the borrower hasn't lived in the home for 12 consecutive months.

>> Possibly, if you do any of the following:

- Fail to pay your property taxes

- Fail to keep up your homeowners insurance

- Let your home fall into disrepair

If you fail to properly maintain your home and it falls into disrepair, the lender may be able to make extra cash advances to cover these repair expenses. Just remember that reverse mortgage borrowers are still homeowners and therefore are still responsible for taxes, insurance, and upkeep.

What do you owe?

The total amount you will owe at the end of the loan (your loan balance) equals

>> All the cash advances you've received (including any used to pay loan costs)

>> Plus all the interest on them — up to the loan's nonrecourse limit (the value of the home)

If you get an adjustable-rate reverse mortgage, the interest rate can vary based on changes in published indexes. The greater a loan's permissible interest rate adjustment, the lower its interest rate initially. As a result, you get a larger cash advance with this type of loan than you do with loans that have higher initial interest rates.

You can never owe more than the value of the home at the time the loan is repaid. True reverse mortgages are *nonrecourse loans,* which means that in seeking repayment the lender doesn't have recourse to anything other than your home — not your income, your other assets, or your heirs' finances.

Even if you get monthly advances until you're 115 years old, even if your home declines in value between now and then, and even if the total of monthly advances becomes greater than your home's value — you can still never owe more than the value of your home. If you or your heirs sell your home to pay off the loan, the debt is limited by the net proceeds from the sale of your home.

How is the loan repaid?

How a reverse mortgage is repaid depends on the circumstances under which the loan ends:

>> If you sell and move, you'd most likely pay back the loan from the money you get from selling your home. But you could pay it back from other funds if you had them.

>> If the loan ends due to the death of the last surviving borrower, the loan must be repaid before the home's title can be transferred to the borrower's heirs. The heirs may repay the loan by selling the home, using other funds from the borrower's estate, using their own funds, or by taking out a new forward mortgage against the home.

As lenders have learned, not all reverse mortgage borrowers end up living in their homes for the rest of their lives. Some folks who originally planned to live in a particular house forever subsequently change their minds. Others develop health problems that force them to move. So it makes sense to plan for the possibility that you may sell and move some day. How much equity would be left if you did?

If, at the end of the loan, your loan balance is less than the value of your home (or your net sale proceeds if you sell), then you or your heirs get to keep the difference. The lender doesn't get the house. The lender gets paid the amount you owe on the reverse mortgage, and you or your heirs keep the rest of the house's proceeds of sale.

TIP

If you take the loan as a credit line account, be sure to withdraw all your remaining available credit before the loan ends. You have access to the money sooner that way, and the amount could be more than otherwise may be left. For example, a growing credit line could become greater than the leftover equity if the home's value decreases.

What's the out-of-pocket cost of getting a reverse mortgage?

The out-of-pocket cash cost to you with a reverse mortgage is usually limited to just two modest items. First is an application fee that covers a property appraisal (to see how much your home is worth). Second is a minimal credit check (to see whether you're delinquent on any federally insured loans).

Other costs, including the loan origination fee, can be financed with the loan. This means you can use reverse mortgage funds advanced to you at closing to pay the costs due at that time and later advances to pay any *ongoing costs*, such as monthly servicing fees. The advances are added to your loan balance and become part of what you owe — and pay interest on.

What are the other reverse mortgage costs?

The specific-cost items vary from one program to another. Many of them are of the same type found on forward mortgages: interest charges, origination fees, and whatever third-party closing costs (title search and insurance, surveys, inspections, document and recording fees, and property taxes) are required in your area.

Two other costs unique to some reverse mortgages are the monthly servicing fee, which can cost up to $35 per month, and a reverse mortgage insurance premium, which can cost up to 2.5 percent of the home's value at closing (this premium is just 0.5 percent if you take no more than 60 percent of the approved funds).

In addition to the upfront insurance charge paid at closing, there is also an annual mortgage insurance premium of 1.25 percent of your reverse mortgage balance. This ongoing premium accumulates and is owed and paid once your loan ends and is paid back.

TIP

Within the federally insured Home Equity Conversion Mortgage (HECM) program, the costs that may be different from one lender to another are the origination fee, the servicing fee, third-party closing costs, and the interest rate. To get the best deal, compare these specific costs.

With HECM loans, there is a maximum origination fee of 2 percent of the first $200,000 of the home's value and 1 percent of the amount above $200,000 to a maximum fee allowed of $6,000. *Note:* Individual lenders may charge lower origination fees at their discretion.

It's difficult to evaluate or compare the true, total cost of reverse mortgages because that amount ultimately depends on the following:

>> How long you end up keeping the loan

>> The cash advances you receive during the loan

>> The interest rate charged on the loan

>> Your home's value when the loan is over

You can, however, compare the costs of different reverse mortgages by evaluating each loan's total annual average loan cost, also known as the total annual rate. The following section talks more about that.

What's the total annual rate?

The total annual rate on a reverse mortgage includes all the loan's costs. On any given loan, total annual rates depend on two major factors: time and appreciation.

Total annual average rates are generally greatest in the early years of the loan and decrease over time, for two reasons:

>> The initial fees and costs become a smaller part of the total amount owed as years go by.

>> The likelihood increases that the rising loan balance will catch up to — and then be limited by — the nonrecourse limit the longer you have the loan.

Total annual rates also depend on changes in a home's value over time. The less appreciation, the greater the likelihood that a rising loan balance will catch up to — and then be limited by — the home's value. On the other hand, when a home appreciates at a robust rate, the loan balance may never catch up to (and be limited by) it.

If you end up living in your home well past your projected life expectancy or your home appreciates at a lower rate than anticipated, you may get a true bargain. But if you die, sell, or move within just a few years, the true cost could be quite high.

When deciding to go with a reverse mortgage, you simply can't avoid the fundamental risk that the true cost can end up being quite high. You just have to understand the risk in general, assess the potential range of total rates on a specific loan, and decide whether the risk is worth the benefits you expect to get from the loan.

Just remember, total annual rates aren't really comparable to the interest rates quoted on forward mortgages because

>> Total annual rates include all the costs.

>> Reverse mortgages require no monthly repayments.

>> Reverse mortgages can provide an open-ended monthly income guarantee or a guaranteed credit line (which may grow larger).

>> You can never owe more than your home's worth, even if its net value is less than what your loan balance would otherwise have been.

How do reverse mortgages affect your government-sponsored benefits?

Social Security and Medicare benefits aren't affected by reverse mortgages. But Supplemental Security Income (SSI) and Medicaid are different. Reverse mortgages will affect these and other public benefit programs under certain circumstances:

» Because they don't count as income, loan advances on a reverse mortgage generally don't affect your benefits if you spend them during the calendar month in which you get them. But if you keep an advance past the end of the calendar month (in a checking or savings account, for example), it counts as a *liquid asset*. If your total liquid assets at the end of any month are greater than $2,000 for a single person or $3,000 for a couple, you could lose your eligibility.

» If anyone in the business of selling annuities has tried to sell you on the idea of using proceeds from a reverse mortgage to purchase an annuity, you need to know that annuity advances reduce SSI benefits dollar for dollar and can make you ineligible for Medicaid. So if you're considering an annuity and if you're now receiving — or expect that some day you may qualify for — SSI or Medicaid, check with the SSI, Medicaid, and other program offices in your community. Get specific details on how annuity income affects these benefits.

Shopping for a Reverse Mortgage

Reverse mortgages give you a new retirement financial option that previous generations of homeowners didn't have. These loans can provide an important new source of retirement cash — without requiring you to leave your home or to make loan payments for as long as you live there.

But you have to proceed carefully. What you don't know about reverse mortgages *can* hurt you. The most important — and perhaps surprising — facts you need to understand are these:

» You may get a lot more cash from one reverse mortgage program than from another.

» The true cost of one program may be much greater than the cost of another.

» A program giving you significantly more cash may also cost less than any other.

>> To find the program that works best for you, you have to take both of the following into account:

- How much total cash would be available to you in growing versus flat credit lines

- The comparative total annual rate on competing loans

>> Lenders offering a variety of plans may try to sell you one plan versus another because they make more money on it.

REMEMBER

Reverse mortgages are a specialty loan product that requires loan officers to receive training to be eligible to work on a reverse mortgage. Most loan officers (even the best ones with decades of experience) don't work with reverse mortgages. When you decide to apply for a reverse mortgage, ask enough questions to make sure the loan officer has done dozens of reverse mortgages. You don't want a loan officer figuring out reverse mortgages on your loan!

Making major choices

Which reverse mortgage plan — if any — would work the best for you?

>> The federally insured Home Equity Conversion Mortgage (HECM) is most likely to provide more cash at a lower cost, especially if you want a credit line, or if you own your home jointly with a spouse or other person. But be aware that $636,150 is the maximum loan limit allowed on a HECM as of 2017.

>> Consider shopping the two private reverse mortgage providers — American Advisors Group and Finance of America Reverse Mortgage — especially if you own a higher value property. Private reverse mortgage providers aren't subject to the same regulations and loan limits as HECM providers.

Although HECM may be more likely to provide significantly more cash at a lot lower cost on the credit lines most consumers prefer, the best plan for you depends on your specific situation. So you need to consider *all* your reverse mortgage options. That's especially important if you

>> Want a monthly loan advance only

>> Live in a home worth substantially more than the average

Later in this chapter, the section "Deciding Whether You Want a Reverse Mortgage" gives you additional considerations to ponder when thinking about whether a reverse mortgage is your best option.

Counseling

To get a HECM reverse mortgage, you must complete a counseling session with a HUD-approved counselor. Visit `www.hud.gov/program_offices/housing/sfh/hecm/hecmlist` to find approved counselors in your area or call 800-569-4287. Reverse mortgages can get complicated quickly, and most folks find them challenging to fully understand. So having to complete counseling before committing to a reverse mortgage is a good thing.

Counselors ask ten questions during each session to be sure borrowers have an understanding of the basics of reverse mortgages. To "pass" the counseling session, the prospective borrowers must answer at least five of the ten questions correctly. If they can't, they may need to go back for more sessions. Counseling fees are reasonable and typically cost about $125, although they may vary based on the borrowers' financial situation and may even be waived for lower-income folks.

Deciding Whether You Want a Reverse Mortgage

Only you can decide what a reverse mortgage is worth to you. The value probably mostly depends on your purpose for the money, such as the following:

>> Increasing your monthly income

>> Having a cash reserve (credit line account) for irregular or unexpected expenses

>> Paying off debt that requires monthly repayments

>> Repairing or improving your home

>> Getting the services you need to remain independent

>> Improving the quality of your life (perhaps fulfilling some of your bucket list items)

One approach is to consider a major alternative: selling your home and moving to a less expensive form of housing. Think about the following questions:

>> How much money could you get by selling your home?

>> What would it cost you to buy and maintain or rent a new one?

>> How much could you safely earn (that is, without exposing yourself to excessive risk) on sale proceeds not used for a new home?

>> Could you tolerate living in the same home or even in that separate but all-too-close "Granny flat" with your relatives?

Selling Your House For Dummies, which Eric Tyson coauthored with real estate expert Ray Brown (published by Wiley), can help you think through the issues. If you do decide to sell your home, Eric and Ray's book will help you get top dollar.

Thanks to continued innovation in the mortgage industry, you can sell your current home, buy a different one, and, at the time of purchase, take out a reverse mortgage. To be eligible for a so-called "HECM for Purchase," which enables you to buy a home in part using proceeds from a new reverse mortgage, you generally need to make a significant down payment (50-plus percent of the purchase price), and the reverse mortgage finances the rest. You do this in place of making an all-cash purchase.

Chapter **3**

Deciding to Sell

Selling your house and moving *can* be an enjoyable (not to mention profitable) experience. Unfortunately, for most people, it isn't. Selling a house not only introduces financial turmoil into most people's lives but also causes them stress.

This chapter aims to help you make the right decision about whether to sell your house. If you do decide to sell, you should get as many dollars and as few upset stomachs from the sale as possible.

The reasons people want to sell their houses are almost as varied as the houses themselves. Because you're reading this book, you're likely thinking about it because your circumstances have changed: You may no longer need so much space, you may want to pare down and live a more simplified, streamlined lifestyle, or you may need to pull the long-built-up equity out of your house to help fund your retirement. But people sell their houses for lots of reasons. Here are some of the common, not-so-common, and downright bizarre reasons:

» Additional debt burden because of layoff, medical expenses, disability, or overspending

» Bad vibes or bad luck associated with the house

» Better job opportunities elsewhere

» House located in a flood, earthquake, or other disaster zone

» Increased space requirements for expanding family

- >> Lack of garage
- >> Neighborhood conditions incompatible with socioeconomic status
- >> Noisy neighborhood
- >> Obnoxious family or business moved next door
- >> Recent death of spouse
- >> Recent marriage or divorce
- >> Serious house defects (such as radon or termites) that owners don't want to or can't afford to fix
- >> Unfriendly neighbors
- >> Unsafe neighborhood
- >> Unsatisfactory neighborhood shopping
- >> Unsatisfactory school district
- >> Unsuitable climate

As you can see from this partial list, most of the reasons people have a desire to sell their houses are based on *wants,* not *needs.* You don't *need* to move because your neighborhood is too noisy or because your house seems too small. You don't *need* to move because the weather in your area isn't nice enough. You don't *need* to live on a quieter, tree-lined street.

All these features are things people desire or *want,* not things they *need.* And people who think they can afford to pay for such things usually get more of what they *want.* Sometimes, though, people spend money moving and still don't get what they want. The weather in the new locale may not be terrific, the neighbors may not be friendly and quiet, and the schools may not turn children into stellar students. You may move to get away from particular problems and then find yourself facing a new set of problems.

You deserve to make the most of your money. Unless you're one of the few who has far more money than you can ever possibly spend, it's a good idea to prioritize the demands on your money to accomplish your most important financial goals.

REMEMBER

Nothing's wrong with spending money to trade in one house for another, but *before* you set those wheels in motion, think about the impact of that kind of spending on other aspects of your life. The more you spend on housing, the less you'll have for your other goals, such as saving for retirement or taking annual vacations, and the more time you may be forced to spend working.

Figuring Out if You Really Need to Sell

Although spending your entire life in the first home you buy is an increasingly unlikely prospect, some people do end up living in the same home for 10, 20, even 30 or more years. Staying put can have its advantages.

If, like most prospective house sellers, you have a choice between staying put and selling, *not* selling has clear advantages. Selling your house and then buying another one takes a great deal of legwork and research time on your part. Whether you sell your house yourself or hire an agent, you're going to be heavily involved in getting your house ready for sale and keeping it pristine while it's on the market.

WARNING

In addition to time, selling your house and buying another one can cost serious money. Between real estate commissions, loan fees, title insurance, transfer tax, and myriad other costs of selling your house and then buying another one, you can easily spend 15 percent or more of the value of the property you're selling.

Fifteen percent sounds like a lot, doesn't it? Well, consider this: Unless you own your house free and clear of any mortgage debt, your transaction costs are going to gobble up an even larger percentage of the money you've invested in your home.

Check out this scenario: You're thinking about selling your $240,000 house. If selling your house and buying another one costs you about 15 percent of the first house's value, then you're taking $36,000 out of your sale proceeds. However, if you happen to owe $180,000 on your mortgage, your *equity* in the home — the difference between the amount the house is worth ($240,000) and the amount you owe ($180,000) — is $60,000. Therefore, the $36,000 in transaction costs devours a huge 60 percent of your equity. Ouch!

Before spending that much of your hard-earned money, make sure you give careful thought and consideration to why you want to sell, the financial consequences of selling, and the alternatives to selling. Before looking at the numbers, consider the qualitative issues.

Good reasons to stay

Whereas some people have clear and compelling reasons for selling their homes, others do so for the wrong reasons. You don't want to make the financially painful mistake of selling if you don't have to or can't afford to.

The following sections offer reasons you may be better off staying right where you are.

You're already having trouble living within your means

TIP

If you're having difficulty making ends meet and you use high-interest consumer credit, such as credit cards or auto loans, to maintain your desired standard of living, you shouldn't spend more money on housing. Even if you're planning to trade your current house for one of comparable value, you may not be able to afford all the transaction costs of selling and buying.

Even if you aren't a consumer-debt user and you're saving a comfortable portion (10 percent or more) of your current earnings, *don't* assume you can afford to trade up to a more expensive home. In addition to a higher mortgage payment, you may also face increased property taxes, insurance rates, and home maintenance costs.

REMEMBER

A mortgage lender may be willing to finance a loan that enables you to trade up to a more expensive home, but qualifying for a loan doesn't mean you can *afford* that home. Mortgage lenders use simplistic formulas, based primarily on your income, to determine the amount they're willing to lend you. Mortgage lenders don't know (or care) how far behind you are in saving for your retirement or how many children you must help with college costs or how much assistance you want or need to give to elderly parents.

Mortgage lenders are concerned about protecting their interests in the event that you default on your mortgage. As long as you meet a few minimal financial requirements (you make a sufficient down payment, and your housing expenses are less than a certain percentage of your income), the mortgage lenders can sell your loan with the backing of a government mortgage agency, effectively wiping their hands clean of you and your problems.

The problems are more in your perceptions

Everybody, at some point, leaps to conclusions based on faulty assumptions or incomplete research in virtually all aspects of their lives. Peter, for example, was a single parent living with his son in a nice neighborhood in an urban environment. When his son started junior high school, Peter grew increasingly concerned with the possibility that his son would become involved with drugs, which seemed to be prevalent in their city.

Despite working in the city, Peter decided to move to an easygoing, suburban community about 45 minutes outside the city. Shortly after the move, Peter's son got mixed up with drugs anyway — perhaps, in part, because the long daily commute meant Peter was around even less.

In addition to ignoring lifestyle issues (such as the length of his commute), Peter made a common human mistake — he assumed things were a particular way without getting the facts. The reality was that the suburban community to which Peter moved had as many problems with teenagers on drugs as the good neighborhoods in his former city.

Crime and safety make up another common realm where people have misconceptions. Some communities often make the evening news with graphic stories and film footage of crimes. Statistically, however, most crimes committed in a given city or town occur in fairly small geographic areas. Local police departments tabulate neighborhood crime rates. If you're concerned about crime and safety, don't guess; get the facts by contacting your local police department and asking them how to obtain the data.

Schools are another hot-button issue. In some areas, people make blanket statements condemning all public schools. They also insist that if you live in such-and-such town or city, you must send your children to private school if you want them to get a good education. The reality, as education experts (and good old-fashioned common sense) suggest, is that you can find good and bad public schools and good and bad private schools. You also need to evaluate whether you're spending too many hours working and commuting just so you can make expensive tuition payments. If that's the case, you may not be able to spend adequate time with your children. The best possible teacher for your children is you.

Selling won't solve the problem(s)

Avoiding problems is another human tendency. That's what Fred and Ethel tried to do. Much to their chagrin, Fred and Ethel discovered that their home had two not-so-visible but, unfortunately, costly-to-fix problems. The new roof they needed was going to cost big bucks because local ordinances required the removal of several layers of existing roofing material when a new roof was installed. Fred and Ethel also had recently found out that their house contained asbestos, a known carcinogen.

Rather than research and deal with these problems, Fred and Ethel decided that the easiest solution was to sell their house and buy another one in a nearby town where they thought they'd be happy. They then attempted to sell their home without disclosing these known defects — a major legal no-no — but were tripped up by smart buyers who found out about the problems from inspectors they hired to check out the property.

Actually, the prospective buyers did Fred and Ethel two big favors:

>> By uncovering the problems early, the buyers saved Fred and Ethel from a costly lawsuit that could easily have resulted if the flaws were discovered after the house was sold.

>> By ultimately deciding to hold onto their home, which they otherwise were content with, Fred and Ethel saved themselves thousands of dollars in selling and buying transaction costs. Those savings more than paid for the cost of a new roof. And Fred and Ethel discovered that, because the asbestos was in good condition and properly contained, it was best left alone.

You can fix some or all of the problems

When they realized that they couldn't run from their home's problems, Fred and Ethel, discussed in the preceding section, discovered how to get those problems fixed. You can address quite a number of possible shortcomings in your home less expensively than buying a new home.

If you think that home improvement projects are going to be too expensive, do some rough calculations to determine the cost of selling your current house and then buying another. Remember, you can easily spend 15 percent of the house's value on all the transaction costs of selling and then buying again.

Instead of trading houses, why not spend those transaction dollars on improving the home you currently own? Do you hate the carpeting and paint job? Get new carpets and repaint. If your home is a tad too small, consider adding on a room or two. Just be careful not to turn your home into a castle if all the surrounding houses are shacks. *Overimproving* your property can be an expensive mistake: After the improvements to your house, you'll own the most expensive house on the block, and you'll have difficulty recouping the cost of the improvements in the form of a higher house sale price.

WARNING

Some people are seduced by the seeming better attributes of other houses on the market. If your house is small, larger ones seem more appealing. If you don't like your carpeting, houses that have hardwood floors may attract you. However, as is true of long-term friends or spouses, you know your current home's defects all too well because you've lived with them. Unless you're incredibly observant, you surely didn't know half of your home's faults and shortcomings before you moved in. The same is true of new homes you may be lusting after.

TIP

Some problems and defects are more easily fixed and more worth fixing than others. When you're deciding whether to fix problems or move away from them, consider these important issues:

>> **What's the payback?** Some home remodeling projects may actually pay for or come close to paying for themselves. Certain remodeling projects increase your home's value by enough to make up for most or even all the cost of the improvement(s).

TIP

Generally speaking, projects that increase the cosmetic appeal or usability of living space tend to be more financially worthwhile than projects that don't. For example, consider painting and recarpeting a home versus fixing its foundation. The former projects are visible and, if done well, enhance a home's value; the latter project doesn't add to the visible appeal of the home or usability of living space. If, however, you *must* do foundation repairs or the house will collapse, spend your money on the foundation.

If you decide to stay put and renovate or improve your current home, you're going to need to find a way to pay for all that work. If you head down the renovation path, don't forget that contracting work often ends up costing more than you (and your contractor) originally expected.

>> **How intrusive will the work be?** As you surely know, money isn't everything. Six months into a home remodeling project that moves you out of your bedroom, spreads sawdust all over your kitchen table, and has you wanting to flee the country, the "payback" on the project doesn't seem so important anymore. In addition to costing more than most people expect, contracting work almost always takes longer than everyone expects.

TIP

Ask yourself and others who've endured similar projects: How much will this project disrupt my life? Your contract with the contractor should include financial penalties for not finishing on time.

Some problems or shortcomings of your current house simply can't be fixed. If you're tired of shoveling snow in the winter and dripping sweat in the summer, you're not going to be able to change your local weather. If crime is indeed a big problem, you aren't going to be able to cut area crime rate anytime soon. Moving may be the best solution.

Reasons to consider selling

If you're in a situation where you really *need* to sell, as opposed to wanting to sell, by all means put your house on the market. And if you *want* to sell, and can *afford* to do so, you should go for it as well. The following sections offer some solid reasons for selling.

You can afford to trade homes

Your desire to sell your current house and buy another one may be driven by a force as frivolous as sheer boredom. But if you can afford to sell and buy again, and you know what you're getting into, why not?

Now, defining *afford* is important. Here, it means that you've identified your personal and financial goals and you've calculated that the cost of trading houses won't compromise those goals.

Everyone has unique goals, but if you're like most people, you probably don't want to spend the rest of your life working full time. To retire or semi-retire, you're going to need to save quite a bit of money during your working years. If you haven't yet crunched any numbers to see where you stand in terms of retirement saving, postpone major real estate decisions until you explore your financial future. And definitely have a look at the chapters in Book 1.

You need to move for your job

Some people find that at particular points in their lives they need to move to take advantage of a career opportunity. For example, if you want to be involved with technology companies, certain regions of the country offer far greater opportunities than others.

When you lack employment, paying bills is difficult, especially the costs involved in home ownership. If you've lost your job or your employer demands that you relocate to keep your job, you may feel a real need to move, especially in a sluggish economy.

REMEMBER

Moving for a better job (or simply for *a* job) is a fine thing to do. However, some people fool themselves into believing that a higher-paying job or a move to an area with lower housing costs will put them on an easier financial street. You must consider all the costs of living in a new area versus your current area before deciding that moving to a new community is financially wise.

And consider that you may be overlooking opportunities right in your own backyard. Just because your employer offers you a better job to get you to relocate doesn't mean you can't bargain for a promotion and stay put geographically. Likewise, during an economic slowdown, if your employer says you must relocate or face downsizing, explore other employment options in your area, especially if you want to stay in the local area.

You're having (or will have) financial trouble

Sometimes, people fall on difficult financial times because of an unexpected event. Check out these two scenarios:

>> After Ryan graduated from college, he landed a good marketing job and seemed financially secure. So he bought a home. After a few years in the home, Ryan discovered that he had a chronic medical problem.

Ultimately, Ryan decided to go into a lower-stress job and work part time. As a result, his income significantly decreased while his medical expenses increased. He no longer could afford his home. It made sense for Ryan to sell his house and move into lower-cost housing that better addressed his reduced mobility.

» When Teri and her husband bought a home, they were both holding down high-paying jobs. Unfortunately, their marriage had problems. After much marital counseling and many attempts to get their marriage on a better track, Teri and her husband divorced. Because neither of them alone could afford the costs of the house, Teri and her husband needed to sell.

In addition to unexpected events, some people simply live beyond their means and can't keep their heads above the financial water of large mortgage payments and associated housing costs. Sometimes people get bogged down with additional consumer debt because they stretched themselves too much when buying their home.

TIP

Selling your house and moving to a lower-cost housing option may be just what the financial doctor ordered. On the other hand, if you can bring your spending under control and pay off those consumer debts, maybe you can afford to remain in your present home. Be sure you're being honest with yourself and realistic about your ability to accomplish your goals given your continuing housing expenses. See the chapters in Book 4 for more on managing budgets and investments.

You're retiring

If you decide to call it quits on the full-time working life, you may find yourself with more house than you need or you may want to move to a less costly area. Instead of trading up, you may consider trading down.

You can free up some of the cash you've tied up in your current house and use that money to help finance your retirement by moving to a less expensive home. But if you're otherwise happy where you're currently living, don't think you *must* trade down to a less expensive home simply to tap the equity in your current property. As discussed in Book 6, Chapter 2, you can tap your home's equity through other methods, such as taking out a reverse mortgage.

Your house is associated with bad feelings

As with other financial decisions, choosing to sell or buy a home isn't only about money. Human emotions and memories can be just as powerful and just as real factors to consider.

Deciding to Sell

If your spouse or child has passed away, you divorced, or your house was badly burglarized, the property may be a constant source of bad feelings. Although selling your house and moving won't make your troubles go away, being in a new home in a different area or neighborhood may help you get on with your life and not dwell excessively on your recent unpleasant experiences. Just be sure to temper your emotions with a realistic look at your financial situation.

Knowing the Health of Your Housing Market

Your personal financial situation clearly is an important factor in deciding whether and when to sell your house, but the state of your local housing market may also influence your decision. Check out the following sections for the lowdown on the housing market and how it affects your sale.

Selling in a depressed housing market

No one likes to lose money. If you scraped and saved for years for the down payment to buy a home, finding out your house is worth less than the amount you paid for it can be quite a blow. Between the decline in the market value of your home and the selling costs, you may possibly even lose your entire invested down payment. And you thought the stock market was risky!

Some homeowners find themselves *upside down,* which means the mortgage on the house exceeds the amount for which the house can be sold. In other words, upside-down homeowners literally have to pay money to sell their houses because they've lost more than their original down payment. Ouch! (This happened to a lot of folks during the severe financial crisis of 2008, which clobbered home values in many parts of the country.)

When deciding whether to sell in a depressed market, consider the factors discussed in the following sections.

If you still have adequate equity

Although your local real estate market may have recently declined, if you've owned your house long enough or made a large enough down payment, you still may be able to net a good deal of cash by selling. If you can make enough money to enable yourself to buy another home, don't sweat the fact that your local real estate market may currently be depressed. As long as the sale fits in with your overall financial situation, sell your house and get on with your life.

All real estate markets go through up and down cycles. Over the long term, however, housing prices tend to increase. So if you sell a house or two during a down market, odds are you'll also sell a house or two during better market conditions. And if you're staying in the same area or moving to another depressed housing market, you're simply trading one reduced-price house for another. If you're moving to a more expensive market or a market currently doing better than the one you're leaving, be sure that spending more on housing doesn't compromise your long-term personal and financial goals.

If you lack enough money to buy your next home

Sometimes homeowners find themselves in a situation where, if they sell, they won't have enough money to buy their next home. If you find yourself in such a circumstance, first clarify whether you *want* or *need* to sell:

» If you *want* to sell but don't *need* to and can avoid selling for a while, consider waiting it out. Otherwise, if you sell and then don't have adequate money to buy your next home, you may find yourself in the unfortunate position of being a renter when the local real estate market turns the corner and starts improving again. So you'll have sold low and later be forced to buy high. You'll need to have an even greater down payment to get back into the market, or you'll be forced to buy a more modest house.

» If you *need* to sell, you have a tougher road ahead. You must hope that the real estate market where you buy won't rocket ahead while you're trying to accumulate a larger down payment. However, you may also want to look into methods for buying a home with a smaller down payment. For example, a benevolent family member may help you out, the person selling you your new home may lend you some money, or you may decide to take out one of the low-down-payment loans that some mortgage lenders offer. If prices do rise at a fast rate, you can either set your sights on a different market or lower your expectations for the kind of home you're going to buy.

If you must move or relocate and don't want to sell in a depressed market, you can rent out your home until the market turns around. Be sure you understand the tax consequences of such an arrangement, because the rent payments will count as additional income. Before becoming a landlord, consider your ability to deal with the hassles that come with the territory. You must also educate yourself on local rent-control ordinances and compare your property's monthly expenses with the rental income that you'll collect. (See the nearby sidebar "Figuring the cash flow on rental property.") If you're going to lose money each month, the constant cash drain may handicap your future ability to save, in addition to increasing your total losses on the property.

FIGURING THE CASH FLOW ON RENTAL PROPERTY

Cash flow is the difference between the amount of money that a property brings in and the amount you have to pay out for expenses. Some homeowners-turned-rental-property-owners can't cover all the costs associated with rental property. In the worst cases, such property owners end up in personal bankruptcy from the drain of negative cash flow (that is, expenses exceed income). In other cases, the negative cash flow hampers property owners' ability to accomplish important financial goals such as saving for retirement or helping with their children's college expenses.

Before you consider becoming a landlord, make some projections about what you expect your property's monthly income and expenses to be.

Income

On the income side, determine the amount of rent you're able to charge:

- Take a look at what comparable properties currently are renting for in your local market.
- Check out the classified ads in your local paper(s).
- Speak with some leasing agents at real estate rental companies.

Be sure to allow for some portion (around 5 percent per year) of the time for your property to be vacant — finding good tenants takes time.

Expenses

On the expense side, you have your monthly mortgage payment. And, of course, you have property taxes. Because you probably pay them only once or twice yearly, divide the annual amount by 12 to arrive at your monthly property tax bill.

You may end up paying some or all of your renter's utility bills, such as garbage, water, or gas. Estimate from your own usage what the monthly tab will be. Expect most utility bills to increase a bit because tenants will probably waste more when you're picking up the bill.

Be sure to ask your insurance company about how your property insurance premium changes if you convert the property into a rental. As is true with your property taxes, divide the annual total by 12 to get a monthly amount.

Don't forget repairs and maintenance! Expect to spend about 1 percent of the property's value per year on maintenance, repairs, and cleaning. Again, divide by 12 to get a monthly figure.

Finding good tenants takes time and promotion. If you choose to list through them, rental brokers normally take one month's rent as their cut. If you advertise, estimate at least $100 to $200 in advertising expenses, not to mention the cost of your time in showing the property to prospective tenants. You must also plan on running credit checks on prospective tenants.

Estimated cash flow

Now, total all the monthly expenses and subtract that number from your estimated monthly income after allowing for some vacancy time. *Voilà!* You've just calculated your property's cash flow.

If you have a negative cash flow, you may actually be close to breaking even when you factor in a rental property tax write-off known as *depreciation*. You break down the purchase of your property between the building, which is depreciable, and land, which isn't depreciable. You can make this allocation based on the assessed value for the land and the building or on a real estate appraisal. Residential property is depreciated over 27½ years at a rate of 3.64 percent of the building value per year. For example, if you buy a residential rental property for $250,000, and $175,000 of that amount is allocated to the building, that allocation means you can take $6,370 per year as a depreciation tax deduction ($175,000 \times 0.0364$).

Selling during a strong market

What could be better than selling your house during a time of rising or already elevated home prices? If you can afford the transaction costs of selling your current house and buying another home, and if the costs of the new home fit within your budget and financial goals, go for it.

Just be careful of three things:

>> **Greed:** Don't get greedy and grossly overprice your house. You may end up getting less from the sale than you expected, and the sale is likely to take much longer than if you'd priced the property fairly. If you price your house too high, when you finally drop the price to the right range, you may face lower offers because your house has the stigma of being old on the market.

>> **Underpricing:** Necessity being the mother of invention, the housing recovery, beginning in 2010, fostered a potentially risky but sometimes profitable pricing strategy. But beware, this strategy will work only during a sustained period of very low supply and very high demand. It entails pricing the home well below the apparent market value. The idea is to create an auction atmosphere and attract so many buyers that they will bid the price well above the low list price and, hopefully, above the price you'd hoped to obtain. The danger with this strategy is that it doesn't always work. You may receive only one offer at or even below the listed price. If so, then this is likely the actual market value of your home. Although you are never obligated to accept an offer, whether at list price or even well above, you can create hard feelings and, therefore, troubled negotiations by turning down offers at the asking price.

>> **Timing:** If you're staying in your current strong market or moving to another strong market, be careful about timing the sale of your current house and the purchase of your next one. For example, you probably don't want to sell and then spend months bidding unsuccessfully on other homes. You may get stuck renting for a while and need to make an additional move; such costs can eat up the cash from your recent sale and interfere with your ability to afford your next home.

Chapter **4**

Exploring the Economics of Selling

As Forrest Gump would've said if he'd been a real estate agent, "House selling is like a box of chocolates . . . you never know what you're gonna get." You never know how much your house is really worth until you reach an agreement with a prospective buyer. And even after you decide to accept an offer, you never know what surprises and costs may crop up before your deal actually closes.

However, although it's an inexact science, there's no reason you can't reasonably *estimate* your expected proceeds of sale. This chapter can show you how.

TIP

If money isn't a constraint for you and you can comfortably make the move that you're proposing, feel free to skip this chapter. Spend the free time reflecting on how fortunate you are!

Estimating Proceeds of Sale

You may need to get a certain amount of money from the sale of your house, or at least know before you can close on a deal how much you'll receive. Take the time to understand the particular probable proceeds of sale under the following scenarios:

>> **You're strapped for cash because you want to buy a more expensive home.** You need to know *before* you sell if you'll have enough money to complete your next purchase. If you don't know this amount, the worst-case scenario is that the sale of your current house doesn't leave you enough money to buy your next one. Although you probably won't end up homeless, you may end up renting for a while and having to make an extra move, or having to scrounge around at the last minute for more money.

>> **You're trading down because you need more money for retirement.** Perhaps you want to receive a certain amount of money from your house sale to afford a particular retirement standard of living. If you're not realistic about how much cash you'll net from the sale, you may end up wasting a great deal of time and money on a house sale that yields less cash than you need or expect.

>> **You're relocating, in part, because of finances.** If you have a choice about taking a job in some other part of the country, you may be tempted to relocate if you think you'll be more comfortable financially. However, if you're simply assuming or guessing that you'll be better off in the new area, you may be wrong. You need to gather and review some facts before you move.

Note: This discussion of estimating house sale proceeds assumes that you don't have an employer who's willing to pay for some of your house selling and moving costs. If you're relocating because of a new job, by all means negotiate to have your new employer pay for some or even all of the expenses related to your house sale. You'll have that much more money to plow into your next home.

Estimated sale price

Clearly, the price at which you can sell your house is the biggest factor in determining how much money you'll be able to put in your pocket from selling your house. The estimated sale price, unfortunately, is also the hardest number to pin down.

You shouldn't allow your *needs* to dictate the price at which you list your house for sale (see Book 6, Chapter 5). Prospective buyers of your house don't care about your needs, wants, or desires — such as, "I need $250,000 from the sale of my house to retire." Your house's asking price should be based on the house's worth — which sometimes may not be to your liking. Your house's worth is best determined by examining the recent sale prices of comparable houses. A good real estate agent can put together a comparable market analysis for you. If you're selling your house yourself, Book 6, Chapter 5 explains how to prepare a comparable market analysis.

Estimated house sale price	$ _____
– Closing costs	– $ _____
– Mortgage payoff	– $ _____
– Moving costs	– $ _____
= Estimated proceeds from house sale	= $ _____

Closing costs

Selling a house costs a good deal of money. Generally, expect to pay about 7 to 10 percent of the house's sale price in various closing costs for which you, as the seller, may be responsible. A *closing cost* is an expense that you incur in the sale of your house and that reduces the total money you receive from the sale. The typical closing costs include the following:

>> **Real estate agent commissions:** If you're selling your house through real estate agents, they typically take a commission of 5 to 6 percent of the selling price. If you work with agents, the commission percentage you pay is negotiable and may be somewhat lower on higher-priced properties.

>> **Repairs:** Unless you've taken really good care of your house over the years or you're selling in a strong local real estate market, you can also expect to shell out some money for corrective work. For example, in some communities, you may need a pest control and dry-rot clearance to sell your property. Inspections of your property may uncover building code violations, such as faulty electrical wiring or plumbing problems, that you must repair. Consider having your house inspected before listing it for sale.

>> **Transfer tax:** Taxes, taxes, taxes — the three sure things in life. Some cities and towns whack you with a transfer tax when you sell your house. Such taxes are typically based on the sale price of the property. Check with your friendly local real estate agent or your local tax collector's office to get an idea about your community's transfer tax rates.

>> **Prorated property taxes:** Depending on the date you close on the sale of your house, you may owe money to bring your property tax payments up-to-date. In most towns and cities, unless you're delinquent with your payments, you probably won't owe more than six months of property taxes. In fact, because many communities require that you pay your property taxes in advance of the period that the payments cover, you may find that you're owed a refund of taxes from the buyer of your property.

Because you can't predict the date your house will sell, estimating the amount you may owe in property taxes at closing is a tad difficult. You do know, however, whether you have to pay your taxes well in advance. If your local community doesn't have such a pay-in-advance payment system or you wait until the last minute to pay your taxes or make delinquent payments, you may want to budget three months or so of property taxes as a closing cost.

>> **Possible credits:** If you've paid ahead on your property taxes, you may get a "refund" from the buyer of your house. You may also get a refund from your homeowners insurance company for the unused portion of your homeowners policy. And, finally, if you put less than 20 percent down when you originally purchased the house, your lender may have required that you pay a portion of your property taxes and homeowners insurance in advance each month and then held these payments in an impound account. (An *impound account* refers to money held in a trust account established by the lender, which is used to pay property taxes and insurance premiums on your behalf when they're due). The lender refunds the unused funds from your impound account money when the sale is complete.

Do the necessary research for the preceding expenses if you want to more closely estimate expenditures on closing costs. Otherwise, for a safe ballpark estimate, assume that 10 percent of the expected sale price of your house will go toward paying closing costs.

Estimated house sale price	$ _____
– Closing costs	– $ _____
– Mortgage payoff	– $ _____
– Moving costs	– $ _____
= Estimated proceeds from house sale	= $ _____

Mortgage payoff

For most people, the need to pay off an outstanding mortgage (or two) greatly depletes the expected proceeds from a house sale. Figuring out your mortgage payoff balance usually is a snap.

Simply review your mortgage lender's most recent monthly statement to find out the amount you still owe as of the date of the statement. You may need to make a couple of adjustments to this amount to make it more accurate.

First, on most mortgages, your outstanding balance should decline each month as you make additional payments. Because you can't sell your house immediately, your balance should decline between now and the date that you close on the sale. If your loan has negative *amortization* (the monthly payment falls short of paying the monthly interest that's accruing), your loan balance may be growing rather than shrinking.

Subtract from your outstanding balance the sum of the principal payments you'll be making between now and the proposed sale date. For example, if your most recent monthly mortgage statement shows that $200 of your payment went toward principal reduction, and you expect to hold onto the house for at least six more months, you can subtract $1,200 from your current outstanding balance.

Add to your balance any penalties that your mortgage lender may charge you for prepaying. Hopefully you avoided that by getting a mortgage without a prepayment penalty.

TIP

If you have any doubts at all about whether your mortgage has a prepayment penalty, find out. You can either check your loan agreement (issued to you at the time you closed on your mortgage) or ask your mortgage lender (check your statement for a phone number). Write down the information you're given, the name of the person you spoke with, and the date. You may also ask that person to send you something in writing to confirm the information you were provided by phone.

TIP

You can try negotiating with the lender to reduce or remove the prepayment penalty. A good bank may offer to cut you a deal if it realizes that you may do more of your future banking there if it keeps you happy. Your lender may also waive or greatly reduce a mortgage prepayment penalty if the buyers of your house use your lender to finance their purchase. If it's a large prepayment penalty, you can ask that the buyers obtain their mortgage from your lender, presuming the lender has competitive loan terms.

Most mortgage lenders assess a nominal fee for sending you a payoff statement that details, to the penny, the cost of paying off your loan balance on a specific day, as well as for other paperwork fees. These fees usually don't amount to more than $100 or so, but if you want to know exactly how much to expect, simply call your lender. If the fee seems excessive or you're willing to haggle, ask the lender to reduce these fees; some will comply with your request.

Estimated house sale price	$ _____
– Closing costs	– $ _____
– Mortgage payoff	– $ _____
– Moving costs	– $ _____
= Estimated proceeds from house sale	= $ _____

Moving expenses

Over the years, you've probably accumulated more stuff than you realize. Whether you've piled knickknacks in your closets, filled your attic with boxes of gadgets, lined your garage with old bikes, or decorated every room with the finest furnishings, you're going to have to pack up all your stuff and have someone haul it away.

Most people don't have the equipment, experience, and muscle power to move all their stuff themselves. If you're like most folks on the move, you call a moving service. As with any other service business, prices and quality of service vary.

The farther you move and the more weight you're moving, the more the costs escalate. Move the contents of a typical one-bedroom apartment about one-third of the way across the United States, and you can easily spend several thousands of dollars. Move the same items all the way across the country, and the cost may double. Moving the contents of a spacious four-bedroom house halfway across the country can run you about $15,000 to $20,000.

TIP

Be sure to research moving costs, especially if you're selling a big house filled with furniture and other personal possessions or if you're moving a great distance. Get bids from several reputable movers and check references. Price and quality of service vary greatly.

Estimated house sale price	$ _____
– Closing costs	– $ _____
– Mortgage payoff	– $ _____
– Moving costs	– $ _____
= Estimated proceeds from house sale	= $ _____

Putting it all together

After you understand the important elements of determining your proceeds from the expected sale of your house, you can work through the numbers to figure out how much moolah you can hope to have coming your way.

Estimated house sale price	$ _____
– Closing costs	– $ _____
– Mortgage payoff	– $ _____
– Moving costs	– $ _____
= Estimated proceeds from house sale	= $ _____

TAX DEDUCTIONS FOR MOVING COSTS

If you're moving to a new job location, you can deduct from your taxable income many of the incurred moving costs that aren't paid for by your employer. These deductions include the cost of moving your household goods and personal effects and the cost of transporting yourself and your family from your old homestead to your new one. However, you can't deduct the costs of house-hunting trips, transaction fees for selling and buying the old and new residences, temporary living expenses, or the cost of meals during relocation travel.

To qualify for the IRS moving tax deduction (which is claimed on IRS Form 3903), you must pass two tests. First, the distance between your former house and your new job must be at least 50 miles greater than the distance between your former house and your old job. For example, suppose you currently work 20 miles from your house. You get transferred to a new office that is 71 miles from your house. Because the difference between the two distances is greater than or equal to 50 miles, you pass the first test.

You must also pass the second test. During the 12-month period following your relocation, you must work at your new job on a full-time basis for at least 39 weeks. If you get fired after 38 weeks, you can't take any deductions.

These rules are even stricter for the self-employed. Refer to a good tax advisor to get more information on these deduction details.

Now that you know what proceeds you can expect from your house sale, what can and should you do with this information? As mentioned earlier in the chapter, this estimate is necessary if you're at all cash-constrained in buying your next home or if you're selling to finance some important financial goal, such as retirement.

Assessing the Financial Feasibility of a Move

In the event that you're staying in the same neighborhood or community, estimating the cost of living in another home should be fairly easy.

WARNING

If, on the other hand, you're relocating to a new area, don't make the common mistake of neglecting to consider possible changes in your overall expenses. Many people simply assume that their finances "will work out," whereas others fall prey to wishful thinking: "Because housing costs are lower in the area we're moving to, I'm sure we'll be financially better off."

Wouldn't it be great if life were that simple. Unfortunately, it isn't.

Researching living costs and employment opportunities

Before you commit to listing your house for sale and sell it, understand what your cost of living will be in the new area. Your property taxes, utilities, food, commuting costs, and many other important items in your personal budget will change when you move into a new home in a different area.

If you don't consider the cost of living in the new location, you may end up facing unpleasant surprises. That's what happened to Joanne and Andy:

> Weary of working long hours to afford the seemingly high cost of living in Northern California, the couple viewed Andy's Midwest job offer as their ticket to financial freedom. Although the pay was about what Andy was receiving in his present job, Joanne and Andy figured they'd be on Easy Street, given how much cheaper home prices were in the town where they expected to live.
>
> So Andy happily accepted his new job offer, and he and Joanne quit their current jobs. They sold their house and decided to rent for a while after they moved so they could better assess exactly where they wanted to live.
>
> After moving, Joanne and Andy spent the next several months in their new Midwest community looking for a home. Although they'd thought that housing would be far less costly in their new area, they discovered that replicating what they had in Northern California — a community with parks, cultural amenities, and a good school system — cost more than they expected.
>
> And then they discovered that some of the other things that they spent money on each month were even more costly in their new area. For example, Joanne and Andy found that their first winter's heating bill eclipsed the total annual utility bill that they'd paid out west. Food was more expensive, as were property taxes. And Joanne had great difficulty replicating her previous job because her profession was less in demand in the new area. When all was said and done, Joanne and Andy's new home in the Midwest put them in the same financial boat they were in in California.

Now, if Joanne and Andy had moved for nonfinancial reasons, then the fact that they didn't end up being better off financially may not have mattered. But, except for the seemingly high cost of living, Joanne and Andy had liked their location in Northern California. As they found, however, high home prices are only a piece of the local personal financial puzzle. You must also consider the other items in your budget and figure out how your income and expenses may change if you move.

Five years after their move, Joanne and Andy moved back to the San Francisco Bay Area. They made some adjustments to their spending so they could accomplish their goals and live in the community of their choice.

USING A BRIDGE LOAN TO TAKE EQUITY OUT OF A CURRENT HOUSE BEFORE A SALE

Some people put themselves in a housing pickle that causes them to incur additional house-selling costs. The pickle results from buying a new home before their current one is sold.

Most people can't afford to own two homes at the same time; they need to get the cash out of their current home to buy a new one. Not surprisingly, the friendly lenders invented a way for people to get around this little inconvenience. It's called a *bridge loan,* and if you qualify, this loan enables you to borrow against the equity in your current property, giving you the cash to buy your new home before your current house sells.

Bridge loans are a bad idea for a number of reasons. First, if you get stuck holding both houses for many months, you face a continuing cash drain from making two (or more) mortgage payments, property tax payments, and home insurance payments, as well as maintaining two houses. Second, the interest rate and fees on a bridge loan are quite high compared to a conventional mortgage. Finally, if housing prices head south, you may end up in deep financial trouble if you're unable to sell your current house for enough money to pay the outstanding loans against it. Also, beware that if you take out a bridge loan on your existing home before you close the sale on your new home, the additional expense may keep you from qualifying for the loan you expect to receive on your purchase property.

Bottom line: You should sell your current house before buying a new one.

TIP

Numerous resources are available for estimating the cost of living in a particular area:

>> The American Chamber of Commerce Research Association (ACCRA) publishes a quarterly cost-of-living index (online at ACCRA's Cost of Living Index website, www.coli.org). It charges $7.95 for a two-city comparison (subsequent comparisons keeping one of the cities the same are reduced to $4.95 each).

>> PayScale.com (www.payscale.com/cost-of-living-calculator) and Salary.com (swz.salary.com/CostOfLivingWizard/LayoutScripts/Coll_Start.aspx) offer free salary calculators that enable you to compare salaries between two different towns or cities. Salary.com also has a nifty tool that allows you to value the benefits offered through a job (swz.salary.com/MyBenefits/LayoutScripts/Mbfl_Start.aspx).

>> The U.S. Department of Labor's Bureau of Labor Statistics calculates the cost of living for major metropolitan areas, and you can access this free information online at www.bls.gov/cpi/home.htm.

Cost-of-living indexes and surveys should be used only as a starting point and as general guidelines. They shouldn't replace a thorough budgetary breakdown that addresses the specifics of your situation. Sure, the indexes may tell you that Louisville is generally a less expensive place to live than Boston, but they ignore the fact that, for example, you never needed a car in Boston because you could walk to work and take public transit almost everywhere else. Your job in Louisville may require you to buy a car, auto insurance, and fuel for commuting, not to mention more airplane trips to visit your family in the Northeast.

Avoiding relocation traps

As Joanne and Andy found, you shouldn't act first (move and buy a new home) and ask questions later (see the section "Researching living costs and employment opportunities," earlier in this chapter). Don't base such a critical decision on assumptions and wishful thinking.

Here are the common pitfalls that ensnare those making relocation decisions, so you can avoid falling into them yourself:

>> **Equating lower housing costs with a lower cost of living:** This was one of the big mistakes Joanne and Andy made. The cost of housing probably accounts for no more than a third of your spending. So if you don't consider the other goods and services you spend money on, you neglect the lion's share of your budget. *Research all the major costs of living in an area before you commit to relocating to the area.*

>> **Not doing an apples-to-apples comparison of housing costs:** Again, Joanne and Andy made this mistake. To a certain extent, you get what you pay for. Housing costs are lower in communities with fewer amenities, inferior schools, poor commuting access, and so on. So if you're looking at relocating to an area with much lower housing costs, you need to be skeptical instead of thinking that you've found the deal of the century. Ask yourself, "What does that area lack that my current area offers?"

>> **Ignoring the overall opportunities in the local job market:** Your next job is just that — your next job. You're probably not going to stay in this job for decades on end. So when you're contemplating moving to a new area, think bigger than just this "next" job. Unless you enjoy the cost and hassle of relocating frequently, consider your chances for finding your next couple of jobs in a given area. Although it's impossible for some people to know what they're going to want to do several years down the road, considering the job market for more than your current job can save you from relocating more than you need to or leaving behind an area you otherwise like.

If you're married, you also need to consider your spouse's job prospects in your new community. In Joanne and Andy's case, they learned the hard way about the pitfalls of focusing on only one person's job.

» **Taking the place where you live for granted:** All too often you appreciate what you liked about a place more after you move away. Maybe, for example, you're tired of the urban congestion and dream of the relaxed pace of a more rural community. After you make the move, however, you really start missing going to the theater and dining at cosmopolitan restaurants. Pretty soon you find yourself spending a great deal of money to escape the "boondocks," traveling back into the city to see musicals and eat Indian food.

Chapter **5**

Determining Your House's Value

Step right up into the time machine, please. You're about to be transported back to the day you began looking for your current home — the house hunt that culminated in the purchase of the home you now own. Ah, there you are, hesitantly wandering from one Sunday open house to the next with the classified ads in your hand and a puzzled look on your face.

When you first started your search, you didn't have a clue about how much any of the houses you toured were worth. Do you remember how the asking prices were meaningless sequences of numbers to you? If, for example, you saw a house being offered at $274,950, you didn't know whether it was a steal at that price or grossly overpriced. The experience you had is common. Everyone goes through that phase during the initial stage of the home-buying process.

A couple of months later you were confidently zipping in and out of open houses. You figured out property values by personally eyeballing as many houses as you could. Then you kept checking the status of the properties to see whether they'd sold and, if they had, at what price. You discovered that sale prices, not asking prices, establish a house's value. Your hard work paid off. You became a market-savvy, educated buyer.

Okay, buckle up for your return to the present. How do you think things will change when you become a seller? Surprise. Where property values are concerned, the rules of the game are identical for buyers and sellers. Being an educated seller is just as important as being an educated buyer. You get educated exactly the same way — by touring houses comparable to yours that are currently for sale in your neighborhood.

TIP

Good news. You don't have to spend every weekend between now and the sale of your house touring properties. If you choose to use the services of a good real estate agent, he can accelerate your learning curve by screening which houses you visit. After seeing no more than a dozen houses comparable to yours in size, age, condition, and location, you'll be an educated seller. (You can spend the time you save gussying up your house for sale!) After you've made these tours, you can set a value on your own house, and this chapter aims to help you determine that price.

Defining Cost, Price, and Value

George Bernard Shaw is often credited with having wryly observed that England and the United States were two countries divided by a common language. Citizens of the two countries use the same words, but the words may have entirely different meanings in each country. For example, folks in Merry Old England buy bangers with pounds. "What an odd country," Americans think. "They purchase hot dogs with weights?"

You don't have to go all the way to England for a verbal joust. A similar breakdown in communication occurs here in the good ol' USA whenever Americans use *cost*, *price*, and *value* interchangeably. This linguistic imprecision creates big problems during negotiations between homebuyers and house sellers.

The fact is: Neither *cost* nor *price* is the same as *value*. After you understand the meanings of these words and how they differ, you can say exactly what you mean and replace emotion with objectivity during price negotiations. Out*fact*ing buyers is always better than attempting to out*argue* them.

Value is elusive

Value is your opinion of your house's worth to you based on the way you use it now and plan to use it in the future. Note that, in the preceding sentence, the words *your* and *you* each appear twice. Because *your* opinion is subjective, the features *you* value may not be the universal standard for all of humanity.

You may, for example, be of the strongly held opinion that the one and only acceptable house color is beet red. Your neighbor may feel just as resolutely that only sky blue houses are gorgeous and all other colors are ugly. No harm done, as long as everyone realizes that a big difference exists between opinions and facts.

Two factors greatly affect value:

>> **Internal factors:** Your personal (internal) situation has a fascinating way of changing over time. Suppose that 30 years ago, when you bought your present house, you put great value on a four-bedroom home with a fenced-in backyard. The house had to be located in a town with a terrific school system. Why? Because 30 years ago, you were the proud parent of two adorable kids.

Now your children are grown and have their own homes. They left you rattling around in your house like a tiny pea in a gigantic pod. Without kids, you don't need the big house, huge yard, or terrific school system. The house didn't change — what changed were the internal factors regarding your use for the house and, thus, its value to you. Divorce and retirement are other examples of internal factors that compel folks to buy or sell houses.

>> **External factors:** Circumstances outside your control that can affect property values also change for better or worse. If, for example, commute time to the big city where you work is cut from 1 hour to 30 minutes when mass transit rail service is extended into your area, your house's value increases. But if a toxic waste dump is discovered next to your house, the house's value takes a hit.

The law of supply and demand is another external factor that affects value. If more people want to buy houses than sell them, buyer competition drives up house prices. If, on the other hand, more people want to sell than buy, reduced demand results in lower property prices.

Cost is history

Cost measures past expenditures — for example, the amount you originally paid for your house. But that was then, and this is now. The amount you paid long ago or the amount you spent fixing up the house after you bought it doesn't mean a thing as far as your house's present or future value is concerned.

For example, when home prices began skyrocketing in many areas of the country during the early 2000s, some buyers accused sellers of being greedy. "You paid $75,000 15 years ago. Now you're asking $250,000," they said. "That's a huge profit."

"So what?" sellers replied. "If you don't want to pay our modest asking price, move out of the way so the nice buyers standing behind you can present their offers."

In a hot sellers' market, people who base their offering prices on the original price paid for a property waste everyone's time.

The market can change radically in a few short years. By 2008–09 in the midst of the Great Recession, prices had declined dramatically in many areas. Sellers would've been ecstatic to find buyers willing to pay them the amount they'd paid less than five years earlier when home prices peaked. In those areas, sellers who priced their houses based on the inflated purchase prices they'd paid years earlier learned a painful lesson: Your potential profit *or loss* as a seller doesn't enter into the equation when determining your house's present value.

Price is the here and now

You put an *asking* price on your house. Buyers put an *offering* price in their contract. You and the buyers negotiate back and forth to establish your house's *purchase* price. Today's purchase price becomes tomorrow's cost, and so it goes.

REMEMBER

Cost is the past, price is the present, and value (like beauty) is in the eyes of the beholder. Neither the price you paid for your house eons ago when you bought it nor the amount you want to get for it today matters to buyers. Don't waste valuable time on fantasy pricing.

Determining Fair Market Value (FMV)

Every house sells at the right price. That price is defined as its *fair market value* (FMV) — the price a buyer will pay and a seller will accept for the house — given that neither buyer nor seller is under duress. *Duress* comes from life changes, such as divorce or sudden job transfer, which put either the buyers or sellers under pressure to perform quickly. If appraisers know that a sale was made under duress, they raise or lower the sale price accordingly to more accurately reflect the house's true FMV.

REMEMBER

FMV is a zillion times more powerful than plain old *value.* As a seller, you have an opinion about the amount your house is worth. Buyers have a separate, not necessarily equal, and probably lower, opinion of your house's value. Values are opinions, not facts. FMV, conversely, is fact. It becomes fact the moment you and the buyer agree on a mutually acceptable price. Just as it takes two to tango, it takes you and a buyer to make FMV. Facts are bankable.

Need-based pricing isn't FMV

Whenever the residential real estate market gets soft and squishy like a rotten tomato, many would-be sellers feel that FMV isn't fair at all. "Why doesn't our house sell?" they ask. "Why can't we get our asking price? It's not fair."

Don't confuse "fair" with equitable or favorable. Despite its amiable name, FMV is brutally impartial and sometimes even cruel. *Need* is not an integral component of FMV. FMV doesn't give a hoot about any of the following:

>> How much money you *need* because you overpaid for your house when you bought it

>> How much money you *need* to replace the money you spent fixing up your house after you bought it

>> How much money you *need* to pay off your mortgage or home-equity loan

>> How much money you *need* from the sale to buy your next home

Here's why *need* doesn't determine FMV. Suppose two identical houses located right next door to one another are listed for sale at the same time. One house was purchased by Marcia for $30,000 in 1990. You made a $60,000 cash down payment when you bought the other house for $300,000 two years ago. As luck would have it, property values declined a year after you bought your house.

You clearly *need* more money from the sale than Marcia. After all, you paid ten times as much for your house. What's more, Marcia paid off her loan five years ago. You, on the other hand, owe the bank big bucks on your mortgage.

Because the houses are identical in size, age, condition, and location, they have the same FMV. Under the circumstances, the fact that they both sold for $285,000 isn't surprising. Marcia got a nice nest egg for her retirement. You barely cleared enough from the deal to pay off your mortgage and other expenses of sale. Fair? Marcia thinks so. You don't.

REMEMBER

FMV is utterly unbiased. It's the amount your house is worth in the market today — not the amount you or the buyers would like it to be.

Median prices aren't FMV

Organizations such as the National Association of Realtors, the Chamber of Commerce, and private research firms gather data on house sales activity in a specific geographic region, such as a city, county, or state. They use this information to prepare reports on housing topics, such as the average cost of houses in an area and the increase or decline in regional house sales on a yearly or monthly basis.

One of the most widely quoted housing statistics is the *median sale price,* which is simply the midpoint in a range of all house sales in an area during a specified reporting period, such as a month or a year. Half the sales during the reporting period are above the median, and half fall below it.

The median-priced house, in other words, is the one exactly in the middle of the prices of all the houses that sold during the specified reporting period. For example, the median sale price of an existing single-family house in the United States was about $265,000 in 2017 — meaning half the houses in the U.S. sold for more than $265,000 and the other half sold for less than $265,000. (In case you're interested, the median sale price was just $118,000 in 1996 when the first edition of *Home Buying Kit For Dummies* went to press.) Unfortunately, all you know about this hypothetical median-priced American house is its price.

You don't know how many bedrooms or baths the mythical median-priced house contains. Nor do you know how many square feet of interior living space the house offers, how old it is, whether it has a garage or a yard, or how well maintained it is. You don't even know where in the United States this elusive median-priced house is located.

As a homeowner, you can use median sale price statistics to measure *general* property value trends. For example, suppose your local Chamber of Commerce says the median sale price of a house in your area was $200,000 five years ago when you bought your house, and it's $240,000 today. Based on that information, you can safely say that median sale prices have increased 20 percent over the past five years.

REMEMBER

Just because the median sale price of a house in your area went up 20 percent doesn't mean the house you paid $250,000 for five years ago is worth $300,000 today. Median sale price statistics aren't any more accurate for determining your house's value than median income statistics are for calculating your paycheck.

You need much more precise information to establish the FMV of the house you're about to sell.

Using a Comparable Market Analysis

The best way to accurately determine your house's FMV is by using a written *comparable market analysis* (CMA) to see how your house compares to other houses like yours that have either sold recently or currently are on the market. If you hire a real estate agent to sell your house, you'll likely get several CMAs during the selection process. You can use these CMAs to fine-tune your asking price.

The "Recent Sales" section of the CMA helps establish the FMV of *your house* by comparing it to all other houses that

>> Are located in the same or similar neighborhood as your house

>> Are of approximately the same age, size, and condition as your house

>> Have sold in the past six months

Houses meeting these criteria are called *comps*, short for *comparables.* Depending on the date you started looking at houses for sale in your neighborhood, you may not have visited all the sold comps. No problem. A good real estate agent can show you listing statements for the houses you haven't seen, take you on a verbal tour of every house, and explain how each one compares with your house.

Every residential real estate office develops its own CMA format. Regardless of the way your agent's office presents its CMA information, Tables 5-1 and 5-2 illustrate the elements that all good CMAs contain. Suppose you live at 220 Oak Street. These tables provide CMA information for your house (abbreviated as YH).

TABLE 5-1   ## Sample CMA — "Recent Sales" Section

Address	Date Sold	Sale Price	Bedrm/Bath	Parking	Condition	Remarks
210 Oak	04/30	$290,000	3/3	2 car	Very good	**Best comp!** Approx. the same location, size, and condition as *your house (YH)* with a slightly smaller lot. 1,867 square feet. $155 per square foot.
335 Elm	02/14	$268,500	3/2	2 car	Fair	Busy street. Older baths. 1,805 square feet. $149 per square foot.
307 Ash	03/15	$285,000	3/3	2 car	Good	Slightly larger than YH, but nearly the same condition. Good comp. 1,850 square feet. $154 per square foot.
555 Ash	01/12	$282,500	3/2.5	2 car	Excellent	Smaller than YH, but knockout renovation. 1,740 square feet. $162 per square foot.
75 Birch	04/20	$293,000	3/3	3 car	Very good	Larger than YH, but location isn't as good. Superb landscaping. 1,910 square feet. $153 per square foot.

TIP

When you analyze the sales in Table 5-1, you find that houses comparable to your house are selling in the range of $149 to $162 per square foot. Putting the sale prices into a *price-per-square-foot format* makes property comparisons much easier. As Table 5-2 shows, any price that's way above or below the norm really leaps out at you.

The "Currently For Sale" section of the CMA compares your house to neighborhood comps that are *currently on the market.* These comps are included in the analysis to check price trends. If prices are falling, asking prices of houses on the market today will be lower than sale prices of comparable houses. If prices are rising, you'll see higher asking prices today than sale prices for comps that sold three to six months ago.

TABLE 5-2   ## Sample CMA — "Currently For Sale" Section

Address	Date on Market	Asking Price	Bedrm/Bath	Parking	Condition	Remarks
220 Oak *(Your House)*	Not on market	To be determined	3/3	2 car	Very good	Quieter location than 123 Oak, good detailing, older kitchen. 1,880 square feet.
123 Oak	05/01	$299,500	3/2	2 car	Excellent	High-end rehabilitated and priced accordingly. 1,855 square feet. $161 per square foot.
360 Oak	02/10	$275,000	3/2	1 car	Fair	Kitchen & baths need work, no fireplace. 1,695 square feet. $162 per square foot.
140 Elm	04/01	$279,500	3/3	2 car	Good	Busy street, small rooms, small yard. 1,725 square feet. $162 per square foot.
505 Elm	1/15	$325,000	2/2	1 car	Fair	Delusions of grandeur. Grossly overpriced! 1,580 square feet. $206 per square foot.

TABLE 5-2 *(continued)*

Address	Date on Market	Asking Price	Bedrm/Bath	Parking	Condition	Remarks
104 Ash	04/17	$294,500	3/2.5	2 car	Very good	**Best comp!** Good floor plan, large rooms. Surprised it hasn't sold. 1,860 square feet. $158 per square foot.
222 Ash	02/01	$319,500	3/2	1 car	Fair	Must have used 505 Elm as comp. Will never sell at this price. 1,610 square feet. $198 per square foot.
47 Birch	03/15	$319,000	4/3.5	2 car	Good	Nice house, but overimproved for neighborhood. 2,005 square feet. $159 per square foot.
111 Birch	04/25	$289,500	3/3	2 car	Very good	Gorgeous kitchen, no fireplace. 1,870 square feet. $155 per square foot.

Playing with the numbers

Suppose today's date is May 15. You and your agent are sitting at the kitchen table looking at two sheets of paper. One page shows all the recent sales of comps in your neighborhood. The other lists houses comparable to yours that currently are on the market in your area. Each set of comps tells you something important.

"Sold" comps indicate probable FMV

Your agent says 210 Oak (refer to Table 5-1) is an ideal "sold" comp because it's two doors away from your house, is roughly the same size as your house, and is in about the same condition as your house. Furthermore, no major changes have occurred in your local real estate market since 210 Oak sold two weeks ago for $155 per square foot. The only other recent sale at a higher price per square foot was 555 Ash, but that comp isn't as good because the house is in better condition than your house (no offense).

TIP

Factually establishing your house's probable sale price based on its square footage is easy after you know how. Multiply your house's square footage by estimated FMV expressed in a price per square foot. In this case, because your house (220 Oak) has 1,880 square feet multiplied by $155 per square foot, it should sell for about $291,400. Simple.

"Currently For Sale" comps define asking price

You've toured every one of the comparable properties listed in the "Currently For Sale" section of your agent's CMA. Having seen 104 Ash (refer to Table 5-2) with your own eyes, you agree that it's more like your house than any other property now on the market in your area. Even so, it isn't a perfect comp because 104 Ash is smaller than your house and has only two and a half baths versus three full baths in your house. You know enough about property values to realize that the house is priced to sell at $158 per square foot.

Even though 123 Oak and 360 Oak are closer to your house than 104 Ash, neither house is as good a comp as the Ash Street property. The house at 123 Oak is totally renovated, has a wonderful kitchen, and should sell for a higher price per square foot than your house. Whether they can get $161 per square foot remains to be seen. The house at 360 Oak, on the other hand, is smaller than your house, doesn't show well, and has one less bath and a smaller garage. No way will 360 Oak sell for $162 per square foot.

All things considered, you decide to base your asking price on $158 per square foot. For one thing, that amount is the upper limit of the asking prices of comparable houses. The extra $3 per square foot over your house's probable FMV gives you a little room to negotiate with buyers. Multiplying 1,880 square feet times $158 per square foot equals $297,040, which is an odd asking price. To make the asking price more exciting for prospective buyers, you round it down to an even $295,000.

This example is rather straightforward. Pricing in the real world, however, is usually somewhat complicated.

REMEMBER

Give sale prices more weight than asking prices when determining your house's asking price. Don't guess about your house's worth. Analyze the sale prices of comparable houses. Your CMA should note any price reductions made while the comps were on the market as well as the credits sellers gave buyers for corrective work repairs.

Interpreting CMA adjustments and flaws

CMAs beat the heck out of median price statistics for establishing FMV, but keep in mind that CMAs aren't perfect. Buyers and sellers have used exactly the same comps and arrived at stunningly different opinions of FMV. Here's where discrepancies can creep into your CMA:

>> **Incomplete comps:** Your CMA must be comprehensive. It should include *all* comp sales in the past six months and *all* comps currently on the market. Be sure the comp sales data reflects price reductions during the marketing period and credits given for corrective work repairs. Getting an accurate picture of FMV may be difficult if parts of the puzzle are missing.

>> **Old comps:** Like milk in your refrigerator, comps have expiration dates. Lenders rarely accept as comps houses that sold more than six months ago, because their sale prices don't reflect current consumer confidence, business conditions, or mortgage rates. As a rule, the older the comp, the less likely that it represents today's FMV.

TECHNICAL STUFF

Why six months? Because six months generally is accepted as long enough to represent a good cross section of comparable sales, but short enough to have fairly consistent market conditions. This time period, however, isn't carved in stone. If, for example, the biggest employer in your area had a massive layoff three months ago, six months is too long for a valid comparison. Conversely, if houses in your area rarely sell, you'll probably have to use comparable sales that occurred more than six months ago.

>> **House condition:** No two homes are the same after they've been lived in. Suppose two identical tract homes are located next door to one another. One, owned by an older couple with no children or pets, is in pristine condition. The other, owned by a family with five small kids and three large dogs, resembles a federal disaster area. It's Guesstimate City when trying to determine the cost to repair the wear-and-tear damage in the second house. A good CMA, however, makes adjustments for this type of difference between houses.

>> **Site differences within your neighborhood:** Even though all the comps are in the same neighborhood, they aren't located on precisely the same plot of ground. How much is being located next to the beautiful park worth to a buyer? How much will a buyer pay to be seven blocks closer to the bus stop during the rainy season? These value adjustments are subjective and, thus, imprecise.

>> **Out-of-neighborhood comps:** Suppose that, in the past six months, no houses sold in your neighborhood. Going into other areas to find comps forces you and your agent to make value adjustments between two different neighborhoods' amenities (schools, shopping, transportation, and so on). Comparing different neighborhoods is a lot more difficult than making value adjustments within your neighborhood.

>> **Noncomp house sales:** What if five houses sold in your neighborhood in the past six months but not one was remotely comparable to yours in age, size, style, or condition? You and your agent must estimate value differences for three-bedroom versus four-bedroom houses, old versus new kitchens, small versus large yards, garages versus carports, and so on. If your house offers a panoramic view and none of the other houses have any view at all, how much does the view increase your house's value? Guesstimates like these are highly subjective.

WARNING

A valid comparison of your house to the other houses is impossible if you and your agent have only read about the comps in listing statements. Seeing is believing. Most listing statements (one-page property descriptions) are exaggerated to greater or lesser degrees. You don't know how overstated if you haven't seen the house for yourself. You may discover that a "large" master bedroom is tiny. A "gourmet" kitchen's only distinction may be an especially fancy hot plate. That "sweeping" view from the living room may be visible only if you're as tall as LeBron James. Of course, you won't know any of these things if you only read the houses' puff sheets instead of visiting each house in person.

Floor plans also greatly affect a house's value. Two houses, for example, may be approximately the same size, age, and condition yet vary wildly in value. One house's floor plan flows beautifully from room to room; the rooms themselves are well proportioned with high ceilings. The other house doesn't work well because its floor plan is choppy and the ceilings are low. You can't tell which is which just by reading the two listing statements.

TIP

Eyeballing — touring houses and noting important details inside and out — is the *best* way to decide which houses are true comps for your house and which differences you must adjust for in your comparable analysis. Regard with a certain degree of skepticism any written description of a house written by someone else. Check it out yourself.

Considering appraisals versus CMAs

If you're the suspicious type, you may want to double-check your agent's opinion of value before putting your house on the market. You can do so by paying several hundred dollars for a professional appraisal of your house.

Getting an *unbiased* second opinion of value is always reassuring. Appraisers, unlike agents, have no reason to tell you what you want to hear to get a listing. Whether your house sells or not, an appraiser gets paid. On the other hand, if you think a professional appraisal is vastly superior to your agent's opinion of value, think again. A good agent's CMA usually is as good as an appraisal for purposes of marketing your house. Conversely, if a professional appraisal is vastly superior because your agent is a lousy judge of property values, get a better agent.

In any given area, appraisers don't usually see as many houses as do agents who focus on that area. Appraisers aren't lazy; they use their time in other ways. Formal appraisals are time-consuming. An appraiser inspects a property from foundation to attic, measures its square footage, makes detailed notes regarding everything from the quality of construction to the amount of wear and tear, photographs the house inside and out, photographs comps for the house being appraised, writes up the appraisal, and so on. Agents can tour 15 to 20 houses in the same amount of time an appraiser requires to do one appraisal.

As a result, appraisers frequently call agents to find out about houses the agents listed or sold that may be comps. Regardless of how good an agent's description of the house, eyeballing property is better. Any appraisal's accuracy suffers if the appraisal is based on comps the appraiser hasn't seen.

WARNING

Agents also call each other about houses they haven't seen, so don't jump to the conclusion that appraisers are the only ones who do such things. Reading listing statements and picking other agents' brains to find out about property is no substitute for firsthand eyeballing. If your agent hasn't seen most of the comps used in your CMA, get an agent who knows your local market.

TIP

Unless you're pretty darn uncertain about your house's worth or are considering selling your house yourself, don't waste money on an appraisal.

Bidding Wars

In a perfect world, buyers and sellers would use only facts to establish property values, and sales would be fast and easy. Unfortunately, the world is far from perfect. The following sections provide two reasons.

How buyers and sellers get to FMV

Buyers and sellers zero in on a house's FMV from utterly different directions. Buyers bring their offering price *up* to FMV because they don't want to overpay. Sellers, conversely, ratchet their asking price *down* to FMV because they don't want to leave any of their profit on the table.

Even though sellers and buyers approach FMV from opposite directions, note that they end up at exactly the same place. That result is no surprise. If you and the buyers rely on the same data — the asking prices and sale prices of comparable houses — to determine FMV, you're bound to reach the same conclusion sooner or later.

Why "buying a listing" ruins property pricing

One crucial aspect of selling a house is correctly establishing its initial asking price. If a seller prices a house near its FMV, the house usually sells quickly for top dollar. If, on the other hand, a seller grossly overprices a property, it tends to linger on the market month after month until the owner corrects the problem.

Why would you be tempted to overprice your house? Because an unprincipled real estate agent takes advantage of your legitimate concern about underpricing your property, or, perhaps, the agent just wants to exploit your greed. A bidding war develops among the agents who're competing to list your house for sale. The first victim of this bidding war is, unfortunately, the concept of FMV. Here's what happens:

"Thanks for giving me a chance to represent you during the sale of your handsome house," says Tommy Truthful, an agent from Honest Realty. "As you can see from the CMA I prepared today, 142 houses sold in your neighborhood during the past six months. Two are considerably larger than yours, so they aren't good comps. The 140 properties comparable to your house in size, age, location, and condition sold in a price range of $225,000 to $227,500. Based on this astonishing abundance of undeniable, irrefutable, incontestable, indisputable, incontrovertible, unquestionable facts, I recommend an initial asking price of not more than $229,500."

"Wait just a second," cautions Sally Slick from Aim to Please Realty. "You may be leaving money on the table if your asking price is $229,500. Comps aren't everything. Your chimney is made of better quality bricks than any of those other 140 houses' chimneys. Even more important, not one of the 140 houses has an ostrich-sized birdbath in its front yard. These special features, in my humble opinion, are easily worth an additional $20,000. I recommend that you ask $249,500."

"Facts, schmacts," oozes Otto Outrageous from Sky High Realty, who figures he won't get your listing unless he outbids the other two agents. "I think $249,500 isn't even close to what you should ask. We'll feature your house on our web page linked to our affiliate offices in Paris, London, Rome, and Nome. Massive exposure is the key to maximizing your sale price. I'm sure that if we look long enough and hard enough, we can find a buyer in some secret nook of this vast planet who'll pay $275,000 for your wonderful house."

WARNING

This deceptive approach — when several agents give a seller increasingly outrageous opinions of a house's value — is called *buying a listing.* Agents who use this ploy think the best way to get listings is to tell sellers what they want to hear — that their house is unique and is worth way, way, waaaaaaaaaaay more than any comparable house. Greed conquers reason.

This ruse may be a successful tactic for getting listings, but it's a rotten way to sell them. Property owners who succumb to fantasy pricing are condemned to waste their time until they finally return to real-world economics. These misguided homeowners confuse the act of listing a house with the act of selling it. Unless their listing agent intends to buy the house, the owners and agent are playing an expensive game of Let's Pretend.

REMEMBER

The price you and your listing agent agree on doesn't really matter. Until you find a buyer who agrees with you, your house won't sell. Resist the temptation to base your asking price on

>> The amount that you want your house to be worth

>> The amount you need to receive from the sale to be able to buy your dream home

Let the comps tell you the price your house is worth. Unlike unscrupulous agents, comps don't lie.

Index

Numerics

4 percent rule, 267

90 percent rule, safe harbor method *vs.*, 86–87

100 percent join and survivor option, for pensions, 293

401(k), 120–123, 289, 395

403(b) plans, 117

529 plans, 38, 168

A

AAFD (American Association of Franchisees & Dealers), 73

AAI (Accredited Advisor in Insurance), 204

AARP Employer Pledge, 19

AARP Foundation (website), 26

AARP Social Security For Dummies (Peterson), 44

AARP's LifeReimagined (website), 58, 59

abatement, 273

accidental death insurance, 196

Accion (website), 63

accountants, estate planning and, 160–161, 350

accounting

about, 75

establishing a system, 76–80

keeping tax records, 80–83

accounts receivable, 334

ACCRA (American Chamber of Commerce Research Association), 477

Accredited Advisor in Insurance (AAI), 204

AccuQuote (website), 253

ACTEC (American College of Trust and Estate Counsel) (website), 160

activities, in retirement communities, 435

actual expenses, 268

adapt, ability to, 29

adjusted future estate value, 419

adjusted gross income (AGI), 320

administrator, 368

advisors, 202–203

AFA (American Franchisee Association), 73

afford, 462

Affordable Care Act (2010), 220, 440

age of retirement, 108

ageism, 27–30

AGI (adjusted gross income), 320

Aging Workforce survey, 9

AICPA (American Institute of Certified Public Accountants), 160, 350

alcohol, heart health and, 258

Alfred P. Sloan Foundation, 9

alternative payee, 394

American Advisors Group, 452

American Association of Franchisees & Dealers (AAFD), 73

American Chamber of Commerce Research Association (ACCRA), 477

American College of Trust and Estate Counsel (ACTEC) (website), 160

American Franchisee Association (AFA), 73

American Institute of Certified Public Accountants (AICPA), 160, 350

amortization, 473

ancillary probate, 367

angel investors, 63

annuities

about, 285–286

contributing during working years, 286–287

deferred, 288–289, 322–323

F

health maintenance organizations (HMOs), 220

health savings account (HSA), 46

healthcare
  expenses for, 278
  housing near, 435
  jobs in, 17–18

Healthcare.gov (website), 46

heart health, 258–259

HECM (Home Equity Conversion Mortgage), 436, 444, 445, 449, 452

"HECM for Purchase," 454

heirs, determining intended, 146–149

help
  with estate planning, 346–352
  getting, 59–61
  seeking, 27
  for social entrepreneurs, 69

HMOs (health maintenance organizations), 220

hobbies, turning into profit, 58

holographic will, 178

home equity, as a retirement plan component, 105

Home Equity Conversion Mortgage (HECM), 436, 444, 445, 449, 452

home equity line of credit
  defined, 35
  financing with, 62–63

home equity loan
  reverse mortgages vs., 439
  second mortgage vs., 443–444

home healthcare, under Medicare Part A coverage, 214

home office, writing off, 42–43

hospital stays, under Medicare Part A coverage, 213

hospitality and leisure jobs, 18

HourlyNerd, 52

housing
  about, 431, 455–456
  calculating value of homes, 354–355
  determining your need for, 457–464
  expenses for, 81, 273–275
  financial feasibility of a move, 475–479
  health of market, 464–468
  job moves, 462
  location options, 433–436
  moving, 431–436
  pros and cons of moving, 432–433
  rental income, 440
  reverse mortgages, 436–439
  schools and, 459
  selling, 455–468, 469–475
  tax issues, 439–440
  trading, 461–462

housing, value of
  about, 481–482
  bidding wars, 493–495
  comparable market analysis (CMA), 486–493
  cost, 482, 483–484
  determining fair market value (FMV), 484–486
  price, 482, 484
  value, 482–483

"How Work Affects Your Benefits" (website), 44

HSA (health savings account), 46

HUD-approved counselor, 453

hydration, 260

I

IA (Investment Adviser), 349

IBM's Transition to Teaching program, 37

icons, explained, 2–3

Idealist, 69

identifying need for disability insurance, 255–256

identity loss, with self-employment, 67

IFA (International Franchise Association), 74

imaginary property, 336

immediate annuity, 287

impound account, 472

moving costs
about, 474
location options, 433–436
writing off, 42
MSAs (medical savings accounts), 221
mutual fund certificate, 337

N

O

P

About the Authors

Bob Carlson is editor of the monthly newsletter *Retirement Watch.* Bob is also Chairman of the Board of Trustees of the Fairfax County Employees' Retirement System, which has more than $2.4 billion in assets. He has served on the board since 1992. He was a member of the Board of Trustees of the Virginia Retirement System, which oversaw $42 billion in assets, from 2001 to 2005.

His prior books include *Invest Like a Fox . . . Not Like a Hedgehog* and *The New Rules of Retirement,* both published by John Wiley & Sons, Inc. He has written numerous other books and reports, including *Tax Wise Money Strategies* and *Retirement Tax Guide.* He has also been interviewed by or quoted in numerous publications, including *The Wall Street Journal, Reader's Digest, Barron's, AARP Bulletin, Money* magazine, *Worth* magazine, *Kiplinger's Personal Finance* magazine, *The Washington Post,* and many others. He has appeared on national television and on a number of radio programs. He is past editor of *Tax Wise Money. The Washington Post* calls Bob's advice "smart . . . savvy . . . sensible . . . valuable and imaginative."

You can also hear Bob as a featured guest on nationally syndicated radio shows, such as *The Retirement Hour, Dateline Washington, Family News in Focus, The Michael Reagan Show, Money Matters,* and *The Stock Doctor.*

Bob received his JD and an MS (accounting) from the University of Virginia, received his BS (financial management) from Clemson University, and passed the CPA Exam. He is also an instrument-rated private pilot.

N. Brian Caverly, Esq., is a practicing lawyer in Northeastern Pennsylvania with his principal office in Wilkes-Barre. He has practiced law since 1968 and in his practice emphasizes wills and estates, estate planning, and elder law. He is a graduate of Bucknell University in Lewisburg, Pennsylvania, with an AB degree in economics, and from the Dickinson School of Law in Carlisle, Pennsylvania, with a JD degree. He serves on the board of directors of the Angeline Elizabeth Kirby Memorial Health Center in Wilkes-Barre, a major charitable organization. Brian is also chairman of the Luzerne County Planning Commission. He presents lectures and writes articles and papers about various legal topics, including those related to estate planning.

Robert S. Griswold, MSBA, is a successful real estate investor, expert witness, and hands-on landlord/property manager with a large portfolio of residential and commercial rental income properties. He uses print and broadcast journalism to bring his many years of experience to his readers, listeners, and viewers.

He is the author of *Property Management For Dummies* and *Property Management Kit For Dummies* both published by Wiley and for 15 years was the real estate expert for NBC San Diego, with a regular on-air live-caller segment. Robert was the host of a live weekly radio talk show, *Real Estate Today!,* for nearly 15 years, and he's also the columnist for the syndicated "Rental Roundtable" and "Rental Forum" columns.

These popular features are published in dozens of major newspapers throughout the country, and Robert has been recognized twice as the number-one real estate broadcast journalist in the nation by the National Association of Real Estate Editors.

Robert's educational background includes having earned a BS and two master's degrees in finance and business economics, real estate finance, international finance, real estate and urban land economics, and real estate development, all from the Marshall School of Business at the University of Southern California. His real estate investing and managing professional designations include the CRE (Counselor of Real Estate), the CPM (Certified Property Manager), the CCIM (Certified Commercial Investment Member), the ARM (Accredited Residential Manager), the GRI (Graduate, REALTOR Institute), the CCAM (Certified Community Association Manager), and the PCAM (Professional Community Association Manager).

Robert has been retained on more than 2,000 legal matters as an expert in the standard of care, custom, and practice for all aspects of real estate ownership and management in both state and federal cases throughout the country. He is the president of Griswold Real Estate Management, Inc., managing residential, commercial, retail, and industrial properties throughout California and Nevada.

On a personal level, Robert enjoys travel (particularly cruises), sports, and family activities. He truly enjoys real estate and tries to keep life in perspective through humor!

Kerry Hannon is a nationally recognized authority on career transitions and retirement, a frequent TV and radio commentator who speaks about and offers advice on career and personal finance trends, and author of numerous books, including *Love Your Job: The New Rules for Career Happiness* (Wiley/AARP), *What's Next? Finding Your Passion and Your Dream Job in Your Forties, Fifties and Beyond* (Berkley Trade/AARP), and *Great Jobs for Everyone 50+: Finding Work That Keeps You Happy and Healthy . . . And Pays the Bills* (Wiley/AARP).

Kerry is a columnist and regular contributor to *The New York Times,* a contributing writer for *Money* magazine, AARP's Jobs Expert and Great Jobs columnist, contributing editor and Second Verse columnist at *Forbes,* and the PBS website NextAvenue. org expert and regular columnist on personal finance and careers for boomer women. Kerry is a fellow of the Columbia Journalism School and the Robert N. Butler Columbia Aging Center's 2015 Age Boom Academy. She is a former Metlife Foundation and New America Media fellow on aging. On June 24, 2015, Kerry testified before the Senate Special Committee on Aging at the invitation of its chairman, Senator Susan M. Collins (R-Maine), and ranking member, Claire McCaskill (D-Mo.) At the hearing, *Work in Retirement: Career Reinventions and the New Retirement Workscape,* Kerry discussed the challenges that Americans who work in retirement or plan to work in retirement may face and the value that older workers can add to the workplace.

Kerry has been covering careers and individual career choices for more than a decade. In 2006, she developed the *U.S. News & World Report* "Second Acts" feature — a regular column that looked at people who successfully navigated a career change in midlife, focusing on their challenges and their motivations. She has spent more than two decades covering all aspects of business and personal finance as a columnist, editor, and writer for the nation's leading media companies, including *Forbes, Money, U.S. News & World Report,* and *USA Today.* Kerry's work has also regularly appeared in *BusinessWeek, Kiplinger's Personal Finance, The Wall Street Journal,* and *Reader's Digest,* among other national publications. She has appeared as a financial expert on ABC News, CBS, CNBC, NBC Nightly News, NPR, and PBS.

Kerry graduated from Shady Side Academy in Pittsburgh, Pennsylvania, where she serves on the Board of Visitors, and received a bachelor's degree from Duke University, where she is a member of an editorial board.

Kerry lives in Washington, D.C., with her husband, documentary producer and editor Cliff Hackel, and her Labrador retriever, Zena.

Follow Kerry on Twitter @KerryHannon, visit her website at KerryHannon.com, and check out her LinkedIn profile at www.linkedin.com/in/kerryhannon.

Jack Hungelmann's policy knowledge, problem-solving expertise, and coverage analysis skills were gained through more than 2,000 hours of education and 35 years in the insurance business as a claims adjuster, agent, and consultant. He has advised individuals and commercial enterprises on their insurance needs and has earned several distinguished designations. Among these are the Certified Insurance Counselor (CIC), the Chartered Property and Casualty Underwriter (CPCU), and the Associate in Reinsurance (ARe).

Jack graduated from the University of Minnesota in 1969 and has taught professional continuing education classes for the CPCU Society and the National Alliance for Insurance Education & Research. He has been published numerous times in *American Agent & Broker* magazine. More recently, he has written and continues to write quarterly articles on personal risk management and insurance for the website of the International Risk Management Institute (www.irmi.com).

Jack has personally written newsletters for his clients three times a year for more than 20 years. You can check out back issues of the newsletter, as well as subscribe to future electronic versions, at Jack's website (www.jackhungelmann.com). The site also contains Jack's contact information and links to most of his articles from the past several years. Jack lives in Chaska, Minnesota, with his bride, Judy.

Aaron Larson is an attorney practicing law in Ann Arbor, Michigan, where he lives with his wife and daughter. After graduating from the University of Michigan Law School, Aaron started practice as a quintessential small town lawyer, providing legal services that included estate planning, probate, and guardianship services. He subsequently worked for the Institute of Continuing Legal Education in Ann Arbor, Michigan, where he developed professional education programs for lawyers in areas including estate planning, litigation, and family law. His present legal practice focuses on civil appeals. He operates the ExpertLaw website (`www.expertlaw.com`), offering free legal information and assistance to consumers, as well as resources for legal professionals.

Jordan S. Simon is vice president of asset management at Venture West, Inc., a Tucson, Arizona–based investment firm, where he has worked since 1988. Jordan focuses on real estate investments. He received his bachelor's degree from the University of Arizona and his MBA from the University of Southern California, where he was the recipient of the Quon Award for outstanding university and community service. Jordan is the coauthor of *The Computer Professional's Guide to Effective Communications*.

Eric Tyson is an internationally acclaimed and best-selling personal finance book author, syndicated columnist, and speaker. He has worked with and taught people from all financial situations, so he knows the financial concerns and questions of real folks just like you. Despite being handicapped by an MBA from the Stanford Graduate School of Business and a BS in Economics and Biology from Yale University, Eric remains a master of "keeping it simple."

After toiling away for a number of years as a management consultant to Fortune 500 financial service firms, Eric took his inside knowledge of the banking, investment, and insurance industries and committed himself to making personal financial management accessible to all. Today, Eric is an accomplished personal finance writer. His "Investor's Guide" syndicated column, distributed by King Features, is read by millions nationally. He is the author of five national bestselling books, including *Personal Finance For Dummies, Investing For Dummies,* and *Home Buying For Dummies* (coauthor), among others, which are all published by John Wiley & Sons, Inc. *Personal Finance For Dummies* was awarded the Benjamin Franklin Award for best business book of the year.

Eric's work has been featured and quoted in hundreds of publications, including *The Wall Street Journal, Los Angeles Times, Chicago Tribune, Forbes* magazine, *Kiplinger's Personal Finance* magazine, *Parenting* magazine, *Money* magazine, and *Bottom Line/Personal* magazine; on NBC's *Today Show,* ABC, CNBC, PBS's *Nightly Business Report,* CNN, and FOX-TV; and on CBS national radio, NPR's Sound Money, Bloomberg Business Radio, and Business Radio Network.

Eric's website is `www.erictyson.com`.

Publisher's Acknowledgments

Acquisitions Editor: Tracy Boggier

Project Managers: Vicki Adang, Linda Brandon

Development Editors: Vicki Adang, Linda Brandon

Copy Editor: Jennette ElNaggar

Technical Editor: Pierre-Emmanuel Jouve

Compilation Editor: Corbin Collins

Production Editor: G. Vasanth Koilraj

Cover Image: © haveseen/Shutterstock